ETHICS IN A CHRISTIAN CONTEXT

# ETHICS
# IN A CHRISTIAN
# CONTEXT

PAUL L. LEHMANN

1817

HARPER & ROW, PUBLISHERS

New York, Hagerstown, San Francisco, London

To
TIMOTHY LEHMANN
and
MARTHA MENZEL LEHMANN (d. 1954)
through whom
I first learned freedom in believing
and obedience in freedom

# CONTENTS

*Preface*                                                    13

## PART ONE

# CHRISTIAN FAITH AND CHRISTIAN ETHICS

I   CHRISTIAN THINKING ABOUT ETHICS                          23
    1   Ethics and Christian Ethics                          23
    2   Christian Ethics and New Testament Ethics            26
    3   Principal Accents in the History of Christian
        Thinking About Ethics                                32

II  THE CHURCH AS THE CONTEXT OF ETHICAL REFLECTION          45
    1   Christian Ethics as '*Koinonia* Ethics'              45
    2   The Ethical Reality of the Church                    56
        *a.* The Socio-Ethical Understanding of the
        Church in the New Testament                          57
        *b.* The Reformation Doctrine of the Communion
        of Saints                                            63

III  WHAT GOD IS DOING IN THE WORLD                          74
    1   The Political Character of the Divine Activity        81
    2   Biblical Imagery and the Politics of God             86
    3   The Biblical Story                                   95

IV  CHRISTIAN ETHICS AND A THEOLOGY OF MESSIANISM           102
    1   The Trinitarian Basis of Christian Ethics           105
    2   Signs of Redemption Under the Threefold Office
        of Christ                                            112
    3   Second Adam, Second Advent, and Human Ful-
        fillment                                             117

V   THE CONTEXTUAL CHARACTER OF CHRISTIAN ETHICS            124
    1   A Contextual Critique of Ethical Absolutism         124
    2   Random Instances of Contextual Behavior             132
    3   The Crucial Difficulty of a 'Double Standard'       145
    4   A Contextual Ethic as Indicative Ethics             159

# Contents

## PART TWO

## CHRISTIAN AND PHILOSOPHICAL THINKING ABOUT ETHICS

VI   THE SEARCH FOR THE GOOD     165
   1   The Ethical Eudemonism of Aristotle     166
     a. The Highest Good and the Rule of Virtue     168
     b. The Problem of Evil     170
   2   The Ethical Legalism of Immanuel Kant     172
     a. The Highest Good     174
     b. The Rule of Duty     177
     c. The Problem of Radical Evil     181
     d. The Problem of Ethical Motivation     184

VII   THE REDIRECTION OF THE SEARCH     190
   1   William James, An Altered View of Mind     192
   2   On the Boundary Between Religion and Ethics     197
   3   James and the Christian Tradition     201

VIII   THE POWERS OF MAN     205
   1   The Powers of Man: Freedom     206
     a. The Quest for Ultimate Ethical Fact     208
     b. The Problem of Evil     211
   2   The Powers of Man: Mature Self-Love     217
     a. The Task of Humanistic Ethics     219
     b. The Precariousness of Humanistic Ethics     221

IX   ON ETHICS AND LANGUAGE     225
   1   Ethics on the Analytical Model     229
   2   Meta-Ethical Achievements     234
   3   *Koinonia* Ethics and Meta-Ethics     238

✓ X   ON THE BOUNDARY OF ETHICS AND CHRISTIAN FAITH     251
   1   The Consensus of Philosophical Ethics     251
   2   The Thrust of Christian Ethics Toward Philosophical Ethics     253
     a. The Revisionist Thrust: Augustine     254
     b. The Synthetic Thrust: Thomas Aquinas     256
     c. The Dia-Parallel Thrust: Schleiermacher     259

XI  THE INSUFFICIENCY OF PHILOSOPHICAL ETHICS     268
    1   Schleiermacher and Barth     269
    2   The Ethical Inadequacy of Moral Philosophy     277


*PART THREE*

THE QUESTION OF CONSCIENCE

XII  A CRITIQUE OF MORAL THEOLOGY     287
    1   The Nature and Scope of Moral Theology     288
    2   Moral Theology in Operation     292
    3   The Renovation of Moral Theology: A Critique
        from Within by Moral Theologians     295
        *a.* Roman Catholic Criticism     296
        *b.* Anglican Moral Theology     303
    4   A Critical Appraisal of Moral Theology     316

XIII  THE DECLINE AND FALL OF CONSCIENCE     326
    1   The Enemy of Humanization     328
    2   The Domestication of Conscience     330
    3   Duty's Inner Citadel     333
    4   The Dethronement of Conscience     337

XIV  THE ETHICAL REALITY OF CONSCIENCE     344
    1   A '*Koinonia* Ethic' as the Context of Conscience     344
    2   Christian Contextualism and the Ethical Reality
        of Conscience     347
    3   The Roots of a Fresh Possibility     352
    4   The Nexus of Obedient Freedom     360

  *Bibliography*     367

  *Indexes*     371
    1   *Biblical References*     371
    2   *Personal Names*     373
    3   *Subjects*     376

# FOREWORD

IN 1945 the Alumni Association and Board of Trustees of the
Austin Presbyterian Theological Seminary established a
Lectureship, bringing a distinguished scholar each year to
address an annual mid-winter convocation of ministers and
students on some phase of Christian thought.

The Thomas White Currie Bible Class of the Highland Park
Presbyterian Church of Dallas, Texas, in 1950, undertook the
maintenance of this Lectureship in memory of the late Dr
Thomas White Currie, founder of the class and president of the
Seminary from 1921 to 1943.

The series of lectures on this Foundation for the year 1961 is
included in this volume.

DAVID L. STITT
*President*

*Austin Presbyterian Theological Seminary*
*Austin, Texas*

# ACKNOWLEDGMENTS

Grateful acknowledgment is made to the following publishers for permission to quote from works cited:

Harcourt, Brace & World, Inc., for "when god decided to invent" from POEMS 1923-1954 by E. E. Cummings, copyright 1944 by E. E. Cummings.

Holt, Rinehart & Winston, Inc., for lines from "Ballad of Bataan" from THE FOURTH DECADE by Norman Rosten, copyright 1943 by Norman Rosten, and for selections from MAN FOR HIMSELF by Erich Fromm.

Liberal Arts Press Division of The Bobbs-Merrill Company, Inc., for selections from CRITIQUE OF PRACTICAL REASON by Immanuel Kant (translated by Lewis White Beck) copyright © 1956 by The Liberal Arts Press.

Longmans, Green & Company, New York and London, and David McKay Company, New York, for quotations from PRAGMATISM, VARIETIES OF RELIGIOUS EXPERIENCE, THE WILL TO BELIEVE, and A PLURALISTIC UNIVERSE by William James, and Longmans, Green & Company, London, for quotations from THE STRUCTURE OF CAROLINE MORAL THEOLOGY by H. R. McAdoo, 1949.

Oxford University Press, New York and London, for quotations from volume 9 of *The Works of Aristotle,* edited by W. D. Ross, 1915.

Prentice-Hall, Inc., for selections from ETHICAL THEORY: The Problems of Normative and Critical Ethics by Richard B. Brandt, copyright © 1959 by Prentice-Hall, Inc.

Random House, New York, and Faber & Faber, London, for a quotation from THE AGE OF ANXIETY by W. H. Auden, 1947.

Sheed & Ward, Inc., for selections from MORAL AND PASTORAL THEOLOGY, Vol. I, by Henry Davis, S.J., published by Sheed & Ward, Inc., New York.

Yale University Press, New Haven, for quotations from MAN'S FREEDOM, by Paul Weiss, 1950.

# PREFACE

WITH the publication in 1932 of Emil Brunner's *Das Gebot und die Ordnungen*, the interpretation of Christian ethics entered into a new and lively period of discussion. Not since the appearance of Friedrich Schleiermacher's *Die christliche Sitte* nearly a century earlier (1843) had anything fresh and provocative emerged in this area of Christian theology—with the possible exception of the American social gospel. The intellectual lineage of this movement may be traced to the monumental effort of Ernst Troeltsch to face the widening chasm between Christian faith and contemporary culture which was beginning to be evident at the turn of the present century. At mid-century, there are indications that Troeltsch has not said his last word.

But in the interval another kind of task needed to be undertaken. The faith and ethics of the sixteenth-century reformation of the church required a careful and specific re-examination of its ways of thinking about ethics and of giving shape to behavior. Protestantism simply could not stand in the breach glimpsed by Troeltsch unless it could summon a livelier sensitivity to and understanding of the resources of its heritage for dealing with a new and ominous destiny. As Schleiermacher had tried to clarify and to release the creative ethical resources of the Reformation for the mid-nineteenth century, Brunner tried to do the same for the century following. Indeed, the really groundbreaking significance of Brunner's work is that his sharp repudiation of Schleiermacher sharpened the issue common to them both. That issue is whether there are insights and conceptions rooted in the faith and ethics of the Reformation which are possessed of formative power for ethical theory and practice today.

This issue underlies Karl Barth's severe strictures against Brunner and his thoroughgoing attempt to deal with ethics differently. It is this issue too which underlies Reinhold Niebuhr's more moderate reservations with respect to Brunner's effort and his own attempt to explore, over against Barth's christological approach to ethics, an approach from the side of biblical and theological anthropology. In one way or another, what has been happening on the Continent, in England, and in the United States during the past three decades has been an ongoing response to the work of these pioneers, now in this direction, now in that direction; with the accent sometimes more upon the biblical and theological sides, sometimes more upon the philosophical and social sides of the central issue.

The present volume seeks to show that the faith and thought of the Reformation provide insights into and ways of interpreting ethics which give creative meaning and direction to behavior. The Protestant Reformation introduced into the Western cultural tradition a liberating grasp of the ways of God with men and thus also the possibility of ever fresh and experimental responses to the dynamics and the humanizing character of the divine activity in the world. This meant for ethics the displacement of the prescriptive and absolute formulation of its claims by the contextual understanding of what God is doing in the world to make and to keep human life human. It also meant for ethics an open door for the discovery of its genuinely descriptive character. Ethics could now be a *descriptive* discipline, not in contrast to a normative discipline (a distinction which presupposes another context), but in the sense of providing an account of the transformation of the concrete stuff of behavior, i.e., the circumstances, the motivations, and the structures of action, owing to the concrete, personal, and purposeful activity of God.

The extent to which the faith and thought of the Reformation liberate ethical thinking from the abstractness and confinement of principles and precepts may be most cogently exhibited from an investigation of the ethical implications of the fact and the faith of the Christian community. From this community of faith and life, Christian ethics acquires its character and significance as a *koinonia ethic*. When ethical thinking starts with the *koinonia*, the activity and purposes of God become the concrete context from within which behavior can be regarded as both guided and shaped. It cannot be too strongly stressed that the contextual character of Christian ethics, as these pages seek to analyze it, is derived from the ethical reality and significance of the Christian *koinonia*. The contextual character of Christian ethics is not derived from an application to the Christian *koinonia* of a general theory of contextualism.

Such a liberation of ethical thinking cannot, however, be pursued very fully, or even very far, without encountering the haunting question of other ethical options. There are Christian ethics other than Protestant, and religious ethics other than Christian. There is also a long and influential way of thinking about ethics which claims to be neither religious nor Christian, namely, the tradition of moral philosophy. Thus, to think about ethics by starting with the Christian *koinonia* requires an analysis of the methodological issues involved between Christian ethics and moral philosophy and between evangelical (or Protestant) and Catholic ways of dealing with ethical problems. There is a marked difference in ethical theory between Christian ethics and moral philosophy and between Christian ethics and moral theology.

This difference is crucially exposed by the question of conscience. The interpretation of conscience in Christian ethics is involved in a dilemma occasioned by the ambiguity and diversity of ethical experience. The conscience is no clear and certain interpreter of the will of God or of the ethical choices incumbent upon one in obedience to the will of God. The conscience more often functions as the bearer of ethical generalizations increasingly emptied of concrete behavioral meaning and power, and as the seat and source of guilt which paralyzes the nerve of ethical action. Thus, the question of conscience exhibits the fact that Christian ethics, both in theory and practice, has been haunted by the dilemma between ethical irrelevance, on the one hand, and ethical relativism, on the other.

When the Christian *koinonia* is taken as the starting point for ethical reflection, the methodological arrangement of the materials of such an ethic intrinsically suggests itself. Thus, Part One undertakes to describe what the method of a Christian ethic as a theological discipline involves. Part Two seeks to extend the methodological description by a careful differentiation of Christian thinking about ethics from the way of dealing with ethics which has emerged in Western thought through the tradition of moral philosophy. This differentiation is external to the Christian *koinonia*. There is, however, an internal differentiation which must also be made. It is occasioned by another and no less formidable way of thinking about ethics from within the community of Christian faith and life. The tradition of moral theology offers a kind of *koinonia ethic* which carries the methodological clarification of ethical theory to a crucial culmination with the question of conscience. Part Three, therefore, is concerned with moral theology and with the question of conscience.

The decisive issue affecting the validity of an evangelical or Protestant ethic in distinction, on the one hand, from moral philosophy and, on the other, from moral theology is this: *Which account of the conscience is correct?* The present ethical condition of the conscience is such as to require ethical theory either to 'do the conscience in' or to 'do the conscience over'! This means the displacement of an ethic of precept and law by a context for conscience within which the ethical reality of conscience can be exhibited. The discernment and analysis of such a context is the distinctive contribution of the Reformation to ethical theory.

One further comment may be made with regard to two terms frequently employed in the following pages and pivotal to the exposition of the thesis here proposed. These terms are 'maturity' and 'the new humanity'.

Psychoanalytic connotations of the word 'maturity' have been drawn upon whenever the context of the particular discussion seemed to be illuminated by their use. Primarily, however, and basically, we have tried to adhere to the New Testament understanding of 'maturity'. According to the New Testament, 'maturity' means 'human wholeness', the full or complete development of man as an individual and of all men in their relations with one another. When psychoanalytic theory defines maturity as *self-realization through self-acceptance*, it underlines a basic aspect of what is fundamentally *human* in the nature of man and of man's relation to the world and to his fellows. For Christianity, what is fundamentally human in human nature is the gift to man of the power to be and to fulfill himself in and through a relationship of dependence and self-giving toward God and toward his fellow man. Thus, maturity is *self-acceptance through self-giving*. In the pages that follow, the psychoanalytic understanding of maturity is used as a help toward giving concreteness and clarity to the Christian understanding of maturity but *not* as identical with it.

In the fully developed Christian sense, 'maturity' and 'the new humanity' are identical. But what is the relation of this identity of meaning to other connotations of these terms? The problem is to state distinctly, yet inseparably, the various meanings of 'maturity', of 'the wholeness of man', of 'the new humanity'. Maturity is a constituent of human nature as well as an experience of human relatedness. It presupposes the sinfulness and brokenness of man as well as man's need and capacity for forgiveness and his experience of reconciliation. Maturity is always being achieved and in some sense is already achieved. It is at once a gift and a power which came, as Christianity insists, from the relation of Jesus Christ both to the Christian and to all men. This is the meaning of the New Testament claim that Jesus Christ is both Redeemer and he 'in whom all things hold together', both prototype and bestower of the new humanity.

If it be kept in mind that the main concern throughout these pages is with the concrete ethical reality of a transformed human being and a transformed humanity owing to the specific action of God in Jesus Christ, an action and transformation of which the reality of the Christian *koinonia* is a foretaste, it may be possible to understand why the attempt to focus upon the dynamic and concrete reality of all the meanings denoted sometimes by 'maturity', sometimes by 'the wholeness of man', sometimes by 'the new humanity' has been made.

Not least among the factors heightening my own impatience with the protracted completion of these pages has been the strong sense of indebtedness to persons and occasions. To the Rev. John Alexander Mackay, President Emeritus of Princeton Theological Seminary, I wish to say first of all that except for his wisdom and perceptiveness, confidence and encouragement, the inquiries and studies leading to these pages would never have been undertaken. Dr Mackay knew with uncanny and incomparable theological sensitivity what I was to learn only as a consequence of his insistence, namely, that a dedication to systematic theology requires for its true and lively exercise the chastening and the excitement of the discipline of Christian ethics. I trust that he may recognize here a devoted though incommensurate expression of esteem and affection. Upon the recommendation of Dr Mackay, the Board of Trustees of the

Theological Seminary at Princeton made available to me during the year 1954-55 a sabbatical leave, in the course of which the initial draft of these pages was prepared. I hope that the members of the Board will find it possible to accept this belated token of my thanks. To President David L. Stitt and to the members of the Faculty of the Presbyterian Theological Seminary at Austin, Texas, I wish to say how grateful I am for the privilege of their invitation to deliver the Thomas White Currie Lectures at the Seminary in January, 1961. Although what was presented at Austin was the substance of Chapters II, III, IV, XIII, and XIV, the stimulus of their invitation and of their hospitality provided the occasion for the final and greatly expanded scope of the lectures.

During the interval between 1954 and 1961 the present form of the argument was experimentally explored at a number of conferences with college and university students and at pastors' institutes. For these opportunities, and to those who were present, I am especially grateful since they provided the insistent encouragement of attentive and memorable conversations and searching criticism.

My colleagues and fellow students in the Faculty of Divinity at Harvard University have generously favored me with the fruits of their own special competences and researches. To colleagues and students at the Divinity School and to my former colleagues and students at Princeton Seminary I should like to express my appreciation for the experience of comradeship in a community of faith and learning wherein these pages could be both begun and brought to their completion. They will never know how greatly their silence or their gentle inquiries—sometimes with measured hope, sometimes with faintly restrained incredulity—about the progress of the manuscript carried the writing beyond its innumerable frustrations and delays.

I wish to express particular gratitude to Professor Daniel Day Williams of the Union Theological Seminary, New York, for counsel and confidence unfailingly and incommensurably accorded these pages, as a consequence of which they were enormously improved. To my former colleagues at Wellesley College, Miss Louise Pettibone Smith, for her sharp judgment both of substance and of style, and Miss Virginia Onderdonk for her uncommon philosophical competence, and to Mr George

Kalbfleisch of Dartmouth College for a rigorous and critical reading of the present text, I can only gladly acknowledge my indebtedness.

My thanks are also due to three former teaching assistants for generous interest and help in the completion of the manuscript. They are Professor Benjamin Reist, of San Francisco Theological Seminary; Professor Benjamin Milner, of Wellesley College; Professor David Crownfield, of Alma College, Michigan.

Mr Milner S. Ball has greatly facilitated the preparation of the manuscript for publication, especially in verifying not infrequently exasperating notes and references. To him and to Mrs Paul Thompson, Miss Elizabeth Meade, and Mrs Arthur Kooman for their help indispensable to a publishable text I can only say this very inadequate word of my appreciation.

I wish also to thank Mr Ralph Sundguist for very competent assistance in the reading of the page proofs and in the preparation of the Indexes.

PAUL LEHMANN

*Cambridge, Massachusetts*
*31 October 1962*

PART ONE

# CHRISTIAN FAITH AND CHRISTIAN ETHICS

# I

## CHRISTIAN THINKING ABOUT ETHICS

CHRISTIAN ethics and the ethics of Christians are not the same. The difference is due both to the fact that Christians never meet the ethical claims upon their life and to the fact that Christian ethics, in distinction from the ethics of Christians, is an intellectual discipline. Christian ethics, properly regarded, has to do with systematic reflection upon what is involved in the ethical nature of the Christian religion. We are engaged, therefore, in a reflective analysis, rather than in trying to prescribe how Christians ought to behave. The aim is to rethink what the Christian faith implies, as regards their behavior, for those who accept and undertake to live by that faith.

### 1 *Ethics and Christian Ethics*

Christian ethics could be designated as a *science*. But the term 'science' is encumbered by a number of ambiguities and is not indispensable to reflective analysis. We may accordingly speak of ethics as an intellectual 'discipline' rather than as a 'science'. And it will be clarifying to begin our reflection and analysis with a brief glance at the root and the environment of the word 'ethics' itself.

The word 'ethics' is derived from a Greek root, the verbal form of which is εἴωθα; the corresponding noun, τὸ ἦθος. It meant originally 'dwelling', or 'stall'. To this word, τὸ ἦθος, the Latin translation *mos* was given; and from the Latin *mos* our word 'morality' is derived. Now this etymological story sheds an instructive light upon a persistent confusion in all ethical thinking. The confusion attends the understanding of the relationship between 'ethics' and 'morality'. Are 'ethics' and 'morality' synonymous words, or are they to be distinguished?

And if they are to be distinguished, is the distinction a real one or is it a distinction without a difference?

In casual and unreflective usage, 'ethics' and 'morality' tend to be interchanged as though they really were synonymous terms. The lurking sense of a difference between them has, however, never been completely suppressed. This ambivalence is rooted largely in an inadequacy of language due to the failure of language to catch up with experience before repeated and inaccurate translation from one language to another has confused the sense of terms. At all events, 'ethics' in its root meaning, at least as regards the noun τὸ ἦθος, had to do with 'stability' or 'stall'—that is, with the stability and security which are necessary if one is going to act at all. It may be humiliating, but it is instructive to recall that the term was first applied not to human beings but to animals. It was obvious to men that animals needed to be put somewhere for shelter and protection. Thus the germinal idea in the word τὸ ἦθος is the stability and security provided by a 'stall' or 'dwelling' for animals. The verb root εἴωθα means 'to be accustomed to' or 'to be wont to'. Hence the relationship between stability and custom was a kind of elemental datum of experience. It was really the primary office of custom to do in the human area what the stall did for animals: to provide security and stability.

As reflection upon the stability and security fundamental to human behavior continued, a certain distinction came to be made between 'ethics' and 'morality'. Diogenes Laertius, for example, speaks of ethics as that part of philosophy which has to do with 'life and with all that concerns us'.[1] Ethics, according to Diogenes, is concerned with the foundations of human behavior, morality with actual practice or behavior on these foundations. Indeed, the paramount importance of ethics was evident from the example and precepts of the philosophers as well as from the customs of living practiced by the schools, such as the Cynics, Pythagoreans, and Stoics.[2] And so the word 'morality' came gradually to be reserved for behavior according

---

[1] 'Μέρη δὲ φιλοσοφίας τρία . . . ἠθικὸν δὲ τὸ περὶ βίου καὶ τῶν πρὸς ἡμᾶς.' Cf. Diogenes Laertius, Lives and Opinions of Eminent Philosophers. Bk. I, Prologue, par. 18. English translation by R. D. Hicks, in the Loeb Classical Library, Vols. 184 and 185. G. P. Putnam's Sons, New York, 1925.

[2] Ibid., Bk. I, Prologue, par. 19; Bk. VIII, pars. 22, 56; Bk. IX, par. 108.

to custom, and the word 'ethics' for behavior according to reason, that is, reflection upon the foundations and principles of behavior. The German language, for instance, distinguishes between *Sitte* and *Ethik*, the former meaning 'custom', the latter being the more reflective consideration of the foundations and the guidance of behavior (*Tugendlehre*).

This little account of the meaning and use of the word 'ethics' points to the germinal idea that 'ethics' is concerned with that which holds human society together. It is, so to say, the 'cement' of human society, providing the stability and security indispensable to the living of human life. There is a distinction between behavior according to custom and behavior according to reflection. And from the first there has been a certain tension in ethical theory between 'ethics' and 'morality'.

As a theological discipline, ethics involves the same kind of reflection and analysis that we have noted. But the difference between ethics as a *discipline* and ethics as a *theological discipline*, the difference between Christian ethics and either practical morality (behavior according to custom) or reflections upon ethics which come to us from philosophy (moral philosophy), is derived from the *presuppositions* upon which ethical thinking is based. As a theological discipline, ethics involves reflection upon life, upon the cement of human society, and upon morality from the standpoint of certain theological presuppositions. There are theological ethics which are not *Christian* ethics. The ethics of Islam, for example, are theological but not Christian; so also with the ethics of Judaism or of Hinduism. What, then, is *Christian ethics*?

The answer to this question here proposed is this: *Christian ethics, as a theological discipline, is the reflection upon the question, and its answer: What am I, as a believer in Jesus Christ and as a member of his church, to do?* To undertake the reflection upon and analysis of this question and its answer—this is Christian ethics.[1]

---

[1] There is a minor grammatical problem which attends an essay in Christian ethics in the English language. The noun 'ethics' has a plural sound but a singular sense. Since, in a reflective analysis, the sense may be expected to take precedence over sound, the singular form of the verb with the plural (usually) form of the noun will be used in this essay, except where the context obviously requires a plural verb.

## 2  *Christian Ethics and New Testament Ethics*

This definition of Christian ethics encounters at the outset a crucial methodological difficulty. Where does one begin in thinking about Christian ethics, and why? In view of the formative place of the New Testament in Christian thought and life, must not Christian thinking about ethics begin with an account of the ethics of the New Testament and its Old Testament antecedents—in short, with the ethics of the Bible? If the point of departure is a systematic formulation of the nature and task of Christian ethics, rather than the ethics of the Bible, does the analysis not run the risk of producing an elaborate theological construction superimposed upon and stifling the creative source of Christian thinking about anything?

The answer is a dual one. Reflective analysis cannot avoid the risk of abstraction. Whether or not the analysis succumbs to that risk depends upon how steadily and accurately the presuppositions of the analysis and the realities of the human situation are linked together. As regards Christian thinking, however, there is a further and a more important consideration. All Christian thinking involves hermeneutics, either implicitly or explicitly. Although hermeneutics refers generally to the study and formulation of principles of literary interpretation, the word has come to be reserved for that branch of Christian theology which has to do with the principles of biblical interpretation. One cannot think as a Christian without presupposing a certain way of understanding the Bible. The relation between Christian faith and the text of the Bible is too complex to allow a simple derivation of the faith from the text or of the text from the faith. The reality and activity of God, the shaping of a community of faith in consequence of the divine activity, the apprehension of the divine activity and the historical life and destiny of the community of faith—all are involved in the simple act of taking up the Bible to read. To ignore these considerations is to ignore the crucial question of the possibility and validity of theological knowledge and thus to court a greater risk than that of theological abstraction.[1]

[1] In an unpublished doctoral dissertation on 'The Possibility of Theological Understanding' submitted to the faculty of Princeton Theological Seminary (1953), Frederick Herzog, Professor of Theology in the Divinity

This does not mean that a discussion of Christian ethics requires an elaboration of hermeneutical theory at the outset. It simply means that a recognition of the hermeneutical problem shatters an apparently ingrained habit of Christians of beginning with the New Testament, or with the Bible, as though that were obvious. Actually, at the beginning Christians do not seem to have regarded the Scriptures as a photoelectric instrument for discerning the mind and the will of God. Christian ethical thinking, as Ernst Troeltsch has irrefutably pointed out, has from the first been aware that something has happened between the Scriptures and the believers, between the New Testament and the church.[1] This is not to say that the New Testament and the church are not on speaking terms. But it is to say that we do not move easily and smoothly, and without very serious reflection, from the New Testament to the church and from the church to the New Testament.

As Troeltsch has noted, and as biblical criticism has steadily confirmed since he wrote, the New Testament community, centered as it was in the company of disciples who gathered around Jesus of Nazareth, found itself in a very great predicament. The Crucifixion had run counter to long-established

---

School at Duke University, has brilliantly explored the hermeneutical problem and sought to suggest a valid biblical interpretation today. Two recently published discussions of Christian ethics have ignored the hermeneutical problem and have consequently disregarded the basic question of what Christian ethics really is. Cf. Paul Ramsey, *Basic Christian Ethics*, Charles Scribner's Sons, New York, 1950 (SCM Press, London), and George F. Thomas, *Christian Ethics and Moral Philosophy*, Charles Scribner's Sons, New York, 1955. Subordinating the systematic to the genetic approach to Christian ethical analysis, these otherwise able treatments remain external to the kind of involvement required by Christian ethics as a theological discipline. They beg the basic question. By contrast, Reinhold Niebuhr's *An Interpretation of Christian Ethics*, Harper & Row, New York, 1935 (SCM Press, London, 1936), and Emil Brunner's *The Divine Imperative*, The Westminster Press, Philadelphia, 1947 (SCM Press, London, 1947), find it necessary to raise the question of the possibility of a Christian ethics and thus bring to the subject a more intrinsic and authentic treatment.

[1] Ernst Troeltsch, *Gesammelte Schriften*, Bd. I, *Die Soziallehren der christlichen Kirchen und Gruppen*, J. C. B. Mohr (Paul Siebeck), Tuebingen, 1919, *Kap. I*. The English translation is by Olive Wyon, *The Social Teaching of the Christian Churches*, The Macmillan Company, New York, 1931, 1949 (Allen & Unwin, London, 1931), especially chap. I.

messianic expectation. According to Luke 24, two disciples were
going along the road from Jerusalem to Emmaus. Unknown to
them, Jesus approached them and asked what from their point
of view was a rather stupid question. 'What is this conversation
which you are holding with each other as you walk?' And
there came an exasperated reply, 'Are you the only visitor to
Jerusalem who does not know the things that have happened
there in these days?' And he said to them, 'What things?'
And they said to him, 'Concerning Jesus of Nazareth . . . how
our chief priests . . . crucified him. But we had hoped that he
was the one to redeem Israel.'[1]

Or take Acts 1. Forty days after the Resurrection Jesus came
to the disciples and found them gathered together still trying to
understand the meaning of his death. There was, apparently,
no photoelectric evidence on the point. Again an exasperated
interpolation. 'Lord, will you at this time restore the Kingdom
to us?' And he said, 'It is not for you to know the times or
seasons which the Father has fixed by his own authority. But
you shall receive power when the Holy Spirit has come upon
you; and you shall be my witnesses in Jerusalem, and in all
Judaea and Samaria, and to the end of the earth!'[2] On an
earlier occasion Jesus had reminded his disciples of Lot's wife.[3]
She tried photoelectric living, which always reads backwards.
And she has not moved since. The simple inference from these
words in Acts is that the promised expectation had not been
fulfilled. Suddenly the community around Jesus, to whom he
was the Lord of faith and life, was left with the world on its
hands. And then all the trouble began! One could say that the
literature of Christian ethics reflects nothing so much as the
attempt [on the part of those who undertook in the world to
follow Jesus Christ] to understand and to interpret their responsibilities and their behavior. The literature of Christian ethics
is thus one of the most important pieces of evidence for the
fact that New Testament ethics and Christian ethics are not
identical.

What then are we to do with the New Testament—discard it?
To take this course would be to attempt a short cut to the

---

[1] See Luke 24.13-21. All biblical quotations will be from the Revised
Standard Version, unless otherwise indicated.
[2] See Acts 1.6-8            [3] Luke 17.32.

problem from the other side. For such an attempt there is no warrant whatever in the literature of Christian ethics. To enlarge our figure of speech a bit, the fact that Christians have not only the world on their hands but the New Testament itself on their hands makes of Christian ethics an intense and complex matter. Unless we are prepared to say that the history of the church from subapostolic times onwards is a history of defection from the original perfection of the primal Christian community, we have to face the fact that an analysis of Christian ethics involves a kind of running conversation between the New Testament, on the one hand, and our situation, as heirs of the New Testament, on the other.

If we look, therefore, at another possibility, we see that New Testament ethics and Christian ethics are *related*, though not identical. To do this is to be able to take seriously two very important subapostolic developments in the life of the church. The first is the development which led to the formation of the Canon. Thinking about Christian ethics by starting with the New Testament encounters the impressive difficulty that the church was never able to proceed in this way. Had this been possible, the church would never have become involved in the struggle over the Canon. The struggle over the Canon means that the church had to take thought about the sense in which the Scriptures are to be regarded as the point of departure for Christian faith and life. Had the authority of the Scriptures been self-evident, the Canon would have been self-evident. To consult the Scriptures as one would consult an oracle (or to modernize the allusion, a telephone directory) is a procedure inadequate both to the catechetical and to the anti-heretical responsibilities of the church. The decision about the Canon implies a decision about the Scriptures which avoids a very acute dilemma. On the one hand, the Canon means an avoidance of the absolutization of the Scriptures. One cannot go to the text—as text—for guidance. The Canon means that one goes to the text in the context of the faith and the life of the church. On the other hand, the decision about the Canon means the avoidance of the absolutization of tradition. We are not saying that the faith and life of the church, still less that the mind of the church, are in and of themselves normative for Christian thinking and Christian living. Neither the 'sectarian' attempt to work from a pure text nor the 'catholicizing' attempt to work from an exalted tradition is consonant with the fact and the significance of the Canon. What the decision about the Canon points to is the delicate balance between the Scriptures and the believing community (and *pari passu*, also the life of the believer in a community of believers) which it was the genius of the Reformation to underline.

This is the second subapostolic development in the life of the church which illuminates the relation between New Testament ethics and Christian ethics. Three maxims may be drawn from the theology of the Reformers and are worth recalling in this connection. The first is:

> *Scriptura est singularitas et perspicuitas veritatis fidei* (Scripture is the characteristically clear truth of faith).

The second is:

> *Tota Scriptura est verbum dei* (The Scripture as a whole is the Word of God).

The third is:

> *Testimonium internum Spiritus sancti* (The internal witness of the Holy Spirit).

These maxims have, of course, functioned chiefly as the watchwords of Protestant Orthodoxy. The theological treatises of the seventeenth century elaborate a doctrine of Holy Scripture with great care and comprehensiveness because of the authoritative importance assigned to the Bible in matters of faith and conduct. In these treatises, more plainly than anywhere else except in the confessional statements themselves, the exaltation and substitution of the Bible for the teaching office of the church as the primal and final authority in religious matters become plain. It must always be remembered that what was meant in the seventeenth century by these maxims was a doctrine of scriptural authority little short of verbal inerrancy. On this reading, the first maxim would be understood as asserting that the Bible is the particular and precise truth of faith, the second as asserting that the whole Scripture equally in every part is the Word of God. The third maxim, however, opens the way for another possibility. It may be read, and for the most part was read by Protestant Orthodoxy, in an almost dictational sense and thus as guaranteeing the claims of the other two maxims.[1] Yet the internal witness of the Holy Spirit is scarcely identical with the external witness of the Holy Spirit, and thus the strictly dictational operation of the Holy Spirit as presupposed by the doctrine of Scripture in Protestant Orthodoxy included and concealed the catalyst of its own dissolution. It is this consideration which gives heightened significance to the fact that the third maxim in the form stated is a conspicuous part of the way in which the original Reformers viewed both the Bible and the church. Protestant Orthodoxy overstated what the original Reformers were trying to express. And it is this overstatement which is corrected when we read the maxims in the non-literalistic sense in which they have been stated.

In this sense the maxims may serve to underline the point that the Canon is the work of the Holy Spirit in the church and that, as members of the church, believers encounter the Scriptures and find themselves in a continuous conversation with the Scriptures.[2] This is why Christian ethics and other disciplined reflection upon the nature and content of faith are theological matters. It is the office of theology to analyze and to work out the terms of the running conversation between the

---

[1] Actually the form of the first two maxims is synthetic. The phrases are variously distributed through the treatises and nowhere seem to come together in precisely the combination suggested here. The context, however, not only allows such a synthetic formulation but virtually requires it if we are to understand what the orthodox doctrine of Scripture was getting at. The third formulation does occur as stated and at many different points in the discussion of the doctrine of the Scripture. This maxim, however, also occurs frequently and as stated in the writings of the original Reformers. A conveniently available survey of the seventeenth-century Reformed literature on this point is to be found in Heinrich Heppe, *Reformed Dogmatics*, English translation by G. T. Thomson, revised and edited by Ernst Bizer, Allen & Unwin, London, 1950. Chapter Two will particularly want to be consulted. The translation is based upon Vol. 2 of Heppe's *Reformierte Dogmatik*, which first appeared in 1861. For a similar presentation of *Lutheran Dogmatics*, see Emanuel Hirsch, *Hilfsbuch zum Studium der Dogmatik*, 3. Aufl., Walter de Gruyter and Company, Berlin, 1958.

[2] Obviously this does not exclude the possibility that one may read the Scriptures and be illuminated by the Holy Spirit, i.e., become a believer, apart from membership in the church. We are concerned here with a systematic, not a chronological, point. It is equally obvious, however, that were one *so* to read the Scriptures, and *so* to come to faith, one could not stop short of participation in the life and the faith of the church.

Scriptures and ourselves. And for this reason we begin, not with the New Testament as such, but with the question of what is involved in Christian ethics as a theological discipline.

### 3 *Principal Accents in the History of Christian Thinking About Ethics*

The tension between New Testament ethics and Christian ethics has largely pervaded Christian ethical reflection from the beginning. With one or two possible exceptions, the literature of the church through the fourth century had no systematic Christian ethics. This literature, like that of the New Testament itself, reflects what might be called a 'situational ethics'. The Corinthian letters, for instance, deal with concrete problems of conduct and decision which had arisen for members of the Christian community in that city. Should Christians eat meat which had been bought at shops whose business it was to prepare and sell viands for the pagan sacrifices?[1] What should a man or woman who happened to have been converted from paganism to Christianity, and who happened also to be married, do about the unconverted partner? Did membership in a Christian community under these conditions disrupt the marriage relation?[2] Should Christians settle their grievances before a pagan court or before the church?[3] In a previous letter to the Christian community at Corinth, St Paul had been unmistakably direct and concrete in dealing with ethical matters. 'Don't mix with the immoral', he had written. But very soon afterwards he had found it necessary to explain what he meant. The initial injunction, translated into a principle consistently carried out, had not solved the problem.

> I didn't mean, of course, that you were to have no contact at all with the immoral of this world, or with any cheats or thieves or idolaters— for that would mean going out of the world altogether! But in this letter I tell you not to associate with any professing Christian who is known to be an impure man or a swindler, an idolater, a man with a foul tongue, a drunkard or a thief. My instruction is: 'Don't even eat with such a man.' Those outside the Church it is not my business to judge. But surely it is your business to judge those who are inside the Church—God alone can judge those who are outside. It is your plain duty to expel from the Church this wicked man![4]

---

[1] I Cor. 8.1ff.          [2] Ibid., 7.12ff.          [3] Ibid., 6.1ff.
[4] Ibid., 5.9-13 (Phillips' translation).

Plainly, membership in the Christian Church involved, at the beginning, an unequivocal break with specific kinds of behavior which had come to be condoned, if not approved, by the larger society of which the church was part.

This acute awareness of the difference in behavior between those who were Christians and those who were not is common to the New Testament ethical literature and to the ethical writings of the subapostolic period. Indeed, the conviction that the Christian faith somehow makes a noticeable difference in behavior between those who profess it and those who do not never disappears from Christian ethical reflection. What happens is that Christian ethical analysis shows a slowly and steadily emerging awareness of the difficulty of marking precisely what the distinction between Christian and non-Christian behavior is.

The subapostolic literature is more zealous about the boundary than the New Testament is. In distinction from the Corinthian letters, treatises like the *Didache* or the *Shepherd of Hermas* manifest such a zeal for differentiating between Christian and pagan behavior that ascetically tinged homilies of moral instruction and guidance are the result. It is not noticed that the Pauline caution about 'going out of the world altogether' and about 'judging the world' has been disregarded. Nor is there an awareness of a shift in motivation. The appeal is not, as with St Paul, to the 'dying and rising with Christ'[1] but to 'the Two Ways': 'righteousness and unrighteousness', 'purity and impurity', 'life and death'. 'There are two ways,' begins the *Didache*, 'one to life and one to death; and there is a great difference between the two ways. The way of life is this:

First, you must love God who made you, and second, your neighbor as yourself. And whatever you want people to refrain from doing to you, you must not do to them.

What these maxims teach is this: 'Bless those who curse you,' and 'pray for your enemies.' Moreover, fast 'for those who persecute you.' For 'what credit is it to you if you love those who love you? Is that not the way the heathen act?' But 'you must love those who hate you,' and then you will make no enemies. 'Abstain from carnal passions.' . . . If someone deprives you of 'your property, do not ask for it back.' (Yóu could not get it back anyway!) 'Give to everybody who begs from you and ask for no return.' For the Father wants his own gifts to be universally

---

[1] II Cor. 4.1ff.

shared. But alas for the man who receives! If he receives because he is in
need, he will be guiltless. But if he is not in need he will have to stand
trial why he received and for what purpose. He will be thrown into
prison and have his action investigated; and 'he will not get out until
he has paid back the last cent.' Indeed, there is a further saying that
relates to this: 'Let your donation sweat in your hands until you know
to whom to give it.'

But the way of death is this: first of all, it is wicked and thoroughly
blasphemous: murders, adulteries, lusts, fornications, thefts, idolatries,
magic arts, sorceries, robberies, false witness, hypocrisies, duplicity,
deceit, arrogance, malice, stubbornness, greediness, filthy talk, jealousy,
audacity, haughtiness, boastfulness.

See 'that no one leads you astray' from this way of the teaching, since
such a one's teaching is godless.

If you can bear the Lord's full yoke, you will be perfect. But if you
cannot, then do what you can.[1]

And in the same vein, but with perhaps more stress upon
negative and positive traits, Hermas declares:

'Restrain yourself in regard to evil, and do it not; but exercise no restraint
in regard to good, but do it. For if you exercise restraint in the doing of
good, you will commit a great sin; but if you exercise restraint so as not
to do that which is evil, you are practising great righteousness. Restrain
yourself, therefore, from all iniquity, and do that which is good.' 'What,
sir,' say I, 'are all the evil deeds from which we must restrain ourselves?'
'Hear,' says he: 'from adultery and fornication, from unlawful revelling,
from wicked luxury, from indulgence in many kinds of food and the
extravagance of riches, and from boastfulness, and haughtiness, and
insolence, and lies, and backbiting, and hypocrisy, from the remembrance
of wrong, and from all slander. These are the deeds that are most wicked
in the life of men. From all these deeds, therefore, the servant of God must
restrain himself. For he who does not restrain himself from these, cannot
live to God. . . .'

'But listen,' says he, 'to the things in regard to which you have not
to exercise self-restraint, but which you ought to do. Restrain not yourself
in regard to that which is good, but do it.' 'And tell me, sir,' say I, 'the
nature of the good deeds, that I may walk in them and wait on them, so
that doing them I can be saved. . . .'

'First of all there is faith, then fear of the Lord, love, concord, words of
righteousness, truth, patience. Than these, nothing is better in the life
of men. If any one attend to these, and restrain himself not from them,
blessed is he in his life. Then there are the following attendant on these:
helping widows, looking after orphans and the needy, rescuing the
servants of God from necessities, the being hospitable—for in hospitality

---

[1] *The Didache*, 1.1-6; 5.1; 6.1-2. Edited and translated by Cyril C.
Richardson, in *The Library of Christian Classics*, The Westminster Press,
Philadelphia, Vol. I, 1953 (SCM Press, London, 1953), pp. 171-72, 173-74.

good-doing finds a field—never opposing any one, the being quiet, having fewer needs than all men, reverencing the aged, practising righteousness, watching the brotherhood, bearing insolence, being long-suffering, encouraging those who are sick in soul, not casting those who have fallen into sin from the faith but turning them back and restoring them to peace of mind, admonishing sinners, not oppressing debtors and the needy, and if there are any other actions like these.

'Keep, therefore, this commandment. If you do good, and restrain not yourself from it, you will live to God.'[1]

Here, as Bishop Nygren has pointed out, though with special reference to the *Didache*, 'the causal motivation' (i.e., of *agape*) has been replaced by 'a teleological motivation'.[2]

This way of dealing with ethical problems was characteristic of the church, at least until toward the end of the fourth century. Tertullian, for example, wrote on many ethical subjects, but they were all specific and separate matters: on the kind of clothes one is to wear, on modesty, on fasting, on chastity.[3] The problem which again and again occupies the literature of the early church is the problem of virginity. But from the *Didache* to Tertullian the ethical orientation of the New Testament is either recalled for use as precepts applicable to particular ethical problems or casuistically employed in support of an ethical position really taken on other grounds.

The fourth century discloses what is, perhaps, the first use of the term 'ethics' in a Christian treatise. Basil of Caesarea about A.D. 361 drew up approximately eighty rules for the Christian life under the title 'The Principles of Ethics'.[4] Similarly, though more systematically, Bishop Ambrose of Milan published in 391 a work *On the Duties of the Clergy*, in three books.[5] Here again can be noted a strange mixture of New Testament

---

[1] *The Shepherd of Hermas*, Book Second, Commandments, VIII. *The Ante-Nicene Fathers*, The Christian Literature Company, Buffalo, Vol. II, 1885 (T. & T. Clark, Edinburgh).

[2] Anders Nygren, *Agape and Eros*, The Westminster Press, Philadelphia, 1953 (SPCK, London, 1953), p. 261.

[3] Cf. *The Ante-Nicene Fathers*, Vol. IV.

[4] Basil of Caesarea, *APXH TΩN HΘIKΩN*, Migne, PG, 31, 1857. See also the *Prolegomena* in *The Nicene and Post-Nicene Fathers* (*NPNF*), Second Series, The Christian Literature Company, New York, Vol. VIII, 1895, p. li.

[5] *De Officiis Ministrorum* is perhaps the first systematic treatise on Christian ethics. Cf. Migne, PL, 16, 1866; *NPNF*, Second Series, Vol. X, 1896.

insights and the ascetic tradition of the fourth-century priests. Two or three passages from Ambrose are worth citing in order to get the flavor of what he is concerned about. 'We know', wrote the Bishop with remarkable contemporary relevance, 'that contempt of riches is a form of justice.'[1] 'Mercy never fails but always finds means of help.'[2] And in a passage in the first book, the Bishop addresses himself to matters pertaining to the behavior of his clergy, matters which have not entirely disappeared in clerical circles in the interval.

> Ye remember, my children, that a friend of ours who seems to recommend himself by his assiduity in his duties, was nevertheless not admitted by me into the number of the clergy because his gestures were too unseemly. Also that I bade one whom I found already among the clergy never to go in front of me because he actually pained me by the seeming arrogance of his gait. That is what I said when he returned from his duties after an offence committed. This alone I would not allow, nor did my mind deceive me, for both these men have left the Church. What their gait betrayed them to be, such were they proved to be by the faithlessness of their hearts. Some there are who in walking perceptibly copy the gestures of actors, and act as though they were bearers in the procession and had the motions of nodding statues to such an extent that they seemed to beat a sort of time as often as they changed their step. Nor do I think it becoming to walk hurriedly except when a case of some danger demands it, or a real necessity. For we often see those who hurry come up panting and with features distorted. But if there is no reason for the need of such hurry, it gives just cause for offence. I am not, however, talking of those who have to hurry now and then for some particular reason, but of those to whom by the yoke of constant habit it has become second nature. In the case of the former, I cannot approve of their slow, solemn movements, which remind one of the forms of phantoms. Nor do I care for the others with their headlong speed. For they put one in mind of the ruin of outcasts. A suitable gait is that wherein there is an appearance of authority, and weight and dignity, and which has a calm collected bearing. But it must be of such a character that all effort and conceit may be wanting, and that it be simple and plain. Nothing counterfeit is pleasing. Let Nature train our movements; indeed, if there is any fault in Nature, let us mend it with diligence, and that artifice may be wanting, let not amendments be wanting.[3]

Such moralistic advice abounds in the ethical literature of the early church. It is not dissociated from the Scriptures, which find their way into the discussion either through allusions or as proof texts. But it is also plain that the focus of attention is upon specific problems of conduct, many of which

[1] *De Officiis*, II, 27, 133.        [2] Ibid., III, 7, 47.        [3] Ibid., I, 18, 72ff.

are foreign to the ethical situation of the New Testament. The disposition of these problems, moreover, is not only unsystematic; but in so far as presuppositions are evident, they seem to be drawn as much from Platonic, Stoic, and monastic ethical reflection as from the Bible. A work by Gregory the Great, which included a discussion of the four cardinal virtues in the course of a *Commentary on the Book of Job*, indicates how confused the systematic picture was.[1] The one conspicuous exception to this unsystematic and occasional literature is Augustine's *On the Morals of the Catholic Church*, which does offer, at the instance of a doctrine of virtue, a carefully reasoned synthesis of Platonic and New Testament ethical reflection.[2]

Turning to the Middle Ages, we mention two works which continue the tradition of the past, though in a somewhat more elaborate form. The first, from the early Middle Ages, is the *Rule of Saint Benedict*; the second, from the late Middle Ages, is the *Imitation of Christ* of St Thomas à Kempis.[3] Benedict's *Rule* is an attempt to set out the duties of the monastic life and to correct certain excesses and inadequacies which had arisen in monastic practice before his time. The work is marked by a shrewd combination of the demands upon the Christian under

[1] Gregory the Great, *Moralium Libri, sive Expositio in Librum B. Job*, Liber secundus, XLIX, pp. 592-93, Migne, PL, 75, 1862.

[2] Augustine, *De moribus ecclesiae catholicae*, Migne, PL, 32, 18; *NPNF*, First Series, The Christian Literature Company, Buffalo, Vol. IV, 1887. The well-known passage from the fifteenth chapter of this treatise admirably expresses its synthetic aim and character. Virtue is defined as 'nothing else than perfect love of God', and the cardinal virtues of Greek moral philosophy are said to be 'forms' of this love. Augustine then declares that 'temperance is love keeping itself entire and incorrupt for God; fortitude is love bearing everything readily for the sake of God; justice is love serving God only, and therefore ruling all else, as subject to man; prudence is love making a right distinction between what helps it towards God and what might hinder it'. But it must be remembered that the treatise on the *Morals of the Catholic Church* is a companion of the treatise on the *Morals of the Manichees*, so that its occasion is more polemical than constructive.

[3] *Of the Rule of Saint Benedict*, a readable and carefully edited, freshly translated text by Owen Chadwick, is available in *The Library of Christian Classics*, The Westminster Press, Philadelphia, Vol. XII, *Western Asceticism*, 1958 (SCM Press, London, 1958), pp. 290-337. Many editions of the *Imitation of Christ* are available. Attention may be called here to the six-volume edition of Thomas à Kempis, *Works*, K. Paul, London, Vol. 6, *Of the Imitation of Christ*, 1907.

vows and the frailties of human nature. The story of Jacob's ladder is applied to the attainment of humility, the chief virtue of the monk. 'If we want to attain true humility,' Benedict wrote, 'and come quickly to the top of that heavenly ascent to which we can only mount by lowliness in this present life, we must ascend by good works, and erect the mystical ladder of Jacob, where angels ascending and descending appeared to him.'[1] When the monk has mounted twelve steps of humility, he has attained the true love of God which makes it possible for him then to do the will of God in all things.

Among Benedict's shrewd advices out of a due regard for human frailty, those having to do with 'how the monks are to sleep'; with 'the tools and property of the monastery'; with 'the weekly offices in the kitchen'; and with 'the quantity of food' and 'the quantity of drink' are especially striking.[2] As regards kitchen duty, the *Rule* prescribes that 'the brothers are to serve by turns; and no one is exempt from duty in the kitchen, unless he be hindered by ill-health or employed on some business for the good of the monastery. From this service a monk learns charity and gains a greater degree of merit.' On the matter of drink, the *Rule* notes that:

Every man hath his proper gift from God, the one after this manner, and another after that. So it is a nice point to prescribe a certain measure of food and drink for others. Notwithstanding, having regard to the weakness of the sick, I am of the opinion that a hemina of wine every day will suffice. Yet be it known to those whom God has granted the gift of abstinence, that they shall have an especial reward.

If the necessity of the place, or the hard work, or the heat of the summer, makes them need more, it shall be in the power of the superior to add to the allowance; yet always with caution, that they may not fall to the temptations of satiety and drunkenness. Although we read that wine is never for monks, it is hard to persuade modern monks of this. At least we must all agree that we are not to drink to satiety, but with moderation. 'For wine makes even wise men to fall into apostasy.'

Where the poverty of the place prevents this measure being available,

---

[1] Op. cit., chap. 7. The ladder symbolism seems to have permeated Christian piety and ethics, particularly of the monastic sort, from Pseudo-Dionysius the Areopagite (third century) onwards. Though the scheme has been reduced from twelve steps to four by the time of à Kempis, and the mortification of the flesh has given way to the mortification of the self (soul), the ladder symbolism may still be detected.

[2] Ibid., and in the order noted, chaps. 22, 32, 25, 29, 40.

but much less, or even none at all; the monks there are to bless God, and not complain.

I give this especial instruction, that no one shall complain.

Although the ladder symbolism is not absent from the *Imitation of Christ*, the central place in Christian piety and behavior is occupied by the Passion of Christ. 'The whole of the Christian life', Bishop Nygren remarks, 'becomes essentially "*meditatio vitae Christi*", in which the emphasis is laid on the suffering and death, with a view to an "*imitatio Christi*" which shall transform the whole of life.'[1] It must be admitted that this concentration upon the Passion of Christ contributed to the understanding of the sacrificial character of the love of God. But it must also be noted that this 'Passion mysticism', to use Nygren's phrase, was nourished by the Bride figure of the *Song of Songs* as well as by the Crucifixion. The effect of this was to sensualize and even to sentimentalize the love for Christ, a consequence confirmed not only by medieval mysticism but by evangelical hymnody, particularly the Passion hymns. 'Both as regards love and the Passion of Christ,' says Nygren, 'Passion mysticism is governed by a fundamental spirit far removed from that of the New Testament which says: "Weep not for me, but weep for yourselves, and for your children" (Luke 23.28).'[2]

Of course, the most systematic ethical treatise of the Middle Ages is the *Secunda secundae* of the *Summa Theologica* of Thomas Aquinas. This work comprises 189 questions and answers which deal with the theological virtues and related matters like hatred, mercy, and war (QQ. 1-46); with a treatise on fortitude and temperance (QQ. 123-170); and with acts which pertain especially to certain men, that is, with prophecy, contemplation, and perfection, the ascetic crown of the Christian life (QQ. 171-189).[3] It is not accidental that this, as well as other works of Thomas, shows a conspicuous dependence upon both Augustine and Dionysius the Areopagite. The discussion of the theological virtues at the beginning of the *Secunda secundae*, and of the ascetic or contemplative crown of the Christian life at the end, with the treatment of the cardinal virtues in between,

---

[1] Op. cit., p. 663.          [2] Ibid., p. 664.

[3] Thomas Aquinas, *Summa Theologica: Secunda Secundae*, edidit, Commissio Piana, Ottawa, 1953, Vol. III. English Dominican translation, R. T. Washbourne, Ltd., London, 1917-22.

provides substantial confirmation of the fact that both the spirit and the letter of Thomas' argument are marked by the ascetic and mystical approaches to the Christian life which dominated the Middle Ages. The Scriptures are abundantly used. But reflective attention has become so completely absorbed by the problems of piety and ethics arising from an environment compounded of scriptural and Neoplatonic traditions as to overlook the question whether a systematic synthesis of divergent ethical presuppositions offered an authentic alternative to the legalistic morality of the early Christian period.

At least to the extent that this question was raised anew, the Reformation broke fresh ground in Christian ethical thinking and writing. Perhaps the most important ethical treatise of the sixteenth century is Luther's *Sermon on Good Works*,[1] which succinctly states the Reformation ethical position. Here the ladder symbolism, in both its monastic and its mystical forms, and the merit theology of the high Middle Ages are vigorously repudiated, and a fresh attempt is made to search the Scriptures for a different orientation and new lines of ethical analysis. 'The deepest difference between Catholicism and Luther', says Bishop Nygren, 'can be expressed by the following formulae: in Catholicism, fellowship with God on God's own level, on the basis of holiness; in Luther, fellowship with God on our level, on the basis of sin.'[2] The *Commentaries on Romans and Galatians* and on the *Sermon on the Mount* provide the pivotal biblical analyses underlying the position taken in the *Sermon on Good Works*; and the tract on Christian liberty turns out to be a remarkable manifesto of what the ethical reorientation of the Reformation really involved.[3] The most systematic statement of

---

[1] Martin Luther, *Sermon von den guten Werken* (1950), WA, 6, 196/202-76; 9, 226/229-301. For an English translation, the reader may be referred to the *Works of Martin Luther*, Holman edition, Muhlenberg Press, Philadelphia, 1943, Vol. I.

[2] Op. cit., p. 690.

[3] The critical edition of Luther's works in the original is that which since 1883 has borne the imprint of Weimar and come to be known as the *Weimar Ausgabe* (WA). A new and critical edition of Luther's works, carefully selected and freshly translated into English, has already begun to appear under the joint auspices of the Concordia Publishing House in St Louis and the Muhlenberg Press in Philadelphia. A total of fifty-five volumes is projected under the general editorship of Jaroslav Pelikan and Helmut Lehmann. The works mentioned above are noted first in the Weimar

this reorientation is offered in the <u>third book of Calvin's</u>
*<u>Institutes of the Christian Religion</u>.*[1]

From the seventeenth century onward, the term 'ethics'
comes more and more into specific use.[2] Partly owing to the
penchant of a rationalistic habit of mind for precise distinctions,
and partly owing to the altered climate of thought effected by
the Enlightenment and the Idealistic philosophy, the question
of the relation between ethics and dogmatics seemed to require
preliminary clarification in Christian ethical discussion.
Schleiermacher, for instance, wrote a book on the Christian
faith which included, on methodological grounds, propositions
of *Christian Ethics*.[3] The late nineteenth- and early twentieth-

edition and then in the corresponding edition by Pelikan and Lehmann.
This edition is also called the *American Edition*. When referred to in the
following pages, the abbreviation, AE, will be used.

*Vorlesung ueber den Roemerbrief* (1515-16), WA, 56-57. English translation
is projected as Vol. 25 of AE. Meanwhile the reader may be referred to the
translation by Wilhelm Pauck, *Luther: Lectures on Romans*, The Library of
Christian Classics, Volume XV, Philadelphia, The Westminster Press,
1961.

*In epistolam Pauli ad Galatas M. Lutheri commentarius* (1519), WA, 2, 436-618.
English translation is projected as Vols. 26-27 of AE.

*Wochenpredigten ueber Mattaeus 5-7* (1530-32), WA, 32, 299-544; AE, Vol.
21, 1956.

*Von der Freyheit eynes christen Menschen*, WA, 7, 42-49; AE, Vol. 31, 1957.

[1] Ioannis Calvini, *Institutio religionis christianae*, 1559, CR, XXX, Bk. III.
English translation by John Allen, *The Institutes of the Christian Religion*,
The Westminster Press, Philadelphia, 2 vols., 1936.

[2] The sixteenth century apparently knows only the three-volume work
of Lambert Danaeus, which appeared in Geneva with the term 'ethics' in
the title. His *Ethices christianae* was published in 1577. On either side of this
discussion may be noted the *De virtute christianae* (1529) of Thomas Venatorius
and the *Epitome theologiae moralis* (1634) of George Calixt as typifying the
way in which Christian ethical thinking was done.

[3] Friedrich Schleiermacher, *Der christliche Glaube*, G. Reimer, Berlin,
1821-22; English translation by H. R. Mackintosh and J. S. Stewart, *The
Christian Faith*, T. & T. Clark, Edinburgh, 1928, third impression, 1956.
The inclusion of ethical matter within the scope of dogmatics is part of the
enlargement of the revised edition of the *Glaubenslehre*. The general phrase
used for such matters is *Christliche Sittenlehre*. But before this arrangement
had been arrived at, Schleiermacher wrote an elaborate analysis of the
foundations of philosophical ethics upon which he later drew in dealing
with Christian ethics. The earlier work tries to find a basic and at the same
time all-inclusive scientific principle of ethical interpretation and for this
undertaking the term *Sittenlehre* is used—a usage which varies from the

century theologian Wilhelm Herrmann wrote a book which
included a reference to systematic theology only in its subtitle;
and he discussed Christian ethics in a brief volume which bore
the general title *Ethics*.[1] Perhaps the most elaborate treatment
of Christian ethics to come out of the nineteenth century was
the five-volume work by Richard Rothe, which envisages an
immense scope of theoretical and practical ethical discussion.[2]

Christian thinking about ethics since the Reformation appears
to have been divided between the continuation, though not
without considerable adaptation, of the medieval way of
dealing with ethical matters on the part of Roman Catholic
moralists and the attempt on the part of Protestant theologians
to work out the ethical reorientation inaugurated by Luther.[3]

---

general distinction between *Sittenlehre* and *Tugendlehre*, alluded to on page
25 above, and which shows how fluid at the reflective level the distinction
in words can be. (See *Werke*, Dritte Abteilung, *Zur Philosophie*, Erster Band,
G. Reimer, Berlin, 1946. The essay entitled *Grundlinien einer Kritik der
bisherigen Sittenlehre* was first published in 1803 and revised in 1834.)
Schleiermacher's specific treatment of Christian ethics was destined for
posthumous publication and in significance for the history of theological
ethics paralleled the influence of the *Glaubenslehre* upon dogmatics. In aim
though not in substance, the present discussion is in line with Schleiermacher's interpretation of Christian ethics. His lectures on the subject were
edited by L. Jonas and published under the title *Die christliche Sitte nach den
Grundsaetzen der evangelischen Kirche*. (*Werke*, Erste Abteilung, Bd. XII, G.
Reimer, Berlin, 1843.)

[1] Wilhelm Herrmann, *Die Religion in Verhaeltnis zum Welterkennen und zur
Sittlichkeit: eine Grundlegung der systematischen Theologie*, M. Niemeyer, Halle,
1879; *Ethik*, J. C. B. Mohr, Tuebingen, 1901.

[2] Richard Rothe, *Theologische Ethik*, Zimmermann, Wittenberg, 5 vols.,
1867-71. The almost statistical passion for complete and accurate coverage
evident in Rothe's work is nicely indicated by the title of the three-volume
discussion of A. von Oettingen, *Moralstatistik und die christliche Sittenlehre*,
Erlangen, 1868, 1873. One might regard these two extended treatises as
marking a kind of beginning of an evangelical factuality in ethics.

[3] This statement ignores, of course, the ethical tradition of the Greek
Orthodox Church, and of the so-called 'sects'. If our discussion of the
literature of Christian ethics aimed at a comprehensive survey, the omission
would be inadmissible. Since the aim is to suggest how the tension between
New Testament ethics and Christian ethics pervades the literature and that
the Reformation attempted to work out this tension with fresh and full
seriousness, the omission may be allowed. As regards the treatment of
Christian ethics among Orthodox theologians, the broad generalization
may, perhaps, be made that the tension between New Testament ethics

But the fresh articulation in the sixteenth century of the creative and unavoidable tension between biblical ethics and Christian ethics never came fully to expression in systematic ethical reflection from a Christian point of view. The formative character of the biblical ethical insights and the complex character of the always contemporary ethical situation were not adequately expounded, as regards their dynamic interrelatedness.

The attempt to overcome this lack is the real significance of Emil Brunner's *The Divine Imperative*.[1] With notable systematic thoroughness and comprehensiveness, Brunner tries to explore the implications for Christian ethics of the biblical account of God's redemptive activity in the world in the life, death, and resurrection of Jesus of Nazareth. Brunner brings this activity to ethical focus in the Reformation doctrine of justification by faith and by means of this doctrine interprets the will of God in its bearing upon conduct both personal and social. This work of Brunner's, Bishop Nygren's *Agape and Eros*, and Reinhold Niebuhr's *An Interpretation of Christian Ethics* and *The Nature and Destiny of Man* have been perhaps the most influential expositions of Christian ethics in the evangelical or Protestant tradition to the present time.[2] The relatively more recent systematic

---

and Christian ethics is less acutely felt and that the intimate connection between liturgy and life which marks the piety of Orthodoxy is designed to foster the direct implementation of the ethic of the Gospels in and through the ethics of the church. This point is, perhaps, nicely instanced by the circumstance that both Count Tolstoy and Dostoevsky were nurtured in the Orthodox tradition.

As for the so-called 'sects', it may be remarked that they exhibit a tendency opposite to that of the Orthodox. The tension between New Testament ethics and Christian ethics is *more* acutely felt, and a serious attempt is made to encourage the individual Christian as a member of a holy community toward as close an approximation to the ethical behavior of Jesus Christ as the conditions of a sinful world allow. Thus the ethical reorientation inaugurated by Luther became in diverse ways a passionate sectarian concern.

[1] Emil Brunner, *Das Gebot und die Ordnungen*, J. C. B. Mohr (Paul Siebeck), Tuebingen, 1933; translated by Olive Wyon under the title *The Divine Imperative*, The Westminster Press, Philadelphia, 1947 (Lutterworth Press, London, 1947).

[2] Reinhold Niebuhr, *An Interpretation of Christian Ethics*, Harper & Row, New York, 1935 (SCM Press, London, 1936) and *The Nature and Destiny of Man*, Charles Scribner's Sons, New York, 1941, 1943 (Nisbet, London, 1941, 1943).

exposition of Christian ethics by Karl Barth and the fragmentary, still more recently published ethics of Dietrich Bonhoeffer give promise of an even more creative and influential analysis of the insights and resources of an evangelical ethic for the shaping of behavior.[1] Common to all these discussions is the attempt to raise the 'prior question', the question of the correct and fundamental starting point for Christian ethical thinking, especially and precisely in view of the tension between the ethical insights of the Bible and the always contemporary ethical situation.[2]

The subsequent chapters in this volume undertake to participate in this discussion. In so far as they pursue an independent course, they do so, not in disregard of the ferment of ethical discussion in contemporary Christian thought, but rather by raising once again the 'prior question'. It is this question, as formulated at the outset of this chapter, which leads to a different starting point for Christian ethical analysis, and which requires and perhaps also validates a re-examination of the nature and problems of Christian ethics as well as an attempt to state what the context and the structure of Christian behavior are.

[1] Karl Barth, *Die Kirchliche Dogmatik*, Evangelischer Verlag, Zollikon-Zuerich, II/2, 1942, III/4, 1951. Dietrich Bonhoeffer, *Ethik*, zusammengestellt und herausgegeben von Eberhard Bethge, Chr. Kaiser, Muenchen, 1949; translated by Neville Horton Smith, The Macmillan Company, New York, 1955 (SCM Press, London, 1955).

[2] See above p. 26, note 1.

# II

## THE CHURCH AS THE CONTEXT OF
## ETHICAL REFLECTION

IN our thinking about Christian ethics everything depends upon the point of departure. This is really what makes Christian thinking about ethics different from the ethical thinking of other religious traditions and different from philosophical ethics. It is the point of departure which also fundamentally differentiates one interpretation of Christian ethics from another.

When Christian ethics is defined as *the disciplined reflection upon the question and its answer: What am I, as a believer in Jesus Christ and as a member of his church, to do?*, the point of departure is neither vague nor neutral. It is not the common moral sense of mankind, the distilled ethical wisdom of the ages. Not that we can ignore this ethical wisdom, but we do not start with it. Instead, the starting point for Christian thinking about ethics is the fact and the nature of the Christian Church. To put it somewhat too sharply: Christian ethics is not concerned with *the good*, but with what I, as a believer in Jesus Christ and as a member of his church, am to do. *Christian ethics, in other words, is oriented toward revelation and not toward morality.*

### 1 *Christian Ethics as* 'Koinonia *Ethics*'

The sense in which the church is the point of departure for and the context of Christian ethical reflection is best indicated by the way in which, according to the New Testament, the earliest communities or gatherings of Christians appear to have regarded themselves. The semantics of the matter are inconclusive; but the self-understanding of those who came together owing to their common involvement in the claims of Jesus Christ

upon their way of looking at life and of living it is plain.
According to the New Testament, the church is a historical
reality which, as it were, comes upon the historical scene as the
answer of disciples to that which God during the earthly life of
Jesus had done in and through him. This inaugural act of God
appeared to be so tensely on the edge of another and consummating action of God as to give the church a heightened
and urgent sense of its significance and destiny as the people of
God. The people of God are, of course, the people of the 'Age to
Come', the people who are under a new covenant and hold
membership in the true Israel. But so marked is the proleptic
sense of reality in the New Testament that the 'inheritance of
Christ' is viewed not only as a transforming membership in a
brotherhood which is to be but also as the fruit and function of
the Spirit's operation here and now. 'Not only the creation, but
we ourselves, who have the first fruits of the Spirit, groan
inwardly as we wait for adoption as sons, the redemption of our
bodies.'[1] 'He who has prepared us for this very thing is God,
who has given us the Spirit as a guarantee.'[2] 'But it is God who
establishes us with you in Christ, and has commissioned us; he
has put his seal upon us and given us his Spirit in our hearts as
a guarantee.'[3]

The proleptic historical sense of the significance of the church
was informed by Old Testament memories and tradition. It is
not accidental that the Septuagint translates הַקָּהָל by the word
ἡ ἐκκλησία. The consciousness of having been 'called out', of a
peculiar covenantal bond between God and the people and
ultimately also of a saving function among surrounding peoples,
marks the history of the Hebrews, of the 'old Israel' from
Abraham to the second Isaiah. The central place of the Messiah
in the story of the covenant people and the formative connection
between the kingdom of God and the community of the 'true
Israel' we shall have occasion subsequently to notice.[4] But the
sweep of this covenant story and the complex of memories and
traditions of the people of God far exceeded the semantic limitations of the word ἡ ἐκκλησία, or for that matter of the word
ἡ κοινωνία as well.

This story describes the self-consciousness of the church as a

---

[1] Rom. 8.23.    [2] II Cor. 5.5.    [3] Ibid., 1.21-22.    [4] See Chapter III.

*koinonia* and explains how that self-consciousness unmistakably characterized the New Testament accounts of the earliest communities of Christians. In this sense the word ἡ ἐκκλησία does not appear to be as frequently used. But when it is employed, it appears to have acquired a technical connotation strikingly related to the meaning of *koinonia*.[1] This same self-understanding of the church transforms the familiar metaphor of 'the body' from being merely a metaphor of unity into a metaphor designed to express a new 'fellowship-reality' between Jesus Christ and the believers, between the head of the body and its members.[2] Just as there is no Messiah without his people, so there is no real presence of Jesus in history without or apart from the true people of God which as the work of the Holy Spirit is always at the same time a spiritual and visible reality. It is this reality of the *koinonia*, whatever the word for it may be, which denotes the concrete result of God's specifically purposed activity in the world in Jesus Christ. We might, therefore, say that Christian ethics is *koinonia ethics*. This means that it is from, and in, the *koinonia* that we get the answer to the question: What am I, as a believer in Jesus Christ and as a member of his church, to do?

Clearly this is the point which emerges from some of the most influential correspondence of the Apostle Paul. 'God', he once wrote to the existing *koinonia* in Corinth, 'is faithful, by whom you were called into the fellowship (εἰς κοινωνίαν) of his Son, Jesus Christ our Lord.'[3] And toward the end of his life Paul wrote to the existing *koinonia* at Philippi, 'I thank my God in all my remembrance of you, always in every prayer of mine for

[1] The word ἡ ἐκκλησία appears frequently in the New Testament as a kind of *terminus technicus* for the Christian movement (I Cor. 1.2; II Cor. 1.2; Gal. 1.2; and in a somewhat different sense I Thess. 1.1; II Thess. 1.1). But this technical usage cannot be said to be borrowed from the general Hellenistic use of the word ἐκκλησία; nor does it carry discernible marks of the Old Testament; its roots appear to be much more clearly nourished in and by the Qumran brotherhood, where the eschatological sense of the 'true Israel of the end of the ages' seems to characterize the brotherhood in its totality. I am indebted, in making this brief sketch of the semantics and the self-understanding of the New Testament church, to a suggestive article by my colleague Professor Krister Stendahl published under the title *Kirche im Urchristentum* in a revised and third edition of *Die Religion in Geschichte und Gegenwart*, J. C. B. Mohr, Tuebingen, 1929, hereinafter abbreviated to *RGG*.

[2] Compare, for example, I Cor. 12 with I Peter 1.10-12; 2.4-10.

[3] I Cor. 1.9.

you all making my prayer with joy, thankful for your partnership in the gospel from the first day until now' (literally, 'making prayer with joy, because of the fellowship of you'—*ἐπὶ τῇ κοινωνίᾳ ὑμῶν*—'in the gospel').[1]

Perhaps the most impressive passage in which Paul connects the Christian *koinonia* with Christian ethics is in the letter to the existing *koinonia* at Ephesus. Although the term *κοινωνία* does not occur in the passage, its nature and its ethical significance are explicitly set forth, and in terms of the relation between Christ and the church.[2] In view of the intrinsic bearing of the passage upon the *koinonia* character of Christian ethics, it may be cited at some length and then commented upon.

For this reason I, Paul, a prisoner for Christ Jesus on behalf of you Gentiles—assuming that you have heard of the stewardship of God's grace that was given to me for you, how the mystery was made known to me by revelation, . . . When you read this you can perceive my insight into the mystery of Christ, which was not made known to the sons of men in other generations as it has now been revealed to his holy apostles and prophets by the Spirit; that is, how the Gentiles are fellow heirs, members of the same body, and partakers of the promise in Christ Jesus through the gospel. Of this gospel I was made a minister according to the gift of God's grace which was given me by the working of his power. To me, though I am the very least of all the saints, this grace was given, to preach to the Gentiles the unsearchable riches of Christ, and to make all men see what is the plan of the mystery hidden for ages in God who created all things; that through the church (*διὰ τῆς ἐκκλησίας*) the manifold wisdom of God might now be made known to the principalities and powers in the heavenly places. This was according to the eternal purpose which he has realized in Christ Jesus our Lord, in whom we have boldness and confidence of access through our faith in him. . . .

For this reason I bow my knees before the Father, . . . that according to the riches of his glory he may grant you to be strengthened with might through his Spirit in the inner man, and that Christ may dwell in your hearts through faith; that you, being rooted and grounded in

---

[1] Phil. 1.3-5.

[2] This may be one of the internal grounds for raising a question about the Pauline authorship of Ephesians. Current biblical scholarship is apparently still inconclusive on the point, being occupied with the examination of new considerations on both sides of the question. An instructive account of the present state of the discussion is provided by Professor Henry Cadbury in 'The Dilemma of Ephesians', *New Testament Studies*, Vol. V, No. 2, 1958-59, pp. 91-102. But whether Pauline or not, and with due allowance for the greater stress in Ephesians than in Colossians upon Christ as the head of the body, there is no real disparity between what is said here and in the letter to the Colossians about the church.

love, may have power to comprehend with all the saints what is the breadth and length and height and depth, and to know the love of Christ which surpasses knowledge, that you may be filled with all the fulness of God. . . .

I, therefore, a prisoner for the Lord, beg you to lead a life worthy of the calling to which you have been called, with all lowliness and meekness, with patience, forbearing one another in love, eager to maintain the unity of the Spirit in the bond of peace. There is one body and one Spirit, just as you were called to the one hope that belongs to your call, one Lord, one faith, one baptism, one God and Father of us all, who is above all and through all and in all. But grace was given to each of us according to the measure of Christ's gift. . . .

And his gifts were that some should be apostles, some prophets, some evangelists, some pastors and teachers, for the equipment of the saints, for the work of ministry, for building up the body of Christ, until we all attain to the unity of the faith and of the knowledge of the Son of God, to mature manhood, to the measure of the stature of the fulness of Christ; so that we may no longer be children, tossed to and fro and carried about with every wind of doctrine, by the cunning of men, by their craftiness in deceitful wiles. Rather, speaking the truth in love, we are to grow up in every way into him who is the head, into Christ, from whom the whole body, joined and knit together by every joint with which it is supplied, when each part is working properly, makes bodily growth and upbuilds itself in love. . . .

Look carefully then how you walk, not as unwise men but as wise, making the most of the time, because the days are evil. Therefore do not be foolish, but understand what the will of the Lord is . . . always and for everything giving thanks in the name of our Lord Jesus Christ to God the Father.[1]

Here we see that the *koinonia* character of Christian ethics is derived from the nature of the church as the 'body of Christ'. According to the passage cited, the first point to be underlined is that the church, the fellowship which is the body of Christ, the *koinonia*, is the *fellowship-creating reality* of Christ's presence in the world. God's secret (τὸ μυστήριον), the incalculable riches of Christ, has been hidden to past generations of mankind, but now, by the Spirit, it has been made plain to all men. The secret is that the Gentiles are fellow heirs and members of the same body and that the church is the instrument through which the complex wisdom of God is made known. This was in accordance with God's eternal purpose realized in Christ. The church is actually anchored in the structure of God's creation and is itself the fullness of God's purpose. Secondly, this fellow-

---

[1] Eph. 3.1-12, 14, 16-19; 4.1-7, 11-16; 5.15-17, 20.

ship-creating reality of Christ's presence in the world may be
apprehended in a certain way. There is a 'line of revelation', a
prophetic-apostolic line, which is illumined in and to the
fellowship by the Spirit. This line of divine revelation is the
clue to the *koinonia*, the *ecclesiola in ecclesia*, the little church
within the church.[1] The *koinonia* is always there in the com-

[1] The phrase *ecclesiola in ecclesia* is a post-Reformation, not a New Testament, way of underlining the authentic nature of the Christian community.
It emerges in German Pietism, a movement which aimed at the renewal
of the churches and congregations on the basis of personal piety. With
Spener this piety characterized 'those who wanted to be Christians with all
earnestness'; with August Hermann Francke, personal piety characterized
those who had been converted after an inner struggle of repentance
(*Busskampf*); with Count Zinzendorf, the founder of the Moravian community, the stress fell upon the religion of the heart (*Herzenreligion*).
   In a searching and provocative little study Emil Brunner has recently
urged that there is only one clear meaning of 'church' in the New Testament
and that the attempt to distinguish between a true and a false, an invisible
and a visible, a spiritual and an institutional church is as foreign to the
New Testament as could possibly be. 'The *ecclesia*', Brunner declares, 'is
the actual and real fellowship with Christ, as real as are the faith and love
and hope which belong to the *ecclesia*. Furthermore, the *ecclesia* is the fellowship established in Christ among those who are bound together through him,
a fellowship which is as real as are their concern for one another, their
brotherly love towards one another, the sacrifices of funds and goods, of
time and strength, of safety and of life which they make for one another.'
The persistent and widespread and regrettable misunderstanding of the
church is the interpretation of the church as always also an institution—
indeed, as an institution at all. (See Emil Brunner, *Das Missverstaendnis der
Kirche*, Zwingli-Verlag, Zuerich, 1951, especially pp. 96 and 97. The italics
and translation are mine. There is an English translation by Harold Knight
under the title *The Misunderstanding of the Church*, The Westminster Press,
Philadelphia, 1953 (Lutterworth Press, London, 1952).)
   Brunner's insistence upon the *koinonia* character of the church as the
authentic New Testament understanding of the body of Christ eloquently
and evidentially confirms our present concern. If Brunner is correct, one
cannot speak about the *ecclesiola in ecclesia* at all. And yet he does allow that
the various forms of the church's life in the course of her history are attempts
with greater or less fidelity to express or to return to the authentic self-
understanding of the New Testament community as a *koinonia*. It may be
wondered whether Brunner does not overlook the dialectic between the
spiritual and empirical reality of the body of Christ in his zeal to rescue
the church from the peril of institutionalization and to give to the distinction
between the spiritual and empirical reality of the church a trans-institu-
tional and authentic fellowship significance. The Pietist movement also
draws too sharp a distinction between the 'little church' and the 'larger

munity of faith where prophetic-apostolic *witness* to revelation and *response* of the fellowship in the Spirit coincide.

The specific allusion of the passage is, of course, to the problem raised for the Jewish Christian community, on the one hand by the fact of their pre-Christian and presumably continuing membership in the covenant community of Israel, and on the other by the fact that there were Gentiles who also were believers. The original Christian form of the problem of the believers and the unbelievers is, thus, a two-pronged one. In the Letter to the Romans[1] the Apostle Paul addresses himself to the Israelitic aspect of the question and makes the point that the Israelitic community can neither confine nor be cut off from the inheritance of God's saving activity in history. In the Ephesian passage the author addresses himself to the Gentile aspect of the problem and makes the point that the inclusion of the Gentiles within the 'Israel of God'[2] must be understood as the contemporary disclosure or revelation of a previously hidden secret of the divine plan of salvation. The problem of believers and unbelievers has shifted its center of gravity: not Jews as believers and Gentiles as unbelievers, but Jews and Gentiles as believers in distinction from Jews and Gentiles as unbelievers. This means that, in the complex wisdom of God, believer and unbeliever are fellow heirs—not primarily as Jews and Gentiles, or merely as human beings, but as human beings who as members of a 'third race' are proleptic of the transformation and fulfillment of all human beings in the new humanity of which Christ, the head of the body, is also the second Adam, the first fruit.[3] The complex wisdom of God is that, just as the

church', which at least since Augustine's day had been recognized as a *corpus permixtum*. Brunner's point is not the Pietist one. Yet in so far as the Pietist phrase *ecclesiola in ecclesia* forcefully and succinctly expresses the concern for the authentic reality of the church as a fellowship of which Christ is the head and in which Christ is really present and at work in the world, it may be appropriated here both in relation to Brunner's point and more particularly in apposition to the point under discussion in the Letter to the Ephesians. See also the synoptic and admirably factual articles entitled 'Kirche', respectively in *RGG*, Vol. 3, pp. 783-807; and *Evangelisches Kirchenlexikon*, Vol. 2, Vandenhoeck und Ruprecht, Goettingen, 1958, pp. 608-38.

[1] Chaps. 9-11.

[2] To use a strong, and previously used, genuine Pauline phrase from Gal. 6.16.

[3] See Chapter IV, 3.

Gentiles have not been excluded from the Israelitic inheritance, so unbelievers, though not *in principle* excluded from the unsearchable riches of Christ, are not *by definition* included in their benefits. The responsibility of believers is so to make known the unsearchable riches of Christ that the fellow heir in the economy of God is drawn into the *koinonia* and does not remain outside.

In the third place, the body of Christ is a fellowship of diverse gifts. There is no uniformity, no monotony, in the *koinonia*. These diversities of gifts are themselves part of the Creator's purpose according to which Christ functions in the world. They are focused and grounded upon the unity of the head, who is Christ. In the last analysis, it is Christ who is the center of the *koinonia*. The figures are interchangeable: the 'head of the body', the 'center of the fellowship'. In the Synoptic Gospels, the point emerges in a paradoxical form: 'Not every one who says to me, "Lord, Lord," shall enter the kingdom of heaven, but he who does the will of my Father who is in heaven';[1] and, 'Blessed are those servants whom the master finds awake when he comes; truly, I say to you, he will gird himself and have them sit at table, and he will come and serve them.'[2] And the Fourth Gospel, in a less paradoxical way, underlines the interchangeability between the 'head of the body' and the 'center of the fellowship' in words attributed to Jesus, as follows: 'I am the way, and the truth and the life; no one comes to the Father but by me. . . . Greater love has no man than this, that a man lay down his life for his friends. You are my friends if you do what I command you.'[3] An anonymous mid-second-century sermon puts it like this:

> The Bible, moreover, and the Apostles say that the Church is not limited to the present, but existed from the beginning. For it was spiritual, as was our Jesus, and was made manifest in the last days to save us. Indeed, the Church which is spiritual was made manifest in the flesh of Christ, and so indicates to us that if any of us guard it in the flesh and do not corrupt it, he will get it in return by the Holy Spirit. . . . Now, if we say that the Church is the flesh and the Christ is the spirit, then he who does violence to the flesh, does violence to the Church. Such a person, then, will not share in the spirit, which is Christ. This flesh is able to share in so great a life and immortality, because the Holy Spirit cleaves to it.

---

[1] Matt. 7.21.    [2] Luke 12.37.    [3] John 14.6; 15.13, 14.

Nor can one express or tell 'what things the Lord has prepared' for his chosen ones.[1]

So long as one is able to say that 'the church is the flesh and the Christ is the spirit', and to keep eyes open to the dynamism of the Holy Spirit in shaping 'so great a life and immortality', there is an authentic response in the *koinonia* to the diversity of gifts as a witness to the centrality and presence of Christ in the world. In this sense, one can say, 'where Jesus Christ is, there is the *koinonia*'; or as Ignatius would have put it, 'where Jesus Christ is, there is the Catholic Church'. But as soon as one begins to put the matter the other way around, namely, 'where the Catholic Church is, there is Jesus Christ', one has not only begun to distort what 'the Bible, moreover, and the Apostles say that the Church is . . .'; one has also lost the sense for the ethical reality of the *koinonia* in the world.

A fourth consideration suggested by the Ephesian passage has to do with the goal and *esprit* of the Christian life, of life in the *koinonia*. The point and goal of the Christian life are 'mature manhood'.[2] This is the fruit of 'the unity of the faith

[1] *An Early Christian Sermon*, usually called II Clement, edited and translated by Cyril C. Richardson, *The Library of Christian Classics*, The Westminster Press, Philadelphia, Vol. I, 1953 (SCM Press, London, 1953), p. 199. Contemporary biblical and systematic theological discussion has alerted us to the possibility of distorting what 'the Bible, moreover, and the Apostles say' by an unguarded appropriation of the Hellenic distinction between flesh and spirit. This is, however, not the point at issue here. The passage from the sermon puts with imagination and force exactly what is involved in the hiddenness and in the visibility of the *koinonia* in the world. Already in the second century the tension between 'hiddenness' and 'visibility' was being weakened, if not slowly stratified, by the process of institutionalization. Ignatius can still say firmly, 'Where Jesus Christ is, there is the Catholic Church'. But he does not do so without attaching this affirmation to a previous clause: 'Where the bishop is present, there let the congregation gather, just as etc.' Ibid., p. 115. But it is important to remember that, when the apposition of the two clauses which Ignatius had maintained came to be dissolved, as later happened, and men began to think and feel that 'where the Catholic Church is, there is Jesus Christ', then the figure of the 'head and the body' was no longer interchangeable with the figure of 'the center of the fellowship', and the understanding of the *koinonia* as the clue to the mystery and the reality of Christ's presence and work in the world was lost.

[2] Or, as Canon Phillips has phrased it, 'real maturity'. J. B. Phillips, *Letters to Young Churches*, The Macmillan Company, New York, 1950 (Geoffrey Bles, London, 1947), Eph. 4.13.

and of the knowledge of the Son of God'. Maturity—that is 'that measure of development which is meant by "the fullness of Christ"!'[1] The ethical reality of the church is the building up of itself in love, as Christ the head works in it; and this ethical reality is the *koinonia*.

We come here upon another far-reaching revision of Christian ethical understanding required by the *koinonia* as the point of departure for Christian thinking about ethics. It has already been emphasized that Christian ethics is oriented toward revelation rather than toward morality. A corollary must now be emphasized, namely, that *Christian ethics aims, not at morality, but at maturity.* The *mature* life is the fruit of Christian faith. Morality is a by-product of maturity.

'Rather, speaking the truth in love, we are to grow up in every way into him who is the head, into Christ, from whom the whole body joined and knit together by every joint with which it is supplied when each part is working properly, makes bodily growth and upbuilds itself in love.' The Greek text says: εἰς ἄνδρα τέλειον, 'towards a complete man', or 'towards a whole man'.[2] The contrast is between the full bodily growth of an adult and the incomplete physical development of an infant or boy. The organic vitality of the physical thrust toward wholeness is appropriated by the author of Ephesians in order to illuminate the organic vitality of the structure of the *koinonia*. *Integrity in and through interrelatedness* characterizes bodily growth toward maturity. This growth is marked by a pattern according to which the individuality of each several part is achieved and expressed in and through its own proper functioning, i.e., its own being what it is in interrelatedness with all other parts. Just so, the interrelatedness between Christ, the head, and the several members of the fellowship of diverse gifts which is Christ's body is structured in the world in a pattern of integrity in and through interrelatedness. And participation in this pattern is at once the mark and the means of that organic vitality which carries forward toward wholeness, or maturity, the several members individually and the body as a whole. What psychology knows as the problem of integration, what

---

[1] So in Eph. 4. 13. The RSV translates, 'the measure of the stature of the fullness of Christ'.

[2] Eph. 4.15, 16; 4.13 (Nestle).

sociology knows as the problem of community, Christian faith discerns and delineates as the problem of the head and the body. The resolution of the problem belongs to the possessor of the secret of maturity. For maturity *is* the integrity in and through interrelatedness which makes it possible for each individual member of an organic whole to be himself in togetherness, and in togetherness each to be himself.

This is maturity. And it has subtle and far-reaching implications for the bearing of Christian faith upon the living of the Christian life. When one thinks, for instance, of the way in which the Christian Church has ever and again succumbed to an unholy and unhealthy rhythm between dogmatism, on the one hand, and pietism, on the other, one gets some measure of the pathological immaturity that frustrates the body of Christ as a *koinonia* in the world. According to this rhythm, a believer is never willing to take his fellow man, whether believer or unbeliever, as he is, but always wants to impose upon his fellow, as a precondition of their fellowship, the doctrinal pattern of his own belief. And when this attack upon the integrity of the other succumbs to the enervating futility of rational formulations, the other side of the coin presently turns face up. The believer then gets emotional about his faith, as though the *koinonia* could be authenticated by internalization. But *maturity*, which is the fruit of Christian faith and the goal of *koinonia* living, makes it unseemly for a Christian either to walk about with head in the clouds as though he were God or to rouse the feelings as though they were the principal instruments for glorifying God. It is unseemly because such behavior is a violation of the fundamental humanity of man, the humanity with which Christ identified himself in his incarnation, which Christ restored through his humiliation, and which Christ glorifies in his resurrected and ascended body and through the *koinonia* which is his body in the world.

The signs and the practice of this maturity touch the deepest springs of human motivation and the farthest range of human interrelatedness. The intricate complexity of maturity is never denied; but neither is it surrendered to. Complexity, in the context of the *koinonia*, is an occasion for the fulfillment, not the frustration, of the rich diversity of Christ's giving. The confidence of the Christian is that this is what God is working at in the world and that sooner or later, come what may, the promise and the prospect of maturity will be consummated.

> Finish, then, with lying and tell your neighbor the truth. For we are not separate units but intimately related to each other in Christ. If you are angry, be sure that it is not out of wounded pride or bad temper. Never go to bed angry—don't give the devil that sort of foothold.
>
> If you used to be a thief you must not only give up stealing, but you must learn to make an honest living, so that you may be able to give to those in need. . . .
>
> Let there be no more resentment, no more anger or temper, no more violent self-assertiveness, no more slander and no more malicious remarks. Be kind to each other, be understanding. Be as ready to forgive others as God for Christ's sake has forgiven you.[1]

The succeeding chapter extends this motivational analysis so as to include, directly and by implication, the whole range of human interrelatedness. The relations between wives and husbands, children and parents, servants and masters—indeed, all the interrelationships of men—are drawn into the orbit of the way life looks from within the *koinonia*. The thrust of the *koinonia* into the world means that all ordinary conduct is *socialized* rather than *universalized*, because in the *koinonia*, and this means in the ethical reality of Christian faith, the maturity and the humanity of man stand or fall together. A mature humanity and the 'new humanity' are identical.

## 2 *The Ethical Reality of the Church*

If what we have been saying about the church as the point of departure for Christian thinking about ethics, and, in consequence, about the *koinonia* character of Christian ethics, is valid, two considerations press for further clarification lest they remain as troublesome objections to the present course of the argument. One of these considerations has to do with the possible objection to a *koinonia* ethic from the side of the individual. The other has to do with an objectionable source of confusion, namely, the sense in which, if at all, the *koinonia* is to be distinguished from the empirical reality of the church. These considerations and possible objections arise from an inadequate grasp of the way in which Christian ethics as *koinonia* ethics underlines the *ethical* reality of the church.

[1] Eph., 4.25-31 (Phillips).

## a. The socio-ethical understanding of the church in the New Testament

It has become axiomatic, and on the alleged authority of Jesus himself, to link Christianity with the exaltation of the individual. Jesus' major concern, so the claim runs, was with the individual. He discovered the individual. He came to redeem the individual. What happens to this individualism in a *koinonia* ethic?

It must be admitted that the teachings of Jesus express a very real and basic concern with individuals. The parables of the lost sheep, and the lost coin, together with the classical instance, the parable of the prodigal son, make Jesus' concern with and for individuals undeniably plain.[1] One thinks also of the moving passage: 'Are not two sparrows sold for a penny? And not one of them will fall to the ground without your Father's will. But even the hairs of your head are all numbered';[2] and again of Jesus' injunction to his disciples that they are to 'rejoice that [their] names are written in heaven'.[3]

And yet, just as Jesus stressed God's concern with and for the individual, so also this concern with and for the individual is not a separate concern. Whatever accent upon the individual there is in Jesus' thought is always related to the context of his preaching and teaching; and most of all, Jesus' alleged individualism must be understood with reference to his own conception of himself. It is not accidental that Mark declares, 'Jesus came . . . preaching the gospel of God, and saying, "The time is fulfilled, and the kingdom of God is at hand; repent, and believe in the gospel." '[4] Jesus did not come saying, 'Are you saved?—You! and You! and You!' He did not come with an invitation to come forward, give yourself to Christ, fill out a card, and join the church! Individuals are 'saved' into the *koinonia*, not one by one! Jesus came preaching the gospel of God, which is: 'The time is fulfilled, and the kingdom of God is at hand; repent, and believe in the gospel.' Even the prodigal son, when he comes to himself, returns to the Father's house and is received again into a *family*. The lost sheep, for whom the shepherd leaves the ninety and nine behind, is restored to the *flock*. Being restored to the flock, to the family, the individual with whom God is concerned and who has lost his individuality,

[1] Luke 15.   [2] Matt. 10.29-30.   [3] Luke 10.20.   [4] Mark 1.14-15.

that is, his selfhood, is drawn back into the orbit of God's way of working with men in the world. And as Jesus' life and ministry move on, the records implicitly or explicitly indicate an increasing identification of himself with the Messiah, who is unintelligible apart from the covenant community, the corporate structure of God's activity in the world. The Synoptic insistence upon the qualified nature of Jesus' concern for the individual is underlined as well by the Fourth Gospel, whose metaphors of the 'vine and the branches', the 'shepherd and the sheep' are eloquent cases in point.[1]

To be sure, Jesus was concerned with and for the individual, but not with a 'rugged individual'. Jesus' concern centered upon a 'redeemed individual'; and 'redeemed individual' and 'rugged individual' are contradictory terms. A redeemed individual is the individual whose individuality is the by-product and the fruit of the fellowship of Christ's body, that is, of the *koinonia.* Thus, it is simply an error to say that the great thing about Jesus is that he exalted the dignity of the individual. Christianity does not affirm the *dignity* but the *sanctity* of the individual. The dignity of the individual is derived not from Jesus but from the Stoic and Deist exaltation of the worth of man. Christianity, on the other hand, is concerned about the sanctity of the individual—with or without dignity—because of Jesus' perceptive claim that when individuals are degraded or destroyed the purposes of God are obstructed. It is God's fellowship-creating mystery, purposed from before the foundation of the world and disclosed in the *koinonia*, that is violated whenever the individual is disproportionately exalted (as in revivalistic pietism) or disproportionately abased (as in political totalitarianism).

The individualistic misunderstanding of the mind of Jesus has also involved the Apostle Paul. Perhaps the most that can be said for the extension of this error is that it serves as a further, though negative, confirmation of the faithfulness with which Paul entered into and interpreted the mind of Jesus. The principal refuge of this misinterpretation both of Jesus and of Paul is lodged in passages which underlie the other troublesome misunderstanding of a *koinonia ethic.* Thus, the attempt to clarify the relation between the *koinonia* and the church serves as an

[1] Cf. John 15 and 10.

additional bulwark against the individualistic error. Indeed, it is not too much to say that confusion about the significance of the individual and confusion about the significance of the church in Christianity are correlative confusions. The ethical reality of the church forcefully exposes the one error with the other.

Two metaphors chiefly characterize Paul's developing thought about the nature of the *koinonia* as the fellowship-creating reality of Christ's presence in the world. One is the metaphor of 'the temple'; the other is the metaphor of 'the body'.[1] In general, it may be said that the individualistic error has distorted the relation between the *koinonia* and the church in Pauline thought by individualizing the Apostle's conception of the 'temple' and the 'body'. Thus, the fundamental interchangeability of these metaphors has been obscured, and the sense for God's fellowship-creating activity in the world has been dulled. It is this divine activity in Christ which gives to the *koinonia* its crucial significance for an authentic Christian understanding, both of the individual and of the church.

The root of the difficulty seems to be that Paul uses the metaphor of the 'body' chiefly and rightly in a social sense, but occasionally also in an individualistic sense. In the latter case, certain moral behavioral injunctions are directed toward individual Christians, and on the ground that their individual bodies are a 'temple of the Holy Spirit within [them]'. What has not been sufficiently noticed in the course of this too rapid leap to a conclusion is that the use of the temple metaphor which occurs in the context of a discussion of bodily immorality has been prepared for by a use of the temple metaphor in the context of a discussion of what it means to be a member of the 'body of Christ' in Corinth. 'The body is not meant for immorality, but for the Lord, and the Lord for the body', says I Cor. 6.13; and it concludes with the familiar interrogative injunction: 'Do you not know that your body is a temple of the Holy

---

[1] On the 'temple', cf. especially I Cor. 3.16; 6.19; II Cor. 6.16; Eph. 2.21. On the 'body', cf. especially, in addition to the passage in Ephesians already noted, Col. 1.18, 24, where 'body' and 'church' are synonymously used; 2.19 and 3.15, where 'body' is described in terms of organism much in the manner of the Ephesian passage; and above all, the well-known discussion of the 'body and its members' in I Cor. 12.

Spirit within you, which you have from God?'[1] But before this apparently individualistic conclusion has been reached, Paul puts another question which prevents (or at least modifies) a reading of his mind in so individualistic a way. 'Do you not know that your bodies are members of Christ?'[2]

It is hard to see how this question, individualistically understood, could have any meaning other than a literal identification of the physical bodies of believers with the physical or quasi-physical resurrected body of Christ. Which is to say, the question, understood in this way, is meaningless. It would have been meaningless for Paul also. For the context plainly shows that Paul was interested in quite another point. Toward the end of the third chapter of I Corinthians the same question occurs, as at the end of Chapter 6. 'Do you not know that you are God's temple, and that God's Spirit dwells in you? If any one destroys God's temple, God will destroy him. For God's temple is holy, and that temple you are.'[3] The basis and the nature of the Christian life, as life in a certain kind of community, are the central concerns of this chapter. 'You are God's field, God's building', Paul declares. 'According to the commission of God given to me, like a skilled master builder I laid a foundation, and another man is building upon it. Let each man take care how he builds upon it. For no other foundation can anyone lay than that which is laid, which is Jesus Christ.'[4]

In this passage, the 'temple' is inferentially related to the bodily individuality alluded to in Chapter 6. As the later allusion has to do with immorality, so the earlier reference concerns building rightly upon a foundation already laid. But these are derivative responsibilities of the individual Christian which make sense only if he is clear about what it means to be a Christian in the first place. The decisive point is that both in I Cor. 3.16 and in 6.19 the second personal pronoun *plural* is used. 'You are God's temple.' 'Your body is a temple of the Holy Spirit within you.' The plural 'you', in all these instances, refers to the Corinthian congregation, the *koinonia* of believers, to whom Paul is writing. How fundamentally this is the case is indicated by what is virtually a commentary upon these Corinthian passages in the second chapter of Ephesians. Here

[1] I Cor. 6.19.    [2] Ibid., v. 15.    [3] I Cor. 3.16-17.    [4] Ibid., vv. 9-11.

the explicit allusion to 'a holy temple in the Lord' is expressly anchored in the fellowship character of the 'body', so fully elaborated in the later chapters of the Ephesians letter.

> So then you are no longer strangers and sojourners, but you are fellow citizens with the saints and members of the household of God, built upon the foundation of the apostles and prophets, Christ Jesus himself being the chief cornerstone, in whom the whole structure is joined together and grows into a holy temple in the Lord; in whom you also are built into it for a dwelling place of God in the Spirit.[1]

On the one hand, of course, there is nothing more individual than the body. Even an architectural glance at a building can scarcely exclude the impression that the whole consists of individual parts. But on the other hand, nothing is more patent than the organic and social character of the body. The architectural reality of a building includes style and *esprit* as well as stones, and this is a matter of 'corporate' or 'social' wholeness. This is exactly the point that is so eloquently expressed in Paul's celebrated description of the body and its members.[2] It may, accordingly, be concluded that when Paul deals with the behavior of Christians, that is, with the ethical reality of the Christian life, he starts from the ethical reality of the church as a *koinonia*, a fellowship of maturity in love. In structuring this fellowship, Paul works with the metaphor of 'temple' and of 'body' and with the idea of the structuring activity of God in Christ and in the Spirit. As his thought unfolds, various nuances of meaning emerge which tend toward the hyphenization of 'temple' and 'body' into 'temple-body' and toward a kind of dynamic polarity between 'temple-body', on the one hand, and the Holy Spirit, on the other. The point would seem to be that the Spirit of God dwells in the individual and in the fellowship alike. The crucial question is where one gets on the track, so to say. The answer is that one gets on the track by being, to use a eucharistic phrase, 'very members incorporate in the mystical body of thy Son, which is the blessed company of all faithful people'.[3]

In an illuminating discussion the Dean of the Cathedral at

---

[1] Eph. 2.19-22.     [2] I Cor. 12.
[3] From the concluding prayer of the Order for Holy Communion, *Book of Common Prayer*, Thomas Nelson and Sons, New York, 1929 (various editions, London), p. 83.

Liverpool explores at some length the biblical conceptions which bear upon the societal character of Christian faith and life. Concerning the metaphors which we have been considering, Dr Dillistone makes the suggestive point that in Paul's usage there was a natural transition from the 'temple' to 'temple-body' and then to the 'body' itself. If this be correct, further support would seem to be at hand for the view that, whether Paul refers to the 'embodiment of Christ' or to the 'embodiment of the Spirit', his central thought is that it is in the *koinonia*, in the fellowship of believers, that this embodiment occurs. Commenting upon the best-known passage in which Paul uses the metaphor of the body Dean Dillistone remarks:

> In this great passage the various strands of Paul's thinking are woven together into a unified whole. The thought of Christians being baptized into Christ and becoming one man in Christ Jesus (Gal. 3.28), the thought of their receiving the Spirit of the Son into their hearts (Gal. 4.6), the thought that the Christian is a new creation in Christ (Gal. 6.15), the thought of the Christian community as the temple of the Holy Spirit (I Cor. 3), the thought that the individual Christian's body is a member of Christ and a temple of the Spirit (I Cor. 6), the thought of all Christians partaking of the one body in the Eucharist (I Cor. 10)—all these strands woven into the already existing fabric of humanity as a body become the finished pattern of the Church, the people of God's new creation and the shrine of the Holy Spirit. It is unnecessary to single out this strand or that as being more influential than another in the development of Paul's thought. We see the material, we see the finished product, and in between there is the vivid creative imagination of the Apostle himself fashioning one of the truly archetypal images of the Divine society in its historical realization.[1]

Here we have not only a discerning and persuasive summary of the Pauline evidence regarding the ethical significance of the church but also an indication of how the New Testament itself conceives of Christ's real presence in the world. The 'body of Christ' is the characteristic New Testament way of speaking about the church; and the metaphor of the body underlines the point that in so far as the church is a *koinonia*—a fellowship relationship in which each individual functions properly himself in relation to the whole, and the whole functions properly in so far as each individual is related to it—the church is authentically church. According to the New Testament, the

[1] F. W. Dillistone, *The Structure of the Divine Society*, The Westminster Press, Philadelphia, 1951 (Lutterworth Press, London, 1951), p. 65.

ethical reality of the church is the presence in the world of a community within which the achievement of maturity is always both a possibility and a fact.

### b. The Reformation doctrine of the Communion of Saints

This New Testament conception of the ethical significance of the church is the basic rediscovery of the Reformation. It is often said, at least often enough to have become a commonplace, that Protestantism and individualism belong together. The argument runs that the Reformation accorded the individual his full religious significance: uninhibited access to God. In a way which had not been true for centuries before, if ever, the Reformation made the individual believer the fulcrum for the understanding of Christianity. This argument is false. It is not false in the sense that there is no element of truth in it. But the error lies in the contention that religious individualism is the characteristic stress and principal fruit of the Reformation. A succinct and cogent textual refutation of this error was published many years ago under a title that could scarcely have been more aptly designed to deter prospective readers. The book was called *Unitive Protestantism*. Actually what the book provides is a remarkable discussion of what the principal Reformers thought that they were really doing and of what they really thought about the church.[1] Its principal thesis is that the Reformation had no sooner begun than the Reformers addressed themselves chiefly to the task of bringing the true *church* to light.

According to Professor McNeill, the basic conception of the Reformers is the conception of the *communio sanctorum*, the communion of saints, or, as we have been saying, the fellowship of believers. 'The Holy Christian Church', says Luther, 'is the principal work of God for the sake of which all things were made.'[2] 'I take God and his angels to witness', writes Calvin,

---

[1] Cf. John T. McNeill, *Unitive Protestantism*, Abingdon Press, Nashville, 1930. I am especially indebted to Professor McNeill for having drawn my attention to the Luther material which follows. In some instances I have slightly altered his translations and expanded his citations on the basis of the original texts.

[2] 'In the Church', Luther continues, 'great wonders daily occur, such as the forgiveness of sins, triumph over death (*Tod wegnehmen*), the gift of righteousness, and eternal life; which only faith discerns. . . . Unbelief sees nothing, not even the sun, the heavens and the earth, or at least does not

'never since I became a teacher of the Church have I had any other purpose than the Church's advancement.'[1] For Calvin, this *communio sanctorum* was the whole body of the elect; for Luther, it was the society of the justified. But it was a *society*. 'All the saints', says Luther, 'are members of Christ and the Church, which is a spiritual and eternal city of God; and whoever is received into this city is said to be received into the communion of saints and to be incorporated into the body of Christ and made his member.'[2] In the same sermon, Luther explains that '*communio* is fellowship (*Gemeinschaft*), and *communicare* means in Latin, to receive this fellowship, as we say in German, "to go to sacrament" '.[3] Obviously, 'communicate' in this sense has a meaning at variance with contemporary usage. But the New Testament and Elizabethan sense of the word is more basically to the point than is its contemporary variant. 'To communicate' is not merely 'to talk to somebody'—surely an idle use both of time and of the basically human in us all. 'To communicate' is to be in an actual relationship with somebody in which you give yourself to him and he gives himself to you. Luther shared the New Testament discernment that to communicate in this way takes a bit of doing. It requires, in fact, a redemptive ingredient. Thus, he declares that 'Christ with all saints takes on, through his love, our estate (*Gestalt*), strives with us against sin, death, and all evil, wherefore, we, inflamed with love, take on his estate (*Gestalt*), entrust ourselves

regard them as works of God; but uses them as does a cow or a sow, for unbelief does not speak about these things nor praise the creator for them.' Commentary on Ps. 143.5, in *Kleine exegetische Schriften*, XVI, *Saemtliche Schriften*, edition Johann Georg Walch, Halle, 1743, Band IX, 1386.

[1] '*Ioannes Calvinus Lectori . . . ipsum et angelos testes habeam, nihil ex quo officium doctoris in ecclesia suscepi, mihi fuisse propositum quam ecclesiae prodesse. . . .*' Preface to the 1559 edition of the *Institutes of the Christian Religion*, CR, XXX.

[2] '*Mit Christus geystlichem corper vorleybet und seyn glyd gemacht.*' *Eyn Sermon von dem Hochwuerdigen Sacrament des Heyligen Leychnams Christi und von den Bruderschaften*, 24 December 1519, WA, 2, 743.

[3] Ibid., Luther's phrase is '*zum Sakrament gehen*'. It is germane to think also in this connection of the King James translation of Heb. 13.16. 'But to do good and to communicate forget not (τῆς δὲ εὐποιίας καὶ κοινωνίας) for with such sacrifices God is well pleased.' In the same interpersonal sense, κοινωνεῖν is translated in the AV as 'communicate' in Gal. 6.6; Phil. 4.14; I Tim. 6.18.

to his righteousness, life and blessedness'. 'The sacrament', he goes on, 'is nothing else than a divine sign in which Christ is peculiarly declared and given to all believers, with all their works, sufferings, services, graces, and possessions, for the consolation and support of all who are in anxiety and distress, persecuted by the devil, sin, world, flesh and all evil. . . .'[1] Christ is declared and given to all believers, just as they are, with all that they are: works, sufferings, services, graces, possessions! Nothing is left out! The wholeness of everybody in the wholeness of all—this is what the sacrament points to and expresses! The communion of saints is, according to Luther, the fellowship of believers who 'go to communion'. To 'go to communion' is to engage in a twofold act: an act of receiving and of sharing. The celebration of the sacrament is the celebration of the miracle of authentic *transubstantiation*, 'which means', in an unforgettably vivid phrase, 'through love being changed into each other!'[2]

The *koinonia* is either a eucharistic achievement or a conjurer's trick. And this is why it makes all the difference in the world to which church you belong, in what context your ethical insights and practices are nourished. 'This is what it means to say, "I believe in the holy Spirit, the holy, catholic Church." What is it to believe in the holy Church other than to believe in the communion of saints? How do the saints communicate? Actually, by all good and evil: all are of all (*omnia sunt omnium*), just as the sacrament of the altar shows in bread, and wine, when we are said by the Apostle, to be one body one bread, one drink (*potus*).'[3] Here is the real starting point, the authentic orientation of the Christian's life in Luther's mind.

For Calvin it is the same. The difference between Luther and Calvin concerns only the origin, not the significance, of the

---

[1] Ibid., WA, 2, 748, 749.  [2] Ibid., 750.

[3] *Tessaradecas consolatoria pro laborantibus et oneratis*, Wittenberg, February 1520. The tract is entitled *The Fourteen*, or *Consolation for such as labor and are heavily laden*. It was prepared for the dying Frederick of Saxony, as a reminder of seven grievous ills which are not to be compared to the sufferings of Christ, and of seven blessings which indicate the riches of divine grace. The Latin test appeared on 5 February, the German in a translation by Spalatin on 11 February 1520. WA, 6, 131-32. An English translation of this tract is available in the *Works of Martin Luther*, Holman edition, Muhlenberg Press, Philadelphia, 1943. See Vol. I, pp. 103-72.

*communio sanctorum.* Calvin grounds the community of believers
in the divine election, Luther in the assurance of justification.
Yet even here the difference is less marked than it seems, since
the assurance of justification was for Luther also an operation
of the divine election. 'All the elect of God', Calvin declares, 'are
so connected in Christ that just as they depend upon one head,
they also coalesce as in one body, compactly cohere among
each other as members of the same body; being made truly one,
who likewise live by the same spirit of God in one faith, hope,
and love, being called, even now, not only to the same inheritance of eternal life but also to a participation in one God and
Christ.'[1] Commenting upon the Ephesian passage, cited at
length above, Calvin remarks that the phrase, ' "the edifying of
itself" means that no increase is advantageous unless it responds
in the whole body. Therefore, he errs who desires to grow by
himself. . . . Just so, if we wish to belong to Christ, let no man
be anything for himself: but let us all be whatever we are for
each other (*nemo sibi aliquid sit: sed alii aliis simus quidquid sumus*).'[2]

Calvin juxtaposes the subjunctive and indicative moods of
the verb *to be* in a pointed and exciting play on words. *Simus:
sumus* means, literally, 'let us be what we are!' Exactly as with
Luther's 'through love being changed into each other', so
Calvin's 'let us be whatever we are for each other' means the
rejection of preferential differentiation and its displacement by
organic interrelational differentiation as the true significance of
*koinonia.* We are what we are in and through God's action in
Christ, bringing our authentic humanity to pass through
authentic belonging. Our being at all, our being what we are,
is our being in this community. This is the *communio sanctorum,*
the fellowship of Christians, in the world. It does not mean that
there are no diversities in the fellowship. But it does mean that
diversities, whether in society or in the church, cannot be

[1] *Institutes,* IV, 1, 2. CR, XXX, II, 747. Translation mine.

[2] John Calvin, *Commentary on the Letter of Saint Paul to the Ephesians,* CR,
LXXIX, 203. The phrase *in aedificationem sui facit* is singled out by Calvin
from the last clause of v. 16, *incrementum corporis facit in aedificationem sui, in
caritate.* The Greek text says, τὴν αὔξησιν τοῦ σώματος ποιεῖται εἰς οἰκοδομὴν
ἑαυτοῦ ἐν ἀγάπῃ, literally, 'makes an increase of the body towards the
building up of itself in love'. And it is this phrase which Phillips paraphrases
as 'grows by the proper functioning of the individual parts to its full maturity
in love'.

preferentially used to disrupt and destroy the fellowship. They are diversities designed to express the reality and maturity of the fellowship. We are what we are, our humanity stands or falls by the 'being what they are' of all the members of the body in their constitutive relation to the head. Always, as we all, on the same level, have received from the head our life, we are the church.

'This view of the Christian communion', says Dr McNeill, 'is substantially shared by all the Reformers.'[1] Its bearing upon another misunderstood aspect of the Protestant heritage must be briefly pointed out because it also concerns the ethical reality of the church. The individualistic error has perpetuated itself, perhaps most stubbornly, in the formula that Protestantism stands for the 'priesthood of all believers', which means that every man is his own priest. But this is not the Reformation teaching at all. The Reformation teaching is, as McNeill underlines, not every man his *own* priest, but every man his *neighbor's* priest.[2] As Luther puts it: 'Who then can comprehend the riches and the glory of the Christian life? . . . But alas in our day this life is unknown throughout the world; . . . we are altogether ignorant of our own name and do not know why we are Christians or bear the name of Christians (*cur Christiani simus et vocemur*). Surely we are named after Christ, not because he is absent from us, but because he dwells in us, that is, because we believe in him and are Christs one to another and do to our neighbors as Christ does to us.'[3] The link in Luther's thought between this view of the *priesthood of all believers* and the *communio sanctorum* is supplied by the priesthood of Christ. It is this priesthood which makes a priest between man and God, or between man and Jesus Christ, superfluous. It is this priesthood which has superseded and dispensed with any other than a congregationally derived priesthood. Otherwise, the Letter to the Hebrews would seem to have been superfluous; in which case, it is hard to see how one is to understand the intimate

[1] Op. cit., p. 31.   [2] Ibid., p. 36.
[3] Martin Luther, *Tractatus de libertate christiana*, 1520, WA, 7, 66. It is instructive that, although not engaging in a play on words, Luther also uses here the word *simus*, in the same sense in which the word appears in Calvin's commentary on Eph. 4.16. The translation is from AE, Vol. 31, p. 268.

relation, not to say identity, between priesthood and the chosen people, as a nation and a kingdom, in I Peter 2.9-10, not to mention Rev. 1.6; or the *koinonia* character of the body of Christ in the New Testament.[1]

Every man his neighbor's priest, 'one the Christ of the other' —this is the Christian life, life in and of the *koinonia*! The incarnate, resurrected, and ascended Christ has no real presence in the world apart from this fellowship-creating relationship in which the 'one' confronts the 'other' in the maturing humanity of man. This is what the 'head and the body' in the New Testament, and in the Reformation doctrine of the *communio sanctorum*, are all about. We have to do with a society in which all the parts properly function in so far as all the parts, in one way or another, minister Christ to all the other parts.

Thus, the self-understanding of the New Testament church as a *koinonia*, as a way of spelling out what the 'body of Christ' means, is also the central concern of the Reformation in its attempt to define the point of departure for the Christian life, for Christian thinking about ethics. It is with the ethical reality of the church that an answer to the question: What am I, as a believer in Jesus Christ and as a member of his church, to do? begins to come into view.

So marked a stress upon the *koinonia* character of the church inevitably raises the question of the relation between the ethical and the empirical reality of the church. If, according to the New Testament, the 'body of Christ' is thought of as a *koinonia*; if the *communio sanctorum*, as the Reformers thought of it, is a *societal* rather than an *institutional* reality, the 'true church' would seem to be either so overlaid by the empirical church as to make it 'invisible' beyond recognition, or to be so markedly

---

[1] 'But you are a chosen race, a royal priesthood, a holy nation, God's own people; once you had not received mercy but now you have received mercy.' I Peter 2.9-10.

'To him who loves us and has freed us from our sins by his blood and made us a kingdom, priests to his God and Father, to him be glory and dominion for ever and ever. Amen.' Rev. 1.5b, 6.

The circumstance that I Peter is addressed to a *koinonia* in exile does not alter the point. Indeed, the German church struggle during the days of National Socialist rule provides illuminating confirmation of the fact that the church under persecution, and in this sense also in exile, both rediscovers and lives by its *koinonia* character.

different from the empirical church as to lead us in the direction
of an ecclesiological 'double standard'. According to this
standard, there would seem to be two churches: the one
invisible and true; the other visible and false. And yet, so
radical a disjunction of the 'church of God' was never espoused
either by the New Testament writers or by the Reformers or
by the intervening teachers of the church.[1] Even Wyclif, who
probably went farther toward such a disjunction than anyone
else, does not allow himself to sever every link between the
invisible and the visible reality of the church. 'Thus, it has been
shown: the universal or catholic church contains in itself, by
definition (*eo ipso . . . ipsa continet in se*) all the predestinate.' But
the predestinate are also members of 'holy mother church'.[2]
And while for Wyclif the members of 'holy mother church' are
all the predestinate, and all the predestinate are members of
'holy mother church', the maternity of the church nevertheless,
and in some undecipherable way, links the *ecclesia predestinatorum*
with the *particularis ecclesia*, with the local and visible church.[3]

Wyclif was an Augustinian; and it was Augustine who,
perhaps more than any other teacher of the church, wrestled
with the problem posed by the New Testament itself concerning
the church, at once hidden and empirical, invisible and visible.
It is the remarkable achievement of Augustine's analysis to have
kept these two facets of the reality of the church, as 'the
redeemed family of the Lord Christ' and the 'pilgrim city of
King Christ', in dynamic and dialectical interconnection. 'But
let this city bear in mind', Augustine remarks, and he means
the visible church of which 'all the predestinate' are also
members,

---

[1] Cf. 'the church of God which is at Corinth' (τῇ ἐκκλησίᾳ τοῦ θεοῦ τῇ
οὔσῃ ἐν κορίνθῳ). I Cor. 1.2; II Cor. 1.1. τῇ οὔσῃ is grammatically the
feminine particle of εἰμί ('to be'). Its use in this connection strongly asserts
the *visibility* of the assembled people of God, the called, that is, the *koinonia*.
The phrase 'church of God' occurs also in I Cor. 11.22; 15.9; Gal. 1.13;
I Thess. 2.14; I Tim. 3.15. See also above p. 47, note 1.

[2] Johannis Wyclif, *Tractatus de Ecclesia*, edited by J. Loserth, The Wyclif
Society, London, 1886, cap. I, E, 11. 22ff.; o, 1. 17.

[3] Ibid., R, 1. 7. And especially, '*Oportet autem . . . primo cognoscere quiditatem
sancte matris ecclesie ad modum loquendi scripture sacre et sanctorum qui sensum eius
elucidant. Oportet secundo cognoscere materiam predestinacionis divine, quanto sit
nobis incognita.*' T, 11. 1-6.

that among her enemies lie hid those who are destined to be fellow-citizens, that she may not think it a fruitless labor to bear what they inflict as enemies until they become confessors of the faith. So, too, as long as she is a stranger in the world, the city of God has in her communion, and bound to her by the sacraments, some who shall not eternally dwell in the lot of the saints. Of these, some are not now recognized; others declare themselves, and do not hesitate to make common cause with our enemies in murmuring against God, whose sacramental badge they wear. These men you may today see thronging the churches with us, tomorrow crowding the theatres with the godless. But we have the less reason to despair of the reclamation even of such persons, if among our most declared enemies there are now some, unknown to themselves who are destined to become our friends. *In truth, these two cities are entangled together in this world, and intermixed until the last judgment effect their separation.*[1]

There is really no more satisfactory account of the dynamic and dialectical interrelations between the *koinonia* and the empirical reality of the church. The biblical roots of it are unmistakable. As the religious development of Israel tended toward a differentiation between the empirical reality of the covenant people and the hidden reality of the remnant, so in the New Testament a differentiation and tension may be noted between the hidden reality of the *koinonia* and the empirical reality of the church. The phenomenology of the situation is that there is a people whose 'story' is the focal point of God's concrete activity in the world. But the dynamics and direction of God's activity are always toward bringing to light, from the foundation and center of the 'story' of his people, an actual foretaste of God's consummating purposes for them and for the world.

This twofold, dialectical and dynamic, New Testament sense of the church passed via Augustine into the language of theology and became the distinction between the invisible and the visible church. During the Middle Ages, as Professor McNeill points out, the dialectical reality of the church, so vitally maintained by Augustine, was gradually dissolved. The *invisibility* of the church came to be reserved for the church's reality beyond the plane of history, being applied, on the one hand, to the communion of the Christian on earth with those who had passed into the next life, and, on the other, to children yet unborn but

---

[1] Augustine, *The City of God*, edited by Marcus Dods, T. & T. Clark, Edinburgh, 1881, Bk. I, chap. 35. Italics mine.

already in the plan of God belonging to the holy fellowship.[1]
It is not difficult to understand that such a view of *invisibility*
should have made room for and gradually succumbed to the
identification of the 'true' with the *visible* church. Indeed,
whenever the dialectic between the invisibility and the visibility
of the church is weakened or lost sight of, a fateful consequence
sooner or later follows. The attempt is made to affirm and
safeguard the integrity of the church by so greatly stressing the
invisibility of the church as to aggravate and accelerate the
secularization of the visible church which has already begun
with the weakened force of the dialectic between the two. It is
a kind of vicious circle in which the more invisible the church
becomes, the less it visibly becomes the church.

By the time of the Reformation, the dialectic of the New
Testament sense of the church was in urgent need of restoration.
Thus, Calvin can go so far as to say that we must 'leave it to
the Lord, . . . sometimes to remove from human observation all
external knowledge of his Church', and also that the church is
'the principal theatre of [God's] glory (*praecipium est gloriae eius
theatrum.*)[2]' The invisibility of the church is both a divine
punishment upon the impiety of men and God's way of
protecting the church pending some better way of increasing
and extending it.[3] Thus, for Calvin, as Professor McNeill
remarks, 'the task of a Reformer was that of bringing the
invisible to visibility again'.[4] 'It is the will of God', Calvin
declares, 'that the communion of his Church should be maintained in the external society.'[5] And while he greatly stressed
the instrumental character of the church and concerned himself
with the ordering of its life, it was by the twofold sense of the
church in the Scriptures that his thinking about the church was
shaped.[6] The Calvinistic mind, succinctly expressed in the
Westminster Confession of Faith (1647), speaks on this point
for the Reformation as a whole. After acknowledging the

[1] McNeill, op. cit., p. 23.

[2] Calvin, *Institutes, Praefatio ad Regem Galliae*, CR, XXX, 23; *Commentarii
in Isaiam Prophetam*, Cap. LXVI, 9; CR, XXXVII, 445.

[3] *Institutes*, CR, XXX, 23. '*Anno vero se Dominus multo admirabiliorem
praebebit in augenda et multiplicanda ecclesia.*' *Commentarii in Isaiam Prophetam*,
CR, LXV, 445.

[4] Op. cit., p. 44.

[5] Calvin, *Institutes*, IV, 1, 16; CR, XXX, 759.

[6] Ibid., IV, 1. 7; CR, XXX, 752, 753.

catholic or universal church both as invisible and visible, the Confession declares that 'this catholic church hath been some-times more, and sometimes less visible. . . . The purest churches under heaven are subject both to mixture and to error; . . . Nevertheless, there shall be always a Church on earth to worship God according to his will.'[1]

We may conclude, then, that the sense in which the *koinonia* is to be related to and distinguished from the empirical reality of the church is to be understood in the light of the New Testament view of the church as an ethical reality.[2] The hidden ($\varkappa o\iota\nu\omega\nu\acute{\iota}a$) character of the church and the empirical ($\dot{\varepsilon}\varkappa\varkappa\lambda\eta\sigma\acute{\iota}a$) character of the church are dynamically and dialectically related in and through God's action in Christ, whose headship of the church makes the church at once the context and the custodian of the secret of the maturity of humanity. Regarded in this way, the reality of the church is an ethical reality because what God is doing in the world becomes concrete in the trans-formation of human motivation and of the structures of human relatedness which are the stuff of human fulfillment. What is real about the Christian life is always hidden in the fellowship of the *koinonia*. The *koinonia* is, however, neither *identical* with the *visible* church nor *separable* from the visible church. *Ecclesiola in ecclesia*, the little church within the church, the leaven in the lump, the remnant in the midst of the covenant people, the *koinonia* in the world—this is the reality which is the starting point for the living of the Christian life and for our thinking about Christian ethics.

There is, of course, one marginal possibility which must always also be kept in mind. Indeed, it emerges precisely in the context and course of God's action in Christ in the fellowship of believers in the world. The marginal possibility is that God himself is free to transcend—*ubi et quando visum est Deo* ('where and when it pleaseth him')—what he has done and continues to do in and through the church. God's action and God's

[1] The Westminster Confession of Faith, chap. XXV, 4, 5. Philip Schaff, *The Creeds of Christendom*, Harper & Brothers, New York, 1877, Vol. III, p. 658. See also pp. 11-12 for a similar, though less precise, statement from the Augsburg Confession.

[2] It is necessary to bear in mind here the reference to Emil Brunner's interpretation of the New Testament understanding of the church. See above, p. 50, note 1.

freedom are never more plainly misunderstood than by those who suppose that God has acted and does act in a certain way and cannot, therefore, always also act in other ways. Of course, God is bound *to* what he does and has done. But he is not bound *by* what he has done. It may therefore always be possible that the distinguishable, though inseparable, relation between the *koinonia* and the church may be strengthened, or corrected, or even set upon an entirely fresh track, by the unexpected eruption into visibility of the invisibility of God's purposed fellowship in Christ. If and when such a marginal possibility occurs, it can only be welcomed by those who belong to the *koinonia* anywhere.[1]

Meanwhile, those who have raised the question what, as believers in Jesus Christ and as members of his church, they are to do will have more than enough to engage their minds and give direction to their behavior. For when the church is the context of ethical reflection, Christian ethics becomes contextual. What God is doing in the world radically revises the ethos of the Christian life, the fabric that holds the Christian life together.

[1] See above, Chapter I, p. 31, note 2.

# III

## WHAT GOD IS DOING IN THE WORLD

THERE is an obvious pretension in the attempt to write about 'what God is doing in the world'. Such an oracular claim might be appropriate to the world of 'gods and heroes', but scarcely to the world of time and space and things. This analysis of what is involved in Christian thinking about ethics, however, disclaims all oracular information. It is not by direct, divine illumination, but by reason of the contextual character of the self-revelatory activity of God in the church, dialectically understood, that we venture to embark upon the considerations of this chapter. Will Rogers, celebrated American humorist of the first third of this century, used to remark: 'All I know is what I read in the papers.' Just so, all that is here claimed to be known about what God is doing in the world is what we read in the Bible as well as 'in the papers'. Reading the papers may or may not require also a reading of the Bible. But certainly a perceptive reading of the Bible requires also a reading of the papers. Contemporary with Will Rogers' remark is the observation of this century's most celebrated theologian, that 'a wide reading of contemporary secular literature—especially of newspapers!—is therefore recommended to any one desirous of understanding the Epistle to the Romans'.[1]

The reason, of course, is that the Christian life is lived not only in the church but also in the world; and whatever God is doing in and through the *koinonia*, he is doing also in the world. The day-by-day account of the goings on in the world and the day-by-day account of God's doings in the world belong inevitably together if what is happening is not to get out of

---

[1] Karl Barth, *Der Roemerbrief*, 2te bis 6te Auflage, Chr. Kaiser, Muenchen, 1929, p. 411; English translation by Sir Edwyn Hoskyns, Oxford University Press, London, 1933, p. 425.

focus. 'The problem of ethics is . . . a great disturbance. How, indeed, can it be otherwise? For human behavior must inevitably be disturbed by the thought of God. . . . If our thinking is not to be pseudo-thinking, we must think about life; for such a thinking is a thinking about God. And if we are to think about life, we must penetrate its hidden corners, and steadily refuse to treat anything—however trivial or disgusting it may seem to be—as irrelevant.'[1]

The first important consequence of starting to think about ethics with or from within the *koinonia* is that a familiar but much-blurred answer to the question of what Christians are to do begins to come into focus. Too long, and too quickly, has it been known that Christians are to do 'the will of God'. This reply to the definitive question of Christian ethics has all the marks of a cliché. Nothing is more obvious than that a person who tries to think about ethics from a religious point of view, above all as a Christian, should know that he is to do the will of God. Furthermore, and this too is obvious, the real problem of Christian behavior is not *knowing* that one is to do the will of God but *doing* the will of God which one knows. If men would abandon the sometimes bald, and sometimes subtle, evasion that they really would do the will of God if they knew what it was; if men would, instead, really begin to will to do the will of God which they knew, Christian behavior would be at least more honest if not more apparent in the world. Do we not have it upon the highest authority that 'if any man's will is to do his will, he shall know whether the teaching is from God or whether I am speaking on my own authority'?[2] What other answer would a religious man, and above all a Christian, expect to the question: What am I to do? than: *The will of God*?

These questions are rhetorical because they cluster around a cliché. What makes a cliché of 'the will of God', as an answer to the ethical question, is that to answer in this way is to espouse a half-truth. Ethics, as Kant has eloquently and elaborately

[1] Barth, ibid., pp. 410-11; English translation, pp. 424-25. See also the more recent and somewhat different way of making the same point, Karl Barth, *Kurze Erklaerung des Roemerbriefes*, Chr. Kaiser, Muenchen, 1956, p. 189. The stress here is rather upon the Christian's life in the *koinonia* and in the world.

[2] John 7.17.

explained, is intrinsically volitional, being concerned with the willing acceptance of a claim. The Johannine account of Jesus' stress upon the will has been profoundly and elaborately transmitted to the Christian ethical tradition through the mind of Augustine, and nothing is more characteristic of Christian piety and ethics than decision. It cannot be nor need it be denied that men who seriously ask, as religious men, what they are to do know that the answer is 'the will of God'.

Nevertheless, however self-evident and valid it may be to urge upon men the doing of the will of God, this is only half the truth. The other half is that 'the will of God' is not a simple answer to a simple question but a complex answer to a complex question. To assume that the question, What am I to do? is a simple one, put from off the surface of life to penetrate whatever lies beneath, is not only naïve but irresponsible. The fact is that men ask concerning the will of God, not merely evasively, pretending that they do not know they are to do the will of God when they really do know, but because they are genuinely perplexed by the diversity and complexity of human motivation and of behavioral options which make up the stuff of the ethical situation. The truth is that the more ethically sensitive a person is, the more likely he is to know (1) that a simple admonition to do the will of God is so remote from the actualities of the ethical situation as to amount to a frivolous platitude, and/or (2) that even if he is prepared to acknowledge that he is to do the will of God, he comes thereby only to a still more troublesome perplexity, namely, what is the will of God which he admits he is to do?

At just such a point as this, Jesus himself appears to have drawn the line between the Pharisaic sense of the ethical situation and his own. For the former, the will of God is simple, no matter how complex the human situation to which it applies. It is set down in 'the law', and in the 'tradition of the elders'. For Jesus, the will of God is always problematical enough to have to be unpretentiously asked for and trusted. 'What do you think? A man had two sons; and he went to the first and said, "Son, go and work in the vineyard today." And he answered, "I will not"; but afterward he repented and went. And he went to the second and said the same; and he answered, "I go, sir," but did not go. Which of the two did the will of his father?' They said, 'The first.' Jesus said to them, 'Truly, I say to you, the tax collectors and the harlots go into the kingdom of God before you.'[1] 'And I tell you, Ask, and it will be given you; seek, and you will find; knock, and it will be opened to you. For every one who asks receives, and he who seeks finds, and to him who knocks it will be opened.'[2]

Thus, it is not merely the question concerning the will of God which is complex; the answer is complex too. Asking for and trusting the will of God are recommended by Jesus not only because of the complexity of the ethical situation but also, and more basically, because of the complexity of the will of God itself. The fact is that the dynamics of the divine behavior in the world exclude both an abstract and a preceptual apprehension of the will of God. There is no formal principle of Christian behavior because Christian behavior cannot be generalized. And Christian behavior cannot be generalized because the will of God cannot be generalized. A generalized persuasion of the will of God may have mystical or emotive intensity but is devoid of ethical content and behavioral significance. And even if such a generalized persuasion of the will of God were given propositional formulation for purposes of ethical counsel and guidance, the result would be a maxim or a precept, good for edifying repetition but devoid of behavioral precision. It cannot be too strongly stressed that the Decalogue presupposes the covenant and, in a world in which God is at work and man is destined to find fulfillment in the service of God, sharply focuses upon the concrete human occasions of obedience. Nor can it be overlooked—though in the tradition of Christian thinking about ethics nothing seems to have been more persistently overlooked—that the most preceptually rigorous account of the behavior to be adopted by the covenant community refuses to give a preceptual account of the divine will. Says the Book of Deuteronomy,

> When your son asks you in time to come, What is the meaning of the testimonies and the statutes and the ordinances which the Lord our God has commanded you? [that is, what really *is* the will of God?] then you shall say to your son, 'We were Pharaoh's slaves in Egypt; and the Lord brought us out of Egypt with a mighty hand; and the Lord showed signs and wonders, great and grievous, against Egypt and against Pharaoh and

---

[1] Matt. 21.28-31.  [2] Luke 11.9-10; see also Matt. 7.7-8.

all his household before our eyes; and he brought us out from there, ihat he might bring us in and give us the land which he swore to give to our fathers. And the Lord commanded us to do all these statutes, to fear the Lord our God, for our good always, that he might preserve us alive as at this day. And it will be righteousness for us, if we are careful to do all this commandment before the Lord our God, as he has commanded us.'[1]

In short, what God requires is meaningless apart from the dynamics of the divine activity, and the dynamics of the divine activity define the context within which 'all this commandment' is to 'be righteousness for us', indeed, is to be carefully done.[2]

[1] Deut. 6.20-25.

[2] The Reformers saw this point clearly, as Calvin's discussion of the Decalogue in the second book of the *Institutes*, chap. 8, and Luther's treatment of the commandments in the Larger and Smaller Catechisms (and indeed the Reformation catechisms generally) make plain. It is this inner meaning of the law, moreover, which enabled Luther and Calvin to subsume the Decalogue under the law of love and to speak of the 'Two Tables' of the law, that is, the love to God and the love to neighbor. See especially John Calvin, *Institutes of the Christian Religion*, II, viii; III, xix, 4-7. Also Martin Luther, *Treatise on Good Works* (in the *Works of Martin Luther*, Holman edition, Muhlenberg Press, Philadelphia, 1943), Vol. I; *The Freedom of a Christian* and *The Sermon on Two Kinds of Righteousness*, the American edition (see chap. I, p. 40, note 3), Vol. 31. It is not accidental that Luther in the *Treatise on Good Works* makes frequent use of the Sermon on the Mount. Indeed, on the basis of an inner meaning of the law, the Reformers were right in seeing an intrinsic parallelism between the Sermon and the Decalogue. On the other hand, when the Reformers take up the question of the law in relation to the gospel, and particularly the question of natural law, they tend to make a different use of the intrinsic parallelism between the Decalogue and the Sermon on the Mount. They seem in these contexts to find the Decalogue, the Sermon, and natural law interchangeable and to take up the doctrine of the 'threefold office of the law' and to be led by this route back to a preceptual reading of the law. I say 'back to' because a preceptual reading of the law falls below the level of the position taken in the catechisms and in the discussion of Christian liberty and allows the pre-Reformation tradition on the matter to overshadow the creative rediscovery of the Bible which had propelled the Reformers on their reforming way. Some account of the evidence and the significance of the extent to which the Reformers accepted the tradition in their interpretation of the law is conveniently available in an article by Professor John T. McNeill, 'Natural Law in the Teaching of the Reformers', *The Journal of Religion*, Vol. 26, No. 3, July 1946; in an appendix to Emil Brunner, *Man in Revolt*, The Westminster Press, Philadelphia, 1947 (Lutterworth Press, London, 1939), pp. 516ff., and in the essay by Karl Barth, 'Rechtfertigung und Recht', *Theologische Studien*, I, 1938, translated into English by G. Ronald Howe, *Church and State*, SCM Press, London, 1939.

More recent scholarly attention to the Book of Deuteronomy has underlined its significance not as    .

> divine law in codified form, but preaching about the commandments. . . . Deuteronomy proclaims Yahweh's election and promise of salvation. . . . All the departments of Israel's life are laid claim to in the light of this great new order in which the statute about the unity and the singleness of Yahweh operates specially for the cult as the means by which all is bound together and united. . . . Thus we have in Deuteronomy the most comprehensive example of a theological restatement of old traditions which in the later Israel could become at the same time the message of Yahweh.[1]

Thus Deuteronomy is an interpretation of Israel's faith which became the basis of reform. It seeks to recapture the true spirit and meaning of the Mosaic covenant and in so doing establishes and interprets obligation in a covenant context which first of all is a matter of the heart.[2] Deuteronomy is thus to be aligned with the prophetic protest against the preceptual misinterpretation of the law.

As Mark reports it, Jesus takes up the same point against the Pharisees. In a passage in which Jesus cites the fifth commandment and some other provisions of the 'Law of Moses', he quotes the prophet Isaiah against those who honor God with their lips but not from the heart, and concludes that the authorities on the will of God, the teachers of the law, are 'making void the word of God through your tradition which you hand on'.[3] On another occasion Jesus is, as Luke quotes

---

[1] See Gerhard von Rad, *Deuteronomium-Studien*, Vandenhoeck und Ruprecht, Goettingen, 1948, pp. 10, 49-50, the English translation by David Stalker bears the title *Studies in Deuteronomy*, Alec R. Allenson Inc., Naperville, 1953 (SCM Press, London, 1953), pp. 15, 70-71. I am indebted to my colleague Professor G. E. Wright for drawing my attention to Professor von Rad's studies, and also for his own illuminating introduction to Deuteronomy in *The Interpreter's Bible*, Abingdon-Cokesbury Press, New York, 1953, Vol. 2. See especially p. 312.

[2] Deut. 6.3-4.

[3] Mark 7.6-13. Matthew, although he rearranges the material, follows Mark (15.1-9). Isaiah is quoted from 29.13, albeit from the Septuagint rather than from the original text. As Mark used it, the passage reads: 'This people honors me with their lips, but their heart is far from me; in vain do they worship me, teaching as doctrines the precepts of men.' The context of the original passage gives even stronger emphasis to the connection which 'the heart' provides between the activity of God and the doings of his people.

him, still more blunt. 'Woe to you lawyers! For you have taken away the key of knowledge; you did not enter yourselves, and you hindered those who were entering.'[1]

To ask simply, 'What am I to do?' and simply to reply, 'The will of God!' ignores both what God is doing in the world and the ethical reality of the human situation. The fact is that outside the context of the divine activity it makes no sense to talk about the will of God; and within the context of the divine activity, the question about the will of God exposes the paradoxical character of the ethical situation of man. The paradox is that *we do not know the will of God which we will and we do not will the will of God which we know.* It marks every serious struggle to know and to do what God wills. The more earnestly a man asks what the will of God is, the more clearly he discovers that he both knows and does *not* know, both wills and does *not* will to do the will of God concerning which he asks. Christian thinking about ethics, beginning as it does with and from the *koinonia*, uniquely recognizes the pivotal ethical significance of this paradox. It requires a thoroughgoing revision of the interpretation of ethics. The analysis of ethical goals or values, of ethical motivation, of means and ends, of virtues and character, undergoes a transformation which amounts to a radical reductionism. The focus of ethical attention is deliberately concentrated upon the paradoxical reality and vitality of what is involved in doing the will of God. Indeed, it is the *koinonia* context and character of Christian ethics that give ethical sense and substance to the seeking and the doing of God's will. For in the *koinonia*, and owing to the *koinonia*, man is concretely and inescapably involved in what God is doing in the world. 'For which of you, desiring to build a tower, does not first sit down and count the cost, whether he has enough to complete it? Otherwise, when he has laid a foundation, and is not able to finish, all who see it begin to mock him, saying, "This man began to build, and was not able to finish." . . . So therefore whoever of you does not renounce all that he has cannot be my disciple.'[2] The radicality of this renunciation is the beginning of the dissolution of the paradox in clear obedience.

[1] Luke 11.52; 'enter', that is, the kingdom of heaven, as Matthew explains, 23.13.
[2] Luke 14.28-30, 33.

1 *The Political Character of the Divine Activity*[1]

The renunciation exacted of him who as a Christian sits down to count the cost of the tower he desires to build is a single-minded appraisal of and obedience to what God is doing in the world. Of this single-mindedness, the Christian Church and the behavior of Christians in our time are no exemplary spectacle. In his brief but imaginative and vigorous account of 'the Christian mission', Canon Max Warren, General Secretary of the Church Missionary Society, tells of a young Muganda woman studying at an English university. She was interpreting to an English audience the dilemma of young Africans who find it difficult to bridge the gap between their Christian schooling and life. 'Many Africans', she said, 'are seeking answers to their questionings but the Church is not playing its full part in helping young people to face the problems of society. To them God is the God of the Church: He is not the God of politics and social life. They need help to see Him as one God: to see that the Church is concerned with the whole of life.'

' "The God of the Church: He is not the God of politics"— so, apparently', says Warren, 'they have learned Christ, these Africans, and discovered in Him not integration but divorce, not atonement but separation. A great gulf is fixed between the Scripture lesson and education for a career, between what happens in church and "the high tumultuous lists of life".'[2] This divorce was not, of course, intended by the Christian mission; but it happened. It is not confined to Africa but echoes as a murmuring sound of protest from many places in the earth, indeed, wherever the church has been 'content to separate what God has joined together, and to treat the Christian faith as a Scripture lesson out of any relation to the rest of life's curriculum'.[3]

[1] The analysis in this and the two subsequent sections of the present chapter was first and more briefly explored in an unpublished lecture on the Settles Foundation at the Presbyterian Theological Seminary at Austin, Texas, in January 1954. This is a belated but no less grateful acknowledgment of my indebtedness for the invitation, for rewarding conversation over these matters, and for warm hospitality to President David Stitt, Dean James McCord, and the faculty and students of the Seminary. Dr McCord is now the President of the Theological Seminary at Princeton, New Jersey.

[2] Max Warren, *The Christian Mission*, SCM Press, London, 1951, p. 9.

[3] Ibid., p. 9.

Such a separation becomes inevitable whenever Christian thinking about ethics becomes divorced from Christian thinking about anything else. In this case, the failure to 'sit down and count the cost' of what is involved in the propagation of the gospel in and across the world has been exposed in the failure to discern what God is really doing in the world. And this is the crucial case because the integrity of the Christian mission stands or falls by authentic Christian witness in word and act to the activity of God—in Canon Warren's phrase, to 'the peculiar saving content of the Gospel'.[1] Evangelism without ethics means that the thrust of the gospel has lost its cutting edge, that human behavior is not being transformed by the fulfilling power of a life-giving faith.

What, then, is God doing in the world? The answer to this question, we have been saying, is attempted outside the *koinonia*, but only sensible from within the *koinonia*. From within the *koinonia* it makes sense to say that what God is doing in the world is his will. It makes sense because in the *koinonia* the will of God is no pious platitude but a clear and concrete matter of politics. In short, 'the God of the Church' *is* 'the God of politics'! But, says another report from the missionary frontier, always authentically the frontier of the church in the world,

> without realizing it, we have drifted back into the old polytheism against which the prophets of the Lord waged their great warfare. The real essence of paganism is that it divides the various concerns of a man's life into departments. There is one god of the soil; there is another god of the desert. The god of wisdom is quite different from the god of wine. If a man wants to marry he must pray at one temple; if he wants to make war he must take his sacrifice elsewhere. All this is precisely where the modern paganism of our secular society has brought us today. Certain portions of our life we call religious. Then we are Christians. We use a special language. We think in terms that we never use in any other context. . . . We call that our Christianity—and there we stop. We turn to another department of life called politics. Now we think in quite different terms. Our liturgy is the catchwords of the daily press. Our divine revelation is the nine o'clock news. Our creed is 'I believe in democracy.' Our incentive is the fear of—we're not sure what. But it certainly isn't the fear of the Lord.[2]

The God whom in the *koinonia* we come to know as real, as the only God there is, the only God worth talking about, is not

[1] *The Christian Mission*, p. 10.          [2] Quoted by Canon Warren, ibid.

divided but one; and the God who is one is the God of politics. This use of the word 'politics' may seem initially to be arbitrary, a semantic *tour de force*. Certainly it is not usual to think *theologically* about God in political terms. Nor is it usual to think *politically* about God at all. The images which come immediately to mind when talking about the 'God of politics' are the images of rulers of states, of governmental structures and policies, and in any neighborhood of the United States of the ward committeeman. These images, although they are indirectly and ultimately also related to the political character of the divine activity, do not give the primary and direct sense of what the phrase 'God of politics' means. God may be a 'mathematician', as has been suggested,[1] but he is certainly not a ward politician. The present adoption of the word 'politics' as applied to the activity of God has to do, not with these pragmatic and passing manifestations of political behavior, but with that to which the word 'politics' fundamentally and centrally refers. In this precise and basic sense, it is possible to say that God, if he is denotable by one phrase more characteristically than by another, is a 'politician'.

The risk of such a denotation is the risk of substituting a slogan for sober theological analysis. It may be hoped however, that the careful reader will not be beguiled by misleading oversimplifications but consider instead the vitality and substance inherent in an interpretation of the activity of God in terms of politics.

In the Western cultural tradition, pre-eminence in matters of definition belongs to the philosophers of ancient Greece. It will be useful, therefore, to recall what Aristotle has to say about the science of politics. According to Aristotle, ethics is a branch of politics. This is because, while ethics is the science of the Good, politics is the science of the highest or supreme Good.

---

[1] Cf. Sir James Jeans, *Physics and Philosophy*, The Macmillan Company, New York, 1943 (Cambridge University Press, Cambridge, 1942), p. 16: 'Kronecker is quoted as saying that in arithmetic God made the integers and men made the rest; in the same spirit we may perhaps say that in physics God made the mathematics and man made the rest.' More cautiously, Sir Arthur Eddington remarks, 'Doubtless the mathematician is a loftier being than the engineer, but perhaps even he ought not to be entrusted with the Creation unreservedly'. Sir Arthur Eddington, *The Nature of the Physical World*, The University Press, Cambridge, 1928, p. 209.

Every art and every investigation, and likewise every practical pursuit or undertaking, seems to aim at some good: hence it has been well said that the Good is that at which all things aim. . . . If therefore among the ends at which our actions aim there will be one which we will for its own sake, while we will the others only for the sake of something else . . . , it is clear that this one ultimate End must be the Good, and indeed, the Supreme Good. . . . If this be so, we ought to make an attempt to comprehend at all events in outline what exactly this Supreme Good is, and of which of the sciences or faculties it is the object. . . . But such is manifestly the science of politics.

. . . the Good of man must be the end of the science of Politics.[1]

Politics, then, is the study or theory of the political community.[2] There is a phenomenology of this community which has to do with the variety of governmental forms and constitutions, with property relations, and with the relations between the political community and other forms of human associations. But the great significance of Aristotle's study of the political community is the way in which he explores the phenomenology of politics in the light of the question of the nature of the political community as such. This is fundamentally a question of the nature of man.

. . . We take for our special consideration [Aristotle says] the study of the form of political community that is the best of all forms for a people able to pursue the most ideal mode of life. . . . The partnership finally composed of several villages is the city-state (κοινωνία τέλειος πόλις) ; . . . and thus, while it comes into existence for the sake of life, it exists for the good life. Hence every city-state exists by nature, . . . and nature is an end, since that which each thing is when its growth is completed we speak of as being the nature of each thing. . . . From these things therefore it is clear

---

[1] Aristotle, *Nicomachean Ethics*, Loeb Classical Library, G. P. Putnam's Sons, New York, 1926 (Heinemann, London, 1934), Book I, i, ii. Aristotle's vocabulary is fluid and variable. For example, in referring to politics, he sometimes says μέθοδος ('investigation'), sometimes γνῶσις ('knowledge'), and sometimes the noun ἡ πολιτική, to convey the whole phrase 'science of politics'. Similarly, when he refers to the object of political science, he uses ἡ πόλις (state) ; and when he thinks of the phenomenology of human relatedness which provides the materials of political science, he speaks of πᾶσαν πόλιν κοινωνίαν τινὰ οὖσαν('every state is . . . a sort of partnership'), and of πόλις καὶ ἡ κοινωνία ἡ πολιτική ('the partnership entitled the state, the political association'). For the last phrase, see the translation of the *Politics*, in the Loeb Classical Library, G. P. Putnam's Sons, New York, 1932 (Heinemann, London, 1932), Book I, i.

[2] θεωρῆσαι περὶ τῆς κοινωνίας τῆς πολιτικῆς. *Politics*, Book II, i.

that the city-state is a natural growth, and that man is by nature a
political animal (ὅτι ὁ ἄνθρωπος φύσει πολιτικὸν ζῷον).[1]

In short, politics, as Aristotle saw it, is the 'science of the polis';
and the 'polis', although concretely it is the 'city-state', is
always also the ideal form of human association which is 'by
nature' the precondition for and the expression of the fulfillment
of human life.

When we say, then, that God is a 'politician', and that what
God is doing in the world is 'making or doing politics', it is the
Aristotelian *definition* and the biblical *description* of what is going
on that we have in mind. According to the *definition*, we may
say that politics is activity, and reflection upon activity, which
aims at and analyzes what it takes to make and to keep human
life *human in the world*. According to the *description*, what it
takes to make and to keep human life human in the world is
'the unsearchable riches of Christ . . . the plan of the mystery
hidden for ages in God who created all things; that through the
church the manifold wisdom of God might now be made known
to the principalities and powers in the heavenly places . . .
until we all attain . . . to mature manhood, to the measure of
the stature of the fullness of Christ'.[2]

It will have been noted that Aristotle uses, with reference to
the phenomenological starting point for the understanding of
the πόλις, the same word that so markedly and specifically
conveys the New Testament understanding of the phenomenological consequences of God's activity in Christ in the world.
The word is, of course, κοινωνία. For Aristotle, and for the
Greek world generally, the word connoted the basic *relatedness*
between human beings. It meant 'having a part in' or 'being
a party to' the affairs or doings or life of another person, or a
group of persons. It could be used to cover the whole range of
human relatedness, as well as to express a focal concept, as in
Aristotle's linking of κοινωνία with πόλις, or as with Epictetus,
for whom κοινωνία, κοινωνός usually refers to the fellowship of
men with one another and in relation to God. 'Greek philosophy
(Plato) carries the idea of fellowship with God beyond the
cultic experience and celebrates it as the highest and most

[1] *Politics*, Book II, 1; Book I, 2.
[2] From the Letter to the Ephesians; see above, pp. 48-56.

blessed fellowship.'[1] If in the Old Testament, and consequently in the Septuagint, the word κοινωνία drops into the background owing to the inability of Israelitic and rabbinic piety and thought to express intimacy between God and man, the word κοινωνία and its connotation reappear in the New Testament, particularly with the Apostle Paul. In Pauline thought, the use of the word κοινωνία undergoes the almost definitive restriction of expressing the fellowship or relatedness of Christians with Christ and consequently with one another.[2] The linguistic link between the Aristotelian *definition* and the biblical *description* is not chiefly a matter of philological similarity but one of semantic difference. The contextual analysis of a common referent makes it plain that the *Politics* and the *Bible* are not dependent upon but independent of one another. Both are concerned with the phenomenology of the *koinonia* as the starting point for an exploration of what it takes to make and to keep human life human. But there is a world of difference between the respective accounts of what it takes. The measure of the difference must be taken by imagination rather than by logic, by images rather than by concepts.

## 2 *Biblical Imagery and the Politics of God*

In a brilliant and illuminating attempt to explore 'the content of believing' by a 'method [which] may be called *depth-theology*', Professor Abraham Heschel has reminded us of the presymbolic character of religious knowledge and of the perennial perils of religious thinking.[3] 'Religious thinking', Rabbi Heschel declares, 'is in perpetual danger of giving primacy to concepts and dogmas and to forfeit the immediacy of insights, to forget that the known is but a reminder of God, that the dogma is a token of His will, the expression the inexpressible at its minimum. Concepts, words must not become screens; they must be regarded as windows. . . . The roots of ultimate insights are

[1] See the article on κοινωνός and its cognates in Gerhard Kittel, *Theologisches Woerterbuch zum neuen Testament*, W. Kohlhammer, Stuttgart, 1938, Vol. 3, pp. 798ff. The passage quoted is at p. 800.

[2] Recall the discussion of the self-understanding of the New Testament in Chapter II above, pp. 45-51ff.

[3] Abraham Heschel, *God in Search of Man*, Farrar, Straus, and Cudahy, Inc., New York, 1955, p. 7.

found . . . not on the level of discursive thinking, but on the level of wonder and radical amazement, in the depth of awe, in our sensitivity to the mystery, in our awareness of the ineffable.'[1] Faithful to his ancient forebears, whose remarkable sensitivity to mystery drew a veil over the etymological pilgrimage of the word κοινωνία en route from the Old Testament and its Semitic environment via a Hellenic environment to its emergence in the New Testament, Professor Heschel draws a line against description as well as against definition, against imagination as well as against conceptual formulation. 'Few of us', he says, 'are able to think in a way which is never crossed by the path of imagination, and it is usually at the cross-roads of thought and imagination that the great sweep of the spirit swerves into the blind alley of a parabolic image. . . . However subtle and noble our concepts may be, as soon as they become descriptive, namely, definite, they confine Him [i.e., God] and force Him into the triteness of our minds. . . . To form an image of Him or His acts is to deny His existence.'[2]

[1] Heschel, ibid., pp. 116-17.

[2] Ibid., p. 187. In order to avoid a possible confusion of meaning, attention is here called to the relation between the literary and/or religious meaning of 'parable' and its geometric meaning. Some disparity on the point appears from the comparison of the *New English Dictionary* (Oxford unabridged, 1909) and Webster's *New International Dictionary* (2nd edition, 1956). According to Oxford, the literary and/or religious meaning of 'parable' is primary; the geometric meaning secondary. Webster, on the other hand, suggests the word 'parabolical' for the literary and/or religious meaning and reserves 'parabolic' for the geometric meaning. However, whether we read Rabbi Heschel's phrase 'the parabolic image' in the sense of 'pertaining to a parable' or of 'pertaining to a parabola' is a less formidable difficulty than at first appears. For a *parable*, at least in the biblical sense, has to do with an imaginative juxtaposition of what is incommensurable, namely, the ways of God and the ways of man. Similarly, a *parabola*, according to Webster, is 'characterized by the equality or coincidence of two elements;—from the fact that a parabola is tangent to the line at infinity while the other conics have two real or imaginary intersections with that line'. In the case of the *parable*, 'equality of two elements' in the qualitative sense would be excluded. But in the mathematical sense of 'equality or coincidence', of a 'tangent to the line at infinity' related to other conics which have 'two real or imaginary intersections with that line' a parabola could express diagrammatically the kind of incommensurable relation between the ways of God and the ways of man which the parable seeks to express. Thus the vocabulary of poetry and the vocabulary of geometry are both useful to the theologian.

As a warning against abstraction, and especially against idolatry, this severe restriction upon the attempt to think and to speak about what God is doing in the world is as necessary as it is inescapable. Calvin, indeed, is as emphatic as is Rabbi Heschel, 'that a true image of God is not to be found in all the world', and he sees 'God's fearful vengeance' upon those who 'shall have dared to think of God otherwise than is right'.[1] And the Westminster Larger Catechism (1729) goes even farther in its express prohibition against 'the making any representation of God . . . either inwardly in our mind, or outwardly in any kind of image or likeness of any creature whatsoever. . . .'[2] But Calvin, in distinction both from the Larger Catechism and from Professor Heschel, sees that the Bible makes room for another dimension of the imagination than mere fancy or idolatry.

In a discerning passage which undertakes to comment upon what is involved in the prohibition against graven images in the second commandment, Calvin notes the difficulty that, despite the fact that the thrust of the commandment is against representation of God 'by any outward similitude (*externa aliqua similitudine eum exprimere*)', God 'has more than once taken upon Himself a visible form (*formam aliquam visibilem non semel sumpsisse*)'.[3] But Calvin concludes that this involves God in no inconsistency, partly because 'this must be accounted as a peculiar circumstance, and not be taken as a general rule', and partly because 'the visions shewn to the patriarchs were testimonies of His invisible glory, rather to elevate men's minds to things above than to keep them entangled amongst earthly elements'.[4] And then with an intriguing psychological penetra-

---

[1] John Calvin, *Commentarium in Quinque Libros Mosis*, Pars. II. CR, XXIV, pp. 377, 388. An English translation by the Reverend Charles Bingham, M.A., has been published in Edinburgh for the Calvin Tract Society. See *Commentaries on the Last Four Books of Moses*, Vol. II, 1853, pp. 108, 124. The last phrase contains an important nuance in the original which is not given in the translation. Calvin wrote: '*si aliter quam fas est de ipso sentire ausi fuerint*', that is, 'if they have dared to think about him otherwise than God has ordered (*quam fas*)'.

[2] *The Larger Catechism*, The Presbyterian Board of Christian Education, Philadelphia, 1928, Q. 109, p. 201.

[3] Calvin, *Commentarium*, pp. 377, 385.

[4] Ibid., p. 385; English translation, p. 120.

tion he observed that visible manifestations of God to the Israelites were an exception which ought not to obscure the significance of the fact that God apparently preferably 'manifested Himself . . . by a voice, and not in a bodily form. . . . This conclusion, therefore, always remains sure, that no image is suitable to God, because He would not be perceived by His people otherwise than in a voice.'[1]

A generation that has not yet had sufficient time to explore the image-making powers of television, and thus to settle the question of relative imaginative purity (e.g., freedom from idolatrous corruption) as between the eye and the ear, may nevertheless observe with appreciation the subtlety and potential accuracy of Calvin's observation. The scriptural preoccupation with a God who speaks, who is known in and through 'his Word', points to a power of imaginative apprehension which rejects definition but does not forswear description as man's way of responding to and reflecting upon what God is doing in the world. Professor Kroner has rightly pointed out that

the imagination of the biblical writers subserves the revelation of . . . God and is the vehicle of that revelation. In Biblical history the *mythos* is not and cannot be differentiated from the actual history, and the *history* in its turn is not to be separated from the *mythos*. History becomes mythical because it is experienced in the spirit of pious imagination, instead of being the product of objective inquiry and scientific research. Biblical history is *mythological* because it narrates what God has done. At the same time, Biblical mythos is *historical* because it narrates what the people of God have done. Biblical history is mythological because it is the history of God's revelation addressed to His people. Revelation and religious imagination, therefore, complement each other.[2]

If, then, we consider the New Testament claim that Jesus of Nazareth is the Son of God, the Word of God, that is, the revelation of God in and through whom all other apprehensions of God's activity are to be criticized and comprehended, 'the peculiar kind of images used by Jesus are of the utmost importance for understanding the connection between revelation and imagination'.[3] It is not accidental that Jesus 'taught them in

[1] Calvin, ibid., pp. 384, 385-86; English translation, pp. 119, 121. The original says, with regard to the suitability of images, '*non quadrare Deo imaginem*', 'to make a sketch of God'.

[2] Richard Kroner, *The Religious Function of Imagination*, Yale University Press, New Haven, 1941, pp. 46-47.

[3] Ibid., p. 51.

parables', as did in all crucial instances the prophets before him. For the parabolic image, far from being a 'blind alley', is the image which more precisely than any other juxtaposes 'inconfusedly [and] inseparably'[1] the ways of God and the ways of man. The formative biblical images partake of this parabolic power. Consequently, they are the stuff of authentic reflection upon and description of the activity of God. For these images point precisely to 'the realness of God' and the responsiveness of man of which the knowledge of faith is comprised.[2] The dynamics of biblical imagination make not only for a 'theology in depth' but for an 'ethic in depth' as well, that is, for an ethical analysis which tries to spell out what is involved in human maturity as the final fruit of being 'firmly fixed in love . . . able to grasp . . . how wide and deep and long and high is the love of Christ . . . by His power within us [who] is able to do far more than we ever dare to ask or imagine. . . .'[3]

Perhaps the most enduring fruit of the higher criticism of the Scriptures will be the liberation of biblical images. Biblical investigation from Wellhausen to Bultmann may be credited, among its many achievements, with having set the biblical images free—free from their confinement by the text, free for the literary and historical context in which biblical imagination could give pointed expression to what God is doing in the world.

Now the formative biblical images which point to and describe the divine activity in the world are *political* images, both in the phenomenological and in the fundamental senses of the word. God, according to the Bible, chooses a 'people'. He makes a 'covenant' with them, delivers them from 'slavery', and gives to them a 'land'. During the 'wilderness-wanderings' of the 'people' from 'slavery' 'to go in to take possession of the land',[4] God spells out in his 'law' the implications of life in 'covenant-relation' with himself. Once in the 'land', the affairs of the 'people' are administered by 'judges', who are sometimes priests, sometimes prophets, and sometimes military leaders; and then, under circumstances that are as fluid and complex

---

[1] *The Symbol of Chalcedon.* See Philip Schaff, *The Creeds of Christendom*, Harper & Brothers, New York, 1877, Vol. II, p. 62.

[2] Heschel, op. cit., pp. 116-17.

[3] Eph. 3.18-21 (Phillips).

[4] Josh. 1.11. Cf. also Gen. 15, 17; Ex. 13, 14, 34; Deut. 5.

as the policy is dubious—dubious to God as well as to the 'people'—God gives to them a 'king'.[1]

The 'kingship' of the 'covenant-people' becomes the focal point of their historical destiny as a 'political' people. On the one hand, the 'kingship' leads to a time of 'national' greatness, too quickly overtaken by a protracted decline as the fortunes of 'rulers' and of 'battle' rise and fall. On the other hand, the 'kingship' becomes the bearer of the ancestral 'blessing' and the sign of the 'people's' redemption, of their deliverance and fulfillment in accordance with the promises and terms of the 'covenant'.[2]

At this point, an interruption of the recital of the political images, which point to and point up God's behavior, is indicated. We have come upon the crucial image as regards the rest of the recital, and meanwhile also upon Professor Martin Buber's fascinating and instructive account of the environment of the images already noted.[3] A brief exploration of Professor Buber's argument may help to clarify and to fortify our attempt to understand the biblical understanding of politics.

Originally planned as the initial part of a three-volume study of messianic faith, particularly of the rise of messianism in Israel, Buber's discussion of the kingship of God has for personal and circumstantial reasons been published on its own. The volume seeks, by way of a commentary upon Gideon's refusal of kingly power, and by literary-critical and comparative historical methods of investigation, to show that the roots of the idea of divine kingship lie deep in Israel's pre-Canaanitic past and are to be rightly understood, not as etiological recollections superimposed upon memory and tradition from a later time, but as positive data belonging to the emerging traditions themselves.[4] 'The actualization of the all-inclusive rulership of God

[1] Judg. 21.25; I Sam. 8-10.

[2] Gen. 12.1-3; Ex. 3.13-17; II Sam. 7.

[3] Martin Buber, *Koenigtum Gottes*, Lambert Schneider, Heidelberg, Dritte neu vermehrte Auflage, 1956.

[4] Cf. Judg. 8.22-23: 'Then the men of Israel said to Gideon, "Rule over us, you and your son and your grandson also; for you have delivered us out of the hand of Midian". Gideon said to them: "I will not rule over you, and my son will not rule over you; the Lord will rule over you." ' Cf. also Buber, op. cit., Preface to the first edition, pp. xff., xv, xvi; Preface to the second edition, pp. liii, liv, and 99ff.

*(Gottesherrschaft)* is the beginning and the end *(das Proton und Eschaton)* of Israel.'[1]

The messianic theme, however, is Buber's central preoccupation. 'The principal content of Israel's messianic faith', he writes, 'is . . . the steady preoccupation with and expression of *(das Ausgerichtetsein auf)* the fulfillment of the relation between God and world in a complete kingly rule of God *(in einer vollkommenen Koenigsherrschaft Gottes)*.' However one may explain the origins of this faith, it cannot be phenomenologically denied that its uniqueness lies in its historical-political character. Lagarde's remark that the monotheism of the Jews is 'on a level with the report of a military subaltern . . . who lists only one instance of whatever he sees' betrays according to Buber 'a remarkable confusion of a relationship of faith with a world-view *(Weltanschauung)*'.[2]

> The vital basis of monotheistic faith *(die Einzigkeitslehre)* is after all not established by counting how many gods there may be. . . . It is the exclusiveness which permeates the relationship of faith; . . . more precisely: the claim to totality and the total effectiveness of exclusiveness *(in der Ganzheitsgeltung und Ganzheitswirkung der Ausschliesslichkeit)*. Israel's faith in God is ultimately characterized by the fact that the relationship of faith applies essentially to the whole of life and operates in everything. . . . He who says to his King and God, from his inmost depths, this singular, 'Thou,' cannot meanwhile linger in areas to which He is strange: he must subordinate them all to Him.[3]

This is the decisive significance of the conflict in the Old Testament between God and the half-gods, or idols. The mark of deviation—and the focus of the conflict—is to have simply a *private*, in this context *tribal*, god.

This theocratic conflict persisted from the earliest pre-monarchic times, and, indeed, so steadily and forcefully asserted itself against the myths and cults of Israel's neighbors as to become the basis for the opposition between authentic and idolatrous worship, and the ground on which Israel rejected her religious and political environment.[4] The religio-political

[1] Buber, op. cit., Preface to the third edition, p. lxiv.
[2] Ibid., p. 76.                    [3] Ibid., pp. 76-77.
[4] Ibid., p. xl. On merely philological grounds, Buber's thesis appears to be unconvincing. See the article by G. E. Wright in *The Journal of Biblical Theology*, Vol. LXXVII, 1958, pp. 43-44, note 5. Professor Wright suggests that the sparse use of the term *melek* for God in the earliest tradition is

depth and pervasiveness of the 'primitive theocracy' adumbrates, already in Gideon's refusal to rule, and more explicitly in the Sinai covenant and in the historically formative event and memory of the Exodus, the ultimate paradox of Israel's unique theocracy.[1]

> The paradox of all original and immediate theocracy [is] that it intrudes upon the limitlessness of the human person, the impulse of man to be independent of his fellow-man, but intrudes not for the sake of a freedom but for the sake of a highest bondage. The existential depth of this paradox is evident in this, that the highest bondage knows no pressure, that its implementation is uninterruptedly entrusted to the believing behavior of him who is bound (*der Glaubenssphaere des Gebundenen ueberantwortet ist*), who under theocratic authority either strives toward a perfect fellowship in freedom, a kingdom of God, or under cover of this aspiration can succumb to an inert or wild disorder.[2]

At all events, 'the usual historical separation of religion from politics is suspended in an authentic paradox'.[3] The theocratic paradox is the stuff of Israel's history and of her religion as a

---

evidently testimony to a difficulty inherent in it. But since the appearance of Buber's book, instructive archaeological and political evidence has emerged which gives striking confirmation to Professor Buber's point. Professor George Mendenhall of the University of Michigan has noted the correspondence in form between the particular type of political covenant found in certain treaties of the second millennium B.C. in western Asia and the Mosaic covenant in the Old Testament. Mendenhall accordingly believes that 'the covenant at Sinai was the formal means by which the semi-nomadic clans, recently emerged from state slavery in Egypt, were bound together in a religious and political community'. These early treaties appear to be of two types. One was a parity treaty between equals. The other was a treaty between a suzerain, i.e., not a king among other kings, but a ruler who believed himself to be the king of kings, and a vassal. Thus there is an immemorial and intimate relationship between the covenant and the divine rulership of God at the basis of Israelite society and of Israel's historical life. See George E. Mendenhall, 'Law and Covenant in Israel and the Ancient Near East', *The Biblical Archaeologist*, Vol. 17, No. 2, May 1954, pp. 26-46, and No. 3, September 1954, pp. 49-76. Professor Mendenhall's article has also been separately published by The Biblical Colloquium, Pittsburgh, Pennsylvania, 1955. The implications of his discoveries without reference to Buber's thesis but with reference to the relationship between the covenant and the kingship of Yahweh have been clearly and succinctly set out by Professor G. E. Wright, *The Book of the Acts of God*, Doubleday and Company, New York, 1957 (Duckworth, London, 1960), pp. 88-98.

[1] Buber, op. cit., pp. 3-10, 118f., 88-89.
[2] Ibid., p. 118.    [3] Ibid., p. 89.

historical religion. 'The spirit of an historical religion is nothing more nor less than the life-and-death passion for transmitting a tradition (*Leidenschaft des Ueberlieferns*) which has been decisively awakened through an event (*Ereignis*).'[1]

The historical operation of the theocratic paradox, however, culminates in a political crisis which brings with it the 'initial tremors of eschatology (*die ersten Schauer der Eschatologie*)'.[2] The crisis is inspired by the theocratic impulse itself and erupts in the conflict between the advocates of monarchical unification and the advocates of the kingship of God. The consequence of this conflict is a further and deeper crisis, 'the crisis out of which the human king of Israel, the follower of JHWH . . . , emerges as the "Anointed", meshiach JHWH, χριστὸς κύριος'.[3]

We may now resume the recital of the political images in terms of which the Bible points to and points up God's behavior with a clearer grasp not only of how formative they are of biblical imagination but also of how and why it is that the crucial political image is the image of the Messiah. The 'tremors of eschatology' never cease their rumbling beneath the surface of Israel's historical and political life. From David's line he comes, the 'Anointed of God', on an appointed 'day of the Lord'. The day of his coming is put forward again and again, as 'exile' and 'captivity' and 'restoration' and 'revolt and the wars of independence' lead the 'covenant-people' through virtual abandonment of their hopes for his 'kingdom' to an abortive attempt to 'take it by force'.[4]

The Messiah is to come as the inaugurator and the consummator of the 'kingship of God'. The Messiah has come. The 'new age' has begun to break across the world in the power and the pattern of God's rule in and over the world. It is this messianic boundary which both connects and separates the Old Testament from the New Testament. The Messiah teaches as 'one having authority', does 'signs and wonders and mighty works' which among others put the demons to flight, and rules over all 'principalities and powers'.[5] In him, that is, in 'Christ Jesus the Lord the whole fulness of deity dwells bodily, and you have come to fulness of life in him, who is the head of all

---

[1] Buber, ibid., p. 100.                [2] Ibid., p. 118.
[3] Ibid., p. 149. Cf. also I Sam. 12.13-15 (RSV).        [4] Matt. 11.12.
[5] Matt. 7.29 and parallels; Luke 4.33ff.; Col. 2.15.

rule and authority'.[1] 'And when all things are subjected to him, then the Son himself will also be subjected to him who put all things under him, that God may be everything to everyone.'[2] This is the day when the 'tremors of eschatology' shall have been quieted in and by the complete consummation. It involves the transcendence and the transfiguration of the heavens and the earth, of all history and politics. There shall be 'a new heaven and a new earth'.[3] What they shall be like and what their goings on shall be surpass knowledge and defy description. Yet, in the end, as in the beginning, the images which point to and point up what God is doing in the world are political images. 'There were loud voices in heaven, saying, "The kingdom of the world has become the kingdom of our Lord and of his Christ, and he shall reign for ever and ever." '[4]

### 3 *The Biblical Story*

If we now ask what are the fundamental sense and significance of the politics of God to which the biblical images point, the answer is given by the 'biblical story'. What Professor Buber has called Israel's 'life-and-death passion for transmitting a tradition' takes intrinsically narrative form. The story concerns God's ways with men and centers upon his will and purpose for men in the world and upon the conflict between his will and theirs. It is God's will not to be himself by himself but in fellowship with 'a people for God's own possession'.[5] The people whom God thus wills are the 'people of the covenant'. For their sakes, and for their destiny, God makes the world, upholds and governs it. 'The covenant,' Karl Barth has discerningly observed, is 'the internal ground of creation . . . creation . . . the external ground of the covenant.'[6] The people, however, are unable to withstand the great temptation; '*eritis sicut Deus*' ('you will be like God'),[7] and launch the great rebellion, the sinful act wherein the attempt is made to recon-

---

[1] Col. 2.9-10 (RSV). It must be remembered that the LXX translates the Hebrew מָשִׁיחַ (mashiach) by the Greek word χριστός.

[2] I Cor. 15.28.    [3] Rev. 21.1.

[4] Ibid., 11.15.    [5] I Peter 2.9 (ASV).

[6] Karl Barth, *Kirchliche Dogmatik*, Evangelischer Verlag, Zollikon-Zuerich, III/1, 1945, pp. 258, 103.

[7] Gen. 3.5 (Vulgate).

stitute the terms of the covenant, the terms on which the world
has been made. God's will to fellowship is displaced by man's
will to power; and in consequence man has lost the secret of
his humanity and the key to the meaning of his life and of the
world in which he cannot help but live it out. The fullness of
life now, as always, awaits the fullness of time. God neither
breaks off the covenant nor destroys the world. God uninterruptedly wills his will, but man pervertedly and superfluously
wills himself. What was a gift has become a quest in which man
seeks what he does not know and knows what he does not seek.
Refusing to trust the risk of trust, man has become the creature
of the backward look at the end of which only questions lurk
and mystery is filled up with foreboding rather than fulfillment.
As E. E. Cummings has put it:

> when god decided to invent
> everything he took one
> breath bigger than a circus tent
> and everything began
>
> when man determined to destroy
> himself he picked the *was*
> of *shall* and finding only *why*
> smashed it into *because*[1]

So—man lives, not in the age of maturity but in the 'age of
anxiety',—

> . . . his tired mind
> Biased toward bigness since his body must
> Exaggerate to exist, possessed by hope,
> Acquisitive, in quest of his own
> Absconded self yet scared to find it
> As he bumbles by from birth to death
> Menaced by madness; whose mode of being,
> Bashful or braggart, is to be at once
> Outside and inside his own demand
> For personal pattern . . .
>                                             All that exists
> Matters to man; he minds what happens
> And feels he is at fault, a fallen soul
> With power to place, to explain every
> What in his world but why he is neither

---

[1] E. E. Cummings, *1 × 1*, Henry Holt and Company, New York, 1944,
XXVI. Italics mine.

> God nor good, this guilt his insoluble
> Final fact, infusing his private
> Nexus of needs, his noted aims with
> Incomprehensible comprehensive dread
> At not being what he knows that before
> This world was he was willed to become.[1]

As the biblical story unfolds, it appears that fulfillment, which, in the context of God's willed purposes of fellowship with man and for man, is movement toward consummation, has become a movement toward consummation via deliverance. To the paradox of the great defection has been juxtaposed the paradox of the great denouement. Creation: sin—judgment: redemption! These are the twin anvils upon which the humanity of man is being hammered out and hammered into being. The goal is 'the prize of the upward call of God in Christ Jesus', 'the measure of the stature of the fullness of Christ'.[2] A divinely willed order of life, in which all created things are instrumental to the possibility and the power given to man—through fellowship with God—to be himself in being related to his fellow man, has been inverted by the will to power by which man subdues his environment, including his 'brother', to the will to be himself by himself. Over against, and working against, this inverted order is a divinely renewed order of life in which the will to power has been transformed into the power to will what God wills by the power of God's Messiah. The destroyed community is being winnowed away by the advent of the messianic community in the world. In the messianic community, the secret and the experience of maturity are being expressed and achieved against the time when 'God will be everything to everyone'.[3]

The juxtaposition of these two paradoxes, together with their corresponding communities, is as inexorable and intimate as a dead stump in the wilderness from whose unproductive and utterly unpromising decay a tiny shoot may be observed. There is no intrinsic connection between the stump and the shoot except that the shoot is the surviving remnant of the not yet and soon to be decayed. But the juxtaposition points to another and radically extrinsic alternative. The shoot out of the stump is a

[1] W. H. Auden, *The Age of Anxiety*, Random House, New York, 1947 (Faber & Faber, London, 1948), pp. 23-24.
[2] Phil. 3.14; Eph. 4.13.          [3] I Cor. 15.28.

sign, a messianic sign, that when all intrinsic possibilities of renewal have been played out, God's fresh possibility of deliverance and fulfillment breaks out. This is God's messianic action. Its political thrust and character are plain. For by this action God sets up and spells out in the world a community of life, in the context of which human maturity becomes both a possibility and a fact.

The messianic image was, as we have seen, not born with the Isaianic vision. But it is not too much to say that the Isaianic vision marks the traumatic perception of and response to the politics of God to which the messianic image refers. 'There shall come forth a shoot', so the vision runs,

> from the stump of Jesse,
> and a branch shall grow out of his roots.
> And the Spirit of the Lord shall rest upon him,
>     the spirit of wisdom and understanding,
>     the spirit of counsel and might,
>     the spirit of knowledge and the fear of the Lord.
> And his delight shall be in the fear of the Lord.
>
> He shall not judge by what his eyes see,
>     or decide by what his ears hear;
> but with righteousness he shall judge the poor,
>     and decide with equity for the meek of the earth;
> and he shall smite the earth with the rod of his mouth,
>     and with the breath of his lips he shall slay the wicked.
> Righteousness shall be the girdle of his waist,
>     and faithfulness the girdle of his loins.
>
> The wolf shall dwell with the lamb,
>     and the leopard shall lie down with the kid,
> and the calf and the lion and the fatling together,
>     and a little child shall lead them.
> The cow and the bear shall feed;
>     their young shall lie down together;
>     and the lion shall eat straw like the ox.
> The sucking child shall play over the hole of the asp,
>     and the weaned child shall put his hand on the adder's den.
> They shall not hurt nor destroy in all my holy mountain;
> for the earth shall be full of the knowledge of the Lord
>     as the waters cover the sea.
>
> In that day the root of Jesse shall stand as an ensign
> to the peoples; him shall the nations seek, and his
>     dwellings shall be glorious.[1]

---

[1] Isa. 11.1-10.

It is not accidental that involvement in the politics of God should be a traumatic affair. Maturity is a traumatic experience compounded of deliverance and fulfillment. In short, maturity is salvation. According to the biblical story, as the humanity of man is being hammered into being by the political dynamics of the divine activity, the soteriological question is forced from the depths of the trauma. In its initial and old covenantal form, the question is: 'How long, O Lord?'[1] In its new covenantal form, the question is: 'What must I do to be saved?'[2] The question is precipitated and its two forms are conjoined by the prophetic-apostolic indication of the thrust into the human situation of what God is doing to make and to keep human life *human* in the world.

The prophetic-apostolic indication of God's politics is that 'line of revelation' which points to and points up what in the Letter to the Ephesians is called 'the incalculable riches of Christ'.[3] The line declares that God is at work 'to pluck up and to break down, to destroy and to overthrow, to build and to plant'.[4] He has 'scattered the proud in the imagination of their hearts, . . . put down the mighty from their thrones, and exalted them of low degree. . . .'[5] The line centers in the advent of the Shepherd-king, 'born . . . in the city of David a Savior, who is Christ the Lord . . . : a babe wrapped in swaddling clothes and lying in a manger'. And 'behold, this child is set for the fall and rising of many in Israel, and for a sign that is spoken against'.[6] He came, as we have said, preaching the kingdom of God, which he defined in terms of another Isaianic vision: 'good news to the poor . . . release to the captives and recovering of sight to the blind, . . . liberty [to] those who are oppressed, . . . the acceptable year of the Lord'.[7] Upon still another Isaianic vision he drew for the pattern of his suffering and death.[8] And on the night in which he was betrayed, 'he took bread, and blessed, and broke it, and gave it to them, and said, "Take; this is my body." And he took a cup, and when he had given thanks he gave it to them, and they all drank of it. And he said to them, "This is my blood of the covenant, which is poured out for many. Truly, I say to you, I shall not drink again of the

[1] Isa. 6.11.　　[2] Acts 16.30.　　[3] See above, pp. 48-49.
[4] Jer. 1.10.　　[5] Luke 1.51-52.　　[6] Luke 2.11-12, 34.
[7] Luke 4.18-19; Isa. 61.1-2.　　[8] Isa. 53.

fruit of the vine until that day when I drink it new in the kingdom of God." '[1]

The textual and historical problems surrounding the accounts of the consummation of the first advent and the expectations of the second advent do not affect their messianic center and consummation. The *koinonia* of which Jesus Christ (Messiah) is meanwhile the head is faithful to its foundation and to its ethical resources when it celebrates in the world over which he rules as Lord, in recollection and in hope, his sovereign presence and power in the midst of the people. 'The cup of blessing which we bless, is it not a participation in the blood of Christ? The bread which we break, is it not a participation in the body of Christ? Because there is one loaf, we who are many are one body, for we all partake of the same loaf.'[2]

---

[1] Mark 14.22-25. The parallels are Matt. 26.26-29; Luke 22.17-19.

[2] I Cor. 10.16-17. The Greek text says: οὐχὶ κοινωνία ἐστὶν τοῦ αἵματος τοῦ χριστοῦ; . . . οὐχὶ κοινωνία τοῦ σώματος τοῦ χριστοῦ ἐστιν; and then concludes, οἱ γὰρ πάντες ἐκ τοῦ ἑνὸς ἄρτου μετέχομεν ('for we all partake of the same loaf'). Μετέχομεν means literally, 'to have among or amid', that is, 'to be what one is in belonging'. To translate κοινωνία by 'participation' and μετέχομεν by 'partake' overlooks the point that Christianity is exactly *not* a mystery cult. The language is technically cultic-sacramental but its connotation here has been transformed by the political context and character of biblical messianism. The language does not seem to be violated by translating: 'The cup of blessing which we bless, is it not a *fellowship of belonging* in the blood of Christ? The bread which we break, is it not a *fellowship of belonging* in the body of Christ? Because there is one loaf, we who are many are one body, *are what we are in belonging* to the same loaf.' Italics are mine. Or if not this, at least J. B. Phillips' translation is nearer the sense of the passage than the RSV: 'The Cup of blessing which we bless, is it not a very sharing in the Blood of Christ? When we break the Bread do we not actually share in the Body of Christ? The very fact that we all share one Bread makes us all one Body.'

The synoptic connection of the Lord's Supper with the messianic banquet supports this interpretation of the political character of the Supper. The celebration on the part of Jesus with his disciples was an anticipation of the coming banquet with the Messiah when the latter has assumed his role as earth's ruler. Christian faith affirms that the Messiah has already come in the life, death, resurrection, and ascension of Jesus of Nazareth and since his exaltation has already assumed his lordship over all things in heaven and in earth. Thus the Lord's Supper becomes a celebration both of Christ's sovereign presence and activity in and over the church and the world and an anticipation of the consummation of his work in the new heaven and the new earth and the new humanity. The political and messianic inter-

The penultimate chapter of the biblical story is the story of the eucharistic community in the world. Here is a *laboratory of maturity* in which, by the operative (real) presence and power of the Messiah-Redeemer in the midst of his people, and through them of all people, the will to power is broken and displaced by the power to will what God wills. The power to will what God wills is the power to be what man has been created and purposed to be. It is the power to be and to stay human, that is, to attain wholeness or maturity. For maturity is the full development in a human being of the power to be truly and fully himself in being related to others who also have the power to be truly and fully themselves. The Christian *koinonia* is the foretaste and the sign in the world that God has always been and is contemporaneously doing what it takes to make and to keep human life human. This is the will of God 'as it was in the beginning, is now, and ever shall be, world without end'.[1]

---

pretation of the Supper has, however, assumed even larger importance in view of the messianic materials which are part of the Dead Sea Scrolls. On this point, see Frank M. Cross, Jr., *The Ancient Library of Qumran,* Doubleday and Company, New York, 1958 (Duckworth, London, 1958), pp. 177-79; Krister Stendahl, *The Scrolls and the New Testament,* Harper & Row, New York, 1957 (SCM Press, London, 1958), pp. 10-11.

[1] *The Book of Common Prayer,* the Order for Morning Prayer, in which the *Gloria* follows upon the Absolution and the Lord's Prayer, and is repeated following the *Venite,* and/or the Psalms, the *Benedictus es, Benedictus,* and *Jubilate.*

# IV

## CHRISTIAN ETHICS AND A THEOLOGY OF MESSIANISM

THE eucharistic liturgy is the dramatic presentation of the reality and the power of what God is doing in the world. Ethical analysis and criticism must steadily accompany liturgical behavior lest liturgy obscure rather than express the dynamics of the divine activity. It is, perhaps, no accident that the intrinsic semantic connection between liturgy and ethics re-emerges in the messianic community of the New Testament.

Work and worship are correlative forms of behavioral service to God. The laborer is the philological precursor of the worshiper. The New Testament use of λειτουργεῖν, λειτουργία, the words which lie at the root of our word 'liturgy', reflects this development. Semitic and Hellenistic associations illuminate by contrast the specific accent of the New Testament. Popular Greek usage meant by 'liturgy' any kind of work as a service.[1] But the word 'liturgy' also carried technical connotations, both cultic and political. In the Septuagint it refers to acts of the community of God's people at worship.[2] The more

---

[1] See Gerhard Kittel, *Theologisches Woerterbuch zum neuen Testament*, W. Kohlhammer, Stuttgart, 1938, Vol. 4, p. 234. 'The New Testament use of λειτουργεῖν, λειτουργία', writes Kittel, 'connects . . . partly with the weakened popular usage (Rom. 15.27; II Cor. 9.12; Phil. 2.30), partly it relates to the pre-Christian Old Testament cultus (Luke 1.23; Heb. 9.21; 10.11), partly [to] an isolated metaphorical application of the terminology of the LXX to the significance of Christ (Hebrews), or to a characterization of the missionary work of Paul prepared for martyrdom, or to a Christian attitude towards life on the part of the congregation (Phil. 2.17).' The 'weakened popular usage' to which Kittel refers is the generalized denotation of any kind of work as a service.

[2] The New Testament significantly goes beyond the Septuagint where the words, λειτουργεῖν, λειτουργία (שָׁרַת, עֲבֹדָה), are technical cultic terms.

characteristic Greek usage referred to service to the people as a
political community. The earliest *liturgies* were celebrations of
benefactors to the *polis*. The New Testament, however, adopts
neither the technical-political nor the technical-cultic meaning
for the Christian's characteristic service to God. The words
λειτουργεῖν, λειτουργία are infrequently used; and when used,
the sense is predominantly ethical rather than cultic. The
emphasis lies upon the *societal* rather than upon the *sacerdotal*
understanding of God's relation to his people.[1] The *koinonia*
celebrates neither benefactors to the community nor cultic
offices. 'The new community (*Gemeinde*) had no priests because
it consisted of nothing but priests. "For through the blood of
Christ, we can enter the sanctuary with confidence" (Heb.
10.19). Thus, we may conclude that the scarcity with which
these terms are used in the New Testament in particular, but
even more the complete absence of any parallel terms for
expressing the relations of the christian community is characteristic of the radical newness of the Christian gospel.'[2] As the
politics of God give to the eucharistic liturgy its occasion and
significance, so the ethical reality of the *koinonia* gives to the
celebration of the Eucharist its integrity.

The connection between the politics of God and the ethical
reality of the *koinonia* is evident not only from the integrity of
liturgical action but also from the integrity of theological
reflection. Life in the *koinonia* requires both liturgical and
theological nourishment. By thoughts as well as by words and
deeds, the *koinonia* exhibits the integrity of its self-understanding,
that is, of the account which is given in the *koinonia* of its
'common knowledge of the Son of God', of God's revealed
behavior.[3] The role of theology in such an account is defined
by the concern for dogma. Dogma is not, as in Roman Catholicism, a 'truth of revelation' defined by the church. On the con-

---

Although שָׁרַת, 'to serve', is exclusively cultic, עָבַד, 'to worship', indicates
the semantic relation between cultic and ethical ideas even in the Old
Testament.

[1] See Chapter II, pp. 56-63. Λειτουργεῖν occurs in the New Testament
three times, one of these in Hebrews; λειτουργία occurs six times, two of
these in Hebrews. See Kittel, op. cit., p. 232.

[2] Ibid., p. 235.

[3] Eph. 4.13; see above, pp. 48-56.

trary, dogma, as Karl Barth has rightly put it, is 'the concurrence (*Uebereinstimmung*) of the church's proclamation with the revelation attested in the Bible'.[1] But as with liturgy, so with theology: without ethical analysis and criticism the dynamics of the divine activity are obscured rather than expressed. This happens whenever the concern of theology with and for dogma becomes an end in itself and hardens into dogmatism. This does not mean that there is no liturgical action, no service of God appropriate to God as he is in himself. Nor does it mean that there is no theology as such, no distinguishable and indispensable concern with and about dogma. Liturgy and theology are not devoured by ethics. Without ethical analysis and criticism, however, the political thrust of the divine activity attested by the biblical story and its images is insufficiently discerned and responded to in the liturgical and theological life of the *koinonia*.

The messianic image which emerges from the biblical story is, as we have seen, the crucial image which illuminates what God is doing in the world. Consequently, theology, as reflection upon the biblical witness to revelation, acquires a messianic character. Christian theology is *ex animo* theology of messianism. The politics of God gives to the church's concern with and about dogma a christological focus and to Christian thinking about ethics a christological foundation.

Contemporary discussions of Christian ethics have been notably careless at this point. They have tended to draw upon theological anthropology for what little dogmatic groundwork may be discerned in them. It is somehow assumed that the nature of man—as creature and sinner, as made in the image of God and made over by grace—is the obvious link between theology (dogmatics) and ethics. But as is often the case with the obvious, it becomes trite and tedious with handling, having strayed off base. The doctrine of man supplies materials for a theological analysis of ethics as relevant as the materials supplied by a doctrine of grace or of the Holy Spirit. The doctrine of man is even more directly relevant to a theological analysis of ethics than, for example, the doctrine of inspiration, or of the attributes of God. But unless it is clear that the theo-

[1] *Kirchliche Dogmatik*, Evangelischer Verlag, Zollikon-Zuerich, I/1, 1932, p. 280.

logical base of Christian thinking about ethics is a christological one, Christian ethics is caught in a dilemma between a capricious doctrinal selectivity, on the one hand, and the abandonment of its theological character, on the other.

We have, then, to explain those christological affirmations which involve basic implications for conduct. When doctrines are viewed from the perspective of ethics, it is remarkable how the substance and the impact of the theological concern for dogma come alive. A theology of messianism is theology with the accent upon the politics of God, that is, upon what God has done and is doing in the world to keep human life human. For such a theology, three christological affirmations acquire particular significance. They are the doctrines of the Trinity, of the threefold office of Christ, and of the Second Adam and the Second Advent. The various elements of the church's christological thinking may be and have been differently designated and arranged for purposes of strictly dogmatic exposition. But a *koinonia* ethic derives its theological foundation and focus from the way in which these doctrines define the meaning and direction of the divine behavior, and thus also of human behavior.

### 1  *The Trinitarian Basis of Christian Ethics*

The doctrine of the Trinity is the most comprehensive statement of the christological dogma. It is the supreme theological achievement of the early church. The christological dogma expresses the fact that the revelation attested in the Bible and proclaimed and taught by the church is God's messianic action in the life, death, resurrection, and ascension of Jesus of Nazareth. This action is the center and criterion of Christian faith and life. It is an action in which God, at one and the same time, gives himself to be known as he is and accomplishes the deliverance and fulfillment of human life in this world and the next. 'God was in Christ reconciling the world to himself. . . .'[1] Or as Athanasius was later to put it:

> As, then, if a man should wish to see God, who is invisible by nature and not seen at all, he may know and apprehend Him from His works: so let him who fails to see Christ with his understanding, at least apprehend Him by the works of His body. . . . Let him marvel that by so ordinary

---

[1] II Cor. 5.19.

a means things divine have been manifested to us, and that by death immortality has reached to all, and that by the Word being made man, the Word of God as author and governor and His providence over all are known. *For he was made man that we might be made God.*[1]

And if the endeavor of the early church to 'see Christ with . . . understanding' came to be absorbed by his person rather than his work, Athanasius' attempt to redress the balance, and, as it were, to see Christ whole, is a reminder of the messianic occasion, contest, and point of the christological dogma.

Athanasius was, of course, primarily absorbed by the problem of the relations between the first and second persons of the Trinity. It remained for Western theologians, particularly Ambrose and Augustine, to explore more fully the significance of the third person of the Trinity in himself and in relation to the other two. Actually the history of doctrine goes far toward proving that the attention to the Holy Spirit is largely an unfinished assignment. The reason is, in considerable part, that the Athanasian view of the central significance of the Trinity and its implications was obscured. Attention was focused, instead, upon the relations between the Father and the Son, and upon an ecclesiastical-sacramental theory of grace as a way of interpreting the work of the Holy Spirit as the Sanctifier of human life. Nevertheless, as Professor Charles Cochrane has put it, the Christian doctrine of the Trinity, formatively shaped by Athanasius, provided a 'principle of intelligibility' (ἀρχή) and a 'moral and spiritual release' whereby ultimate reality, as well as life in this world, could be understood and responsibly

---

[1] Athanasius, *Incarnation of the Word*, in *The Nicene and Post-Nicene Fathers*, Second Series, The Christian Literature Company, New York, Vol. IV, 1892, par. 54. I have departed from Mr Archibald Robertson's translation in concluding the second last sentence. Cf. Migne, PG, Vol. 25, col. 192, par. 54. The italics read in the original: Αὐτὸς γὰρ ἐνηνθρώπησεν, ἵνα ἡμεῖς θεοποιηθῶμεν. The θεοποιηθῶμεν can scarcely mean apotheosis. Athanasius does not say that the Word was 'humanified' that we might be 'deified'. He is trying to show that the Incarnation and the Atonement are so intimately drawn together in the Person of Christ as to be the basis and the guarantee of human fulfillment. It is as though Athanasius were paraphrasing Paul: When God is everything to everyone (I Cor. 15.29) then men will be 'like God', that is, everything to everyone. The *eritis sicut deus* has lost its sinful fang, and its providential foundation and purpose have been fulfilled. See also ibid., par. 19; and Charles Cochrane, *Christianity and Classical Culture*, Oxford University Press, New York, 1940, pp. 37-72.

lived. In this way Athanasius both associated himself with classical ways of thought and transformed them, making them in the last analysis expendable. 'In the new *arche* or starting-point,' says Cochrane, Athanasius

> claimed recognition for a principle which, because of its unique character, transcended the normal processes of apprehension. To grasp it, therefore, required a vigorous effort of thought and imagination and, in particular, it was necessary to expel from the mind the anthropomorphisms of pagan science. . . . For, as the source of Being, this principle was not to be apprehended 'objectively'; it eluded analysis in terms . . . which yield a knowledge of the phenomenological world. But, although not cognizable as an object, it was not therefore reducible to terms merely of subjective feeling, for its reality was presupposed in all the various manifestations of conscious life, of speculative as well as practical activity.[1]

The fundamental point at issue was the recognition of and response to the historic Christ as the disclosure and the bearer of the divine economy. According to this economy, the structure and the destiny of the world and of human life in the world were at once full of movement and of meaning. It made sense, in the context of such an economy, to be a human being; and to be a human being meant to be on the way toward the new humanity to be consummated in the 'second Adam' and the 'second Advent'. Once it has been established and understood that the structure and destiny of the world are directed toward this new humanity, the way is open for the exploration of what its achievement and consummation in Christ involve. Absorbed in an analysis of the relations between the Father and the Son, Athanasius thereby explored and clarified the environment and the fact of the new humanity in Christ. At the same time, he laid the foundation for an understanding of the nature and activity of the Holy Spirit in relation to the Father and the Son, thereby explaining the power by which this new humanity was being achieved and could be achieved. From this point of view, in Cochrane's phrase, 'The panorama of human history may be conceived as a record of the divine economy, the working of the Spirit in and through mankind, from the creation of the first conscious human being to its full and final revelation in the Incarnate Word.'[2]

If the successors of Athanasius had been as clear about the

[1] Cochrane, op. cit., p. 363. See the whole of Part III, chap. X.
[2] Ibid., pp. 367-68.

range and intricacy of this panorama of human history as the work of the Spirit as Athanasius was about its focus and foundation, the trinitarian substance of Christian faith could have been spared much metaphysical and liturgical sterility. It is understandable that in the environment of classicism, theology should have been disproportionately engaged by an ontological rather than an economic interpretation of the Trinity. But it is hard to see how the politics of God, without which theology lacks both content and context, can lead to any other than an economic Trinity. For it is the divine economy of Father, Son, and Holy Spirit which exhibits, both as regards inner-trinitarian and as regards extra-trinitarian relations, the revealed and the dynamic character of the divine activity.

Any interpretation of the Trinity runs the risk of modalism. The economic trinity, at least as initially suggested by Tertullian, is no exception. As Welch rightly points out, it 'contains nothing which would exclude the possibility of a Sabellian interpretation'.[1] Nevertheless, under the impact of the Athanasian defense of the Nicene faith, it is plain that the inner-trinitarian relations between Father, Son, and Spirit, are not compromised by their extra-trinitarian relations. This is because, for Athanasius, theology is really reflection upon the biblical witness to revelation, upon the incarnation of the Word. Therefore, what God is in himself can only be hinted at from his self-disclosure in his activity. It makes all the difference in the world whether one says ὁμοούσιον (of one substance) or ὁμοιούσιον (of like substance) in analyzing the relations between the Father and the Son. The difference is between a world the Redeemer and the Creator of which are one and the same God and a world with at least two gods, one who creates, the other who redeems. It is the difference between a world in which men have been redeemed, set upon a new and living way, in the *same* world, and redemption in a world *toto caelo* other than the one in which men have been set down and, even after the incarnation of the Word, continue to live.

[1] Claude Welch, *In This Name*, Charles Scribner's Sons, New York, 1952, offers an illuminating analysis of the revival and lines of trinitarian thinking in contemporary theology. Appendix A, pp. 293-94, of Professor Welch's discussion offers a succinct account of the distinction between an 'economic' and an 'immanent' or 'ontological' Trinity.

What the ὁμοούσιον is to the relations between the Father and the Son, the *filioque* is to the relations between the Father and the Son, on the one hand, and the Spirit, on the other. Reinhold Niebuhr rightly protests against the tendency in Catholic theology to 'reduce to simple intelligibility' the mystery of the Godhead at which theology arrives in its response to the revelation attested in the Bible. Yet he goes perhaps too far when he appears to find the *filioque* inextricably imprisoned within abortive speculation.[1] It is not accidental that since Augustine the Latin Church has taught the doctrine of double procession of the Spirit from the Father and from the Son,[2] and that

---

More recently, Professor Cyril C. Richardson, in *The Doctrine of the Trinity*, Abingdon Press, New York, 1958, has urged that the doctrine of the Trinity 'is an artificial construct' and that 'Christian theology might be aided by abandoning such a procedure . . .' (pp. 148-49). Richardson's chief objection to the traditional formulations of the Trinity is their imposition of the mold of 'threeness' upon the biblical terms 'Father', 'Son', 'Spirit', which endeavored to express both God's nature and God's activity (pp. 13-14). The principal issue, according to Richardson, is the paradox of God's absoluteness and God-in-relation.

With Professor Richardson's exposure of a basic error of classical trinitarian doctrine we agree. It is precisely for this reason that we have stressed the *economic* as against the *ontological* Trinity. But we are not yet ready to abandon the doctrine altogether, particularly where the theological foundations of ethics are under discussion. To do so would be to set aside an important traditional safeguard against basing ethics upon theological anthropology. Furthermore, when ethical analysis derives its orientation and direction from a trinitarian account of the divine activity, the paradoxical character of God's self-revelation in Jesus Christ, far from being obscured, remains steadily in view and steadily concrete. Thus it is God's activity which preserves and points up the mystery both of God's nature and of God's revelation through providing behavior with the context and the concreteness without which action is sundered from faith and delivered over to fresh speculations (of which God's absoluteness and his being in relation may well be one more) for interpretation and guidance. It is regrettable that Richardson does not refer to Cochrane's interpretation of classical trinitarianism, for here the narrow confines of 'threeness' are transcended and the classical contribution to precisely the sort of variability and viability in setting forth what is involved in God's reconciling action in the world, for which Professor Richardson is seeking to make room, is strikingly analyzed.

[1] Reinhold Niebuhr, *Faith and History*, Charles Scribner's Sons, New York, 1949 (Nisbet, London, 1949).

[2] Philip Schaff, *Creeds of Christendom*, Harper & Brothers, New York, 1877,

Augustine was, with Athanasius, the most biblically oriented among the early Fathers of the church.[1] Once again, what is at stake in the *filioque* is the faithful and intelligible account of what God is doing in the world. Whether one says '*qui ex Patre Filioque procedit*' ('who proceeds from the Father and the Son'), with the Latin and Reformation churches, or '*ex Patre procedentem*' ('proceeding from the Father'), with the Eastern churches, makes a great deal of difference.[2] The subtle distinctions which seek to define and to connect the eternal and the temporal activities of the Godhead involve more than classical rhetoric and metaphysics. The question is critical whether the Spirit 'proceeds' from the Father, or from the Father and from the Son, because it involves the question of whether 'history' or 'nature' is the key to the understanding of God's self-revelation in Christ; and if history, whether there are in actual history signs of redemption which 'are not merely extensions of human wisdom or human virtue [or even human power] but are the consequence of a radical break-through of the divine spirit through human self-sufficiency'.[3]

While the church waits upon a re-examination and a fresh exploration of the meaning and implications of the *filioque*,[4]

---

Vol. I, p. 26. The first clear creedal trace of the *filioque* is, according to Schaff, in the Nicene Creed at the third Council of Toledo in Spain, A.D. 589.

[1] Augustine, *On the Trinity*, Marcus Dods edition, T. & T. Clark, Edinburgh, 1873, Bk. XV, especially chap. XXVI, where Augustine makes plain that the Scriptures ascribe the Spirit both to the Father and to the Son, to God and to Christ.

[2] The Nicaeno-Constantinopolitan Creed. Cf. Schaff, op. cit., Vol. II, pp. 57-61.

[3] Niebuhr, op. cit., p. 168.

[4] Karl Barth has begun such an exploration in the context of his interpretation of the doctrine of the Trinity as the 'prologomena' to dogmatics. The *filioque* rightly leads Barth to the doctrine of *perichoresis* (literally, 'indwelling' or 'permeation'), according to which the ancient church stated its view of the dynamic interrelatedness in unity and community of the three persons of the Godhead. Perichoresis is 'a further delimitation of the homoousion of the Father, the Son, and the Spirit'. So Barth; and he goes on to point out how the doctrine of perichoresis strengthens the force of the *filioque* in preventing an independent anthropological interpretation of the application of the gifts of the Spirit—independent, that is, of a trinitarian response by theology to the self-revelation of God in Jesus Christ. Barth's fully developed doctrine of the Spirit is, of course, still pending. But it is instructive that, in such anticipations of it as we have, Barth fails to indicate

Christian ethics, as reflected in the church, may quicken dogmatic sensitivity and attention to this task. A *koinonia* ethic can only be faithful to its messianic occasion and character upon a trinitarian foundation. This foundation is none other than he who, as the Lord's Anointed (Messiah) is 'of one substance (ὁμοούσιον) with the Father', whose Spirit, proceeding from the Father and the Son (*filioque*), is 'the Lord and Giver of life; who with the Father and the Son together is worshipped and glorified'.[1]

The trinitarian dogma provided, in Professor Cochrane's telling phrase, the 'logos of power' in terms of which Christianity effectively displaced the attempt of Graeco-Roman classicism to adapt the Augustan experiment in 'creative politics' to the changing circumstances of life in this world, and thus to make the world 'safe for civilization'.[2] With trinitarian Christianity, a radical transvaluation of the context, meaning, and direction of life in this world, and accordingly of human behavior, became a live option. The point of departure for and the thrust of this transvaluation were the redemptive reality, dynamics, and direction of the activity of God. Contrary to Professor Cochrane's view, the trinitarian achievement of the church was not so much a new 'metaphysic of ordered process' as a new context of apprehension and behavior within which the whole process and complexity of human inquiry and conduct made intelligible and behavioral sense.[3] Contrary to those strains of

---

the bearing of the *filioque* upon the work of the Spirit. Thus, the link between the inner-trinitarian and the extra-trinitarian dynamics of the divine activity is weaker than it might, and indeed ought to, be; and the constructive line of a rediscovery of the *filioque* is imperiled by doctrinal speculation. Cf. Barth, op. cit., I/1, pp. 509, 513; IV/1, pars. 62, 63. Such a danger has been correctly foreseen by Wilhelm Pauck, *Karl Barth*, Harper & Row, New York, 1931, pp. 189ff. But Pauck goes too far in rejecting Barth's trinitarian reconstruction as wholly speculative. The rejection of the *filioque* and the doctrine of perichoresis in contemporary theology before Barth is instructively sketched by Welch, op. cit., pp. 48-54.

[1] The Nicaeno-Constantinopolitan Creed. Cf. Schaff, op. cit., p. 59.

[2] Cochrane, op. cit., chaps. V-VI, pp. 157-58, 361ff., 436-37, 450ff., 480-90.

[3] Ibid., p. 437. Of course, there was also metaphysics—in this case classical metaphysics. Theology cannot and need not avoid metaphysical problems, the language and the insights of philosophy, current in the cultural environment of any given time. The decisive question in such a

Augustine's analysis of the Trinity which forge too intimate a link between the Holy Spirit and the human spirit,[1] the trinitarian achievement of the church links the mystery and the meaning of the reality and activity of God revealed in Christ so as to guarantee signs of redemption in the world in which God became incarnate and the Holy Spirit is at work. These signs are not less real because open only to eyes of faith. They are not less significant for human apprehension and behavior because they are *indicative* rather than *verifiable*. Verifiability, as we have come at long last to see, is itself highly problematical. These signs of redemption are *signs*, and nothing more. But they do occur, as unpredictable fruits of the fact that the world belongs to God and that God is doing in the world what it takes to make and to keep human life human. The New Testament calls these signs of redemption 'mighty works, and wonders and signs'.[2] They mark the advent of the Messiah, the ingression of the 'new age' upon the 'old age', the proleptic inauguration of the kingdom of God. They are also designated as 'the fruits of the Spirit' in contrast to the 'works of the flesh'.[3] Let it be noted that the signs which point to and point up what God is doing in the world are *ethical* signs. What is *indicated* is that the politics of God does make a discernible difference in the world, and the ongoing life of the *koinonia* is the context within which to come in sight of this difference. The *koinonia* is the bearer in the world of the mystery (secret) and the transforming power of the divine activity, on the one hand, and, on the other, of the secret (mystery) and the 'stuff' of human maturity.

## 2  *Signs of Redemption Under the Threefold Office of Christ*

The speculative and ecclesiastical pressures upon the trinitarian achievement of the church have tended ever and again

---

situation is always whether or not a 'metaphysical surrender' has occurred. The significance of a theology of messianism is exactly this, that the faithfulness of its response to the context and dynamics of the activity of God not only excludes such a surrender but sooner or later makes it possible for theology to effect the kind of transvaluation of culture and politics which Cochrane has described.

[1] Karl Barth and Heinrich Barth, *Zur Lehre vom heiligen Geist*, Beiheft Nr. 1 von 'Zwischen den Zeiten', Chr. Kaiser, Muenchen, 1930, p. 105.

[2] Acts 2.22; II Cor. 12.12; also negatively of false Christs, Matt. 24.24.

[3] Gal. 5.16ff.; cf. also Rom. 8.1-17.

to obscure its ethical vitality and significance. It is not accidental, therefore, that at the time of the Reformation the attempt should have been made to restore the apprehension of what the trinitarian dogma meant and implied, and to recover something of its transforming power. This attempt took the form of a fresh statement of the christological 'center of gravity' at the heart of the dogma with rather more attention to the transforming power than to the context of what was involved. John Calvin appears to have broken fresh ground, as regards the messianic character of theology, by introducing into christological analysis the doctrine of the 'threefold office of Christ'.[1]

Midway through the second book of the *Institutes* Calvin comes to the discussion of the person and work of Christ. He argues that both Christ's deity and his real humanity are indispensable to the proper understanding of his life and work as the mediator between God and man. Calvin then devotes a chapter to what he calls 'the consideration of Christ's three offices, prophetical, regal, and sacerdotal, necessary to our knowing the end of his mission from the Father, and the benefits which he confers on us'.[2] The dogmatic and ethical significance of this chapter is that it expresses Calvin's attempt to overcome a conspicuous weakness of the theological tradition. Christian thought before Calvin had never been eminently successful in pointing out the precise connection between the life and death of Christ, on the one hand, and the life of the believer, on the other. This is a shortcoming still current despite Calvin's attempt to correct it. His effort is certainly not to be regarded as the only possibility; but in the ferment of contemporary theological discussion of ethics, the point that Calvin was getting at may recover the importance which he rightly discerned. Calvin expressly takes up the doctrine of the threefold office of Christ in order to indicate what Christ really

---

[1] Cf. Emil Brunner, *The Christian Doctrine of Creation and Redemption*, The Westminster Press, Philadelphia, 1952 (Lutterworth Press, London, 1952), pp. 308-21; W. A. Visser 't Hooft, *The Kingship of Christ*, Harper & Row, New York, 1948 (SCM Press, London, 1948), p. 16; compare Brunner, op. cit., p. 314.

[2] John Calvin, *Institutio religionis christianae*, 1559, CR, XXX, Bk. II, par. 15.

means for us and how we are involved in his mission in the world. As he saw it, this is the link between Christ and the believer; and thus his doctrine also fortifies the present concern with the connection between theology and ethics.

The prophetical, regal, and sacerdotal offices or functions of Christ undergo, as Calvin sets them out, a transformation of the previous and prevailing contexts of these offices. Calvin remarks that although 'the celebrated title of "Messiah" was given to the promised Mediator . . . yet the prophetical and sacerdotal functions have their respective places, and must not be neglected by us'.[1] As regards the prophetical office Calvin quotes the passage which Jesus himself, according to Luke (4.2ff.), quotes from the prophet Isaiah (61.1, 2), the passage which underlines the anointing 'to preach good tidings unto the meek . . . to bind up the broken-hearted, to proclaim liberty to the captives, to proclaim the acceptable year of the Lord'. And while Calvin rightly notes that this anointing by the Spirit meant that Jesus was to be 'a preacher and witness of the grace of the Father; and that not in a common manner', he infers from this distinction that 'the prophetic dignity in Christ is, to assure us that all branches of perfect wisdom are included in the system of doctrine which he has given us'.[2]

At first glance, this is an inference which appears to take us into a formalistic and doctrinal cul-de-sac. But if we keep in mind that Calvin was trying to forge a link between Christ and the Christian by underscoring the link between the mediator and the Messiah, the connection between the 'perfect widsom' of Christ and 'the system of doctrine which he has given us' carries us beyond mere doctrinal formalism. Calvin's language conveys to our time what was concealed from his own time. He was trying, energetically if obscurely, to draw the life of the Christian, as he lives it out in this world, into the orbit of the politics of God. It is the prophetical office of Christ which keeps the believer in the context of the 'signs and wonders and mighty works' which are going on around him as God keeps doing what it takes to make and to keep human life human.

Similarly, as regards the sacerdotal office, Calvin is at pains to stress that 'the sum of the whole is this—that the sacerdotal dignity belongs exclusively to Christ, because, by the sacrifice

[1] *Institutio*, II, 15, 2.          [2] Ibid.

of his death, he has abolished our guilt and made satisfaction for our sins'.[1] The important point is that the significance of this exclusive priesthood of Christ is not cultic, but rather the 'favor with God' from which 'proceeds not only confidence in prayer, but also tranquillity to the consciences of the faithful; while they recline in safety on the paternal indulgence of God, and are certainly persuaded, that he is pleased with whatever is consecrated to Him through the Mediator'.[2] The accent falls upon the redemptive consequences for behavior or, in Calvin's words, the redemptive 'benefits which he confers on us'.

It is, however, the kingship or 'regal function' which most expressly underlines the transformation of the mediatorial office of Christ through the recovery by Calvin of its link with Christ's messiahship. 'The faithful', he declares, 'stand invincible in the strength of their king'; yet this king 'was not enriched on his own private account but that he might communicate his abundance to them who are hungry and thirsty.' The regal function of Christ 'combines the offices of a king and a shepherd', and on this account 'it is the more reasonable that we should all with one consent be ready to obey him and with the greatest alacrity conform all our services to his will'.[3] Thus the doctrine of the threefold office of Christ really comes out at the point of an explicit doctrinal underlining of the christological focus and foundation of behavior. As Comenius, the re-founder of the *Unitas Fratrum*, put it in another connection: 'Christ must find among you not only a pulpit for his prophetic office; not only an altar for his office as priest and bishop; but likewise a throne and a sceptre for his kingly office.'[4]

It has been pointed out that the Reformers were more reserved in their teaching concerning the kingship of Christ than they were about his other offices. This hesitation was due partly to their struggle against the anarchistic political implications of sectarian teaching and influence and partly to the fact that the Reformers were especially concerned with the basis and origin of salvation rather than with its fruit and goal. Consequently, Protestant theology has never sufficiently regarded the world in the light of the victory of Christ. A theological analysis of

---

[1] *Institutio*, II, 15, 6.      [2] Ibid.      [3] Ibid., II, 15, 5.
[4] John Amos Comenius, *The Bequest of the Unity of Brethren*, English edition, Chicago, 1940; quoted by Visser 't Hooft, op. cit., p. 19.

ethics in the tradition of the Reformation would, therefore, seek not only to correct the Reformers at this point but to make the fullest possible use of the resources which they have placed at the disposal of a theological ethic. 'This does not mean that we can afford to forget the prophetic and priestly Christ, but it does mean that we seek to rediscover the royal nature of our prophetic and priestly Lord.'[1]

The bearing of such a recovery of the doctrine of the threefold office of Christ upon Christian thinking about ethics is at least threefold. In the first place, the political character of what God is doing in the world expressed in the trinitarian statement of the divine economy is brought directly to bear upon the life of the believer by means of a functional, christological context and connection. This is not only a reversal of the general tendency of Protestantism, according to which 'Christianity becomes more and more introspective and the Church knows less and less what to do with the world-embracing and world-shaking affirmations of the Bible'.[2] It is also a way of giving to the believer a clear understanding of the environment and direction of what he is to do and thus a firm ethical foundation for behavior. In the second place, the recovery of the doctrine of the threefold office of Christ creatively unites the church and the world in the ongoing story of salvation. This does not mean that the church and the world are identical. But also and no less importantly, it does not mean that the church manifests itself chiefly as church by speaking against the world. The kingship of Christ means that Christ is important not only for those who recognize him but for the whole world. As Dr Visser 't Hooft has put it, 'history deals not only with the fate of individual souls and the destiny of the people of God. God thinks and plans in terms of humanity and of the universe . . . church and world have, therefore, a great deal in common. Both have the same Lord. Both live in the light of the same victory of Christ over the powers of sin and death. . . . The church is the inner circle, the world the outer circle, but both together are the realm over which Christ is king.'[3] In the third place and as a corollary of the point just made, the recovery of the doctrine of the threefold office of Christ safeguards a

[1] Visser 't Hooft, op. cit., pp. 19 and 20.    [2] Ibid., p. 25.
[3] Ibid., pp. 119, 120.

*koinonia* ethic against the peril of a double standard. The christological focus and foundation of behavior mean that believer and unbeliever are both alike in the same ethical situation. Both believer and unbeliever belong to Christ. Both believer and unbeliever are promised in him the secret and the power of maturity. Both believer and unbeliever are being confronted, in the environment being shaped by Christ's royal and redemptive activity, by the decision to accept or to reject the conditions of a new humanity on Christ's terms, not their own. The difference is that for believers, as members of the *koinonia*, the kingship of Christ 'is revealed; in the world (that is, among unbelievers) it is hidden. The church lives as the people who know that the victory has been won. The world lives on as if nothing had happened. The church realizes that the powers which militate against God's plan are under control. The world lives on as if these powers were still able to shape the ultimate destiny of men.'[1] The difference between believers and unbelievers is not defined by church membership, or even, in the last analysis, by baptism. The difference is defined by imaginative and behavioral sensitivity to what God is doing in the world to make and to keep human life human, to achieve the maturity of men, that is, the new humanity.

### 3 *Second Adam, Second Advent, and Human Fulfillment*

What God is doing in the world to make and to keep human life human is to bring about human maturity; in other words, to bring to pass a new humanity. It is this achievement which gives ethical and substantive significance to what Christian theology has from the beginning tried to convey through its doctrines of the Second Adam and the Second Advent. Indeed, just as the trinitarian dogma states the political character of the divine activity in terms of the divine economy as the environment of Christian behavior, and just as the doctrine of the threefold office of Christ states the connection between the action of God and Christian behavior, so the doctrines of the Second Adam and the Second Advent express the actuality and prospect of Christian behavior.

Once again we have come upon a point of authentic response

[1] Visser 't Hooft, ibid., p. 124.

by Christian theology to its messianic occasion and context. And at this point the full revolutionary bearing of the link between the messiahship and the mediatorship of Christ upon Christian thinking about ethics emerges. Specifically what emerges is the *extent* to which a theology of messianism sharply revises both the doctrinal bases of ethics and the substantive ethical concern and claim of Christianity.

Traditionally, the doctrines of the Second Adam and the Second Advent have been taken up for discussion in that part of Christian theology known as eschatology, or the doctrine of the last things. This allocation has been proper enough, but it has had one particularly unfortunate result. The 'last things' have been naturally, but too pedantically, considered 'last'. Consequently, eschatology has served the rather barren purpose of tying together and tidying up in little more than a formalistic way the loose ends of theological reflection, while at the same time haunting the Christian mind with such loose ends as refused to be thus neatly tied. A theology of messianism, however, exposes the fatal flaw in these conventional proceedings and sets out upon a fresh and different course. A theology of messianism exposes the speculative and irrelevant character of all eschatological thinking apart from ethics. It makes no sense to talk about the 'last things' apart from what is going on here and now. And what is going on here and now is not primarily a matter of setting out the punishment of sin and setting up the triumph of the saints; it is primarily a matter of behavior, of what God is doing in the world and of what in consequence man is involved in, of what man is to do and can do.

The doctrine of the Second Adam goes to the heart of this reversal, and no one has more brilliantly and forcefully pointed out its meaning than has Karl Barth.[1] The phrase 'second Adam' is ambiguous and itself requires to be corrected. It seems to say that there is a 'first Adam' in relation to whom a 'second Adam' is to be recognized and understood. This apparent temporal sequence has largely contributed to the eschatological error to which we have just alluded. A closer reading of

---

[1] Karl Barth, *Christ and Adam*, Harper & Row, New York, 1957 (Oliver & Boyd, Edinburgh, 1956). See also *Kirchliche Dogmatik* IV/1, 1953, especially pp. 570-73. We are indebted to Barth's discussion for much of what here follows between pp. 118 and 123.

Rom. 5, however, makes it plain that Paul has precisely the contrary point in mind. The 'second Adam' is 'second', not so much because a 'first Adam' had preceded him in time, but specifically because the real Adam, having come in Christ, is the one with reference to whom it is important to speak about the other 'Adam' at all. Thus a 'christological' rather than a 'temporal' relation exists between the 'second Adam' (Christ) and the 'first Adam' (the primal Adam). 'Here the new point is', says Barth, 'that the *special* anthropology of Jesus Christ— the one man for all men, all men in the one man, constitutes the secret of "Adam" also, and so is the *norm* of *all* anthropology. . . . Man's essential and original nature is to be found, therefore, not in Adam but in Christ. In Adam we can only find it pre-figured. Adam can therefore be interpreted only in the light of Christ and not the other way round.'[1]

The doctrine of the Second Adam thus fortifies the christo-logical focus and foundation of behavior in a twofold way. In the first place, the doctrine of the Second Adam means that it is the new humanity which is at once the subject and the aim or goal of ethical action. This new humanity is a present, not a mere future, reality. It has already become a fact with the reality of the life, death, and resurrection of Jesus Christ. Christian behavior is behavior with a *forward*, not a backward, look. And the actions which make up this behavior are signifi-cant not in themselves but as pointers to or bearers of the new humanity which in Christ has become a fact in the world and in which, in consequence of what Christ is and is doing in the world, we participate.

> Between our former existence outside Christ and our present existence in him there is a natural connection. Our former existence outside Christ is, rightly understood, already a still hidden but real existence in him. Because of that, . . . we dare to glory in our future salvation—we who still have that past, we who today are still the same men who were once weak, sinners, godless, and enemies. Our past cannot frighten us: in spite of it, and even taking it fully into account, we are still allowed and required to confess our reconciliation and glory in our salvation, just because our past as such—namely, the relationship between Adam and all of us—was already ordered so as to correspond to our present and future—namely, the relationship between Christ and all of us.[2]

The difference, then, between those who are inside and

---

[1] Barth, *Christ and Adam*, pp. 26, 29.     [2] Ibid., p. 28.

outside the *koinonia* is not the difference of being inside and
outside of what God is doing in the world. It is not a difference
of being outside of Christ and so under judgment as distinguished from being inside with Christ and so under grace.
Judgment and grace in Christ belong to the humanity which is
common to all men in him. The difference between believers
and unbelievers, both of whom are involved in the new humanity,
is rather the difference between being in a situation which is
hidden and being in one which is open. This openness is a
matter not only of knowledge as against ignorance but also of
behavior expressive of confidence and hope as against anxiety
and despair, of behaving with abandon rather than with calculation, of being all things to all men rather than, in Canon
Phillips' forceful phrase, 'pursuing selfish advantage . . . com-
piling statistics of evil'.[1] In this new humanity all men are
involved; and it is this new humanity which gives a new and
different actuality to the humanity and behavior of every man.

But the doctrine of the Second Adam fortifies the christological focus and foundation of behavior in yet another way.
It removes the last possibility of a surreptitious resort to
anthropology in Christian ethical reflection. As we noted at the
beginning of this chapter, it has become too usual in Christian
ethical analysis to derive its theological moorings from anthropology. The aim of this way of doing things has been to try to
show that the ethical demand was intelligible and relevant
because it presupposed certain original and residual capacities
resident in human nature for recognizing and fulfilling it.
These capacities, in turn, having been corrupted by sin, were,
so the argument ran, restored and rendered operative by the
redemptive work of Christ and the gift of grace. It was insufficiently noticed, however, that these anthropological considerations were really general and extra-Christian presuppositions
which prevented the authentically Christian factor in the
ethical account of behavior from clear articulation and formative significance. On this basis the Christian significance of
behavior was bound to be little more than an addendum to the
residual goodness of the natural man, which, even as a perfec-
tionist addendum, was likely sooner or later to lose its fascina-

[1] I Cor. 13.5, 6 (Phillips). The forms of the two verbs have been changed
to suit the context.

tion. If one could be almost as good without Christ as with him, he seemed scarcely worth loyalty, or even attention. It was all very well to call the triumph of good over evil a work of grace. But so long as such a triumph was anthropologically based there were readier explanations at hand. On such a basis the significance of Christ for behavior remained remote from the concrete circumstances and problems of behavior. Christology served at best as a theological formula ill protected against more cogent substitutes drawn from biological or historical or philosophical conceptions of human nature.

Theological conceptions such as the 'image of God', 'original sin', 'the grace of Christ' are important for the theological understanding of man. But it should have been obvious that it is not man but Christ who makes ethical thinking and acting 'Christian'. The crucial question is *how* Christ does this. And it is this question that a theology of messianism which includes a doctrine of the Second Adam seeks intrinsically to answer. As Wilhelm Pauck has succinctly and strikingly put it in his own commentary upon Barth's discussion of Rom. 5,

> . . . because there is a higher order of humanity than that of Adam, an order disclosed in God's election of man in Christ, the burden of man's sin, guilt and death can never be the first or primary word about man's nature and destiny nor the key to the understanding of them. For, because in Christ God has become man and because God has chosen man in Christ, human nature and human life must be seen as resting upon the foundations that can never be shaken. The destiny of man is grounded upon the promise of God and no human defiance of the ends for which the world was created, can undo it.[1]

The revolutionary significance of the doctrine of the Second Adam affects, however, not only the doctrinal basis of ethics but also the ethical concern and claim of Christianity. It has already been remarked that Christian ethics is primarily concerned not with the good but with the will of God; it aims at maturity, not at morality. The theological reasons for this shift of ethical concern are now apparent. The immediate and direct theological presuppositions of Christian ethics have to do with the context and actuality of the new humanity in Christ, not with humanity in general, humanity apart from Christ. It follows from this shift of concern that Christian thinking about

[1] Barth, *Christ and Adam*, p. 13.

ethics finds it beside the point to take up the question of the nature of an act and of the relation between the nature of an act and the nature of the good. Such an analysis may supply behavior with rational clarification and guidance but says nothing whatever about its Christian character. The Christian character of behavior is defined not by the principal parts of an act but by the functional significance of action in the context of the divine economy and of the actuality of the new humanity. Thus behavior, as Christianity understands it, is not qualitatively but symbolically significant. Or, to put the point in the light of Jesus' characteristic mode of teaching, behavior is ethically defined not by perfections but by parabolic power. It is foreign to the ethical concerns of Christianity to put claims upon behavior in terms of a progressive movement from the partial to the perfect. On the contrary, the Christian interpretation of behavior starts with and stays within the context of the fact of the new humanity. In this context behavior is, if anything, more dynamic, more on the move, and more informal[1] than the pattern of movement from the partial to the perfect can accommodate. The fact of the new humanity, established in and by the second Adam, means that all behavior is a fragmentary foretaste of the fulfillment which is already on its way.

Thus the ethical reality of the second Adam points intrinsically toward the ethical reality of the second Advent. The second Advent is obviously a correlative consequence of the first Advent. It simply means that Jesus Christ who, in and with his historical existence inaugurated a new age and a new humanity, will come again, as the New Testament put its, 'with power and glory', to consummate what he has begun. 'Power and glory' denote the final and radical transvaluation of the whole created and historical order of which the second Adam and the new humanity are a guarantee and foretaste. Here the language of time and space, of being and perfection, of history and humanity, breaks down and must be left behind. 'Power and glory', but especially 'glory', keep this radical and final transvaluation in sight without containing it. And here again, it is not the cosmological but the ethical—that is, behavioral—significance of the second Advent which makes sense of it. The

[1] According to the root meaning of informal: 'unconstructed', 'radical'.

second Advent rounds out the whole dynamic panorama of the divine economy, the point and purpose of which are the new humanity. The consummation is as definite as the fact of the new humanity, and thus the new humanity is protected against ever becoming either the point of all return or the point of no return. The Christian lives neither by his 'Adamic' past nor by his 'Christian' past, but by the future, of which his present is an exhilarating foretaste. That future is that 'when', when God will be everything to everyone and men will be mature (whole) as their Father in heaven is.[1]

Thus the new order of humanity, in which and by which the Christian lives, has its own way of looking at things and its own way of living out what it sees. In this new order behavior is bereft of every prudential calculation, every motivational concern. Instead, it is endowed with that purity of heart which, in Kierkegaard's phrase, 'is to will one thing', and in Jesus' phrase is 'to see God'.

[1] I Cor. 15.29; Matt. 5.48.

# V

## THE CONTEXTUAL CHARACTER OF CHRISTIAN ETHICS

W<sup>E</sup> have been urging that Christian thinking about
ethics starts with and from within the Christian
*koinonia*. In the *koinonia* it makes sense to talk about
the will of God as the answer to the question: What am I, as a
believer in Jesus Christ and as a member of his church, to do?
For it is in the *koinonia* that one comes in sight of and finds
oneself involved in what God is doing in the world. What God
is doing in the world is setting up and carrying out the conditions for what it takes to keep human life human. The fruit of
this divine activity is human maturity, the wholeness of every
man and of all men in the new humanity inaugurated and being
fulfilled by Jesus Christ in the world. The description of this
activity of God provides a *koinonia* ethic with its biblical and
theological foundations.

### 1 *A Contextual Critique of Ethical Absolutism*

When ethical reflection is pursued in the context of the
Christian *koinonia*, the method and materials of ethics acquire a
concrete and contextual character. *A koinonia ethic is concerned
with relations and functions, not with principles and precepts*. It will
help us to see what is involved in this contrast if we take up a
distinction which is not always made, a failure which makes for
confusion in Christian ethical analysis. The distinction is
between *contextual ethics* and what might be called *absolutist
ethics*. Is it, for instance, wrong to tell a lie? Is a Christian
required always to tell the truth, the whole truth, and nothing
but the truth?

Christian ethics, in common with the formative types of non-

Christian ethical theory, has, on the whole, tended to give an affirmative answer to both these questions. For a Christian, it *is* wrong to tell a lie. A Christian *is* required to tell the truth, the whole truth, and nothing but the truth. It has not always been noticed, however, that such an affirmative answer has been based upon a conception or standard of truth which is foreign to the focus and foundations of a Christian ethic. Such a conception or standard of truth presupposed, in the main, an intimate and self-validating connection between the human reason and the idea of the Good and so was regarded as ethical in itself. This is really the hallmark of absolutist ethics. Absolutist ethics declares that the proper answer to the question: 'What am I to do?' is supplied by an 'absolute'. And what is an 'absolute'? Ethically speaking, *an 'absolute' is a standard of conduct which can be and must be applied to all people in all situations in exactly the same way*. The standard may be an ideal, a value, or a law. Its ethical reality and significance, however, lie in its *absolute* character.

But absolutist ethics pays a very heavy price for its claims. The price is abstraction from the complexity of the actual situation out of which the ethical problem arises. There was once a dramatic farce which used to be played, perhaps not uncharacteristically, to crowded audiences on the Chautauqua circuit. Called *Nothing But the Truth* it described the actual predicament in which a person became involved when he set out to tell 'nothing but the truth'. All human and circumstantial relations became a tangled web of turmoil and misunderstanding, with the result that the leading character's stubborn adherence to this maxim made him thoroughly disliked by everyone else and undermined confidence in the human sense of truthtelling. A friend of mine once told me that he had a colleague who arose upon every issue before the faculty for decision to declare that his conscience required him to vote thus and so. Matters at length came to such a pass that the business of the faculty tended to be obstructed because one never could tell at what point this man would arise to do justice to his conscience. At length the president of the faculty adopted the procedure of calling always upon this colleague first so that his conscience could be got out of the way and the business of the faculty could go forward. Perhaps the most telling confirmation of the 'absolutist predicament' is provided by children, and in ways that are both amusing and vexatious. A child I know went through a period of insisting upon eating his food from dishes or with utensils which had been his father's as a child. If assured that this glass or bowl or spoon had been used by his father as a child, he would proceed with breakfast. If the parents demurred, they had a diplomatic tangle on their hands. The Freudian implications of this situation are disconcerting enough, but the ethical hazards are more so. Underneath this diplomatic tangle was a very awkward ethical dilemma. What were the parents to do? Let the child starve for truth's sake? This, and similar dilemmas, suggest what is meant by saying that the price of 'absolutist' ethics is abstraction from the complexity of the actual human and ethical situation. An absolutist ethic can neither escape from nor deal with the very real disparity between the ethical demand and the ethical act, intrinsic to every ethical situation. There is no way of getting precept and practice together except by illusion on the one hand or by hypocrisy on the other.

The ethical discussion of truth from an absolutist point of view has been given classic formulation by Immanuel Kant in a little treatise called *On a Supposed Right to Lie from Altruistic Motives*.[1] Kant's argument is germane to the present discussion not only because of its succinct and forceful character but also because one cannot dispose of the absolutist position without taking quite seriously its claims upon the nature of ethical thinking. The absolutist position has a long and influential tradition behind it which, however much it may have become trivialized, must be fully faced. Kant's treatise was written as a kind of reply to a certain M. Benjamin Constant, whom he identifies as a French philosopher. M. Constant had taken the position that the maxim 'It is a duty to tell the truth', if adopted and practiced, singly and unconditionally, would make any society impossible.[2] The Frenchman was not denying that it is

---

[1] Immanuel Kant, *On a Supposed Right to Lie from Altruistic Motives*, in *Kant's Ethical Writings*, edited by Lewis E. Beck, University of Chicago Press, Chicago, 1949.

[2] Ibid., p. 346. Actually, M. Henri Benjamin Constant de Rebecque (1767-1830) was a writer, statesman, and orator, and in this sense also a political philosopher.

a duty to tell the truth. He was arguing, however, for an important limitation upon this duty: it is a duty to tell the truth, but only to one who has a right to it. For example, he argued, it is a crime to tell the truth to a murderer who asks whether or not one's friend is at home. Kant set out to prove the falsity of this contention by asserting that it is a duty to tell the truth *unconditionally*. His point is that if this cannot be regarded as a duty all declarations lose their credence, all contracts become insecure; and *then* there is no basis for society, for society depends upon the inviolability of contracts. Kant, with dubious accuracy, goes on to observe that under certain circumstances even civil law punishes the benevolent lie.[1] He turns the illustration of the murderer against M. Constant's interpretation. If the supposed murderer were to come into the house and be told that one's friend was not there, while without one's knowledge the friend had in fact slipped out of the house, so that the murderer being turned away by the denial encountered the friend along the way and accomplished his purpose after all, the law would in fact regard the denial that the friend was in the house as establishing complicity in the friend's death. As Kant saw it, this legal provision is based upon the fact that

[1] Kant's point is that through an accident the benevolent lie can become punishable under civil law. He argues that that which escapes liability to punishment only by accident can also be condemned as wrong by external laws. Benjamin Constant, however, did have legal theory and procedure on his side. Kant may have had in mind certain very special and limited provisions of the German law of his time. If so, it is difficult to understand his attempt in this treatise to rest the case for an unconditional morality of law upon so slender a legal analogy. The likelier interpretation of this passage is that Kant was simply mistaken in his legal interpretation. The law, for example, does punish perjury. But in this case the grounds for punishment have to do with the honor and integrity of the court, not with the unconditional duty to tell the truth. The law also protects the individual against the infringement of his right to freedom of speech and against self-incrimination. In these instances falsehoods are not only not punished but allowed, on the ground that the liberty of the individual is a greater good than unconditional truthfulness.

In the present context, Kant's erroneous appeal to law is the more instructive because it underlines the enormous difficulty of ethical absolutism, whether in legal theory and practice or in moral philosophy.

Although he is not responsible for the present interpretation, I am especially indebted to my colleague Professor Harold H. Berman of the Faculty of Law for the clarification of this point.

truth is a duty which admits of no exceptions. 'To be truthful', in his words, 'in all declarations, therefore, is a sacred and absolutely commanding degree of reason, limited by no expediency.'[1]

Now this is a very formidable claim. And while Kant rests his case rather more upon the necessity of reason than upon Christian considerations, it must be remembered that his whole approach to philosophy and to ethics was not unrelated to the fact that he grew up in a Moravian household. He was a Christian and he thought as a Christian, though not in theological terms. It is understandable indeed that the logic of Kant's position should have become part and parcel of the working maxims by which many people still live and govern their actions as regards telling the truth.

What, then, would a contextual ethic have to offer over against this formidable statement of the absolutist position? Let us try to get at it in this way: Suppose a man has a car which he wants to sell.[2] What does it mean to tell the truth? There would seem to be at least three possibilities open. The owner of the car can refuse to tell the buyer anything. He buys "as is" and at his own risk. Or the owner can tell the buyer everything he knows about the car, at the risk of losing the sale. Or the owner can take a mediating position, answering the buyer's questions and risking only the buyer's praise or blame, according to the subsequent performance of the car. An absolutist ethic would urge the second of these courses of action: It is the duty of the owner of the car to tell the buyer everything he knows about the car. But there is no guarantee on an absolutist basis that the owner of the car can or could tell everything he knows about it. He might have forgotten something. And the *intention* of the owner to tell the truth would not cover the fact that he actually had *not* told the truth. Here we come upon one of the most ingenious and tested and tried attempts to bring an absolutist ethic into line with the actual diversity and com-

[1] Immanuel Kant, *Critique of Practical Reason*, Beck edition, University of Chicago Press, Chicago, 1949, p. 348.

[2] This example has been previously used in a preliminary essay dealing with the contextual character of Christian ethics. Cf. 'The Foundation and Pattern of Christian Behavior', in *Christian Faith and Social Ethics*, edited by John Hutchison, Charles Scribner's Sons, New York, 1953.

plexity of the ethical situation. This attempt takes the form of an analysis which very closely relates *intention* and *action* in the human ethical situation, and assigns ethical priority to *intention*. Although Protestant thinking about ethics has been heavily affected and indeed afflicted by the doctrine of intention (not least owing to the influence of Immanuel Kant), the doctrine of intention is really intrinsic to the ethics of Roman Catholic moral theology, with which we shall be concerned in a subsequent chapter.[1]

A contextual ethic begins at the opposite point from the one at which Immanuel Kant begins. Kant's dictum that it is absolutely necessary to tell the truth 'unconditionally' has been impressively and instructively countered by the position taken in a similarly small treatise by Dietrich Bonhoeffer called *What Does It Mean to Tell the Truth?*[2] In this little treatise Bonhoeffer notes that telling the truth is 'a matter of accurate and serious consideration of the actual circumstances. The more complex the circumstances of a man's life are, the more responsible he is; and the more difficult it is for him to tell the truth. Therefore, telling the truth must be learned . . . since it is simply a fact that the ethical cannot be detached from the real situation, the increasingly accurate knowledge of the *situation* is a necessary element of ethical action.'[3] On these terms, telling the truth about the car would obviously not be identical with *optimum verbal veracity*. It would be different for a high school adolescent and for a man in middle life; for a man who had two cars and for a man who had to dispose of the only car he had, in order to pay for his wife's burial; for a humanist and for a Christian. But in each case, telling the truth would be a matter of saying, to use Bonhoeffer's phrase, 'the right word', or better, 'the living word'. 'The living word', says Bonhoeffer, 'is as alive as life itself.'[4]

[1] See Chapter XII.

[2] Dietrich Bonhoeffer, *Ethik*, zusammengestellt und herausgegeben von Eberhard Bethge, Chr. Kaiser, Muenchen, 1949; English translation, entitled *Ethics*, by Neville Horton Smith, The Macmillan Company, New York, 1955 (SCM Press, London, 1955). The translation seems to me to be not altogether a happy one. I have accordingly attempted a translation of my own, noting the reference, however, first in the original and then, in parentheses, in the English edition.

[3] Ibid., p. 284 (327).  [4] Ibid., p. 285 (328).

What is the *living word*? It is the verbal expression of the full complexity and totality of the existing, concrete situation. And what is *ethical* about the existing, concrete situation is that which holds it together. And what, it may be asked, holds the concrete situation together? The answer is: that which makes it possible for human beings to be open *for* one another and *to* one another. In so far as the *right* word, or the *living* word, is instrumental to such an openness of human beings to each other, telling the truth is ethically real. If the buyer and the seller of this car come through the transaction to a true consideration of each other's predicament, and so are linked to each other as human beings, then they do not merely transact business. The business transaction becomes instrumental to their discovery of each other as human beings, and whether much or little is told about the car, whatever is told is the truth. It is this *human* factor in the interrelationships of men which is the definitely *ethical* factor. A Christian ethic seeks to show that the *human* in us all can be rightly discerned and adhered to only in and through the reality of a climate of trust established by the divine humanity of Jesus Christ and the new humanity, however incipient, of all men in Christ.

All of us are aware that the problem of telling the truth actually does vary according to the relationships in which we find ourselves. In the relations between parents and children, between husband and wife, between friends and friends, between teacher and student, between friend and enemy—in all these relationships the truth in the words varies. As Bonhoeffer puts it, 'Our words must not conform to the truth in principle but concretely. Conformity to the truth that is not concrete is not conformity to the truth before God. . . . One . . . must not forget that God is no general principle, but the Living One who has set me down in a living situation and demands my obedience. Whoever says, "God," cannot ignore the given world in which he lives, otherwise he would not be speaking the truth, otherwise he would not be speaking of the God who became incarnate in the world in Jesus Christ.'[1] It is the fact that God became incarnate in Jesus Christ, as this fact is spelled out by a theology of messianism, which requires of

---

[1] Bonhoeffer, ibid., pp. 283-84 (327).

Christian ethics that the diverse relationships in which men find themselves be taken seriously as bearers of ethical reality and significance.

A *koinonia* ethic claims that such human relationships are actualized in the world in consequence of and in the context of the concrete reality of the church. The empirical church violates in many ways the ethical reality which is the true occasion of its existence and without which it cannot be the church. Nevertheless, the empirical church points, despite its ambiguity, to the fact that there is in the world a *laboratory of the living word,* or, to change the metaphor, a *bridgehead of maturity,* namely, the Christian *koinonia.* In the *koinonia* a continuing experiment is going on in the concrete reality and possibility of man's interrelatedness and openness for man. In the *koinonia* ethical theory and practice acquire a framework of meaning and a pattern of action which undergird the diversity and the complexity of the concrete ethical situation with vitality and purpose.

In the *koinonia* valid ethical questions and concerns are different from what they may be outside the *koinonia.* For example, the ethical question—in the *koinonia*—is not 'What *ought* I to do?' but 'What *am* I to do?' because in the *koinonia* one is always fundamentally in an *indicative* rather than in an *imperative* situation. There is, of course, also an imperative pressure exerted by an indicative situation. The 'ought' factor cannot be ignored in ethical theory. But the 'ought' factor is not the primary ethical reality. The primary ethical reality is the human factor, the *human* indicative, in every situation involving the interrelationships and the decisions of men. In the *koinonia* something is already going on, namely, what God is doing in the situation out of which the ethical question and concern arise to fashion circumstance and behavior according to his will. This is why a contextual ethic does not lead to ethical anarchy or ethical expediency. If what God is doing in the world is to relate men to each other in and through an enterprise of the new humanity, if God is setting the conditions for and bestowing the enabling power of maturity—if this is what God is doing, then it is meaningless to say that if one doesn't tell the truth unconditionally the fabric of society will be shredded by mistrust; it is meaningless to say that if one can claim that whatever occurs to him at the moment to say is the truth, the whole field of truth and falsehood is reduced to anarchy and confusion. Such concerns may have standing in some other kind of ethical climate, but for a Christian ethic they are false concerns.

## 2  *Random Instances of Contextual Behavior*

Almost the first more than casual impact of death upon me occurred in the passing of a lady in early middle life who had come to be virtually a second mother to me. She was stricken, as it seemed, quite suddenly, with a particularly virulent form of carcinoma and died under this ghastly, body-wasting disease. When I saw her for the last time, as she lay upon her hospital bed, she said to me, 'What do the doctors say? Is there anything that can be done?' At this moment there came to mind the profound and humiliating observation of Dostoevsky which, it has always seemed to me, ought to serve as the rubric under which the healthy relate themselves to the ill, and in particular as the rubric under which pastoral calls upon the sick are made. 'In every misfortune of one's neighbor', says Dostoevsky, 'there is always something cheering for an onlooker—whoever he may be.'[1] I knew that this lady would never leave her bed of pain alive. I knew, too, that I was leaving the hospital to take a train for my own work and that I was not in the slightest inclined to exchange places. What should I have replied to her question? How white is a lie? And how black can the truth, the whole truth, and nothing but the truth be? What in such a situation *is* the truth?

Is it telling the truth to say in as sympathetic and tactful a way as possible, 'There is no hope!'? Or should one say, 'Don't worry! Everything will come out all right!'?

The point at issue here is not the celebrated ethical question of the right of the patient to the truth.[2] The point at issue is, granted that the patient has a right to the truth, what is the

---

[1] Fyodor Dostoevsky, *The Possessed*, Modern Library edition, New York, 1936, p. 334.

[2] This question has been freshly and instructively discussed by Professor Joseph Fletcher in his Lowell Lectures, *Morals and Medicine*, Princeton University Press, Princeton, 1954 (Gollancz, London, 1955).

truth to which the patient has a right, and how would a *Christian* ethic deal with this right? My own attempt ran something like this: 'The doctors are doing all that they can. But you and I have always been Christians. Part of what that has meant has been that we have said in our prayers and confessed in our faith that Jesus Christ is Savior and Lord. I do not claim to understand all that this involves. But if it means anything at all, it seems to me to mean at least this—when in the next days and weeks the going gets hard, remember you are not alone! Jesus Christ has been there before!'

In some such way as this a *koinonia* ethic seems to me to try to meet this kind of 'truth situation'. Whatever the contingencies of the situation may be, and however much it may fall apart in terms of a calculated consistency that seems to be called for, a *koinonia* ethic moves in quite another context and upon another level. The God of the Bible places little importance upon human consistency. On the contrary, he wades in and wades through to get his purposes accomplished. The cross of Christ is the supreme destroyer of all securities of men—intellectual, political, personal, moral, religious. And unless it is possible that the same Spirit which informs and holds the church together also holds human relationships and responsibilities together, Christian ethics is a delusion. The delusion is that God is doing something when he isn't.

*a strange statement*

Or take the difficult and delicate area of sexual experience. Christian ethics has been conspicuously unconvincing in dealing with this field of human decision. It must be admitted that deeply rooted organic drives and intense and complex human emotions are components of sexuality. Indeed, sexuality seems to be so precariously poised on the boundary between irrationality and rationality, anarchy and sobriety, as to nullify every attempt to bring the counsels of judgment and virtue to bear upon the guidance of sexual behavior. The long course of social experience seems to indicate that sexuality is more safely and thus also more wisely checked and channeled by the tenacious force of tabu.

Christian ethics, however, owing to its understanding of the activity of God and the freedom, responsibility, and destiny of man, has been unable to accept this naturalistic understanding of sexuality and its control. Roman Catholic sexual ethics presupposes the general insistence of moral theology upon the inclusion of sensuous desires and impulses within man's natural end as a creature directed by reason toward goodness and virtue. In turn, the power of reason and virtue to achieve the natural end of man is so severely weakened by the sinful corruption of human nature that the natural man requires the aid of supernatural grace for the attainment of his true end. Thus, Roman Catholic ethics is able to order sexual love as the lowest level of a fourfold structure of love. Sexual love, together with eros, friendship (φιλία), and charity (ἀγάπη), exhibits the ethical nature and variety of human love.[1] Roman Catholic ethics is able also to structure and limit sexual love through the sacramental character of marriage and the insistence upon procreation as the primary end of marriage. Ultimately, the sovereignty of grace and the spirit over natural impulse is maintained by the adroit insistence that the exaltation of the ascetic life contributes gradually to the ennoblement of natural impulse.

Sexual ethics in the tradition of the Reformation presupposes a different understanding of the relations between the life of nature and the life of grace. The accent falls not upon a tidy correlation of man's natural with man's supernatural end. Instead the stress lies upon the radical corruption of human nature by sin and the providential and legal arrangements which God has ordained to check the anarchy and destructiveness of sin pending the slow and painful transformation of nature by grace in this life and the ultimate triumph of grace over nature in the life to come. Consequently, Protestant sexual ethics has rejected the exaltation of asceticism and the sacramental character of marriage and insisted that marriage is an ordinance of God designed both to serve the felicity of the sexual relationship and to check and chasten incontinent sexual desire. With Luther, the felicity of the sexual act was included within an exalted and even exultant view of marriage and characteristically overshadowed by a grim negativity which found in marriage the one effective antidote to incontinence. 'No matter what praise is given to marriage,' he could say, 'I will not concede it to nature that it is no sin.' Marriage is a

---

[1] Joseph Mausbach, *Katholische Moraltheologie*, Elfte verbesserte Auflage, von Gustav Ermecke, Aschendorff, Muenster, 1960, Bd. II, S. 106.

'medicine' and a 'hospital for the sick'.[1] Calvin, on the other hand, was more positive than Luther. He regarded the sexual act as 'undefiled, honorable and holy, because it is a pure institution of God'. The disparagement of the sexual act he attributes to Satan, who 'dazzles us with an appearance of what is right, in order that we may be led to imagine that we are polluted by intercourse with our wives'.[2] Nevertheless, this constructive possibility did not overcome for Calvin the uneasiness about the pleasurable concomitants of the sexual act. In the main, he, too, adhered to the strongly negative approach to sexuality so dominant in Christian ethics from the beginning.

A conspicuous exception to this chorus of misanthropy is provided by Count von Zinzendorf. Zinzendorf's understanding of human relations was so vividly shaped by the bond and pattern of Christ's relation to the holy community of the church as to ascribe not to marriage but to sexuality itself a kind of sacramental quality. Lust must, of course, be overcome. But the basic sexual attraction of man to woman is a gift of the Creator to the creature and thus is good. Undertaken in the context of Christ's headship of the holy community which is his spouse, the sexual act becomes an integral part of the transformed human nature already manifest as a foretaste of the life of the world to come. The marriage of man and woman is a symbol of the eschatological marriage in which Christ is the bridegroom of humanity as such.

The sectarian grasp of the proper setting of the Christian life in the community of believers as a foretaste of the transformed humanity exhibits a fundamental faithfulness to the creative ethical thrust of the Reformation. The Reformation rightly shattered the glorification of celibacy and virginity which—in astonishing disregard of the biblical view of God's humanizing

[1] Quoted by D. S. Bailey, *Sexual Relation in Christian Thought*, Harper & Row, New York, 1959 (*Man-Woman Relations in Christian Thought*—Longmans, London, 1959), p. 171. In this book Mr Bailey, who is Study Secretary of the Moral Welfare Council of the Church of England, offers an admirably instructive discussion of the Christian ethical tradition concerning the most basic of all the problems of sexual ethics. The passage is taken from Martin Luther, *Predigt vom ehelichen Leben, Werke*, Heyder & Zimmer, Frankfurt, 1877, Vol. XVI, p. 541.

[2] In *Epist. I ad Cor.*; on VII, 6; on VII, 5. Quoted by Bailey, op. cit., p. 172.

activity in the world—appears from the beginning to have
fascinated, then tempted, and from Augustine onwards captured
the Christian understanding of sexuality. The Reformation was
rightly in accord with the tradition of Christian thought in
recognizing the inescapable and explosive relation between
*coitus* and continence, between the sexual act and marriage,
and between marriage and the wider social relations of man,
both in the world and in the church. But the Reformation was
mistakenly in accord with the tradition of Christian ethical
thought in its failure to break out of the stranglehold of negativity which regarded marriage as the legitimization of the
sexual act and the precarious guardian both of continence and
of social stability and health where sexuality was involved.

The practical consequences of this default—indeed, defect—
in Christian sexual ethics are enormous. The legalism whereby
both church and state, theology and law have exalted marriage
as the norm of sexual permissiveness and purity is the least of
the evils when compared to the deliverance of countless generations of adolescents over to the destructive depersonalization of
sexual emotions caught between venereal fears and venereal
frivolity; or when compared to the abandonment of countless
generations of those in middle life to the dehumanizing alternative between the grim acceptance of a 'marriage fate' and
the frenzied search for a relatively satisfactory sexual partnership; or when compared to the clinical documentation of the
psychiatric distortion of the human spirit in the wake of
libidinal sexual repression or enlightened libidinal indulgence.

It does no service either to Christian faith or to the Christian
life to deal with sexuality in terms of the marriage criterion
sustained and reinforced by the overwhelming pressure of tabu,
law, fear, and the romantic consummation of love unstained by
sexual experimentation and lost virginity. There can be no
doubt that such an approach to sexuality has achieved a high
degree of sexual conformity. But certainly since Freud, not to
mention Kinsey, it is plain that the conformity not only has
been exaggerated but is also steadily losing effectiveness. What
is called for is an approach to sexuality which accents both the
fundamental importance of the sexual act for the humanization
of man and the setting in which the humanization of man is a
concrete and achievable reality. In such a setting, the risks of

sexual nonconformity may be run. They are being run anyway, subversively rather than freely. In the setting intrinsic to the humanization of man, the sexual act is loosed from the marriage criterion and anchored in the human reality of encounter between male and female under conditions of trust and fulfillment which such an encounter both nourishes and presupposes.

In this context the fateful sexual axiom of the Christian ethical tradition is broken through and turned around. The reversal may be put like this: *It is not marriage which legitimizes the sexual act but the sexual act which legitimizes marriage*. Strictly considered, 'legitimize' is scarcely the proper word for the reversal. Its use is designed to focus upon the error of the tradition and the possibility of an alternative position. Viewed from the perspective of the reversal, the axiom may be more correctly formulated as follows: *It is not marriage which fulfills the sexual act but the sexual act which fulfills marriage*. This does not mean that the sexual act is the primary or the dominant feature of the marriage relationship or of a relationship between a man and a woman which may lead to marriage. It does mean that the sexual act is fundamental to and the most concrete and intimate condition of human fulfillment in marriage. When the sexual act is understood in the context of the human reality of encounter between male and female under conditions of trust and fulfillment, its specific physiological character is included within a complete and transforming partnership which can be neither complete nor transforming apart from what has been finely called 'the communion of the body'.[1] The concern of a Christian sexual ethic is to exhibit the intimate relation of sexuality in all its forms to the freedom and the integrity of human wholeness in the most concrete human encounter of belonging. Such an ethic can offer no sexual guidance according to a blueprint designed to apply to all sexual behavior in the same way.

Nor is a contextual approach to sexuality a sophisticated formula for the encouragement of sexual experimentation. The problem is to understand, interpret, and guide the sexual

---

[1] By Dr Ernst Michel, a Roman Catholic physician, in a book entitled *Ehe: eine Anthropologie der Geschlechtsgemeinschaft*, 1948. Quoted by Karl Barth, *Kirchliche Dogmatik*, Evangelischer Verlag, Zollikon-Zuerich, III/4, 1951, p. 151.

experience of man in such a way as to exhibit the possibility and the power of freedom in obedience to what God is doing in the world as opposed both to conformity in fear and to licentious nonconformity to what man on his own is doing in the world. The sexual act is no more and no less open to this freedom in obedience than is any other human action. But the Christian Church, and consequently the Christian ethical tradition, has lacked the faith, the imagination, and the boldness to include the sexual act among the risks of free obedience. When sexual experience is understood as intrinsic to the fulfillment of human wholeness in and through human belonging, then whether the sexual act occurs within the marriage relationship or on the way toward marriage is a decision which can only be taken aright as a decision in free obedience to what God is doing in the world to make and to keep human life human. If such an ethic should seem to lead to sexual anarchy, let it be considered that sexuality could scarcely be more vulnerable to promiscuity than it is currently, and that, in any case, a Christian sexual ethic has another concern entirely than that of providing a check upon promiscuity and prostitution. This concern is to offer a context within which sexual intensity can be creatively related to sexual sensitivity because sexuality itself has been transformed from a biological to a human fact, from an elemental drive which man has in common with animals to a distinctively human relation 'inwardly shaped and guided by what is specifically human in human nature and by what gives fundamental meaning to human life'.[1] In such a context, promiscuity and prostitution simply have no place. They are *ab initio* sexual deviations.

No ethic can guarantee behavior against default. However, a Christian sexual ethic which has attempted to interpret and guide sexual behavior in terms of the risks and the resources of human belonging in the freedom of obedience will also know how to deal with sexual disappointments, mistakes, and failures. The basic relation of the sexual act to human belonging, of human belonging to marriage, and of marriage to human fulfillment means that sexual failures inevitably imperil human wholeness. Ultimately, it is the awareness of this danger which

---

[1] A formulation of Dr Ernst Michel's; quoted by Barth, op. cit., p. 152.

has prompted the tradition of Christian sexual ethics to take the safer course of encouraging the avoidance of sexual risks through sexual conformity. The tradition has not sufficiently noticed, however, the greater peril to which an ethic designed to avoid risks is exposed. Like the man in the parable who safely kept his own pound 'laid in a napkin', an ethic of safety is 'condemned out of its own mouth'. 'As for these enemies of mine, who did not want me to reign over them, bring them here and slay them before me.'[1] The course of faithfulness is not the course of safety through conformity but of the risk of obedience in faith and hope and love. When, embarked on such a course, faith is met by infidelity, hope by disillusionment, love by loneliness, and the risk of obedience by the haunting sense of disobedience, the point of renewal is discovered again to be where it has been from the beginning. It is the point of encounter with him who reigns in forgiveness and renewal over every human failure and defeat.

The context and the conditions of human wholeness with which a *koinonia* ethic is concerned pivot in the last analysis around precisely this encounter with him who rules and restores, forgives and transforms every human condition. Perhaps at no point of concrete human behavior does it become more apparent than at the point of the sexual relation that a *koinonia* ethic attempts to take up the problem of sexuality where the Reformation glimpsed a positive possibility, from which it unhappily defected, and seeks to indicate a constructive course along which sexual behavior may be provided with ethical meaning and guidance. What such a course involves belongs properly to the substance or content of Christian ethics and not to its methodology. Our present concern is to suggest illustratively how a contextual method of ethical analysis would revise the interpretation and guidance of sexuality. Meanwhile it may be hoped that the proposed 'axiom of reversal' will be recognized as leading toward a heightening rather than a weakening of the integrity of the sexual relation and of fidelity in marriage. All the problems of the sexual and marital life of man—lust, promiscuity, prostitution, adultery, divorce—retain their importance and their urgency. They have, however, been set in a liberating and a humanizing context. The tutelage of

[1] Luke 19.11-27. See also Matt. 25.14-30.

fear, tabu, and law has been exchanged for the transforming options open to men in the freedom wherewith Christ has set them free. It seems to us that such an exchange was among the foremost concerns of Jesus in his own revision of the law and of 'the tradition of the elders' in which he had been brought up.

One further instance of contextual behavior may be mentioned. Think of the confusion, not to say disillusionment, which has afflicted the Protestant Church in our time over the question of the Christian's relationship to war. Can a Christian participate in war or not? On the whole, the church has been uneasy about an absolutist view of this question. Yet it has never been able to put such a view completely aside. Especially in the modern period, there has been in the church a strong minority emphasis upon the claim that a Christian who did not wish to abandon or compromise his faith would refuse to participate in war. War, so this position affirms, is an inadmissible violation of the Christian conscience. Sometimes this view was derived from the sixth commandment, sometimes from our Lord's teaching about love. In either case, the claim was tenable enough—so long as there was no war. But when the peace was rudely broken, many young men who were genuinely trying to live as Christians suddenly found themselves faced with a decision. They had been brought, under the church's own auspices, into an unnecessary turmoil and conflict between what they believed to be Christian teaching and what they found themselves unable to avoid. For many the conclusion was very nearly disastrous: Christianity is a wonderful ideal but one must never really try to live by it. Or they took the other road, of suspecting that preachers of the gospel could talk as they do because they are really not involved anyhow; they do not know life as it is really lived, as ordinary people know it, because they do not after all, to paraphrase Ezekiel, 'sit where they sit'.[1]

One does not, of course, cut the understanding of Christian ethics to fit the cloth of a given human situation. Nevertheless, one cannot in the light of a given human situation refuse to raise the question whether or not such a prescriptive approach to that situation is really consonant with a Christian ethic. A contextual understanding of Christian ethics would indeed

[1] Ezek. 3.15 (AV).

approach a problem like that of war in a different way. A Christian, according to a contextual analysis, would take up the question of his responsibility in war, first of all, with respect to his membership in the *koinonia*. Membership in the *koinonia* means that he is related to what God is doing in the world and that in the light of God's characteristic behavior there is never any one way as against all others for dealing with any human situation. God is not really as devoid of imagination as that. In the *koinonia* each individual, in the midst of the full complexity of all the factors involved, makes a behavioral decision which amounts, in fact, to taking in trust the risk of trust. A second important consideration is that in the *koinonia* ethical action is never, in the last analysis, a matter of having really done the good. Ethical action is a matter of so having lived that God will recognize that one has been on the track of God's doing; of having lived in the confidence that at the point of one's ethical failure God will surround one with the promise and the assurance of his forgiveness. *The complexity of the actual human situation, with which a* koinonia *ethic tries seriously to deal, is always compounded of an intricate network of circumstance and human interrelationships bracketed by the dynamics of God's political activity on the one hand and God's forgiveness on the other.* It is always in such a context that the Christian undertakes to determine what he is to do in the world.

Understandably, such an ethic will be puzzling, even ridiculous, to those who have no eyes to see the signs of the times, who do not know what belongs to their peace. Such knowledge comes by insight, not by calculation. It is the gift of faith available to those who are willing to take seriously what faith knows about the doing of God's will in the world. Thus it came about that when the Federal Council of Churches at its final biennium in November 1950 received the report of a special commission entitled *The Christian Conscience and Weapons of Mass Destruction*, the journalists could not understand what the theologians were saying.[1] The theologians, on the other hand, got themselves involved in an ill-considered piece of public relations. Even so sophisticated a daily as the *New York Times* published an account of the document under the headline

---

[1] *The Christian Conscience and Weapons of Mass Destruction* published by the Federal Council of Churches, December 1950.

CHURCH UNIT BACKS USE OF ATOM BOMB.[1] Since one hasn't
said 'no!' one will always be interpreted as having said 'yes!'
This kind of disregard of ethical complexity and integrity is
exactly what, according to Jesus, a faithful disciple is to avoid.
The disciple is to be 'wise as serpents and harmless as doves'.[2]
He is not to let 'thy left hand know what thy right hand doeth'.[3]
And this is really one basic reason why 'the children of this
world are in their generation wiser than the children of light'.[4]
Jesus was possessed of an unfailing sense for ethical actuality,
for its predicament and its promise. 'He that is without sin
among you,' he said, 'let him first cast the stone at her.'[5]

When the document of the Federal Council of Churches
declared on the one hand that war is never a Christian possibility and on the other hand that war is always a possibility
which a Christian may not be able ultimately to avoid, was the
document engaged in double-talk? It is much easier, ethically
speaking, to be a Roman Catholic or a Christian Scientist than
it is to be an evangelical Christian. A Roman Catholic can
make precise distinctions between just and unjust wars and give
explicit counsel to the faithful about which wars may be engaged
in and which must be abjured. A Christian Scientist may move
from the patent iniquity of war to an acceptance of its unreality.
But an evangelical Christian is prevented by the *koinonia*
character of the ethics to which his faith commits him from the
kind of flight from the complexity of ethical actuality made
possible by nicely calculated degrees of culpability or by the
consistent adherence to some absolute principle.

A *koinonia* ethic would insist that the document of the Federal
Council of Churches was not engaged in double-talk but in
speaking the right or living word. Actually the ambivalent
character of its recommendation concerning the Christian
course with respect to nuclear armaments was forced on it by
the stubborn fact that American Christians, like Americans
generally, could not live out their lives in this world in disre-

---

[1] *New York Times*, 28 November 1950, p. 16. The sub-headline ran:
'Nuclear Attack on U.S. or Allies Made Condition of Sanction.' But this can
scarcely be said to have provided a very effective qualification of the
principal journalistic presentation of the document.

[2] Matt. 10.16 (AV).          [3] Ibid., 6.3 (AV).
[4] Luke 16.8 (AV).            [5] John 8.7 (AV).

gard of fellow Christians and fellow human beings in other parts of the world. A categorical prohibition of the use of nuclear weapons would in fact have exposed the peoples of western Europe to the heightened peril of nuclear attack and have put the American churches in the position of making a Christian judgment from a position of relative safety. A judgment under those circumstances could scarcely be regarded as inspired. But the alternative to inspired judgments is neither no judgments at all nor sentimental ones.

What this comes to is that if what God is doing in the world is bringing to pass a new humanity, and if men are relating themselves to each other in the context of what God is doing, the alternative to an absolutist ethic is not thoroughgoing ethical capriciousness or relativism. On the contrary, a *koinonia* ethic is a concrete, relational ethic in which the possibilities and the actualities of the human situation are continually breaking down and continually running out into what God is doing to put them together again. If one doesn't believe or has no sense for the fact that God can and does pick up the pieces, then one is indeed reduced to the dismal alternative between the irrelevance of ethical absolutism and the expediency of ethical relativism. But if one does believe and lives by the fact that God is picking up the pieces, it is incumbent upon one to be clear about where and what the pieces are.

Ethical decisions, as Christians try to make them, are behavioral acts which exhibit the connection between what God is doing in the world and the diverse and complex circumstances, motivations, purposes, and interrelations which are the 'stuff' of concrete human situations. Such decisions do not function as an attempt to apply a uniform principle to a uniform or even a variegated situation. It is plain that the love of neighbor as a principle of action derived from the love of God excludes acts which initiate war or lead to war. It is also plain that war is a stubborn ingredient of the human situation and cannot be ethically neutral. The fact is that war is ethically ambiguous. War both contradicts what God is doing in the world to bring about a new humanity and is instrumental to this activity. Christians have always taken positions on both sides of this ambiguity. They have been right in doing so although they have not always correctly understood the sense in which they have been right. Christians who have refused to participate in war because war contradicted the love commandment have denied the integrity of obedience to Christians who have participated in war because war was instrumental to the will of God. Similarly, Christians who have participated in war have denied the integrity of obedience to Christians who have refused to participate in war. An ethic of principle must always find such an ambiguity inadmissible. It must reject war altogether as contrary to the Christian ethic or it must find an ethical rule according to which one war is 'just', another war 'unjust'. Such an ethic has the merit of clarity and consistency and the great advantage of appearing to rescue decision making from ambiguity.

Yet this is the vulnerable point of an ethic of principles. One does not eliminate the ambiguity of ethical decision by setting up a principle which excludes or reduces ambiguity. Indeed, the ethical originality of Christianity lies in its refusal to ignore or to weaken ambiguity while at the same time expecting a decision in obedience and indicating the considerations which make such a decision possible. These considerations are derived from the context of God's activity in the world, a context which makes the obedience of faith a meaningful risk. Such a risk necessarily includes both circumstances and the rational judgments which mold circumstances into policies. These circumstances and judgments are given in, with, and under the human condition. Christian decision making seeks to express in behavior the fact that the human condition itself is being shaped by the politics of God. In a dynamic situation such as this, there is never any *one right action*. There are always acts to be done, the *rightness* of which consists in the fact that the actions bear the risk of obedience and as such are potentially instrumental to the divine activity in the world. They are *potentially instrumental* because the freedom of the divine initiative cannot be abrogated by any human decision. Whether and in how far the actions *actually* serve the purposes of God in fashioning a new humanity in the world is a matter of the Christian's hope. Thus, faith and hope combine to transform a human action into an offering of love in the service of God.

It may be that the Federal Council of Churches was more 'prudential' and less 'Christian' in dealing with the concrete human ambiguity exposed by the fact of nuclear weapons. Those unaccustomed to decision making in a Christian context are understandably puzzled, not to say confused, by a 'yes' and 'no' declaration concerning the Christian's responsibility for the use of weapons of mass destruction. In a Christian context, however, decision making finds such an ambiguity a sign not of confusion but of the inevitable embarrassment of the obedience of faith.

### 3 *The Crucial Difficulty of a 'Double Standard'*

If such be the contextual method and character of a *koinonia* ethic, a very formidable difficulty must be faced. It was alluded to in the foregoing chapter and has been implicit in the whole previous course of the present analysis.[1] The crucial problem of Christian ethics in the context of the *koinonia* is how the behavior of Christians is to be related to the behavior of non-Christians. How can a *koinonia* ethic make any ethical claims upon those in society who do not acknowledge the *koinonia* as their point of departure and frankly live neither in it nor by its light? Do we have here a kind of double ethical standard: one for Christians and another for non-Christians?

The prospect of a double ethical standard is so near at hand and so far-reaching in its implications as to call in question the whole of the present analysis. Often in matters of this sort it is easier to be negative than it is to be positive, easier to say how the behaviors of Christians and of non-Christians can*not* be meaningfully related than to say how they may be constructively brought together. It is not, for example, fruitful or consonant with a *koinonia* ethic to say that non-Christians must conform in their behavior to the community of the church. Whenever one tries from within the *koinonia* to regulate behavior by external conformity one endangers ethical by sub-ethical considerations and procedures. Ever and again such attempts arouse the public mind and disturb public tranquillity *ad hoc*. Not too long ago, for instance, a lively controversy occurred in New York City over a policy authorized by the chairman of the board of directors of the City Hospital prohibiting patients in the hospital from receiving contraceptive medical informa-

---

[1] See above, pp. 115-23, see also pp. 69-73.

tion and advice.[1] The Roman Catholic Church, the Protestant Council of the City of New York, and the New York Council of Rabbis had in turn taken up divergent positions with regard to the hospital policy. The situation appeared to be further aggravated by the circumstance that the patient whose medical treatment came under the ban was herself a Protestant. Whatever the merits or demerits of the issue may have been, the controversy underlined the enormous difficulty of ordering a pluralistic religious and areligious society according to a religious ethic.[2] The role of the Roman Catholic Legion of Decency in the matter of censorship is too well known for more than passing mention. But consider what understanding of Christianity is involved, and what people who have no understanding of the church and of the *koinonia* must think about the kind of God at work in the world when they are exposed to this kind of prescriptive conformity in the name of religious faith. A relationship between religious faith and behavior effected and/or maintained by political pressure is scarcely ethical by any rational determination of the Good, and from the standpoint of the *koinonia* it is untenable.

Roman Catholicism has no monopoly on 'legions of decency'. It was not Roman Catholicism but the Protestantism of the United States which fastened upon the Constitution the eighteenth amendment, which required in turn the twenty-first. Prescriptive attempts to achieve conformity of behavior, even if they could be enforced, are ill suited to the kind of responsibility required for human maturity. Law is certainly not without ethical significance. The ethical significance of law, however, is functional, not normative. No law can be the norm or criterion of action in accordance with the will of God. Law orders human relations by exposing crucial danger spots affecting human relations and also indicates the direction of

---

[1] *New York Times*, 6 August 1958, p. 27; 7 August, p. 49; 8 August, p. 20.

[2] A thoughtful analysis of this difficulty with special reference to the controversy over contraceptive information is worth noting here because it offers a judicious assessment of the issue as well as an enlightened Catholic approach to it. Cf. 'Controversy in New York' by James Finn in *The Commonweal*, Vol. LXVIII, No. 24, 12 September 1958, pp. 583-86. Whether Protestant worries about 'Catholic power' lack the 'substantial basis' averred by Mr Finn will require more evidence than Mr Finn's brilliantly stated assurance, and even more of a span in our 'dynamic still-evolving society'.

humanization. Human relations always veer toward the boundary on which the issue of the humanity or the inhumanity of man to man must be fought through, and the direction of God's activity must be sighted again. Law has the function of exposing this boundary and in that sense is instrumental to the divine activity. This is the ethical significance of law, and in so far as a given law cannot be shown to perform *this* function, it violates Christian ethics and thus also the Christian under-standing of law. Thus, the inability to compel ethical behavior is part of the economy of God whereby men are reminded that human wholeness may be served but is never achieved by law.

Another possibility of relating the behavior of Christians to that of non-Christians lies at the other extreme. The attempt here is not so much to compel external conformity to Christian standards but rather to recommend, in the name of the Christian community, the prevailing patterns of the community at large. Until comparatively recently this has been the Protestant position with regard to racial segregation. It has tended to accept segregation as involving no really basic conflict with the orientation of life in the *koinonia*. Another case in point is the way Protestantism has on the whole accommodated itself to the economic ideology of the middle classes. That Protestant-ism and economic individualism stand or fall together is a doctrine which scarcely can be found in the New Testament. Yet it is currently being circulated by a propaganda sheet called *Christian Economics*, which manages a gratis mailing to the Protestant clergy and the editorial board of which includes active and devoted churchmen, ordained and unordained. Quite apart from the spurious economics of this publication, it is an unblushing attempt to harness the Christian Church to the economic patterns of a moribund capitalism. Thus whether one takes the way of conformity by prescription or the way of conformity by accommodation, these two ways of trying to get the behavior of Christians and non-Christians together seem hardly calculated to establish the *koinonia*. The first way alienates the non-Christian and divides the religious community itself; the second ignores or betrays the dynamics and direction of a *koinonia* ethos.

How, then, is the behavior of Christians to be related to the behavior of non-Christians? The tradition of Christian ethical thinking has provided one very influential answer to this question, in the form of the theory of *natural law*. The idea is that there is a common link between the believer and the non-believer grounded in the nature of the human reason which enables both believer and nonbeliever to make certain ethical judgments and to address themselves in concert to commonly acknowledged ethical situations. For reasons which will be subsequently set out, a theory of natural law is ethically inadequate both in itself and as a possibility open to a *koinonia* ethic.[1] If, then, one is not going to adopt or adapt the tradition of natural law, what alternatives are available?

At least two provisional possibilities suggest themselves for further reflection. However, before exploring these possibilities, we must consider the concept of *middle axioms*, a concept first used, I believe, by Dr J. H. Oldham of Great Britain and ably and systematically put forward by Professor John Bennett.[2] Since Bennett addresses himself to a critical examination of contextual ethics, and to stating his own position, some attention must be given at this point to his serious and instructive case for middle axioms. He is as little interested in perpetuating the phrase 'middle axioms' as we are in perpetuating the phrase '*koinonia* ethics'. The important concern connoted by 'middle axioms' is that there be some designation of objectives or judgments which have a *particular* reference to our concrete situation, which are determiners of policy and yet not identical with the most concrete policy guiding an immediate action. Middle axioms are statements of 'objectives or descriptions of some condition of which policy must take account'. They are ways of stating the 'common moral convictions which Christians share with non-Christians and which guide Christians in making decisions about matters of public policy in which non-Christians are also involved'. These 'axioms cannot be derived from Christian love alone but from Christian love as it seeks knowledge

---

[1] As indicated in the Preface, the present essay is principally concerned with *methodological* questions. A subsequent volume will deal with questions of the content and implementation of a Christian ethic and will include a critical consideration of natural law. See also below, pp. 223-24, 346

[2] I am grateful to Professor Bennett for having favored me with a copy of an unpublished paper of his entitled 'Principles and the Situation', read before the Society of Professors of Christian Ethics and Social Ethics at its meeting in Philadelphia at the end of January 1958.

concerning the needs of the community of neighbors'. They are specifications following from certain 'broad criteria' which 'are our ways of spelling out what the good of the neighbor is in the world as we know it'.

Bennett is emphatic about rejecting a 'deductive ethical rationalism or a strict casuistry based upon principles which imply with precision their own application to each situation', as any contextual ethic is. He goes indeed very far toward a new recognition of the contextual approach to ethics and thinks that the issue between 'principles' and 'contexts' is at best a matter of emphasis. But what concerns him is that the 'hard decisions' we are called upon to make should be made 'because of goals which are defensible on the basis of some principles and we should know in the light of what principles the decisions are hard. Otherwise our *ad hoc* decisions would be absurdly blind....'

With Bennett's principal concern, mainly 'to spell out more than is sometimes thought necessary what Christians bring to the situation' in which they act, the present analysis is in cordial agreement. But this is precisely the point in his analysis at which a familiar difficulty arises. The 'broad criteria related to Christian ethics' and the 'more specific objectives' or 'middle axioms' to which these criteria 'should lead us' are not so essential to that which *Christians* really bring to the situation as the account implies. Professor Bennett rightly notes that Christians bring to the situation a resource of wisdom expressed in Christian teaching and transmitted through a tradition of faith and experience. But what is the meaning of ascribing ethical significance to the possibility that the moral convictions to which this Christian wisdom leads 'can still be defended by considerations which have a broader base than the Christian revelation'? However flexibly these 'principles' may be interpreted and applied, they embody the familiar compound of Christian with non-Christian rationalistic elements which has always involved Christian ethics in a methodological ambiguity. Bennett has not carried his concern for what 'Christians bring to the situation' far enough. Either the Christian, as Christian, brings more to the situation than the wisdom of Christian teaching, or what the Christian brings to the situation is ethically extraneous to, and inextricably involved in, a double standard. The complaint against the natural law tradition is not that it relates Christian and extra-Christian ethical elements but that it does so in an artificial way and by obscuring or surrendering the Christian factors. Although Bennett leaves the question of 'an equivalent natural law' open, his analysis seems to be in similar case.

That Professor Bennett's case for 'flexible principles' does not go far enough is evident also from his correlation of 'middle axioms' with 'policy', without sufficiently considering the question of the relation between these 'middle axioms' and Christian ethical goals. These constitute the 'broad criteria' which 'Christians should bring as guidance to each social situation'. Yet if the 'middle axioms' become, as Bennett hopes, 'a part of the mind of the church', it is hard to see why they are not as intrinsic to 'spelling out' the claims of Christian ethics as are the broad criteria of action themselves. Indeed, this intrinsic significance of the so-called 'middle axioms' is exactly what a contextual analysis of ethics tries to take properly into account. Such an analysis insists that the 'stuff of action', as it were, is as significant ethically as are the resources and direction of behavior.

Let us try to make as concrete as possible the difference between the use of middle axioms in a Christian ethic and the way a *koinonia* ethic would seek to guide the formation of social policy. As a case in point, we shall consider an example of a middle axiom which Professor Bennett himself offers. 'Desegregation', he notes, 'is one of the clearest examples that I can give of the kind of objective that needs to be brought to a situation.' It will be recalled that the celebrated decision of the Supreme Court affecting racial relations in education in the United States (1954) displaced in law the previously operative 'separate but equal' formula by a mandate of 'equality by integration with deliberate speed'.

As I understand it, an ethic of principles would hold that Christian love makes the good of one's neighbor a primary obligation. One way of expressing this obligation in conduct is what Professor Bennett calls 'the broad criterion . . . of justice'. Applied to the relations between the Negro community and the white community in the United States, justice would mean *racial justice*, and racial justice has now been defined in law as 'equality by integration'. Thus the application of Christian love to the concrete situation of racial relations through *justice* follows a strict logical order of ethical principles. The obligation of racial justice may be directly derived from the love commandment.

At this point, however, an important qualification must be made. Although the obligation of racial justice may be directly derived from the love commandment, this obligation is not derived from Christian love *alone*. It arises also from specific and variable factors in the human situation. Thus social pressures aiming at the more rapid achievement of greater racial equality contributed to the desegregation decision. These pressures are distinguishable from the ethical principles involved in the situation and operate in part independently of them. It is this relative independence of circumstances which requires a clarification of specific and limited objectives if society is to be guided by social policy and if such guidance is to be ethical (and not, for example, merely administrative). Middle axioms serve the ethical purpose of defining such specific and limited objectives. They are 'middle' because they function as a bridge between a general ethical principle (e.g., Christian love) and a complex and concrete social situation (e.g., racial justice). They are 'axioms' rather than 'principles' because they lack the universal claim and the general consent of a principle, while serving at the same time to guide a given social situation in the direction required by a universal principle. Thus *desegregation* is a middle axiom of racial justice which has certainly carried both the public mind and public policy in the United States considerably farther toward the goal of racial justice than had been the case hitherto. It must also be noted that desegregation, like all middle axioms, has been supported and opposed both by Christians and by non-Christians, by persons who accept the principle of racial justice as a Christian obligation or as a general ethical obligation but disagree in good conscience over the specific objective of desegregation.

We may now ask how a *koinonia* ethic would interpret desegregation. The desegregation decision of the Supreme Court would be as seriously and urgently regarded by a *koinonia* ethic as by an ethic of principles and middle axioms. The difference between a *koinonia* ethic and an ethic of principles and middle axioms is *not* that one denies ethical reality and significance to what the other affirms. The difference lies in the understanding and interpretation of what is *ethical* about the same set of social goals and circumstances. For a *koinonia* ethic the clarification of ethical principles and their application to concrete situations is ethically unreal because such clarification is a logical enterprise and there is no way in logic of closing the gap between the abstract and the concrete. Ethics is a matter not of logic but of life, a certain kind of reality possessed by the concrete. As we have been trying to urge, ethics is concerned to expose and explicate the *human* reality of the concrete. A *koinonia* ethic is uniquely adequate to this concern because it describes and analyzes the context within which the human reality of the concrete is being steadily shaped and exposed.

In such a context, racial justice is indeed 'a way of spelling out what the good of the neighbor is in the world as we know it'. But 'the good of the neighbor' and 'the world as we know it' acquire *ethical* significance not from the attempt to formulate, to clarify, and to apply ethical principles but from what God is doing in the world to make and to keep human life human. In such a situation, desegregation is not a 'middle axiom', or even an 'axiom' at all. Desegregation is a concrete human action which is a *sign* of God's action. Desegregation may take the form of a social policy or of separate and diverse behavioral circumstances. Circumstances are the instruments of ethical behavior. Whether circumstances serve behavior in the aggregate form of a social policy or as *ad hoc* actions, the *ethical* factor in behavior is provided not by a rational principle but by the *sign character* of the behavior. Desegregation is *ethical* behavior in so far as it bears the marks of God's transformation of the world in accordance with his purposes, of the world's resistance to what God is doing, and of God's ultimate overcoming of the world. In short, desegregation is ethical in so far as it is a *sign* of the new humanity which is coming to be in the world in which Jesus Christ lived and died, over which he rules as Lord against the day of his coming again.

All signs of God's activity divide as well as unite men. They divide believers from believers and believers from unbelievers. They unite believers with believers and with unbelievers. The ethical significance of a sign is not derived from universal consent or from uniform procedures and policies. In a world being shaped by the politics of God, the dynamics of society necessarily include both circumstances and the rational judgments which mold circumstances into policies. A *koinonia* ethic does not exclude the fact that desegregation involves historical, sociological, economic, legal, and political factors as well as the full capacity of human analysis and judgment. According to a *koinonia* ethic, the dynamics of society are neither ethically indifferent nor ethically unambiguous. They are always potentially ethical, that is, capable of erupting into ethical signs, signs of the ethical reality and ferment at work in society because of what God is doing in the world.

It does not matter whether an unbeliever supports desegregation because it is a social good and a Christian supports desegregation as a sign of obedience to the will of God. It does not matter that some Christians support desegregation and other Christians disavow it. What matters is that the behavior of Christians shall exhibit—not obscure—the fact that desegregation is ethically significant because it points to what God is doing in the world to achieve the humanization of man. If unbelievers join with believers in such an enterprise of humanization, they do so, of course, because of what is ethically common to them. A *koinonia* ethic, however, regards what is ethically common to them not as proof of a common rational moral nature but as a sign that the humanizing action of God includes all men. A *koinonia* ethic ventures the claim that it has a clearer view of ethical reality as concrete human reality, and thus also of what God is doing and of what man is to do, than is offered by an ethic of principles and middle axioms. It would seem, then, that if middle axioms actually do become part of the mind of the church, it is because their relation to policy includes also their significance as bearers of the Christian character of action. On the other hand, if middle axioms cannot be regarded as behavioral bearers of Christian ethical insights, they can scarcely be regarded as 'more specific objectives' of *Christian* ethics, however effectively they may shape policy.

With Professor Bennett's account of the dangers which any Christian analysis of ethics must avoid we agree. Neither a 'single track devotion to an ethical principle' nor such an 'emphasis on the situation, [that] we may be determined too much by the limitations that it places upon our vision' is a fruitful avenue of Christian ethical reflection. The avoidance of these dangers is the prospect which is offered by the contextual character of *koinonia* ethics. A *koinonia* ethic does not derive the context of action from the situation alone. It insists, however, that the situation is significant *ethically* because it is shaped by, and thus part of, the context of what God is doing in the world. It is thus incorrect to imply, as does Professor Bennett, that a contextual approach to behavior offers no ethical guidance. Indeed, one could even interpret this guidance in terms of 'flexible principles' and 'middle axioms'. But then the distinction between 'principles and the situation', even as a difference of emphasis, would seem to have disappeared. Either 'flexible principles' and 'middle axioms' are ethically significant *contextually*, or they are vestigial remnants of the natural law tradition and ethically expendable. Perhaps the basic difficulty with Professor Bennett's analysis is a theological one. A theological anthropology is simply insufficient to support the method and substance of Christian ethical reflection. A theology of messianism according to which behavior is the parabolic bearer of a new humanity intrinsically connects both 'gospel' and 'situation' and also the behavior of unbelievers with that of believers.

It is the possibility of such an intrinsic connection which enables a *koinonia* ethic to meet the crucial difficulty of a double standard between believers and unbelievers. The prospect of resolving this difficulty has prompted us to take up the conversation with Professor Bennett and leads us now to return to the two suggestions which seem to be more directly implied by the theological foundations underlying the present discussion.

The first suggestion in terms of which a *koinonia* ethic may conceivably surmount the difficulty of a double standard is derived from the dialectical relation between the 'second Adam' and the 'first Adam' in the shaping of the new humanity. It follows from this dialectical relation that the meeting place between the believer and the nonbeliever ethically speaking is not, as the natural law tradition suggested, at the point of constructive ethical wisdom and achievement but rather at the point of what might be called 'the common ethical predicament'. The common ethical predicament is that compound of circumstantial involvement and human striving for maturity which forces into the open the issue of the falsification or the fulfillment of the authentic humanity of every human being. In delineating this predicament, and in the development of a sensitivity for it, ethical analysis and theological analysis have a very intimate relationship. For example, believers sometimes acquire a habit of behaving with more nuisance value than insight by pressing upon unbelievers the question whether they are saved. This question is at best premature; at worst, irrelevant.

But turn the question the other way around so that it is the unbeliever, not the believer, who asks it. Then the question undergoes a significant transformation. When a believer and an unbeliever are met on the level of their common involvement with the issue of the possibility and the integrity of their humanity, and when by reason of this involvement the question 'What shall I do to be what I am?' however it may be formulated, can no longer be suppressed, then the integrative power and the possibility of the Christian gospel are exposed. The New Testament offers no evidence for putting the question 'Are you saved?' *That* is simply not a biblical question. However, the question 'What shall I do to be saved?' *is* a biblical question. It appears also in the form 'What shall I do to inherit eternal life?' The question means, in short, 'What shall I do to be what I am?' The lawyer, trying to justify himself,[1] the Macedonian jailer, who found himself on the threshold of unemployment,[2] put the question of authentic life from the level of an inescapable confrontation with a claim upon them to move in the direction of self-fulfilling self-surrender. It is only out of this kind of authentic human situation that the question of belief and unbelief, the religious question, has integrity.

The second suggestion in terms of which a *koinonia* ethic may conceivably surmount the difficulty of a double standard is derived from what has already been referred to as the 'whole panorama of the divine economy', pointed to by the doctrines of the Trinity and of the Second Advent. The Gospel of John attributes to Jesus a remark which seems to underline the inclusion of unbelievers within the divine economy. The discourse on 'the good shepherd' contains Jesus' comment that

[1] Luke 10.29.　　　　[2] Acts 16.30.

'I have other sheep, that are not of this fold; I must bring them also, and they will heed my voice. So there shall be one flock, one shepherd.'[1] Some years ago, *Time* magazine reported that a considerable movement of land redistribution was under way in India under the leadership of a certain Mr Vinoba Bhave, who was seeking in this way to implement a kind of gospel of love.[2] A wandering ascetic, though uncommonly learned, without place or influence in government or any secular organization, yet better known to the Indian masses than any other save Prime Minister Nehru, this man was going about from village to village preaching no new doctrine but an old doctrine with new urgency. To the wealthy landholders he is reported as declaring, 'I have come to loot you with love. If you have four sons, consider me as the fifth, and accordingly give me my share.' To the impoverished masses he says, 'We are all members of a single human family.' Mr Bhave is a trusted and faithful disciple of Mahatma Gandhi and thus not a self-acknowledged Christian. It is not inconceivable that some Christian images and memories have found their way into his background, but this would scarcely connect his movement explicitly with the Christian *koinonia*. Yet Mr Bhave was in fact implementing in behavior what according to the Christian *koinonia* God is doing in the world. 'After 6,500 miles,' *Time* crisply noted, 'a million acres for the poor.' Would Mr Bhave be numbered among Jesus' 'sheep' or wouldn't he?

The answer would seem to be an affirmative one and for the reason succinctly suggested by Calvin in a passage in which he is discussing the relationship between Jesus Christ and the Holy Spirit. 'Christ', says Calvin, 'was endued with the Holy Spirit in a peculiar manner; in order to separate us from the world, and introduce us into the hope of an eternal inheritance. Hence the Spirit is called "the Spirit of holiness"; not only because He animates us and supports us by that *general power* which is displayed in mankind, and in all other creatures, but because He is the seed and root of the heavenly life within us.'[3]

The same point has been more recently made by Professor Roger Mehl of the Protestant Theological Faculty of the

[1] John 10.16 (RSV).
[2] 'India: A Man on Foot', *Time*, 11 May 1953, pp. 32-37.
[3] John Calvin, *Institutes of the Christian Religion*, III, 1, 2, Italics mine.

University of Strasbourg. Although Professor Mehl is not commenting upon Calvin, his analysis of 'the nub' of what is involved in the communication of the gospel underlines with striking cogency the concrete transformation of the relations between believer and unbeliever owing to the actuality of the presence of Christ in the world:

> The presence of the living Christ is always the presence of him who by his incarnation has profoundly modified the situation of every man and of all men in the world. That incarnation means not only that Christ has been a man among men, that a holy and exemplary man has been inserted into the line of humanity as a kind of file leader behind whom men could march. That incarnation means that Christ has effectively substituted himself for, put himself in the place of every man, regardless of how miserable he may be. . . . If then I wish to communicate the biblical message to the other person, I must not allow myself to be hindered by that solitude, by that other-ness of the other person which interposes among other things I don't know how many irreducible limits to communication. I am authorized to think and to believe that Christ has really taken the other's place, as he really has taken my place. . . . Christ is no longer merely an external mediator who forces into the open a compromise acceptable to both parties. He does not maintain himself between us according to a formula freely expressed in pious language. He is the other and He is I myself. I am genuinely authorized to consider that a new life, evidently hidden in Christ (Col. 3.3), is in the other person as in me and that one day these lives of ours will be manifested.[1]

Now it may be suggested that this 'general power of the Spirit', this 'real presence of Christ' (in this sense of the phrase), provides a clue for dealing with the question of the believer and the unbeliever of which a *koinonia* ethic takes account. This means that those who start with and from within the *koinonia* find themselves on the behavioral level, involved in situations and with people who start from outside the *koinonia* yet whose behavior makes the recognition inescapable that they are sheep belonging to the same fold.

Luther has another way of getting at the same point, when he speaks about the *deus absconditus*, the hidden character of the divine activity. The Lutheran tradition tends to restrict the *deus absconditus* to Luther's thought about the wrath of God, an interpretation which even Emil Brunner rather consistently

[1] Roger Mehl, *La Rencontre d'Autrui*, Cahiers Théologiques, 36, Delachaux et Niestlé, Paris, 1955, pp. 55-56. Translation mine.

follows. Yet it may be suggested that the conception of the wrath of God does not exhaust Luther's notion of the *deus absconditus*. It has been instructively pointed out that Luther's conception of the hidden God, correctly understood, makes it necessary to keep revelation and hiddenness together. For Luther, so the argument runs, hiddenness is itself part of the revelatory activity of God.[1] Such an interpretation, if correct, would nicely combine with Calvin's doctrine of the 'general power of the Spirit' to provide an explanation of the fact that unbelievers can and do bring forth fruits worthy of repentance without being baptized members of the Christian community. To put the matter another way, the specific behavior-forming reality of the *koinonia* does not preclude the free activity of the Holy Spirit. The same Spirit which informs the *koinonia* informs also the shaping of the new humanity in the world.

It makes a considerable difference whether one shifts these considerations from the first article of the creed, concerning God the Creator, to the third article of the creed, concerning the activity of the Holy Spirit. Theological analysis has tended too long and too steadily to deal with the question of the relations between believers and unbelievers under the rubric of the first article. The result has been a rather sterile discussion of the relations between natural and revealed theology, of the image of God and of how much of it remains untarnished by sin, of formal and material humanity. Such considerations were, at least from an ethical point of view, foredoomed to sterility because the attempt to find out how much knowledge of God a believer can or should have without being an unbeliever, and conversely, how much knowledge of God the unbeliever can or should have without being a believer, is a blind alley. It is a blind alley because after one has laboriously settled the credentials of believing, one always sooner or later is bound to encounter another human being who has never been baptized and appears to be totally unaware of, or indifferent to, the *koinonia*, yet who behaves like the Lord's anointed. This may be one of God's happy private arrangements in order to keep baptism from becoming an advertising campaign. However that may be, the general power of the Spirit provides the kind

[1] Cf. John Dillenberger, *God, Hidden and Revealed*, Muhlenberg Press, Philadelphia, 1953.

of theological and ethical substance and sobriety which intrinsically links the divine economy with human maturity and puts believers and unbelievers upon a common level of integrity about what the struggle for human maturity involves, and upon a common level of imaginative discernment about what the secret of maturity is.

'I have other sheep, that are not of this fold; I must bring them also, and they will heed my voice. So there shall be one flock, one shepherd.' A *koinonia* ethic may thus conceivably dispose of the problem of a double standard by including the unbelievers among the other sheep of the Holy Spirit of God.

## 4 *A Contextual Ethic as Indicative Ethics*

Such a contextual approach to an understanding of behavior makes for a radical shift of ethical perspective and emphasis. A contextual ethic deals with behavior basically in *indicative* rather than in imperative terms. This does not mean that there are no ethical demands. It means that such ethical demands as are authentic acquire meaning and authority from specific ethical relationships, and the latter constitute the context out of which these demands emerge and which shapes the demands. This is why the definitive question with which Christian ethics has to do has been formulated, not as 'What *ought* I . . .', but rather as 'What *am* I, as a believer in Jesus Christ and as a member of his church, to do?' The general answer to this question is, as we have already seen, 'The will of God'. We have now come upon a corollary to this general answer: 'I am to do what I am!' To do what I am is to act in every situation in accordance with what it has been given to me to be. Doing the will of God is doing what I am. If this sounds like doubletalk, then the Johannine literature is also engaged in doubletalk. 'He who does what is true', says the Fourth Gospel, 'comes to the light that it may be clearly seen that his deeds have been wrought in God.'[1] What does it mean to 'do the truth'? In the context of the Fourth Gospel it means 'to be what one is in the context of the Truth'. The 'Truth' of which the Fourth Gospel speaks is not an intellectual formulation but a specific

[1] John 3.21.

kind of activity of God. It denotes the behavioral dependability or faithfulness of God. The same point was taken up in the First Letter of John. 'This is the message we have heard from him and proclaim to you, that God is light, and in him is no darkness at all. If we say we have fellowship with him while we walk in darkness, we lie and do not live according to the truth.'[1] Or consider further, 'So God loved the world, that He gave His only begotten Son, that whoever believes in Him should not perish but have eternal life. For God sent the Son into the world, not to condemn the world, but that the world might be saved through Him. He who believes in Him is not condemned; he who does not believe is condemned already, because he has not believed in the name of the only son of God.'[2] Clearly 'belief' is so intimately connected with the 'situation' of light and darkness, of salvation and condemnation, as to be under-lined as a kind of immediate and authentically human response to the actual condition of things.

But we have tended rather to set the cart before the horse, as though God were doing nothing at all. The conditional 'If you believe, then you shall be saved', or 'If you do not believe, then you shall be condemned', is a reversal of the biblical sense for ethical reality. Of course the unbeliever is condemned! But he is condemned not by the judgments which believers make about him but by the incisive indicative of God's activity. 'This is the judgment that the light *has* come into the world, and men loved darkness rather than light. . . . But he who does what is true, comes to the light.'[3] 'If we *say* we have fellowship with him while we walk in darkness, we lie and do not live according to the truth. But if we walk in the light as he is in the light, we have fellowship (κοινωνία) with one another, and the blood of Jesus His Son cleanses us from sin.'[4] It is in this *fellowship* that one begins to understand that the Crucifixion is the catharsis of the new humanity. 'If we *say* we have no sin, we deceive ourselves [even in the *koinonia*], and the truth is not in us. If we confess our sins, he is faithful and just and will forgive our

---

[1] I John 1.5f.

[2] John 3.16-18. I have inverted the order of the first two words as given in the Revised Standard Version, deleting the word 'For', in order to take account of the stress which in the original is given to the word οὕτως.

[3] John 3.19, 21.          [4] I John 1.6, 7. Italics mine.

sins. . . . If we say we have not sinned, we make him a liar and his word is not in us.'[1] *Doing the truth!* 'For me to live, *is* Christ.'[2] This is the indicative character of the Christian ethos which underlies every ethical imperative, underlines the provisional character of such imperatives, and ultimately suspends them. The indicative character of Christian ethics is the consequence of the contextual character of the forgiveness and the freedom with which Christ has set men free to be and to do what they are in the light of what God has done and is doing in him.

[1] I John 1.8-10. Italics mine.          [2] Phil. 1.21.

PART TWO

# CHRISTIAN AND PHILOSOPHICAL
# THINKING ABOUT ETHICS

# VI

## THE SEARCH FOR THE GOOD

I F a *koinonia* ethic is to take full account of the prospect of resolving the problem of a 'double standard', it will need to be differentiated from alternative ways of dealing with this problem. The differentiation is necessary partly because the theological foundations of Christian ethics seem either to contradict or to ignore the insights and labors of non-Christian thinking about ethics, and partly because the 'common ethical predicament', in which unbelievers and believers are alike involved, has been recognized and explored by other types of ethical analysis. There are, as has been noted from the first, alternatives to Christian ethics. Some of these alternatives are religious ethics other than Christian. Some come from the tradition of moral philosophy. If the task of this part of our methodological analysis were to be fully carried out, we should be required to show how Christian ethics is to be differentiated from the ethics of Hinduism, or of Buddhism, or of Islam. However, since Christian thinking about ethics has been, in the course of its historical development, formatively shaped by the presuppositions and the methodology of the most influential moral philosophers, and since the insights of moral philosophy have in some conspicuous instances become part of the ethical commonplaces by which men, at least in the Western cultural tradition, make their daily choices, we may, for the purpose of the present discussion, limit ourselves to an examination of the way Christian ethics is to be differentiated from moral philosophy—that is, from non-Christian philosophical ethics.[1] Such

[1] For an instructive statement of a constructive and integrative relationship between Christian ethics and moral philosophy on the Augustinian model, see George Thomas, *Christian Ethics and Moral Philosophy*, Charles Scribner's Sons, New York, 1955. Professor Thomas rightly prefers the Augustinian synthesis to the Thomistic one. From the standpoint of a

an investigation should enable us also to understand how and why a Christian analyis of ethics uniquely resolves the problem of human behavior.

The task of differentiating between Christian and philosophical ethics may be carried forward by considering those types of philosophical ethics which have a special bearing upon Christian ethical reflection either because of a tenacious impact upon the tradition of Christian ethics or because of a particularly acute confrontation of Christian ethics with a persuasive rival.[1] The contextual character of Christian ethics has had to make its way against a powerful preoccupation with another kind of ethical concern. The dynamics of the divine activity in shaping the environment, direction, reality, and resources of human maturity have been misread and misapplied, owing to the cogency, subtlety, and range of the search for the Good. Thus a kind of ethical diversion has engaged the Christian mind, for which it is to be not so much reproached as reminded of its own creative ethical resources. Meanwhile the enchantment of the search for the Good may be understood and even appreciated when it is considered that the quest was pursued under the aegis of the classical and the critical philosophy. The intrinsic thrust of a *koinonia* ethic apart, the ethical record of the Western cultural tradition itself requires a careful disengagement from eudemonism and legalism as options to the shaping of behavior in the light of Christian faith.

### 1  *The Ethical Eudemonism of Aristotle*

The *Nicomachean Ethics* provides us with perhaps the most formative statement of ethical eudemonism, as well as with the

---

*koinonia* ethic, however, such a synthetic correlation gives insufficient consideration both to the theological foundations of a Christian ethic and to the limitations of philosophical ethics. This does not mean that a *koinonia* ethic must reject the enterprise of moral philosophy, but rather that a different and more dialectical way of stating the relations between Christian ethics and moral philosophy must be adopted. Although Professor Thomas' selection of materials from the tradition of moral philosophy varies somewhat from the materials selected in this part of our analysis, the attempt here is to overcome the difficulty intrinsic to his analysis.

[1] The impact will be before us in this chapter and the next; the rivals in Chapter VIII and the nature and extent of the disengagement of Christian from philosophical ethics will concern us in Chapters X and XI.

substance of Aristotle's views on ethics.[1] The *Nicomachean Ethics* deals in ten books with the nature of the Good, with moral and intellectual virtue, with the questions of pleasure and of friendship and, in conclusion, of happiness. Because Aristotle's general answer to the question of what the Good is, is given in terms of happiness or well-being (ἐνδαιμονία), his ethics may be called eudemonistic.

Beginning 'with things known to *us*',[2] Aristotle declares that 'every art and every inquiry, . . . every action and pursuit, is thought to aim at some good; and for this reason the good has rightly been declared to be that at which all things aim'.[3] Now there are two kinds of ends or goods of action. There are those which we do for the sake of something else; and there are those which we do for the sake of some end in itself, 'everything else being desired for the sake of this'.[4] The task of ethical reflection is the task of relating the ends or goods which are pursued for the sake of something else to the end or goal which is to be pursued for its own sake. Aristotle admits that it is difficult to achieve the utmost precision in these matters and that 'we must be content . . . to indicate the truth roughly and in outline. . . .' Nevertheless, it is incumbent upon ethical inquiry to press toward 'as much clearness as the subject matter admits of'.[5]

As Aristotle explores the relationship between the two classes of goods or ends, he finds that the science of ethics must really be subsumed under the science of politics. Politics 'ordains which of the sciences should be studied in a state, and which each class of citizens should learn; . . . now since politics uses the rest of the sciences . . . the end of this science must include those of the others, so that this end must be the good for man. For even if the end is the same for a single man and for a state, that of the state seems at all events something greater and more complete . . .; though it is worthwhile to attain the end merely for one man, it is finer and more God-like to attain it for a

---

[1] The other treatises are the *Magna Moralia* and the *Ethica Eudemia*. For the relationship between these treatises, and the problem of Aristotelian authorship, cf. Vol. 9 of *The Works of Aristotle*, edited by W. D. Ross, The Clarendon Press, Oxford, 1915.

[2] Aristotle, *Ethica Nicomachea*, in *The Works of Aristotle*, cited above, Vol. 9, 1095b. When cited below, the abbreviation, *EN*, will be used whenever necessary.

[3] Ibid., 1094a.          [4] Ibid.          [5] Ibid., 1094b.

nation or for city-states.'[1] This passage is instructive because it points to Aristotle's method, not only of relating ethics to politics, but also of relating the two classes of ends or goods to each other. The method is that of recognizing and accepting, as intrinsic to the human reason, a movement in thought from the less to the more complete, from the lower to the higher in a logical hierarchy of ends. Thus politics, concerned with the knowledge and regulation of the end which 'must be the good for man', avails itself of the results of ethical inquiry, which has to do with what this good for man is.[2] Ethics is to provide politics with as clear an account as possible of 'the highest of all goods achievable by action'.[3]

### a. The highest good and the rule of virtue

What, then, is the highest good which is the chief end of man? Aristotle's answer is that this highest good is *happiness*. He arrives at his answer by beginning with a kind of general argument from consent; yet as the analysis unfolds, it becomes plain that the precise understanding of what happiness involves points toward happiness as a rational excellence of the soul. 'Both the general run of men and people of superior refinement say that [the highest Good] is happiness, and identify living well and doing well with being happy; but with regard to what happiness is they differ, and the many do not give the same account as the wise.'[4] After discarding wealth, fame, power, and pleasure, as definitions of happiness, Aristotle declares that 'happiness is an activity of soul in accordance with perfect virtue'.[5] This is how it comes about that the greater part of the *Nicomachean Ethics* is given over to an analysis of the nature of virtue. Indeed, it is from the analysis of virtue that Aristotle entitles his treatise *Ethics*. For virtue is not a natural endowment but 'comes about as a result of habit, whence also its name ($\dot{\eta}\theta\iota\varkappa\dot{\eta}$) is one that is formed by a slight variation from the word $\ddot{\varepsilon}\theta o\varsigma$ (habit)'.[6]

The analysis of virtue involves Aristotle in a distinction which has characterized ethical theory from his day onwards, namely, the distinction between 'theoretical' and 'practical' aims of inquiry. Ethics is not a theoretical but a practical science, 'for

---

[1] *EN.*, 1094a and b.    [2] Ibid., 1178a, 1180, 1181.    [3] Ibid., 1095a.
[4] Ibid.    [5] Ibid., 1102a.    [6] Ibid., 1103a.

we are inquiring not in order to know what virtue is, but in order to become good'.[1] To explain what is involved in becoming good it is necessary to examine the nature of actions, and this examination begins with a determination of 'the right rule'.[2] The 'right rule' is a rule of reason; and Aristotle's formulation of it has provided ethics with both a practical principle and a rule of thumb that are as famous as they are familiar.

> Virtue then [Aristotle declares] is a settled disposition of the mind as regards the choice of actions and feelings, consisting essentially in the observance of the mean relative to us, this being determined by principle, that is, as the prudent man would determine it. And it is a mean state between two vices, one of excess and one of defect. Furthermore, it is a mean state in that whereas the vices either fall short of or exceed what is right in feelings and in actions, virtue ascertains and adopts the mean. Hence while in respect of its essence and the definition that states its original being, virtue is the observance of the mean, in point of excellence and rightness it is an extreme.[3]

Again and again we are reminded by Aristotle that virtue finds or chooses 'what is intermediate'—intermediate between, for example, prodigality and liberality, envy and spite, fear and confidence, and the like.

The rational principle, the principle of the mean, would seem to require only to be acknowledged in order to be achieved. But Aristotle is painstakingly aware that such is not the case. Indeed the 'golden' value which tradition has ascribed to the principle of the mean arises as much from the triumph over difficulties as from the prize of happiness which it brings to the man who manages to order his actions in accordance with the rule.

> It is [says Aristotle] no easy task to be good. For in everything it is no easy task to find the middle, e.g. to find the middle of a circle is not for everyone but for him who knows; so, too, anyone can get angry—that is easy—or give or spend money; but to do this to the right person, to the right extent, at the right time, with the right motive, and in the right way, *that* is not for everyone, nor is it easy; wherefore goodness is both rare and laudable and noble.[4]

The achievement of goodness is, for Aristotle, no counsel of

---

[1] *EN.*, 1103b.          [2] Ibid.

[3] Ibid., 1107a. The translation of this passage follows that in the Loeb Classical Library rather than that in the Ross edition.

[4] Ibid., 1109a.

perfection, but a pragmatically calculated more and less, compounded of reasoning and perception.

> Hence he who aims at the intermediate must first depart from what is the more contrary to it. . . . For of the extremes one is more erroneous, one less so; therefore, since to hit the mean is hard in the extreme, we must as a second best, as people say, take the least of the evils; . . . but up to what point and to what extent a man must deviate before he becomes blameworthy it is not easy to determine by reasoning, any more than anything else that is perceived by the senses; such things depend on particular facts, and the decision rests with perception. So much then, is plain, that the intermediate state is in all things to be praised, but that we must incline sometimes towards the excess, sometimes towards the deficiencies; for so shall we most easily hit the mean and what is right.[1]

### b. The problem of evil

The hindrances to the good life are sufficient to dispel ethical oversimplification. But they do not significantly disturb the logical and ontological tidiness of Aristotle's eudemonistic arrangement of ends and means. As Werner Jaeger has observed, 'in Aristotle's teleology substance and end are one, and the highest end is the most determinate reality there is'.[2] The full measure of this lucid and tranquil combination of order with movement, diversity with direction in the search for the good is indicated by the almost complete domestication of evil.

Aristotle implies that evil is thoroughgoing excess and hastens to add that such excess is a theoretical rather than a practical possibility. He notes with reference to anger, for example, that '(one can be angry with the wrong persons, at the wrong times, more than is right, too quickly or too long); yet *all* are not found in the same person. Indeed they could not [be so found]; for evil destroys even itself, and if it is complete becomes unbearable.'[3] Evil 'belongs to the class of the unlimited . . . and good to that of the limited . . . for which reason also one is easy and the other difficult—to miss the mark easy, to hit difficult.[4] Evil lurks in every vice as 'destructive of the originat-

---

[1] *EN.*, 1109a, 1109b.

[2] Werner Jaeger, *Aristotle*, translated by Richard Robinson, The Clarendon Press, Oxford, 1934, p. 385.

[3] Aristotle, op. cit., 1126a, 10. I have added the bracketed phrase to the Ross translation in an attempt to remove what seems to be an obscurity arising from an omission.

[4] Ibid., 1106b, 28ff.

ing cause of action', which originating cause is 'the end at which [things] are aimed'.[1] This domestication of evil on the ethical level presupposes, or at least strikingly parallels, the fortuitous view of evil on the metaphysical level. 'Evil in other words', as W. D. Ross has observed, 'is not a necessary feature of the universe but a by-product of the world process, something that casually emerges in the course of the endeavor of individual things to reach such perfection as is open to them, and then to approximate as nearly as they can to the divine life. . . .'[2]

Aristotle's recognition of the difficulty of ethical achievement —'to hit the mean is hard in the extreme'—led him into a painstaking analytical pursuit of what was involved in taking 'the least of the evils'. By this road he seems to have come to the conclusion, if we may paraphrase his own words, that 'evil is the least'. It is intrinsic to the preoccupation of the *Nicomachean Ethics* with the search for the Good that evil is a parenthetical concern. It is recognized and alluded to but not wrestled with and worried about. Evil is at best an epiphenomenal delay which does not, indeed cannot, seriously impede the Nicomachean program for training in virtue.

Instead, the eudemonism of this treatment of ethics is marked by a clear answer to the question 'What is the good which a man ought to do?'; a clear way of relating the varieties of good to each other and to the highest Good; and a clear rule of action by which the Good as a universal principle, and the complexities involved in its application may be held together. 'The absolute' is neither oversimplified, on the one hand, nor surrendered to ethical relativism, on the other. The Good which a man ought to do is happiness; and happiness is 'an activity of the soul in accordance with perfect virtue'. The chief Good may be related to the variety of goods and these in turn to one another by the rational differentiation of the lower from the higher, the less complete from the more complete. And action may be guided from the lower to the higher, and from the higher toward the highest and chief Good, by the principle of the mean, that right rule of virtue which 'both finds and chooses what is intermediate' between excess and deficiency.

---

[1] *EN.*, 1140b, 15ff.
[2] W. D. Ross, *Aristotle*, Methuen and Company, London, 1923, p. 178.

## 2   *The Ethical Legalism of Immanuel Kant*[1]

The Aristotelian search for the Good has chiefly influenced Christian thinking about ethics through the formative mind of Thomas Aquinas. But if classical eudemonism may be said to be nearer to the ethical thought of Roman Catholicism, a parallel claim may be made as regards the critical philosophy and the ethical thought of the Reformation. Since we are concerned with the ethical significance of the Reformation and since the critical philosophy expressly undertakes to correct the classical tradition, a careful account of this search for the Good must be included in our attempt to discover what relation, if any, philosophical and Christian ethics bear to each other.

Immanuel Kant sets out, as he tells us, to provide the principle on which Greek philosophy, its physics, its ethics, its logic, is based.[2] His aim is to clarify scientific inquiry by establishing, in so far as possible, its pure principles. All rational knowledge, Kant points out, may be regarded in one of two ways. On the one hand, it may be thought of in terms of the distinction between formal and material knowledge. Formal knowledge is the province of logic which is concerned with the universal laws of thought without reference to objects. Material knowledge is concerned with objects and the laws governing the apprehension of objects and their behavior. There are laws of nature with which physics deals and laws of freedom which are the domain of ethics. In the terminology of the time, natural philosophy is to be differentiated from moral philosophy. On the other hand, rational knowledge may be regarded either as empirical or as pure. Empirical knowledge is that based on grounds of experience whereas pure knowledge is that based on a priori principles. In this way, according to Kant, the meta-

---

[1] The standard English translation of Kant's ethical writings is that of T. K. Abbott, *Kant's Theory of Ethics*, Longmans, Green and Company, London, 1883. More recently, the University of Chicago Press has published a translation with notes by Lewis Beck, entitled *Critique of Practical Reason and Other Writings in Moral Philosophy* (1949). The passages quoted in what follows here are given as Professor Beck has translated them, unless otherwise noted.

[2] *Fundamental Principles of the Metaphysic of Morals*, translated and edited by Lewis W. Beck, University of Chicago Press, Chicago, 1949, pp. 50ff. This treatise will be noted hereinafter by the abbreviation *MM*.

physic of morals arises. The pure part of morals is the concern of ethics; the empirical part has to do with what Kant calls 'practical anthropology'.

As regards ethics, Kant notes that Greek ethical theory had not sufficiently shown the relationship between the end of happiness, toward which all things tend and for the sake of which all things exist, and the actual experience of the individual person who was supposed to live by the ethical demand. The remedy which he seeks for this defect is the delineation of the supreme principle of morality, and he proceeds by taking up, as it were, the other end of the stick. 'We have thought', he says, 'of the will as determinable inasmuch as it belongs to an intelligible world and of the subject of this will (man) as belonging to a pure intelligible world. . . .'[1] Greek ethics had been so preoccupied with the ethical end or goal as to give insufficient attention to the ethical subject, the actual doer of the Good. Kant proposes to take up ethical reflection with the ethical subject, the doer of the Good, hoping in this way to arrive at a more adequate statement of the relation between the ethical demand and the ethical act.

It may be objected that a discussion of Kantian ethics under the rubric of 'The Search for the Good' is not strictly appropriate.[2] The real search seems to be not so much for 'the Good'

---

[1] *Critique of Practical Reason*, p. 160. (This work will be hereinafter identified by the abbreviation *CPR*.) And in the *Metaphysic of Morals* the preparation for this way of thinking is explained: 'A metaphysic of morals is therefore indispensable, not merely because of motives to speculate concerning the source of the a priori practical principles which lie in our reason, but also because morals themselves remain subject to all kinds of corruption so long as the guide and supreme norm of their correct estimation is lacking. *For it is not sufficient to that which should be morally good that it conforms to the law; it must be done for the sake of the law.* Otherwise the conformity is merely contingent and spurious, because, though the unmoral ground may indeed now and then produce lawful actions, more often it brings forth unlawful ones. But the moral law can be found in its purity and genuineness (which is the central concern in the practical) nowhere else than in a pure philosophy; therefore, this (i.e. metaphysics) must lead the way, and without it there can be no moral philosophy. . . . The present foundations . . . are nothing more than the search for and establishment of the supreme principle of morality.' See *MM*, pp. 52, 54. Italics mine.

[2] Kant himself acknowledges this objection in the Preface to the second *Critique* and tries to meet it in the second chapter of the *Analytic of Pure Practical Reason*.

as for 'the determining ground of the will'. This voluntaristic preoccupation, it may be argued, leads Kant to reverse the ethical field. The teleological eudemonism of the *Nicomachean Ethics* is displaced in the critical analysis of the *Pure Practical Reason* by the a priori and indisputable character of the moral law. Kant's reversal of the ethical field must be conceded. But this does not mean a reversal of the ethical aim. Indeed, for all its legalism, Kantian ethics retains the eudemonistic goal of the classical tradition. This goal is both pointed to and presupposed by the postulates of the moral law. And the crux of the search is the right (i.e., intelligible and rationally unalloyed) connection between virtue and happiness.

## a. *The highest good*

Book Two of the *Critique of Practical Reason* notes that 'as pure practical reason it [i.e. the reason] . . . seeks the unconditioned for the practically conditioned (which rests in inclinations and natural need); and this unconditioned is not only sought as the determining ground of the will but, even when this is given (in the moral law), is also sought as the unconditioned totality of the object of the pure practical reason, under the name of the *highest good*'.[1]

[1] *CPR*, pp. 212-13. Attention is also called to the way in which Kant distinguishes between the supreme Good (*supremum bonum*) and the highest Good (*summum bonum*) in the attempt to improve upon Greek ethics by seeking precisely the *proper* relation between virtue and happiness. Ibid., pp. 214ff.

This undertaking finally carries him beyond morality to religion. Kant's point is that religion, specifically the idea of God as necessary Being, cannot be regarded as a guarantee of the life of virtue, as eighteenth-century ethical theory was wont to insist. On the contrary, the idea of God 'arises out of morality and is not its basis. . . . Morality . . . leads ineluctably to religion. . . .' Morality answers the question *how* a man ought to act by means of an analytical account of human freedom. Religion answers the question *whither* an action undertaken from the command of duty alone can be said to lead. 'What is to result from this right conduct of ours?' This question 'cannot possibly be . . . of indifference to reason'. And reason finds in religion the possibility of 'a synthetic a priori proposition', i.e., that there is a God, a possibility which solves within the limits of pure reason, i.e., not heteronomously, the problem of the proper connection between the command of duty and the highest good. See *Religion Within the Limits of Reason Alone*, the edition by Theodore M. Greene and Hoyt H. Hudson, Open Court Publishing Company, Chicago, 1960 (Hamish Hamilton, London, 1960).

As Aristotle had done before him, Kant sets out from 'things known to *us*'. This point of departure poses the question of what in the experience of the individual person, of the doer of an action, can be said to be definitely *ethical*. The answer to this question must express as clearly as possible what, over and above all variety, complexity, and change, can be said to be *ethical* in the sense that, if this factor is absent, one cannot speak of ethical experience at all. Such an 'indispensable condition' of the ethical Kant defines as follows: 'Nothing in the world—indeed nothing even beyond the world—can possibly be conceived which could be called good without qualification, except a *good will*.'[1] There are many things, Kant notes, which are good: intelligence, wit, judgment. But these and other ends may ever and again become subservient to a bad will, and thus must be regarded as not good at all. 'Thus the good will seems to constitute the indispensable condition even of worthiness to be happy.'[2]

Kant admits that singling out the will in this way may seem like 'high blown fancy' in spite of 'the agreement even of common sense'. For it is plain that 'the good will is not good because of what it effects or accomplishes . . . it is good only because of its willing, that is, it is good of itself. . . .'[3] Yet, common reason, able as it is to come as far as this, requires a more critical examination in order to establish the supreme principle of morality. Even a cultivated reason requires such a critical examination. It is at this point that Kant's improvement upon Aristotle emerges. In language different from that of Aristotle, he recognizes that all things tend toward some end, and that ethical reflection seeks to answer the question, What is the chief end of man? Kant agrees with Aristotle that the chief end of man is happiness. But unlike Aristotle, Kant notes that reason is not well suited to a being, the proper object of whose nature is happiness. 'In fact, we find that the more a cultivated reason deliberately devotes itself to the enjoyment of life and happiness, the more the man falls short of true contentment.'[4] Thus, the negative ground for singling out the will is the inadequacy of reason; but there is a positive ground also.

---

The quotations are from the Preface. This treatise will be identified hereinafter by the abbreviation *Rel.*

[1] *MM*, p. 55.   [2] Ibid.   [3] Ibid., p. 56.   [4] Ibid., p. 57.

The actuality of moral experience provides the positive ground for singling out the will as the supreme principle of morality. 'As nature had elsewhere distributed capacities suitable to the functions they are to perform, reason's proper function must be to produce a will good in itself and not one good merely as a means, for to the former reason is absolutely essential. . . . We have, then, to develop the concept of a will which is to be esteemed good of itself without regard to anything else. It dwells already in the natural sound understanding and does not need so much to be taught as only to be brought to light.'[1] Every man knows that there are some things which he ought to do and some things which he ought not to do. And if one asks how man comes by this knowledge, the answer is that the very distinction between 'ought' and 'ought not' involves a principle of volition according to which it must be assumed that man actually has the will to do or not to do what he knows that he ought to do. In a word, *I ought, therefore, I can!*[2] Conversely, if it is to be claimed that a man ought to do what he cannot do, moral experience is subjected to a contradiction which deprives it of all meaning.

The recognition of the givenness or unconditioned character of the good will, however, is only the starting point of correct ethical analysis. The end of happiness requires that more be said in order to show that the good will is indeed intrinsic to the moral nature of man. This Kant attempts by analyzing what he calls 'the conditions of a good will'. The argument carries him from the isolation of the good will to 'the categorical imperative of duty', and, in turn, to 'the maxims of the categorical imperative'.

The categorical imperative of duty is a way of contrasting the disinterestedness of the good will with mere inclination, or with a will motivated by fear. 'An action done from duty', he declares, 'does not have its moral worth in the purpose which is to be achieved through it but in the maxim by which it is determined. Its moral value, therefore, does not depend on the reality of the object of the action but merely on the principle of volition by which the action is done without any regard to

[1] *MM.*, p. 58.
[2] 'For when the moral law commands that we *ought* now to be better men, it follows inevitably that we must *be able* to be better men.' *Rel*, p. 46.

the objects of the faculty of desire.'[1] The 'principle of volition' intrinsic to the good will is two-pronged. On the one hand, it is a rational inference from the will in action; on the other hand, it is the kind of rational inference which points to the fact that the will in action is also under a law.

Thus Kant's correction of Greek ethics involves the subordination of happiness to law, the ultimate displacement of eudemonism by legalism in ethics. Whereas Aristotle's analysis of ethics had subordinated virtue to happiness, Kant reverses the order and subordinates happiness to virtue.[2] By so doing, Kant claims to have improved upon Aristotle's analysis of happiness because, when happiness is subordinated to virtue, the chief Good is linked with a 'right rule' which more adequately connects the chief end of man with the diversities of action than does the rule of the 'golden mean'.

> The moral law is given, as an apodictically certain fact, as it were, of pure reason, a fact of which we are a priori conscious, even if it be granted that no example could be found in which it has been followed exactly. . . . This kind of credential for the moral law, namely, that it is itself demonstrated to be the principle of the deduction of freedom as a causality of pure reason, is a sufficient substitute for any a priori justification, since theoretical reason had to assume at least the possibility of freedom in order to fill one of its own needs. For the moral law sufficiently proves its reality even for the critique of speculative reason by giving a positive definition to a causality thought merely negatively, the possibility of which was incomprehensible to speculative reason though this reason was compelled to assume it. The moral law adds to the negative concept a positive definition, that of a reason which determines the will directly through the condition of a universal lawful form of the maxims of the will.[3]

## b. The rule of duty

Kant's substitute for the principle of the mean is the principle of the categorical imperative of duty with its explanatory maxims. Having brought action under law, Kant notes that law regulates action by command. The commands in terms of which law governs action are of two kinds, corresponding to

---

[1] *MM*, p. 61.           [2] *CPR*, p. 215.

[3] Ibid., pp. 157-58. '. . . one of its own needs'—Kant is alluding here to the discussion in the first *Critique* of the antinomy between freedom and necessity. Cf. the third antinomy, in the *Transcendental Dialectic* of the *Critique of Pure Reason*, translated by F. Max Mueller, The Macmillan Company. New York, 1896, pp. 362-69.

Aristotle's differentiation between ends which are pursued for the sake of something else and the end which is pursued for its own sake. An action which may be called good as a means to something else comes under the *hypothetical* command of law; an action which may be said to be good in itself comes under the *categorical* command of law. Now duty must be a universal and a priori principle of the reason. As Kant puts it, 'Duty is the necessity of an action done from respect for the law'.[1] Thus the categorical command of duty serves as the 'principle of volition' which makes sense of the moral experience of a rational being.

A moral act involves, however, a subjective principle of volition as well as an objective one. The subjective principle of an act Kant calls a *maxim*. Maxims vary according to the conditions of the subject: ignorance, for example, or inclinations. But maxims must always be tested by the objective, or imperative, principle of action, which is valid for every rational being. As Kant puts it: a maxim is 'the principle according to which the subject [*does*] act'; an imperative is 'the principle according to which the subject *ought* to act'.[2] Kant offers a variety of cases in point, one example of which must suffice here. Suppose a man is forced by circumstance to borrow money. He knows that he will not be able to repay what he borrows. He knows also that he will not be able to arrange a loan unless he promises to repay within a certain time. He desires to make the promise but he realizes also that it is improper to borrow knowing he cannot repay. If such a man reasons with himself that, since he is in need, he will borrow and promise to repay although he knows he is unable to do so, he is acting from a subjective principle of self-interest—Kant says 'self-love'. But if he should then change this subjective principle into a law, he would be required as a rational being to conclude that his action was morally wrong since he could not will that the subjective principle should become a universal law.[3] Suppose, however, that the maxim of an action and the imperative of an action correspond. In that case, the maxim of an action must be regarded as necessary and the law to which it conforms must be recognized as universal, i.e., it commands without exception. 'There is, therefore,' Kant declares, 'only one categorical imperative.

[1] *MM*, p. 61.    [2] Ibid., p. 80. Italics mine.
[3] Ibid., pp. 80-82.

It is: Act only according to that maxim by which you can at the same time will that it should become a universal law.'[1]

Thus far we have been exploring Kant's account of the *Foundations of the Metaphysic of Morals*. Kant is best known, of course, for his three impressive *Critiques* of the reason, the second of which is given over especially to ethical reflection.[2] Having already explored the limits of the theoretical reason and pointed toward its *pure* character, Kant observes that if *pure* reason can be shown to be 'actually practical, it will show its own reality and that of its concepts in actions, and all disputations which aim to prove its impossibility will be vain'.[3] Thus in the second *Critique* Kant carries further the analysis of the *Foundations of the Metaphysic of Morals* by supplying clearer and more unmistakable supports for the principle of duty as a fact of reason.

The rational supports for the categorical imperative parallel the a priori categories of the pure theoretical reason, but they are now called 'postulates'. They are called 'postulates' because, unlike the pure theoretical reason, the practical reason does not require a demonstration of its own reality and structure. These are given in the fact of moral experience. What is required is as clear a grasp as possible of the rational implications of moral experience. Thus Kant returns to the starting point provided by the good will. Plainly the dictum 'I ought, therefore, I can',

---

[1] *MM.*, p. 80. There are two variant formulations of the categorical imperative which read: 'act as though the maxim of your action were by your will to become a universal law of nature'; and 'act so as to treat humanity, whether in your own person or in that of another, always as an end and never as a means only'. Ibid., pp. 80, 87.

[2] The *Critique of Pure Theoretical Reason* analyzes our knowledge of the world of nature, as the empirical world, the world of sense data. It turns upon the distinction between the *noumenal* and *phenomenal* worlds and seeks to show by way of a transcendental deduction of categories and an account of the antinomies of the reason both what the pure principles of reason are and what the limits of the reason are in its pure and empirical forms. The *Critique of Practical Reason* explores the noumenal world as the world of freedom and tries to arrive at the principles and postulates which give intelligibility to the moral life. In the Preface to the second *Critique*, Kant explains that he does not speak of the 'pure practical reason', although the parallel structure of the two *Critiques* would seem to require a parallel title. (*CPR*, p. 118.) The third *Critique* is a *Critique of Judgment* and is concerned, on the model of the previous two *Critiques*, with an analysis of aesthetics.

[3] *CPR*, p. 118.

which may be inferred from the good will, presupposes a genuine alternative. A genuine alternative is unintelligible, Kant argues, apart from the postulate of freedom—that is, that the will, in the act of willing, actually chooses one course of action rather than another.[1] The good will, moreover, although its moral worth is determined by its direct and intrinsic exhibition of duty as the highest Good (*summum bonum*) may also, when conjoined with happiness, be regarded as the complete Good (*supremum bonum*). The normal span of life is, however, insufficient for the attainment of happiness through the exercise of freedom so that a time beyond the lifetime not only of a single individual but of all mankind must be presupposed as a further support for the intelligibility of moral experience. This time is an infinite time which requires the postulate of the immortality of the rational soul, the ethical subject.[2] The exercise of freedom in an infinite time, however, would involve moral experience in an infinite indefiniteness if there were no ultimate adjudication of virtuous as against vicious actions. Such an ultimate moral arbitration presupposes the existence of God as the final judge of actions done from duty and those ignobly done, and thus as the final guarantor of happiness.[3]

It must be set down to the immense perspicacity and integrity of Kant's ethical analysis that he did not lose sight of the factor of limit also in the domain of the practical reason. The account of the 'pure theoretical reason' had found in the limits of theoretical reason a liberating occasion for the statement of its pure principles. The factor of limit, however, virtually threatened to invalidate Kant's painstaking effort to isolate and support a supreme principle of morality.

The problem which gives him no rest and which strains his analytical powers to the utmost is whether the categorical imperative of duty has been impregnably protected against heteronomy and securely founded upon the autonomy of the will (freedom) as a necessary condition of the practical reason. A moving passage about midway through the second *Critique* declares that

> it is a very beautiful thing to do good to men because of love and a sympathetic good will or to do justice because of a love of order. But this is not the genuine moral maxim of our conduct, the maxim which is

---

[1] *CPR.*, pp. 118ff.    [2] Ibid., pp. 225ff.    [3] Ibid., pp. 227ff.

suitable to our position among rational beings as men, when we presume, like volunteers, to flout with proud conceit the thought of duty and, as independent of command, merely to will our own good pleasure to do something to which we think we need no command. We stand under a discipline of reason, and in all our maxims we must not forget our subjection to it, or withdraw anything from it, or by an egotistical illusion detract from the authority of the law (even though it is in accordance with the law) elsewhere than in the law itself and in respect for it. Duty and obligation are the only names which we must give to our relation to the moral law. We are indeed legislative members of a moral realm which is possible through freedom and which is presented to us as an object of respect by practical reason; yet we are at the same time subjects in it, not sovereigns, and to mistake our inferior position as creatures and to deny, from self-conceit, respect to the holy law is, in spirit, a defection from it even if its letter be fulfilled.[1]

At the two crucial points, Kant's philosophical integrity calls into question the fidelity of his adherence to the moral law as 'the sole determining ground of the pure will'.[2] The first point has to do with the persistence of *radical evil*, the second with the problem of *ethical motivation*. The doctrine of radical evil engages Kant in the treatise on *Religion Within the Limits of Reason Alone*. By means of it, he tries to dispose of a perplexity affecting the *subjective* principle of volition. The motivational problem left dangling toward the close of the second *Critique* arises from a perplexity affecting the *objective* principle of volition. Kant tries to dispose of this perplexity by a radical revision of his earlier position. The revision occupied him at the very end of his life and was published after his death. It is not accidental that his latest works expose his deep and devout concern for the fate of his whole philosophical undertaking on the boundary between morality and religion. Let us, then, conclude this analysis of the Kantian ethic with a brief exploration of these crucial difficulties, beginning with the problem of evil.

### c. The problem of radical evil

The *Dialectic of Pure Reason*, in its effort to define the highest Good, notes in passing that the facts of evil raises difficulties for a rational view of the world and for the rationality of a morality of freedom.[3] But the question how a will solely determined by the moral law can also will an action in opposition to duty is

---

[1] *CPR.*, p. 189.     [2] Ibid., p. 214.
[3] Ibid., chap. II and chap. VIII.

left unanswered. To this question Kant returns at the outset of the treatise on *Religion*, and his answer provides what might be called a 'negative presupposition' of the ethical persuasiveness of the Christian religion.

In the *Foundations of the Metaphysic of Morals* Kant had distinguished between the subjective principle of volition (maxim) and the objective principle of volition (law).[1] This distinction now serves him in analyzing the difference between good and evil in human nature. The persistence of evil cannot be ascribed, according to Kant, to natural impulse arising either from the original constitution of human nature or from an inherited transmission of the consequences of an original defection or fall. For such a view of evil would undermine man's freedom of choice implicit in the moral law as the sole determining ground of the will.[2] Evil is, thus, a *moral* or *noumenal*, not a *natural* or *phenomenal*, fact. It is to be understood as a *propensity* rather than as a *predisposition* because, 'although it can indeed be innate, it ought not to be represented merely thus; for it can also be regarded as having been . . . *brought* by man *upon himself*'.[3] Nevertheless, evil is *radical* because, although brought upon us by ourselves, it is somehow 'rooted in humanity itself' and ineradicable.[4]

How, then, are we to explain moral evil? Kant's answer is that its origin or cause 'remains inscrutable to us'.[5] The best that reason can do is to show that an evil choice is possible and ascribable to the subjective principle of volition, i.e., to a choice by an individual of a maxim of his action contrary to the moral law. 'When we say, then, Man is by nature good, or Man is by nature evil, this means only that there is in him an ultimate ground . . . of the adoption of good maxims or of evil maxims (i.e. those contrary to law), and this he has, being a man; and hence he thereby expresses the character of his species.'[6]

[1] *MM*, p. 62.

[2] Recall the note in the Preface to the *Critique of Practical Reason* in which Kant declares that there is no 'inconsistency when I say that freedom is the condition of the moral law and later assert that the moral law is the only condition under which freedom can be known. I will only remind the reader that, though freedom is certainly the *ratio essendi* of the moral law, the latter is the *ratio cognoscendi* of freedom.' *CPR*, p. 119.

[3] *Rel*, p. 24. Italics are Kant's.        [4] Ibid., p. 28; see also p. 32.
[5] Ibid., p. 38.                          [6] Ibid., p. 17.

Radical evil is thus a 'point of no return' for an ethic based upon the rational analysis of the implications of human freedom. Ultimately, reason can neither deny nor account for moral evil. It can only be acknowledged as a 'thorn in the flesh' of the moral law. Yet while this is as far as reason can go in fidelity to its own pure principles, reason is not on that account forbidden to reflect upon other interpretations of evil. Such interpretations can neither establish nor confirm what reason has demonstrated but they can assist what reason cannot manage.

Kant has already availed himself of such assistance as an addition which carries him beyond his philosophical warrant. 'We may add further', he declares, 'that the will's capacity or incapacity, arising from natural propensity, to adopt or not to adopt the moral law into its maxim, may be called *a good or an evil heart.*'[1] But whence comes this extraneous allusion to the heart? And why?

The answer is, From the Bible. Kant, of course, does not exegete the Bible but penetrates its human significance, i.e., the way in which the biblical narrative illuminates 'the weakness' and 'the wickedness of human nature or the human heart'.[2] The Bible points to the ethical resources of Christianity for dealing with the very problem which the pure principles of the practical reason cannot resolve. Radical evil is the negative presupposition of Kant's consideration of Christianity because it sharpens the issue of the springs of human motivation and of 'the Restoration to its Power of the Original Predisposition to Good'.[3]

> But if a man is to become not merely *legally* but *morally* a good man . . . that is, a man endowed with virtue in its intelligible character (*virtus noumenon*) and one who, knowing something to be his duty, requires no incentive other than this representation of duty itself, *this* cannot be brought about through gradual *reformation* so long as the basis of the maxims remains impure, but must be effected through a *revolution* in the man's disposition. . . . He can become a new man only by a kind of rebirth, as it were a new creation . . . , and a change of heart.[4]

Kant alludes to the Fourth Gospel (3.5) and to the first chapter of Genesis. By so doing he wished to reinforce his suggestion that the scriptural narrative of man's fall into sin

---

[1] *Rel*, p. 24. Italics are Kant's.    [2] Ibid.    [3] Ibid., p. 40.
[4] Ibid., pp. 42-43. Italics are Kant's.

from a state of innocence corresponds exactly with the facts of moral experience as regards both the inexorability and universality of corruption and the possibility and hope of restoration to the good. Of all religions, Christianity 'alone is moral' because it points the way to self-improvement: (1) by denying that God can make man happy without his 'having to do anything more than to *ask* for it'; and (2) by affirming as a 'basic principle that each must do as much as lies in his power to become a better man, and that only when he . . . has made use of his original disposition to become a better man, can he hope that what is not within his power will be supplied through co-operation from above'.[1]

Morality, however, 'leads ineluctably to religion'[2] not only by way of the negative instance of radical evil and the shadow cast by it upon the *subjective* principle of volition. There is also a kind of positive movement from morality to religion by means of which Kant endeavors further to purify the *objective* principle of volition, i.e., reason's account of the moral law. This brings us to the problem of ethical motivation, objectively considered.

### d. *The problem of ethical motivation*

Toward the close of the *Dialectic of Pure Reason* Kant takes up the question of the relation between the hypotheses of the pure reason in its speculative use and the postulates of the pure reason in its practical use.[3] By way of the two *Critiques*, he has been able to show that 'the moral law, by the concept of the highest good as the object of pure practical reason, defines the concept of the First Being as that of a Supreme Being. . . . Therefore, the concept of God is one which belongs originally not to physics, i.e. to speculative reason, but to morals.'[4] But the point to which so far the critical philosophy has *not* been able to come is whether the postulates which are necessary implications of the absolute character of the moral law can be said to command not only *implicitly* via the law of duty but also *explicitly* via an actuality which they express, given with the moral experience of freedom. In a word, is God a *real* Being as well as a *necessary* Being? Having rejected the ontological

---

[1] *Rel*, p. 47. Italics are Kant's.  
[3] *CPR*, p. 243.  
[2] Ibid., p. 5.  
[4] Ibid., p. 242.

argument on the ground of its failure to provide a speculative affirmation of the reality of God and substituted a moral argument for God's existence, Kant is still haunted by the question of the conclusiveness of the moral proof.

> Is our knowledge really widened in such a way by pure practical reason, and is that which was transcendent for speculative reasons immanent in practical reason? Certainly, but only from a practical point of view. For we thereby know neither the nature of our soul nor the intelligible world nor the Supreme Being as they are in themselves, but have only united the concepts of them in a practical concept of the highest good as the object of our will and have done so a priori through pure reason. . . . But how freedom is possible, and how we should think theoretically or positively of this type of causality is not thereby discovered.[1]

It is not, however, this *theoretical* agnosticism that continues to perplex Kant's mind but the *practical* agnosticism of a mere concept of God. Could it be that the idea of God is somehow more than a postulate of the practical reason—indeed, is immanent within it? Unless this question could be clarified, and in fact affirmatively resolved, Kant's critical search for the Good would culminate at best in inconclusiveness, at worst in failure. How *are* the moral law as the determining ground of the will and the highest Good as the object of the moral will to be joined together without surrendering morality either to inclination or to heteronomy? The first (inclination) would reduce the good will to desire; the second (heteronomy) would subordinate it to necessity, i.e., some kind of determinism. In either case, the will would cease objectively to be *good*. It has not always been clearly or sufficiently understood that Kant's analysis of freedom involves a 'built-in' teleological dynamic, an internal movement of duty toward the Good which gives him no rest.

We have already noted an exceptional instance of this dynamic in the treatise on *Religion*, where Kant admits that, having shown *how* a man ought to act, he has been unable to show toward what end or *whither* an action ought to be directed.[2] This exception had been anticipated, however, already in the *Critique of Practical Reason*, marking a kind of irresistible advance toward the boundary of religion.

In the context of the passage which gives us the famous defini-

---

[1] *CPR.*, p. 236.          [2] See above, p. 174, note 1.

tion of religion,[1] Kant observes that 'the moral law commands us to make the highest possible good in a world the final object of all our conduct'.[2] Immediately and with impressive candor, he then acknowledges the awkward fact that the next question is the question of implementing what is commanded. 'This I cannot hope to effect', he declares, 'except through the agreement of my will with that of a holy and beneficent author of the world.'[3] Here then is the rub! How is this agreement to be worked out both as a possibility and as a real experience? Kant has been able to show *how* a man ought to act but not *why* a man ought to act as he ought. Duty is persuasive as a *law* but not sufficiently persuasive as an *incentive*. Or as Kant puts it, 'therefore, morals is not really the doctrine of how to make ourselves happy but of how we are to be *worthy* of happiness. Only if religion is added to it can the hope arise of someday participating in happiness in proportion as we endeavored not to be unworthy of it.'[4]

It is precisely this addition which does *not* lie within the limits of reason alone. Kant even glimpses the fact that this is what distinguishes Christian ethics from his own.[5] But he does not explore the distinction, partly because he sees 'the doctrine of Christianity' as having a moral implication which is separable from its religious formulation, and partly because he does not see how to resolve the problem of religious immanence, that is, how to explain the idea of God as *intrinsic* to and not merely a *postulate* of practical reason. Thus he must content himself with an acknowledgment and with a risk. The acknowledgment is that the Christian conception of the kingdom of God is 'a concept of the highest good . . . which is alone sufficient to the strictest demand of the practical reason'.[6] The risk is that such a 'pure practical faith' will be misunderstood as a 'rational faith'. 'It might almost seem', he remarks, 'as if this rational faith is here decreed as a command to assume as possible the highest good. But faith that is commanded is an absurdity.'[7] The best that Kant can do is to affirm the *possibility* that rational

---

[1] 'Religion is the recognition of all duties as divine commands. . . .' *CPR*, p. 232.

[2] Ibid.          [3] Ibid.          [4] Ibid. Italics are Kant's.

[5] Ibid., p. 231, at the end of the note on 'the doctrine of Christianity'.

[6] Ibid., p. 231.          [7] Ibid., p. 245.

beings in the world may possess happiness in proportion to virtue. The *actual* possession of happiness is impossible to establish by the critical analysis of the pure principles of the practical reason.

It is this religious preoccupation forced by the dynamics of duty that gives special significance to the *Opus Posthumum*. Kant was untiringly engaged in the effort to extend as widely as possible the range of the transcendental method. This preoccupation led him to attempt to narrow the gap not only between metaphysics and physics but between the theoretical and the practical reason as well.[1] Among the consequences of his continuing labors was the increased urgency of the problem of religious immanence—in Professor Kemp-Smith's words, 'the nature and extent of our knowledge of noumenal realities'.[2]

Of cardinal importance to the present discussion is the way Kant appears to have set aside the moral argument for God with which he had previously disposed of the speculative arguments of natural theology. What he seeks is the purging of the moral proof of the speculative or theoretical residuum which appears to him to have adhered to it. And the route he follows is to reject the question of the existence of God altogether and to transform the idea of God as a *postulate* of the practical reason into a *datum* of the pure practical reason itself, that is to say, into an idea of God as immanent.

A curious fluctuation in the distinction between *hypothesis* and *postulate*[3] points up not only Kant's reconsideration of the relation between the first and second *Critiques* but also the latest direction of his thought. Apropos of a passage in the *Opus Posthumum* which begins by acknowledging God's existence as a practical postulate and ends by denying it, Adickes explains that Kant has allowed 'two opposites of different kinds to commingle: the one, the distinction between theoretical and practical reason; the other, the strictly scientific and transcen-

---

[1] I am following here Norman Kemp-Smith's discussion of the *Opus Posthumum*, in Appendix C to his *Commentary to Kant's Critique of Pure Reason*, 2nd edition, Macmillan & Company, London, 1923, and certain passages from the edition of the *Opus Posthumum* by Erich Adickes in *Kant—Studien*, No. 50, Reuther and Reichard, Berlin, 1920. Hereinafter the *Opus Posthumum* will be identified, in the translation, by the abbreviation *OPS*; in the original, by *OPA*.

[2] *OPS*, p. 612.      [3] See above, p. 184 and note 3.

dental as against the practical and personal way of thinking (*Weltanschauung*)'.[1]

Our suggestion is that such a fluctuation is Kant's response to the dynamics of duty which has been carrying his thought tortuously but surely toward an immanentist revision of the moral proof. The concluding pages of the first manuscript sheaf of the *Opus Posthumum* contain three remarkably forthright statements of this revision. 'God', Kant wrote, 'is not a being outside me but merely a thought in me. God is the morally practical self—legislating Reason. . . . Therefore only one God in me, around me and over me.' 'The proposition: "there is a God," says nothing more than "there is a highest Principle in man's morally self-determining Reason which recognizes that it is determined by and required to act in accordance with such a principle without exception." ' 'God can only be sought in us.'[2] Thus Professor Kemp-Smith rightly observes that 'the whole tenor of [Kant's] argument is towards substituting a proof of a more strictly moral character, all the emphasis being laid upon the direct relation in which the Idea of God stands to the moral imperative'.[3] And having established the immanental rational necessity of the idea of God, Kant borrows the content of the idea from what he calls 'the doctrine of Christianity'.

The legalistic eudemonism of Immanuel Kant's account of ethics supplies an inquirer, as was the case with Aristotelian eudemonism, with a clear answer to the question what is the Good or man's chief end; with a clear method for pursuing the Good; and with a clear way of bringing together the absolutist claims upon action and the diversities and complexities of behavior. The Good is the good will; and the good will is that supreme principle of morality which assures happiness as the fruit of virtue. The good will may be discerned in the shaping

---

[1] *OPA*, pp. 802-03. Translation mine. The passage reads: 'A being which, in accordance with the laws of duty (the categorical imperative) of the moral-practical reason, can justifiably command all other rational beings, is God. The existence of such a being, however, *can only be postulated*, namely, the necessity so to act as though, in the recognition of all my duties as divine commands, I stood under this awful yet redemptive (*heilbringenden*) direction and support (*Gewaehrleistung*). Nevertheless the existence of such a being expressed in this formulation *cannot be postulated*, for this would be a contradiction in terms.' Translation mine.

[2] *OPA*, p. 819. Translation mine.          [3] *OPS*, p. 638.

of action by means of the categorical imperative of duty and its maxims concerning universality and humanity. And as the ethical subject makes his way between 'the commanding decree of reason' and the diversity and complexity of choices of which the stuff of action is made, he may steadily adhere to the path of virtue over which duty presides in the rational confidence in God, freedom, and immortality. Here indeed is an ethic which has acquired an even more axiomatic status in the ethical thought and practice of people who do not ordinarily give much thought to these matters than has the ethic of Aristotle. Every man knows that there is a 'right' which he is to do and a 'wrong' which he is to avoid. The right is that which commands action with the force of duty. And the force of duty is always such as to indicate that action as 'right' which can be willed universally, and which expresses a respect for humanity as an end in itself and never merely as a means. That such an ethic was unable to sustain itself without crossing the boundary between ethics and religion, specifically Christianity, is a point to which we shall return.[1]

[1] See Chapter X.

# VII

## THE REDIRECTION OF THE SEARCH

UNHAPPILY the contemporary ethical situation finds us
in trouble both with Aristotle and with Kant. The
difficulty has been due partly to the persuasiveness with
which the critical philosophy shifted the focus of ethical attention from the ethical object to the ethical subject. It has been
due also to the prescriptive formalism with which the Kantian
ethic undertook to tidy up the complexity and diversity of
action under the commanding law of obligation. The result has
been that the moralists have continued to seek out a more
adequate way of bringing the norm and the stuff of action
together; and they have pursued it mainly in terms of a more
refined analysis of the inner motivations and of the external
sanctions of behavior.[1]

We are, however, also in trouble with the heritage of philo-

---

[1] Attention may be called especially to Hegel's *Philosophy of Right* (1820);
John Stuart Mill's *Utilitarianism* (1863); Herbert Spencer's *Principles of
Ethics* (1879); Francis Bradley's *Ethical Studies* (1876); Thomas Hill Green's
*Prolegomena to Ethics* (1883); and James Martineau's *Types of Ethical Theory*
(1885). These treatises show the degree to which the Kantian philosophy set
the context of ethical reflection. The third chapter of Mill's work, for
example, deals with 'the ultimate sanction of the principle of utility' and
argues that all moral standards require a sanction or binding force which
motivates moral conduct. A distinction is made between external and
internal sanctions, the former of which, such as fear, piety, the hope of
favor, are common to all men; the latter of which, such as duty and conscience, are rooted in individual feeling, most deeply the feeling for society.
The feeling for society is the bond between external and internal sanctions
and explains why it is that the principle of utility is no mere counsel of
expediency but another way of stating the 'right rule' of reason by which
conduct may be guided. Mill defines the principle of utility in terms of
the maxim 'The greatest good of the greatest number' (*Utilitarianism*,
chap. II).

sophical ethics bequeathed to us by Aristotle and by Kant because as children of our time we have become profoundly unconvinced about the degree to which ethical ends or ethical motives can be so specified by reason as to generate persuasive ethical behavior. We live, in short, in a relativistic and post-relativistic ethical situation. So far-reaching is the unpersuasiveness of the tradition of moral philosophy that its unsteady absolutism peers out, as it were, from behind an apologetic which urges that, unless one offers people clear-cut and unambiguous ethical guidance, ethical responsibility will collapse and men will be headed back toward their brutish estate. It still seems difficult to avoid ethical relativism except by the insistence upon some kind of absolutism of ends or of law in ethical behavior.

The relativistic position in ethics may be summed up by saying that there is no 'Good'; there are only 'goods'; and goods are those aims and actions which serve to satisfy individual circumstance, inclination, and need.[1] Ethical relativism emerged under the aegis of the positivist, pragmatist, and instrumentalist movements of the latter part of the nineteenth and first half of the twentieth centuries. Auguste Comte, William James, and John Dewey are among the pioneers of the philosophical shift of perspective in our time which has also forced a re-examination of the Kantian treatment of ethics. And if we recall that Kant was endeavoring to improve upon Aristotle, we might also say that these architects of ethical relativism were exploring a way of overcoming the ethical inadequacy of the whole Western intellectual tradition.

---

[1] Satisfaction, however, not in the sense of the gratification of impulse or the indiscriminate interests of the individual but rather in the specific sense of an aim or an action which can be said to have met the recognizable conditions imposed by environment and by the act of knowing; thus satisfactory for a particular purpose, and under particular circumstances. See, for example, William James, *The Meaning of Truth*, Longmans, Green and Company, New York, 1914, pp. 190ff.; also R. B. Perry, *The Moral Economy*, Charles Scribner's Sons, New York, 1909, p. 83.

The original version of ethical relativism is that of Protagoras, who taught, in effect, according to Plato, that moral principles cannot be shown to be valid for everybody and that people ought to follow the customs of their own group. Cf. *Theaetetus*, 152ff.

### 1 *William James, An Altered View of Mind*

The principal aspects of this reconstruction, having most directly to do with our present concern, may be perceived by recalling the philosophical labors of William James. It has been suggested that William James undertook to re-examine 'every traditional problem' and expressed 'through the medium of personal genius the characteristic tendencies of an epoch'.[1] He began, as Aristotle and Kant before him had begun, 'with things known to us'. But what he found required him resolutely to break with what might be called the '*an sich* tradition' in metaphysics and ethics. He undertook, instead, a radical investigation both of what is it we 'think with' and also of what it is we do when we 'think'. Under James' careful scrutiny, the 'mind', as well as the act and the context of 'knowing', takes on a new and different look. James, says Professor Perry, 'adopts a standpoint which he never leaves. His object is man, the organism, saving himself and asserting his interests within the natural environment. These interests, the irreducible "teleological factor," must be the center and point of reference in any account of mind.'[2] The mind is not a 'mirror', but a kind of 'antenna'. It is a special kind of human agency which functions, to use a vigorous metaphor of James', as 'a theatre of simultaneous possibilities'.[3]

There are, perhaps, two consequences of this altered view of mind requiring particular stress in this connection. One is the rational or contextual character of knowledge and experience. Experience is a compound of interest and environment. Knowledge is the fruit of the attempt of man, through the agency of mind, to make contact with this manifold of experi-

---

[1] Ralph Barton Perry, 'The Philosophy of William James', in *Present Philosophical Tendencies*, Longmans, Green and Company, New York, 1929, p. 349. The essay is admirable, not only for its succinctness, but for the combination of an introduction into James' central concerns with a perspective upon the significance of his work as a whole. The rereading of Professor Perry's essay has made clear to me the extent to which my own approach to ethics has been affected by the intellectual climate so formatively shaped, if not inaugurated, by James.

[2] Ibid., p. 350.

[3] William James, *Principles of Psychology*, Henry Holt and Company, New York, 1890 (Macmillan, London), Vol. I, p. 288.

ence. This is the way 'cognition in the concrete' looks.[1] For James, all knowledge is virtually direct, though not necessarily in the usual order from sense perception to ideas. The point is that the usual order exhibits the relational character 'of the things known to us'. 'Insofar as there is here any difference between the knowing and the known, the knowing is simply the context, the company in which the thing known is received. . . . The function of such knowledge is evidently to get things thus directly acted on, or thus directly introduced into life.'[2] Thus, the old dualism between something known from the 'inside' and from the 'outside', between consciousness and its object, has been overcome.

Clearly, this changes the approach to and interpretation of the problem of truth. Truth is to be identified neither with fact nor with belief nor with propositions nor with reference to some 'hypothetical omniscience'. On the contrary, 'truth is something which happens to ideas owing to their relation to their objects, that is, to the things which they are "about" '.[3] To put it another way: 'The true is the name of whatever proves itself to be good in the way of belief, and good, too, for definite, assignable reasons.'[4] Thus truth and its context are inseparable; and this is as much a matter of ethics as of knowledge. This is the fundamental point of James' pragmatism as regards its account of knowledge. He was not unaware of its trivialization by those too facile with or impatient of its subtleties. Pragmatism is not, as James observed, 'a characteristically American movement, a sort of bob-tailed scheme of thought, excellently fitted for the man on the street, who naturally hates theory and wants cash returns immediately'.[5] Pragmatism, rightly understood, emphasizes 'the particular and presentable consequences of ideas, and is thus opposed to verbalism, to abstractionism, to agnosticism, and to loose and irrelevant speculation'.[6] 'The name "pragmatism," ' James wrote, 'with its suggestions of

[1] Perry, 'The Philosophy of William James', p. 356.
[2] Ibid., pp. 356-57.          [3] Ibid., p. 360.
[4] William James, *Pragmatism*, Longmans, Green and Company, New York and London, 1909, p. 76. This work will hereinafter be identified by the abbreviation *Prag*.
[5] James, *The Meaning of Truth*, p. 185; hereinafter identified by the abbreviation *MT*.
[6] Perry, 'The Philosophy of William James', p. 363.

action, has been an unfortunate choice . . . and has played into
the hands of' its critics. Ideas work not only 'in the physical
environment . . . but they work indefinitely inside of the mental
world also. . . . This pragmatist doctrine, exhibiting our ideas
as complemental factors of reality, throws open . . . a wide
window upon human action, as well as a wide license to
originality in thought.'[1]

The other consequence of James' revised way of starting
'from things known to us'—of his radical empiricism—is his
pluralism. The manifold of experience is known not only in a
context of relations but in a plurality of contexts.[2] 'For pluralism, all that we are required to admit as the constitution of
reality is what we ourselves find empirically realized in every
minimum of finite life. Briefly, it is this, that nothing real is
absolutely simple, that every smallest bit of experience is a
*multum in parvo* plurally related, that each relation is one aspect,
character, or function, way of its being taken, or way of its
taking something else; and that a bit of reality when actively
engaged in one of those relations is not *by that very fact* engaged
in all other relations simultaneously.'[3] Unlike what James calls
'the bugaboo empiricism', which its rationalist opponents accuse
of 'chopping up experience into atomistic sensations', and unlike
those same rationalists who insist upon 'a purely intellectual
principle' which has 'swooped down upon them [i.e., the
atomistic sensations] from on high and folded them in its own
conjunctive categories', James insists that his ' "multiverse"
still makes a "universe" . . . through the fact that each part
hangs together with its very next neighbor in inextricable inter-
fusion'.[4]

James introduces, and for the most part explores, this
pluralism 'in a purely intellectual way'. It is pragmatism's way
of avoiding 'equally . . . absolute monism and absolute pluralism',[5] of breaking with the irrelevance of absolutism without
succumbing to thoroughgoing relativism. But James leaves us

[1] *MT*, pp. 184-86.

[2] *Prag*, Lecture IV, 'The One and the Many', especially pp. 156ff.

[3] William James, *A Pluralistic Universe*, Longmans, Green and Company,
New York and London, 1909, pp. 322-23; hereinafter identified by the
abbreviation *Pl U*.

[4] Ibid., pp. 325-26.          [5] *Prag*, p. 156.

in no doubt that he is concerned about more than a theory of knowledge. 'James' field of study,' Professor Perry has observed, 'the panoramic view within which all his special problems fell, was the lot of mankind.'[1] And among these 'special problems' none is more carefully and significantly considered than is the study of religion. Indeed, the pluralistic ontology[2] to which James' search for the Good propelled him serves not only to dispose of the problem which haunted Kant's account of religion and ethics to the end but to anticipate certain contextual possibilities open to an interpretation of Christian ethics.

Kant, it will be recalled, had moved toward immanence in the attempt to close the gap between the practical reason and the reality of God in experience. Consequently the idea of God became more than a postulate of the practical reason; it became a datum of the moral consciousness itself. As James saw it, this road was the wrong road, 'classical in its exaggeration'.[3] He was emphatic on the point that 'the attempt to demonstrate by purely intellectual processes the truth of the deliverance of religion is absolutely hopeless'.[4] Like Kant, James explored the nature and knowability of religion by dissociating it as far as possible from its institutional character and forms. Like Kant, his constructive religious position presupposed the Christian

[1] Perry, 'The Philosophy of William James', p. 375.

[2] 'It is because so many conjunctions of experience seem so external', James wrote, 'that a philosophy of pure experience must tend to pluralism in its ontology.' *Pl U*, p. 361.

[3] William James, *The Varieties of Religious Experience*, Longmans, Green and Company, New York and London, 1902, p. 55; hereinafter identified by the abbreviation *Var*.

[4] Ibid., p. 455. Kant would have replied that he was engaged in no such attempt; that on the contrary, he was engaged in demonstrating 'by purely intellectual processes' *not* the truth of religion but the true foundations of ethics. If such an undertaking had brought more clearly into view the boundary between ethics and religion, he had never overlooked the fact that the link between ethics and religion was *implicit*, i.e., exactly *not* capable of demonstration. Yet James' charge is not thereby disposed of for he is really raising the prior question of the adequacy, viz., validity, of the rational enterprise itself, at least in its Aristotelian (logical) and Kantian (critical) forms. For James, adequate ethical thinking must proceed in quite another way. Christian ethical analysis makes a similar claim. See also below, pp. 205-06, 217-27.

tradition. And while the outcome was different, James tried, as Kant had tried, to break away from 'the theological machinery that spoke so livingly to our ancestors'[1] and to make a fresh case for the intelligibility and cogency of what they both called 'theism'. What they meant was 'Christian theism'.

But unlike Kant, James rejected 'the transcendentalist reasonings'[2] about religion root and branch. Kant had put before us 'the strange phenomenon . . . of a mind believing with all its strength in the real presence of a set of things of no one of which it can form any notion whatsoever'.[3] Even the immanentism of the *Opus Posthumum*, had he known the work, would have left James unconvinced. His strictures against Principal Caird let us in on James' fundamental reservations.[4] However ardently one presses beyond the sphere of morality into religion, and however adequately 'the phenomenon of the religious consciousness' is described, it is, in James' view, simply inadmissible that religion can be intelligibly derived from a datum of universal consciousness or that 'religion can be transformed into a universally convincing science'. On the contrary, 'what religion reports . . . always purports to be a fact of experience: the divine is actually present, religion says, and between it and ourselves relations of give and take are actual. If definite perceptions of fact like this cannot stand upon their own feet, surely abstract reasoning cannot give them the support they are in need of.'[5]

We have suggested that Kant's approach to ethics involved a reversal of the course taken by Aristotle. From James' point of view Kant's case for the ethical subject failed, and failed because Kant was actually nearer to Aristotle than James was to either. If Aristotle's account of ethics ignored the ethical subject, Kant's account of ethics obscured the ethical subject. James tried to retrieve the ethical individual on the boundary between ethics and religion where Kant irretrievably lost him. In this attempt James succumbed to an exaggeration of his own. Nevertheless, the exaggeration was on the right track— at least so far as the present account of Christian ethics is concerned.

[1] *Pl U*, p. 29.    [2] *Var*, p. 454.    [3] Ibid., p. 55.
[4] Ibid., pp. 451ff.    [5] Ibid., pp. 454-55.

## 2  *On the Boundary Between Religion and Ethics*

James' theory of religion is, perhaps, best remembered for his answer to the question 'What kind of being would God be if he did exist?'[1] His theory of ethics has been, perhaps, most misunderstood because of his answer to the question 'How avoid complete moral skepticism on the one hand, and on the other, escape bringing a wayward personal standard of our own along with us, on which we simply pin our faith?'[2]

The ethical question, it will be noted, is a variant of the dilemma between ethical irrelevance and ethical relativism which occasioned our own rejection of ethical absolutism in Christian ethics. The religious question is, as we have tried to show, correctly put from within the Christian *koinonia*. Had James not succumbed to an exaggeration, his answers to these questions *might* have carried him nearer to an authentic Christian ethics than they did. They *could* have carried him that far.

To the question about God, James replied that God must be conceived as 'a power not ourselves . . . which not only makes for righteousness, but means it, and which recognizes us'.[3] To the ethical question, James replied, 'in seeking for a universal principle, we inevitably are carried onwards to the *most* universal principle—that *the essence of good is simply to satisfy demand*'.[4] Until the concerns of philosophy and theology shifted altogether from the issues posed by the effort to get beyond Kant, James' *religious* answer served ethical theists with virtually epigrammatic authority while his *ethical* answer worried them. It worried them, and less friendly critics even more, because it was incautiously regarded as the boldest kind of hedonistic relativism. Actually, James was more circumspect than friends and enemies alike insisted in their interpretation of him.

God, as 'the power that makes for righteousness' served James, not as a support for ethical theism, but as a concrete fact of religious experience in a pluralistic context. His rejection

---

[1] William James, *The Will to Believe*, Longmans, Green and Company, New York and London, 1904, p. 20; hereinafter identified by the abbreviation *WB*.

[2] Ibid., p. 199.      [3] Ibid., p. 122.

[4] Ibid., p. 201. Italics are James'.

of materialism in favor of spiritualism,[1] of dualistic and of monistic theism because they make us 'outsiders and . . . foreigners in relation to God',[2] was informed by his conviction that the demand for satisfying intimacy in man's relations with the universe was an *individual* demand, and a legitimate one. It was legitimate, however, as an individual demand not in *isolation* but in *plurality*. 'Thus does foreignness get banished from our world, and far more so when we take the system of it pluralistically than when we take it monistically. We are indeed internal parts of God and not external creations. . . . Yet because God is not the absolute, but is himself a part when the system is conceived pluralistically his functions can be taken as not wholly dissimilar to those of the other smaller parts,—as similar to our functions consequently.'[3]

The alternative to foreignness is *intimacy*. And this intimacy is the functional participation of all the parts of a pluralistic world in the order and movement, in the relational variety and structure of the whole. This is why 'to satisfy demand' can be said to be 'the essence of good' without a surrender to prudential relativism. There are levels of relational participation which provide both line and limit to the satisfaction of demand. The oldest of these is the level apprehended by common sense. 'Our fundamental ways of thinking', says James, 'are discoveries of exceedingly remote ancestors, which have been able to preserve themselves throughout the experience of all subsequent time.'[4] And while these discoveries have been corrected and added to by scientific and critical philosophical efforts 'laboriously . . . to part fancies from realities in our experience',[5] they neither displace common sense nor disallow other and further ways of dealing *truly* with the *real* in experience. 'Common sense appears thus as a perfectly definite stage in our understanding of things . . . that satisfies in an extraordinarily successful way the purposes for which we think.'[6] But whether common sense or some other type of thinking is 'the more absolutely true'[7] remains an open question. Indeed, it is this very openness which occasions

---

[1] 'Materialism means simply the denial that the moral order is eternal, and the cutting off of ultimate hopes; spiritualism means the affirmation of an eternal order and the letting loose of hope.' *Prag*, p. 107.

[2] *Pl U*, pp. 24, 26.     [3] Ibid., p. 318.     [4] *Prag*, p. 170.

[5] Ibid., pp. 176-77.     [6] Ibid., p. 181.     [7] Ibid., p. 190.

'a presumption favorable to the pragmatist view that all our theories are *instrumental*, are mental modes of *adaptation* to reality, rather than revelations or gnostic answers to some divinely-instituted world enigma'.[1]

We have now reached the point at which the exaggeration to which James himself succumbed most clearly presents itself to view. James' treatment of religion had preceded his pragmatistic pluralism. In the earlier work, he had noted that 'God is the natural appellation, for us Christians at least, for the supreme reality. . . . God is real because he produces real effects.'[2] But what is puzzling is that he did not find it possible to indicate 'a mental mode of adaptation to reality', an instrumental account of these effects, except as an 'over-belief'. 'Over-belief' was James' term for those interpretations of religious experience which could not be sufficiently related to the scientific and philosophical corrections of common sense. In consequence, they could not be offered as a hypothesis capable of a wider consensus and probable verification. An over-belief is a private religious experience, concept, or claim, incapable of connecting meaningfully with common sense within the terms reached by pragmatistic pluralism as he had come to advocate it. 'I believe the pragmatic way of taking religion to be the deeper way', James observed in a moving passage toward the close of *The Varieties of Religious Experience*. 'It gives it body as well as soul, it makes its claim, as everything real must claim some characteristic realm of fact as its very own. What the more characteristically divine facts are, apart from the actual inflow of energy in the faith-state and the prayer-state I know not. But the over-belief in which I am ready to make my personal venture is that they exist.'[3]

The venture remained a venture because James could not get beyond the *individualistic* and *psychological* aspects of religion. 'By being religious', he declared, 'we establish ourselves in possession of ultimate reality at the only points at which reality is given us to guard. Our responsible concern is with our private destiny after all. . . . Whatever it may be on its *farther* side, the "more" with which in religious experience we feel ourselves connected is on its *hither* side the subconscious continuation of

---

[1] *Prag*, p. 194.    [2] *Var*, pp. 516-17.    [3] Ibid., p. 519.

our conscious life.'[1] This was as far as James could go and 'preserve a contact with "science" which the ordinary theologian lacks'.[2] And he was not unaware that this was a reduction of religion 'to its lowest admissible terms . . . on which it may be hoped that all religious powers may agree'.[3]

Undoubtedly James had provided a noetic and functional account of truth and goodness which, on the boundary of religion, forges a link between individual experience and universal claims. The account is concrete, viable, and discriminating. Here is an alternative to absolutism which does not succumb to aimless or prudential relativism. Here is a pluralism with a 'built-in' movement toward a goal. The goal is a 'universe . . . in possession of the maximum amount of rationality practically attainable by our minds. [Our] relations with it, intellectual, emotional, and active, remain fluent and congruous with [our] own nature's chief demands.'[4] The 'built-in' movement is 'the more living divine reality with which it appears certain that empirical methods tend to connect men in imagination'.[5]

Yet it is regrettable that James has left us exactly where Kant left us, except for a reversal of the field. James, like Kant, arrived at an immanental religious consummation and validation of the search for the Good. But unlike Kant, for whom the boundary between ethics and religion was crossed from the side of an immanental universality of the divine command, James draws the line at the point where individual experience and over-belief are joined. 'We have in *the fact that the conscious person is continuous with a wider self through which saving experiences come*, a positive content of religious experience which, it seems to me, *is literally and objectively true as far as it goes*.'[6] But beyond the concrete effects and effectiveness of individual religious experience and the tough-minded faith-venture into cosmic or psychocosmic universal possibilities—over-beliefs which 'are in fact what are needed to bring the evidence in'[7]—James saw no further way.

---

[1] *Var*, pp. 500-01, 512.      [2] Ibid., p. 512.       [3] Ibid., p. 503.
[4] *Pl U*, p. 319.              [5] Ibid., p. 318.
[6] *Var*, p. 515. Italics are James'.                     [7] *Prag.* p. 301.

### 3 *James and the Christian Tradition*

Unable to accept either popular Christianity or scholastic theism, James understandably turned away from the institutional and dogmatic forms of the Christian tradition. Yet he firmly disavowed atheism[1] and regarded his 'pragmatistic or melioristic type of theism'[2] as not totally uncongenial with a supernaturalism 'of the piece-meal or crasser type'.[3] Especially, then, in view of the circumstance that his own over-belief could be formulated in terms of a God who is both personal and active in the world, we may be permitted to wonder about what he might have concluded had the further reaches of his over-belief led James in a direction other than that offered by 'the phenomena of psychic research so-called'.[4] Might he have come to a different view of revelation from that which offered merely diverse options or 'gnostic answers to a divine world-enigma'?[5] Had James' radical empiricism been as radical as it purported to be, e.g., had it *ultimately* as well as *initially* broken away from a strict adherence to canons of sensory observation, classification, and verification, and into effective consonance with a concrete and pluralistic universe, he might indeed have done so. If 'God is real because he produces real effects', if 'everything real must claim some characteristic realm of fact as its very own', it is hard to see how James could have failed to notice the concreteness, complexity, and dynamics so characteristic of the biblical view of revelation.

Pragmatism, James had once declared, 'will take a God who lives in the very dirt of private fact—if that should seem a likely place to find him'.[6] If such a private fact should be found in the Christian *koinonia* with its experience and exploration of the political character of the divine activity, here might be a further context particularly adapted to the tough-mindedness which James' pragmatistic pluralism requires.

Lacking this context, James was unlike Kant in another significant respect. He was unable to deal with evil in the radical sense of the fact. It remained, to paraphrase his own metaphor, a dirty fact, but not dirty enough. 'The course of history', he wrote in an early work, 'is nothing but the story of

---

[1] *Prag*, p. 299.     [2] Ibid., p. 301.     [3] *Var*, p. 521.
[4] *Pl U*, p. 315.     [5] *Prag*, p. 196.     [6] Ibid., p. 80.

men's struggles from generation to generation to find the more and more inclusive order. *Invent some manner* of realizing your own ideal which will also satisfy the alien demands,—that and that only is the path of peace! . . . There is always a *pinch* between the ideal and the actual which can only be got through by leaving the ideal behind.'[1] Five years later, and in the context of an elaboration of his pragmatistic pluralism, he wrote, 'the way of escape from evil . . . is *not* by getting it "aufgehoben," or preserved in the whole as an element essential but "overcome"! *It is by dropping it out altogether, throwing it overboard and getting beyond it, helping to make a universe that shall forget its very place and name.*'[2] It is indeed possible, as James noted, to live 'seriously' in such a 'drastic kind of a universe'.[3] But if one is to live thus 'seriously', there must be more than a 'pinch' between the ideal and the actual. Getting beyond evil must be the fruit of something other than an 'invention', or even an 'over-belief'.

Suppose the most drastic thing about this universe is the radicality of evil, which can be 'overcome' only in so far as God lives in 'the very dirt' of it, breaking its power, and in a redemptive context setting humanity free 'to make a universe that shall forget its very place and name'. James did not see the way to include these suppositions as part of the over-belief needed 'to bring the evidence in'. Revelation possessed for him no concreteness and no context with reference to which the concreteness of revelation could be described. One need not claim for James' pragmatistic pluralism an apologetic significance which he neither implied nor intended. It may be claimed, however, that the formative significance of his search for the Good lies in the displacement of absolutism by pluralism while avoiding a thoroughgoing relativism as regards truth and goodness. James has provided an instrumental vehicle for an interpretation of ethics which seeks to understand and shape behavior in terms of the dynamics and the pattern of the politics of God.

But the first decade of the twentieth century was culturally and theologically unready to bring this kind of evidence in. Meanwhile, both in the church and in the wider cultural

---

[1] *WB*, pp. 205, 202. Italics are James'.
[2] *Prag*, p. 297. Italics are James'.                [3] Ibid.

situation the post-Kantian battle between formalism and its critics continued inconclusively apace. The church, on the whole, adhered to the formalistic tradition while assorted varieties of empiricists, pragmatists, naturalists, and positivists (soon greatly to multiply) left both the formalistic tradition and the church farther and farther behind. Broadly speaking, up to the First World War, people who were intimately or even remotely influenced by the church tended on the whole to be governed by the maxims of the categorical imperative in the apologetic which they made for their conduct, if not in their conduct itself. Since the First World War, on the other hand, people intimately or even remotely influenced by the church have tended more and more toward the view that if the Christian life is recommended as one of pure ethical possibilities, whether of ends or of motives, this proves nothing so much as that the minister is living in another world, which nobody who is anybody nowadays is really interested in. This statistical circumstance does not, of course, establish the adequacy of ethical relativism, but it does provide a warning against misreading the ethical situation in which we find ourselves. As regards that situation, it may be said that relativism has made its case—at least a very important part of the case. It is impossible any longer to go back to an ethic of the categorical imperative, or of a fixed and theologically established end or goal of behavior. The relativistic protest against the formalism of traditional ethics, against the widening gap in that tradition between the ethical demand and the ethical act, is irrevocable.

But there is another and no less significant aspect of the case for ethical relativism: the case for relativism has been no sooner made than overtaken. It is beginning to be plain that if we are to do justice to ethical reality, some structure or pattern or framework in terms of which behavior can be interpreted and guided must be provided. In how far this 'post-relativistic' ethical situation can be derived from the fact that meanwhile the world has been ravaged by another global conflict is perhaps impossible to determine. Nevertheless, the Second World War hastened the decline of easygoing relativistic self-confidence. It also exposed the logical trickery by which ever and again it was thought possible to dispose of relativism by the cliché that 'every relative presupposes some kind of absolute'. The fact is that the manifold of behavioral options has itself been sharpening the question of a behavioral sense of direction. In this situation, if Christians continue to expound the bearing of the gospel upon behavior in such a way as to take no serious account of ethical relativism, they will be not only talking nonsense to people but deserting them at a critical moment of their own search for a way of life. 'Or what man of you, if his son asks him for bread will give him a stone? Or if he asks for a fish, will give him a serpent?'[1]

[1] Matt. 7.9-10 (RSV).

# VIII

## THE POWERS OF MAN

THE attempt of the philosophical moralists to get beyond both Kantianism and relativism in ethics has markedly altered the climate within which ethical thinking is being and can be done. Old problems have not been discarded. They are being radically restated. A new context has emerged: the resurgence of ethical humanism. An energetic and penetrating analysis of the powers of man has broken through and broken away from the tranquil diversity and movement of a pluralistic universe, shattered its melioristic theism, shunned its positivistic oversimplifications, and proposed a more radical correction of 'radical empiricism' with its context of relations, 'the company in which the thing known is received'.[1] Consequently, philosophical ethics has acquired fresh data and terms of discussion, and Christian ethics has been confronted by a vigorous and persuasive critic and rival. Ethical humanism does not reject relativism. It corrects relativism by taking constructive account of ethical pluralism. Ethical humanism does not reject absolutism. It corrects absolutism by taking constructive account of the ethical requisites of behavior: flexibility, direction, and goal.

Meanwhile, Christian thinking about ethics has not been merely awaiting the next philosophical move. Christian ethical analysis has also been engaged in the attempt to get beyond Kantianism and relativism in ethics.[2] And from its own point

[1] Ralph Barton Perry, 'The Philosophy of William James', in *Present Philosophical Tendencies*, Longmans, Green and Company, New York and London, 1929, pp. 356-57.

[2] E.g., notably by Karl Barth, *Kirchliche Dogmatik*, Evangelischer Verlag, Zollikon-Zuerich, II/2, 1942, III/4, 1951, IV/4, 1959; Dietrich Bonhoeffer, *Ethik*, Chr. Kaiser, Muenchen, 1949; N. H. Søe, *Christliche Ethik*, Chr. Kaiser, Muenchen, 1949; and Helmut Thielicke, *Theologische Ethik*, J. C. B. Mohr, Tuebingen, Bd. I, 1951, Bd. II/1, 1955.

of view and presuppositions Christian ethics has been steadily moving toward an encounter with resurgent humanism. The time has come to raise the issue directly and to face it frankly. Otherwise Christian and philosophical ethics cannot be clearly or correctly related and differentiated. And failing this, the cogency and commendability of a *koinonia* ethic cannot be understood.

The special force of humanism—and with more than one occasional explicit or implicit allusion to Christian ethics—has been brilliantly and cogently expounded in two widely different treatments of the theme. The implications are as tempting as they are enormous. The battle indeed is on! We may begin with the one most readily suited to the immediate course of our discussion, a contemporary statement of a *metaphysic of morals* called *Man's Freedom*, by Paul Weiss of Yale University.[1]

### 1  *The Powers of Man: Freedom*

As Aristotle and Kant before him have done, Professor Weiss also has set out from 'things known to us'. And like his predecessors, he seeks to keep analysis and observation rigorously together. 'A careful inquiry presupposes nothing beyond what is required to explain fully what is observed.'[2] But unlike Aristotle and Kant, what Weiss observes enables him to avoid the polarity between the ethical object and the ethical subject which has foredoomed the tradition of moral philosophy to its own insufficiency. According to Weiss, what is really most known to us is not that we are rational animals or agents of a principle of volition but that we are human beings, characterized by a particular kind of wholeness called 'human nature'. 'Human nature' is compounded of a complex of needs and aspirations, purposes and passions, and a context of interconnected relationships and possibilities. 'A man', he declares, 'is a being in double disequilibrium, with an essence partly in the future and an existence partly at a distance. He recovers the one in part in the form of a guiding meaning, the other in the form of a limiting status. The more of the meaning and the

---

[1] Paul Weiss, *Man's Freedom*, Yale University Press, New Haven, 1950 (The University Press, Oxford, 1950).

[2] Ibid., p. 27.

higher the status he achieves, the more mature he is, for he thereby makes himself from within one with what he is from without.'[1]

As beings of this sort in this kind of situation, 'men make ethical judgments all the time'.[2] The judgments and the human situation underlying and expressed in them constitute the 'ethical facts' which are at once the substance of humanity and the starting point of valid ethical analysis. 'Man', says Weiss, 'makes himself . . . and . . . in a nature permeated by values.'[3] What this ethical activity and its context are like is described in a forceful passage as follows:

> Wanton murder, injustice, betrayal are absolutely wrong, all of us believe. The wrongness, all of us hold, does not depend on how we happen to judge such acts; it is not jeopardized by changes in customs or morality, by shifts in goals or in the nature of our chosen ultimate ends. These acts are essentially wrong, intrinsically wrong; they and wrongness together make an irreducible ethical fact which it would be folly to deny. He who does not know such facts, who does not know that peace is good, that the world is not the best possible and should be improved, that men can be guilty for crimes committed years ago, that love is better than hate, is insincere or mad. Or so we all believe, and many of us say.[4]

We begin here to come in sight of the way to put the directional and the diverse factors in behavior together. The *judgment* and the *act* of wrongness are inseparable and irreducible; and the fact that this irreducibility marks merely the beginning, not the conclusion, of a course of ethical reflection opens up a way of doing justice to the absolutist and relativistic ethical concerns, while avoiding playing the one off against the other. 'The true question is: what ought to be accepted, what ought to be rejected as ultimate ethical fact? Not, are there ultimate ethical facts?'[5] The trouble with Aristotle's eudemonism was, according to Weiss, that it universalized as absolute ethical fact a supreme Good and a scheme of values correlative with it which were really the values of well-born Greeks who had reached middle age. 'We cannot', he says in the course of this amusing aside, 'start anywhere but at the place where we now are. That means that whatever now appears to be an ethical fact must be a datum with which the inquiry must begin.'[6]

---

[1] Weiss, ibid., p. 23. This formulation is strikingly reminiscent of the point with which Reinhold Niebuhr's Gifford Lectures begin.

[2] Ibid., p. 178.    [3] Ibid.    [4] Ibid., p. 179.    [5] Ibid., p. 182.    [6] Ibid.

*a. The quest for ultimate ethical fact*

The quest for ultimate ethical fact provides the principal substance of Professor Weiss' ethics. Not all ethical facts are ultimate and unimpeachable. 'The decision as to what to take as basic truth must be forged by each man in a living act of inquiry. . . .'[1] Such a living act of inquiry is neither an ethical abstraction nor ethically neutral. The particular connection between human nature and the nature of things is established by the 'double disequilibrium' in which man finds himself and whereby he 'makes himself from within one with what he is from without'. This same 'double disequilibrium' makes it possible 'in a living act of inquiry' to establish the objectivity of values—indeed, to establish it in such a way as to take full account of the relativity of values. Weiss declares that 'because inquiry has value, . . . because the values it presupposes are interlocked with the natures of the things with which it is concerned, values must be recognized to be objective, grounding the reality of ethical facts'.[2] Relativity is no more to be identified with subjectivity than objectivity is to be identified with an unvarying absolute value. 'The relativist and the absolutist can be reconciled by recognizing that the standard may be known without being known in detail, and that general principles have diverse, and sometimes even conflicting illustrations.'[3]

According to Weiss, Plato and implicitly Christian theology from Origen to Calvin have gone too far in their account of the nature of the Good and of ethical obligation. Their insistence that the Good cannot be benefited by man but man is benefited by the Good has tended to exalt selfishness. Furthermore, their insistence upon evil as privation of good has put man in the erroneous ethical position in which the more he desires the Good, the more he must be evil, since desire itself betokens a lack and is therefore bad. The relationship which Weiss sees between ethical judgments and ethical action enables him, on the contrary, to insist that since men desire a goodness which they do not have, they are to be regarded not as evil but as good. Perfection, moreover, is good not in the sense of being finished and complete but as an ideal which becomes perfected in the course of its being realized. 'The good', he declares, 'is

---

[1] Weiss, ibid., p. 183.    [2] Ibid.    [3] Ibid., p. 191.

not very good. Perfection is not perfect. Nor is humanity human, thoughtfulness thoughtful, honesty honest. Plato was misled by words when he held that the good was good, holiness holy, and the idea of dirt somehow dirty.'[1]

Thus Weiss proposes that the ideal of perfection is meaningful because it expresses the relationship between the absolute and the relative. 'The concern for perfection', he observes, 'is a dynamic relation between two beings, one concrete and here, the other abstract and remote. The concern draws the two together, enriching the one and promoting actions which draw them still closer together.'[2] In this relationship—between God and the soul, between the perfect and the imperfect, between the ultimate and the proximate, between the ground of being and value and ethical facts—the good is a standard of excellence for all and functions as such a standard. 'The standard is a universal, a meaning, an object of reason which though related to actual values, transcends and tests them all, and can be obtained by abstracting the constant value which everyone incorporates. It has application to all things and to all situations in which they find themselves, being the meaning which all contain and ought to exhibit. It provides a basis for judging men, societies, sub-human beings . . . and is invoked by every man and grasped to some degree by each at every moment.'[3]

Having established a meaningful and actual relation between the absolute and the relative, between perfection and the lesser actions which compose the process of realizing perfection, Weiss addresses himself to the problem of working out a formulation of this viable good. He calls the formulation 'the primary ethical principle', and it serves as his counterpart to 'the golden mean', and 'the categorical imperative', as the 'right rule' for governing action according to reason. In a notable reversal of the Kantian inference that 'I ought, therefore I can', Weiss infers that 'I can, therefore I ought'. Since the perfection possible to a being ought to be realized in it, 'some being must, through the use of a single all-inclusive possibility, convert the often opposing possibilities of the rest into a single harmonious totality of inter-related possibilities'.[4] Man is this being and this is the office of selfhood. Man makes ethics possible because only man makes himself responsible for what ought to be.

[1] Weiss, ibid., p. 193.     [2] Ibid.     [3] Ibid., p. 197.     [4] Ibid., p. 201.

What, then, is 'the primary ethical principle' according to which the good is to be realized in action? Here the rigorous logic of man's freedom is fully exposed to view. Weiss defines 'the primary ethical principle' in terms of the proposition 'it is absolutely wrong to reduce values'.[1] He tries to show that this proposition admits of no exceptions in logic and in act by demonstrating that the proposition 'it is absolutely wrong to reduce values' is equivalent to the proposition 'it is absolutely wrong to kill a friend wantonly'.[2] The affirmations that 'it is absolutely *right* to kill a friend wantonly' and that 'it is absolutely *right* to reduce values' are statements of actions which attempt to destroy the good which they presuppose and so are meaningless. Since man is both a doer of the good and the being with reference to whom the good alone has meaning and value, to kill a friend wantonly is the equivalent of a reduction of value in the ultimate sense. Man 'introduces a new dimension into existence, the dimension of objective though relationally determined ethical values. . . .'[3] The principle that 'it is absolutely wrong to kill a friend wantonly' not only expresses 'an irreducible ethical fact [a fact of judgment and of action] which it would be folly to deny'.[4] It also offers a regulative principle for the realization of the good by directing behavior away from the reduction and toward the increase of value, the increase of value being the objectively established absolute good.

Professor Weiss has provided a post-relativistic metaphysic of morals which must be taken very seriously indeed. Here is a precise and formidable logical resolution of the ambiguity and polarity between the absolute and the relative, between the directional and the diverse actualities and requirements of human behavior. The objectivity of values is grounded in a contextual rather than a speculative conjunction of reason with reality. The ethical object and the ethical subject are both included in an observable human activity which converts all possibilities of judgment and action into 'a single harmonious totality of inter-related possibilities'. Man makes ethics. This is the new dimension both of ethical reality and of ethical reflection in consequence of which ethical behavior and ethical analysis are conjoined in 'a living act of inquiry'. Thus ethics

[1] Weiss, ibid., p. 215.    [2] Ibid., p. 213.    [3] Ibid., p. 203.
[4] Ibid., p. 179.

embodies the secret of man's freedom, which is also the secret of human maturity. The primary ethical principle that 'it is absolutely wrong to reduce values' unites both the universality and the humanity expressed in the maxims of the categorical imperative under a nonlegalistic, humanly concrete rule of reason. Adhering to this principle, man can find his way from one context of values to another in the steady realization of that wholeness wherein he 'makes himself from within one with what he is from without'.

Unlike Aristotle, for whom the religious question, that is, the question of the relation between the good life and the nature and activity of God, remained an open question,[1] and unlike Kant, whose ethics was broadly affected by Christian teaching and at the close virtually crossed over into Christian territory, Professor Weiss so sharply draws the distinction between religion and ethics as to deprive religion of ethical significance. 'Since the good is pertinent to every possibility and fact, ethics has a cosmic sweep, an unlimited scope of application. Its range is as wide as that of physics or chemistry, but unlike them it tells us of a world which exists only so long as there are men. Its penetration is as deep as that of psychology and religion, but unlike them it tells us of a world which is not centered in man or in God. Ethics comes to be and passes away with man, the being who is at his best when he knows himself to be responsible for the universal realization of the absolute good.'[2]

## b. The problem of evil

What is surprising about such a resolute disjunction of religion from ethics is not that it has been made. The preoccupation of ethical humanism with the powers of man could scarcely be expected to come out anywhere else. In addition to its meticulous cogency, the impressive thing about Professor Weiss' account of ethics is its integrity. He does not play fast and loose with the tradition he frankly sets out to correct and extend. *Man's Freedom* offers us an improvement upon Kant in terms of a quasi-Aristotelian model, without ignoring William James' attempt to get beyond Kant upon a model of scientific empiri-

[1] W. D. Ross, *Aristotle*, Methuen and Company, London, 1923, Introduction, pp. xii, xxi.
[2] Weiss, op. cit., p. 202.

cism. We are prepared, therefore, for the rupture of the tenuous link between religion and ethics. What we are not prepared for, however, is Professor Weiss' forceful exhibition of the fact that an ethic separated from religion will find it necessary to deny the radicality of evil. On the boundary of the constructive analysis and the concluding implications of *his* metaphysics of morals, the crucial issue dividing Christian from philosophical thinking about ethics sharply emerges. Like Banquo's ghost, Kant suddenly and eerily obtrudes upon an all but finished enterprise of human power.

We have already seen that Kant had to capitulate to what Aristotle tried to domesticate. Weiss does not capitulate but tries to be casual about what he knows better than to try. Evil is not to be domesticated but explained. And ironically enough, the explanation begins exactly where and why Kant had concluded that no explanation was possible. The locus is the conjunction of the will in the exercise of its creative freedom with 'the insistencies of things; their claim to have a nature and future of their own' which 'so far as they insist on themselves, ... oppose the reassessment we make of them and are so far in conflict with us, evil'.[1] And the why of it, the reason for attempting to explore and explain this conjunction is that 'evil is that which ought not to be. Its occurrence anywhere is sufficient to raise the whole problem of evil and thereby make pertinent the question of what ought to be, why what ought to be does not exist, and what we, with our wills, can do about it'.[2]

Like Kant, but unlike Aristotle and James, Weiss admits that evil is tragic. It is the human struggle between good willed and evil done that makes it so.[3] Like Aristotle and James, but unlike

---

[1] Weiss, ibid., pp. 237-38.    [2] Ibid., p. 238.

[3] In a passage remarkably reminiscent of the description by St Paul of the internal human conflict between good and evil in the seventh chapter of Romans, Professor Weiss declares that 'we constantly commit absolute wrongs in the endeavor to do what is relatively right, and we constantly do what is relatively wrong in doing what is absolutely right. That conflict is inevitable; it is part of the tragedy of man.' Ibid., p. 221. The allusion is rightly unacknowledged. But the question is the more appropriate whether the oversight is due solely or even mainly to the semantic difference between descriptive and confessional statements. It could be that something like a suppression of the confessional dimension in ethical analysis has occurred arising from the marked contextual difference between a metaphysic of morals and a theological ethic.

Kant, evil, for Weiss, does not call into question the ethical enterprise itself, whether as a search for the Good or as a valuation and validation of the powers of man. 'We are left with the alternative that the totality of things and futures has the character of being good. Unlike the evil, that good requires no reference beyond itself.'[1] Unlike Aristotle, Kant, and James, Weiss affirms that an explanation of evil not only cannot be avoided, it can be arrived at, and without reference to God. 'Without turning to God, we can ask the question what relation evil has to good and seem able to answer the question without having to leave the cosmos in which the question was framed.'[2]

As Weiss sees it, evil can be explained because a metaphysic of morals can demonstrate by its own analysis of the observed and the possible that evil is ontologically necessary but not ontologically ultimate. Evil *is* that which ought not to be. But to explain evil as simply correlative with the good is too simple. I still recall from my own initial studies in ethics in the University that it was seriously proposed in effect that 'after all without evil one could not appreciate the good'. The suggestion seemed to me then, as now, specious. It involved an *ad hominem* accommodation to the ugly facts of life that was as misleading as it was neat. It let *me* off too easily; and in addition, the suggestion concealed the failure to distinguish between the order of knowing (*ratio cognoscendi*) and the order of reality (*ratio essendi*). Happily Professor Weiss does not resort to this. 'The *knowledge* of the good', he remarks, 'may perhaps require a reference to a contrasting evil, though this is questionable.'[3] The crucial point affecting the explanation of evil is that evil is both a fact of human action and a natural occurrence. To paraphrase Weiss, evil is both *valuationally* and *ontologically* necessary, but valuational and ontological evil are not necessarily identical.[4]

*Valuationally necessary* evils are those which are 'indispensable instruments for the production of good. . . . Health points up the value of life, disease the value of health.' Of such evils, each of us could make his own list. But these evils, though they may never disappear from the human condition, are 'not ontologically necessary since the universe could continue even though

[1] Weiss, ibid., p. 246.    [2] Ibid., p. 238.    [3] Ibid., p. 246.
[4] Ibid., pp. 238ff.

they were absent'. There is something *intrinsic* about evil, 'evils which remain evils whether needed or not'. It is this *intrinsic evil* which Professor Weiss explains with reference to its ontologically necessary function.

*Ontologically necessary* evil is the evil 'necessary to make a universe be'.[1] The human and cosmic aspects of evil are subsumed under a universe of possibilities and actualities the ultimate referent of which is the absolute Good. To this Good, evil cannot be evil unless it can be referred. And contrariwise, 'the goodness of the universe depends for its possibility on limited defective goods inside it. The universe is good only because there are evils in it.'[2] We must be careful not to identify ontologically necessary evil with natural evil, still less with human evils. The sober fact is that 'insistencies happen to conflict with insistencies' in a universe to which both primary ethical facts and these insistencies *eo ipso* belong. To deny this is to leave not only reason and goodness behind but reality itself, 'to begin a process of alienation from the land of consistent living and almost always end in a spiritual and sometimes in a physical death'.[3] To do this is to commit Professor Weiss' version of sin.

Thus on the boundary of the constructive and the concluding sections of this metaphysic of morals the instructive question is sharply posed: Has Kant, who surrendered consistency of ethical analysis to the radicality of evil, given us a profounder grasp of the dimensions of the ethical problem than Weiss, who has surrendered the radicality of evil to consistency of ethical analysis? Banquo's ghost may stalk the powers of man unburied until man learns that evil spirit 'has a this-worldly reference always, and is concerned with the good open to reason'.[4] On the other hand, there may be a kinship between evil spirit and the spirit of evil—what the New Testament calls 'the spiritual hosts of wickedness in the heavenly places'[5]—which points not to a witch's caldron boiling away on some craggy fastness of the barren human story but to a burial 'where no one had ever been laid'.[6] Kant, it will be recalled, acknowledged that he had inadvertently encountered the Fourth Gospel.[7]

As for Weiss, there is some unsteadiness attending his attempt

---

[1] Weiss, ibid., p. 247.      [2] Ibid.      [3] Ibid., pp. 248-49.
[4] Ibid., p. 249.    [5] Eph. 6.12.    [6] John 19.41.    [7] See above, p. 183.

to adhere consistently to 'the good open to reason'. It is not precisely clear how the ontological correlation of good with evil avoids the triteness of the conventional dictum that evil is necessary to appreciate the Good. The *ratio essendi* of the matter may be more subtle than the *ratio cognoscendi* of it. Yet, if goodness depends upon evil, even though only for its possibility, and even though only upon limited evil, it would seem that there must be evil after all in order to appreciate the Good. The logical priority and the wider range of good over evil do not exclude the determinate correlation, according to which evil is as necessary to good as good is necessary to evil.

Weiss is careful to say that evil is necessary, *not* to make *goodness* be, but 'to make a *universe* be'.[1] He is likewise careful *not* to say explicitly that goodness is necessary to make a universe be. In such a universe, one can understand that there are evils and goods in correlative disequilibrium. One can understand also how in such a universe good and evil are necessary existents. But how a universe can include the cosmos and the Good (and necessary evil) without being itself ethically indifferent or without involving a trans-ethical referent—*this* is not understandable. A trans-ethical referent does not involve, as Weiss with pejorative delicacy seems to assume, 'having to leave the cosmos in which the question was framed' any more than a shift from cosmos to universe involves such a departure. On the contrary, every analysis of the problem posed for the Good by the fact of evil—e.g., the integrity of the Good is called into question—involves a transvaluational thrust beyond good and evil. This is the point which both Jesus and Nietzsche have seen more clearly than Weiss, more steadily than Kant, and more soberly than Aristotle or James.

Weiss wants to explain that evil is 'required by the nature of beings, and . . . why this should be' so.[2] Yet to set *God* aside as a hindrance[3] and propose that *the universe* be accepted as a present help in time of trouble seems anticlimactic indeed. By Weiss' own admission *the universe* is supposed to be 'the whole good' which unites the richness, concreteness, and vitality of the cosmos with the abstract, all-inclusive, and indefinite dura-

---

[1] Weiss, op. cit., p. 247. But this paragraph especially is based upon the whole of chap. 17.

[2] Ibid., p. 241.          [3] Compare, for example, ibid., pp. 191-92, 241-42.

tion of absolute Good.[1] But by the time his 'explanation of evil' has reached the height of this olympian omniscience, the sobriety of his own formulation of the problem of evil has been dissipated by another anticlimax. If the problem of evil is the problem of the conflict of 'creative will' with the 'insistencies of things', and if man is the focus of creative will and the cosmos is the focus of the insistencies of things, it is hard to see how an appeal to the universe can persuade man that the life of virtue is an attractive alternative to the continuing triumph of insistency over creativity. A speculatively consistent case for the good life in a universe of necessary evil may be the best that reason can do. But is this kind of consistency humanly compelling? 'To have the will operate as it should,' Professor Weiss declares, men 'must become virtuous. Lacking virtue they may do much that is good, though this is not likely. Possessing virtue they will still fail to do much that they ought, though they usually will do more good than most. In any case, the evil which they produce they can make less or more, as they will.'[2] How *can* they, if the 'insistencies of things' are insistent enough to come into conflict with creative will? Or is it rather that the conflict lies within the will itself, between the will's insistent and its creative willing? In either case, to urge that men must become virtuous if the will is to operate as it should is idle; to tell them that they can alter the evil which they produce as they will is folly. Caught between a counsel of prudence and a counsel of perfection, virtue has become as pale a shadow of its goodly state as decorum is a pallid form of value.

Professor Weiss' explanation, far from domesticating evil, domesticates creativity instead. One wonders, on this basis, why evil should ever have occurred to men as anything other than a 'built-in' hindrance to creative will, above all as a problem calling into question the significance of creativity itself.

The religion which Kant vainly strove to identify as intrinsic to his analysis of man's freedom was Christianity. The religion which Weiss categorically rejects as irrelevant to his analysis of man's freedom is Christianity. The coincidence is traceable not merely to the ethical story of the Western intellectual tradition. It is due to a decisive issue of ethical substance. The problem of evil marks a fork in the road. The crucial question is *What*

[1] Weiss, ibid., p. 245.    [2] Ibid., p. 251.

*context of ethical analysis is required by an authentic account of man's freedom?*

We may pass over the careless reading of Christian theology which allows Professor Weiss to venture upon a dubious distinction between the writers of theologies and of theodicies.[1] And we may hope that our own reading of Professor Weiss and of the philosophical moralists has been more circumspect. But what cannot be overlooked is the extraordinary suggestion that 'theologies tend to confuse the fact of evil with an origin; theodicies tend to confuse the fact of evil with its locus'.[2] On the record, the facts are quite otherwise. The facts are that theologies have been unable to ignore theodicies and theodicies have been unable to ignore theologies because the radicality of evil does not yield to a reductionist return to 'the land of consistent living'. Consistency of ethical analysis serves in this instance as a disguised route ahead. The fact is that evil aggravates rather than diminishes the concern about its origin *and* locus and ultimately defies both confusion and suppression. Indeed, this is precisely why evil is *radical* rather than explainable, why 'the good open to reason' cannot quiet the question whether *reason* is open to the good. The radicality of evil resists the rationality of evil. The radicality of evil sharpens the urgency of another perspective from which a context may be derived within which to deal both with evil and with good.

Thus the metaphysical humanism of *Man's Freedom* stands in sharpest possible opposition to the methodological and substantive concern of Christian ethics with the freedom of the Christian man, with the maturity for which Christ has set all men free.

### 2 The Powers of Man: Mature Self-Love

The special force of humanism is its persuasive proximity to and sharp rejection of the Christian ethic. Christian and ethical humanism regard the same issues as central so that the decisive question between them has to do with the radicality of their respective probings of ethical reality. Professor Weiss has left us

---

[1] Weiss, ibid., pp. 242-43. One carelessness leads to another. Thus Augustine is counted as a writer of theology although a view which Augustine also held is ascribed to the theodicies.

[2] Ibid., p. 243.

in no doubt about which way the course of wisdom and of good-ness points. Yet the robust intellectual effort required of those who seek to live by his counsel is likely to be less congenial, if not less valid, than is another kind of humanism more widely known, and certainly more readily appealing as a recipe for living. Depth-psychological humanism is significant not only as another attempt to get beyond ethical relativism. It is also the most important alternative to Christian ethics confronting our contemporaries. A persuasive statement of this alternative has been made by Erich Fromm.[1]

Dr Fromm has provided his discussion with the subtitle 'An Inquiry into the Psychology of Ethics'. 'I have written this book', he explains, 'with the intention of re-affirming the validity of humanist ethics, to show that our knowledge of human nature does not lead to ethical relativism, but on the contrary that the sources of norms for ethical conduct are to be found in man's nature itself; that moral norms are based upon man's inherent quality, and that their violation results in mental and emotional disintegration.'[2] On the basis of clinical evidence, Fromm is saying that ethical relativism, which offers no clearly defined way of giving ethical superiority to one course of action rather than another, is not supported by the facts of human nature. What is equally important, however, is that Fromm is persuaded that the alternative to relativism is not a religious ethics but the view that moral norms are based upon inherent qualities in man himself. It is the violation of *human nature* which constitutes an unethical, or immoral, action or situation. 'Not self-renunciation nor selfishness but self-love, not the negation of the individual but the affirmation of his truly human self, are the supreme values of humanistic ethics.'[3] As these are the virtues of humanistic ethics, 'vice' is in the last analysis in-difference to one's own self and any form of self-mutilation.

Clinical evidence, moreover, has confirmed for Dr Fromm the fact that the most serious distortion of ethical understanding and power comes not from moral philosophy but from religion.

---

[1] Erich Fromm, *Man for Himself*, Rinehart and Company, New York, 1947 (Routledge, London, 1949). I mean that depth-psychological humanism is the most persuasive contemporary rival of Christian ethics, not necessarily Fromm's own statement of this humanism.

[2] Ibid., p. 7.                    [3] Ibid.

There is an irreconcilable opposition between humanistic ethics and authoritarian ethics. The great representative of authoritarian ethics is religious ethics—specifically, Christian ethics; and among the varieties of Christian ethics, it is the Protestant Christian version of authoritarian ethics which Fromm resolutely opposes.

Some of the contrasts which he suggests between 'humanistic ethics' and 'authoritarian ethics' are these: According to 'humanistic ethics', virtue is synonymous with the maturity appropriate to each individual character structure; according to 'authoritarian ethics', virtue is synonymous with self-denial and obedience, with the consequent suppression of individuality. Again, 'humanistic ethics' is anthropocentric; 'authoritarian ethics' is centered beyond man, whether in God or in something else. 'Humanistic ethics' is really concerned with the applied science, as Fromm says, 'of the art of living'; and the chief difficulty with an 'authoritarian ethic' is that the source of ethical concern and motivation is outside of man himself. 'Humanistic ethics', he declares, 'is the affirmation of life, the unfolding of man's powers. Virtue is responsibility toward his own existence. Evil constitutes the crippling of man's powers; vice is irresponsibility toward himself.'[1]

This discussion of *Man for Himself* deals forthrightly with a problem which has centrally engaged and perplexed Christian ethical theory, namely, the problem of the relationship between self-love and the love of the neighbor, or altruistic love. According to Fromm, authoritarian ethics makes the great mistake of supposing that self-love is in itself ethically negative; it spends all its energies trying to advise, threaten, cajole, or educate people in the possibilities of *not* loving themselves. Such an enterprise is, in Fromm's judgment, psychologically impossible and is therefore the breeding ground of all sorts of ethical confusion and hypocrisy. 'The first "duty" of an organism is to be alive.'[2] To live is to grow; and for man to be alive is to grow toward maturity.

### a. The task of humanistic ethics

The task of humanistic ethics is to describe man's growth toward maturity and to analyze the structure within and

[1] Fromm, ibid., p. 20.　　　　　　　　[2] Ibid., p. 19.

according to which this growth may be understood and directed. 'The subject matter of ethics is character, and only in reference to the character structure as a whole can value statements be made about single traits and actions.'[1] Although psychoanalytic characterology is still in its infancy, Fromm believes that it is from the insights of psychoanalysis that we derive the necessary knowledge for the development of a mature character structure.

Not all character structures make for maturity. Dr Fromm distinguishes between what he calls the 'non-productive' and the 'productive' character structures. 'Non-productive' character structures are those which find the source of good ouside man, with the consequent depreciation of man's ethical significance. Fromm indicates four types of nonproductive character structures: 'receptive', exploitive', 'hoarding', and 'marketing'.[2] The 'receptive' character structure is marked by the tendency to regard the achievement of maturity or of the good as a gift; the 'exploitive' by the tendency to regard the achievement of maturity or of the good in terms of prestige or property or power and the like. The 'hoarding' character structure inverts the direction of its search for maturity or the good. It erects as it were a 'protective wall' against the outside world, hoarding and saving (thoughts and feelings as well as money and things), while regarding spending itself as a threat to its security. And the 'marketing' character structure, which is the most dominant in our time, tends to transform the achievement of maturity or the good from a human to a commodity value.[3]

Productive character structures, on the other hand, find the source of good in man. 'Productiveness is man's ability to use his powers and to realize the potentialities inherent in him.'[4] It is the necessity and the possibility of a productive character structure that leads Fromm to his version of the 'right rule' for the guidance of behavior toward its end or goal. Aristotle, it will be recalled, had said that '*virtue is a mean* between excess and defect'. Kant had arrived at the categorical imperative and its maxims from the premise '*I ought, therefore I can*'. Professor Weiss has reversed the Kantian aphorism so that, according to him, '*I can, therefore I ought*'; I ought to live by the principle that 'it is absolutely wrong to reduce values'. In his turn, and with

[1] Fromm, ibid., p. 33.    [2] Ibid., pp. 114-16.    [3] Ibid., pp. 62-67.
[4] Ibid., p. 84.

clinical rather than metaphysical evidence before him, Fromm affirms that human personality achieves maturity in and through its behavior—that is to say, '*I am what I do*'.

By this rule, a human individual on the way to maturity may realize the principal secret and fruit of maturity, namely, the productive relationship between love of self and love of neighbor. According to a widespread misconception, Dr Fromm points out, people seem to feel that the chief difficulty in loving is the difficulty of 'being loved'. The fact of the matter, however, is the contrary. The real difficulty with the development of a productive character structure is the achievement of self-love, without which there can be no authentic love of neighbor. 'The doctrine that love for oneself is identical with "selfishness" and an alternative to love for others has pervaded theology, philosophy, and popular thought. . . . [But] love of others and love of ourselves are not alternatives. On the contrary, an attitude of love toward themselves will be found in all those who are capable of loving others. Love, in principle, is indivisible as far as the connection between "objects" and one's own self is concerned.'[1] Self-love is simply the affirmation in thought and practice of man's true self, that is, of his powers and capacities for human growth. Far from implying egotism, psychoanalytic characterology establishes the fact that the love of neighbor is intrinsic to the self-love inherent in man.[2] Thus it is humanistic ethics, not Christian ethics, which meaningfully and fruitfully resolves the problem of love.

### b. *The precariousness of humanistic ethics*

Fromm is not unmindful of the fact that this achievement of humanistic ethics is a precarious achievement. Indeed, with less confidence than Professor Weiss in what man ultimately may be able to achieve, with something of Aristotle's sense of ethical tentativeness and complexity, and with Immanuel Kant's sense of the empirical dubiousness of the good will, Fromm acknowledges that man's powers of self-realization may never quite reach their goal. The reason is that human existence is involved not only in growth but also in 'dichotomy'. Broadly speaking,

[1] Fromm, ibid., pp. 127-30.

[2] Ibid., pp. 97ff., 130ff. See also Erich Fromm, *Psychoanalysis and Religion*, Yale University Press, New Haven, 1950, pp. 86-90.

there are two kinds of dichotomies: 'historical' and 'existential'. 'Historical' dichotomies are temporary and, for all practical purposes, resolvable by the next generation if not by the one in which they appear. The struggle for racial justice in the United States, which has moved in law from segregation to 'separate but equal' to 'integration', might be a case in point. It is a 'dichotomy' because very deeply rooted human divisions over the path to maturity are involved. But it is 'historical', and so temporary, because the steady growth of human capacity for self-realization overcomes the obstacles in its path. So in many ways the vices of one generation become the virtues of the next. But the converse also happens, and this may be understood with reference to the 'existential dichotomies' which beset human life. 'Existential dichotomies' are more serious because they are ineradicable and call in question the foundations and prospects of humanistic ethics. Fromm enumerates three 'existential dichotomies', namely, the dichotomy beween life and death; between actual and potential realization; and between solitude and society.[1] Death contradicts life in a radical way so that growth toward maturity is always exposed to the peril of being robbed at any moment of its fruit. Similarly, even within the boundaries of life and death the achievement of maturity is always more potential than actual, more coming to pass than actually at hand. And while the love of neighbor may be inherent in man, every human individual knows the experience of being never so lonely as when in a crowd. The bridge between the maturity of a single individual and the maturity of all individuals is a suspension bridge with heavily congested traffic. The traffic may never reach the other side, and if it does, the other side may be a destination other than the one originally in view when making the crossing.

These dichotomies introduce a great sobriety into the enterprise of humanistic ethics. But they do not invalidate it, according to Fromm, because the facts of human nature are as they are, and this is the reality with which ethics is intrinsically concerned and which in turn gives to ethics its reality. The development of a mature character structure offers a framework or orientation of behavior which does not require the certainty of consummation for the validation of its dynamic

[1] Fromm, *Man for Himself*, pp. 42-44.

sense of responsibility. It is enough that human nature inherently offers a clear good, namely, the affirmation of life, the unfolding of man's powers; a clear way of pursuing the Good, namely, a development by psychoanalytic self-understanding of a mature character structure; and a clear way of keeping the directional and the diverse factors of behavior together. It is enough to know that 'I am what I do' and to do what I am.

The special force of humanism as the most formidable alternative for those who attempt to think about and to deal with ethical problems as Christians is plain. No longer will it suffice for Christians simply to say that humanistic ethics rests upon an optimistic view of human nature, or that humanistic ethics dispenses with revelation. Fromm is even more concretely aware than is Professor Weiss of the immense complexity and ambiguity of the human struggle toward maturity. Moreover, humanistic ethics, at least in Fromm's version, is an explicitly *indicative* and not an imperative ethics. Indeed, it is precisely at this point that the critical confrontation of Christian ethics by humanistic ethics emerges. Can Christian ethics admit the stricture which Fromm makes against authoritarian—against all characteristically imperative—ethics, namely, that it prevents human maturity by nonproductive character orientation? If so, is it possible then for a Christian ethic so to explore and to implement its own indicative character as to show how and in what sense it is in religion, specifically in Christianity and not in humanism, that the maturity of human personality, of which the Letter to the Ephesians also speaks, is validated and fulfilled?

We have a long row to hoe. For it must be admitted that, as regards the interpretation of Christian ethics, we start with a bad case of arrested development. It may be that the indicative path to maturity is not an ethical possibility open to Christians. But a *koinonia* ethic ventures to take this calculated risk because it is hard to see how on some other basis a Christian account of behavior can be meaningfully offered and implemented. The decisive question is which option is the live option: humanistic or Christian ethics?

The claim of a *koinonia* ethic is that truth and life are in Jesus Christ; and the spelling out of what this claim involves constitutes the constructive substance of Christian ethics as *koinonia* ethics. The elaboration of what is involved in the constructive substance of a *koinonia* ethic lies beyond the scope of the present inquiry and must presuppose the methodological analysis with which these pages are concerned. Only then can a systematic exposition of the content of a Christian ethic exhibit the distinctive orientation with which the gospel provides behavior. And only in the light of such an orientation can the meaning of forgiveness and love, of love and righteousness, of the role of law in the Christian life, and of the difference which being a Christian makes in personal conduct and in social patterns and structures be intrinsically explained. Meanwhile, as regards the way Christians are to go about thinking ethically, the special force of humanism is that humanism, particularly of the depth-psychological variety, not only provides the sharpest alternative to Christian ethics but also underlines the sharp difference between Christian ethics and philosophical ethics in general.

# IX

## ON ETHICS AND LANGUAGE

BEFORE we attempt to formulate the sharp difference between Christian and philosophical ethics, we must take note of a quite different way of thinking about ethics. This way differs not only from the formative types of philosophical ethics, heretofore under consideration, but also from ways of thinking about ethics with which Christian and other moralists have made us familiar and which they have taught us to regard as appropriate. It is proposed, according to this comparatively new mode of ethical reflection, to begin at a very obvious point: the ordinary language of ethical statements.

The moot question is how far and how fruitfully this lead will take us. It is not yet possible to say whether or not the altered climate of moral philosophy is giving ground and shape to another formative type of philosophical ethics. In particular, it is too early to say whether the change in ethical mode and method is an Anglo-Saxon passion come to flower or to funeral in the United States or whether, as has been suggested, a 'second revolution' in philosophy has begun, affecting the Western intellectual tradition as a whole, and cogent and compelling enough to mark a major philosophical preoccupation of the twentieth century.[1] Meanwhile, however, in

[1] Cf. Willem F. Zuurdeeg, *An Analytical Philosophy of Religion*, Abingdon Press, New York, 1958 (Allen & Unwin, London, 1959), pp. 15-17. It depends, of course, upon how one counts. If Kant correctly estimated his own 'Copernican revolution', then Socrates could be regarded as inaugurator of the '*first* revolution', Kant of the *second*, and we should find ourselves now in the *third* revolution. If, however, the focus narrows, the perspective lengthens. If 'the history of philosophy in its relation to the sciences' is under review, a distinction might then well be made between 'modern and traditional philosophy'—the former revolutionary, the latter pre-revolu-

American colleges and universities, notably among the social psychologists, anthropologists, and philosophers, a lively curiosity is abroad about *the significance of how men say what they*

tionary. On this reckoning, the first revolution would be marked by 'the disentangling of those questions which are either empirical ... or formal ..., from the mass of problems which fill the minds of men'. Zuurdeeg here draws upon Isaiah Berlin (*The Age of the Enlightenment*, Mentor Books, New York, 1956 (Muller, London), p. 13) and adds, 'the second revolution, that of the twentieth century' which seeks to disentangle another group of questions from philosophy, viz., God, the meaning of life, what is really good, etc.

Whether or not Zuurdeeg's book will be regarded as competent by the technical philosophers of the 'second revolution' I have not myself the technical competence to say. It seems to me, however, to offer a provocative and instructive exploration of the possibilities of a dialogue between Christian thinkers and the philosophers of the 'second revolution'. Rough-hewn though it is, the book is marked by the solid excitement of a pioneering venture and stands in notable contrast to another attempt from the side of the Christian tradition to take up the conversation. Professor John Hick's *Faith and Knowledge* (Cornell University Press, Ithaca, 1957; The University Press, Oxford, 1957) may prove to have been nearer to the long-range significance of the 'second revolution'. It emanates from the inside at least of the Oxford phase of the altered mode and method of philosophy in the twentieth century, and its discussion of religious cognition is clear, crisp, and pedagogically admirable.

[1] The phrase 'analytical philosophy' has come to denote a special view of the nature, method, and task of philosophy. It may be contrasted, for example, with idealism, naturalism, empiricism, and similar 'movements' or 'schools' with which the history of philosophy is replete. In this instance it is the method which chiefly expresses the nature and task of philosophy. The method of philosophy is *analytical* rather than *formal* (rational, deductive) or *descriptive* (empirical, inductive) and narrows the task of philosophy from the investigation of the relation between reality and knowledge to the investigation of the relation between cognition and statements. Philosophy is still, by nature, the inquiry concerning what is true. But the inquiry is *functional* rather than *speculative* because truth is discoverable and definable through an analysis of its linguistic forms rather than its metaphysical character.

Within this common framework of method and aim, the analytical movement is as diverse and contentious as any philosophical movement has ever been. Its adherents would not claim that they have made philosophy so completely over as to leave it a mere shadow of its former self. Instead, they have attempted to take a fresh look at old problems and to provide stalemated issues (e.g., the one and the many, being and knowledge, mind and matter, 'is' and 'ought') with livelier prospects of significance and solution. Some contemporary analytical concerns seem to have been anti-

*think*. As regards philosophy, this curiosity means that philosophy has become *analytical*.[1] 'It is the function of philosophy to analyze languages.'[2]

Linguistic analysis began by bringing grammar to the side of logic in the definition of what is true. Forms of utterance, the structure of sentences, the variety and significance of predication prompted considerations admirably suited to a tidy journey from premises to their conclusions and a clearer indication of the relation between reasoning and its referents. Linguistic analysis seemed suited also to a promising resolution of the not always dispassionately illuminating debates among positivists, rationalists, and empiricists over the bearing of the scientific method upon the question of truth. The adopted procedure was to diversify signification and thereby to reserve 'truth-signification' for statements whose referent could be tested against empirical data and verification while assigning to other kinds of statements and their referents other kinds of signification.[3] That the procedure should dissolve metaphysics and leave theology without a conversation partner could scarcely fail to be discerned even by the slow of mind. The more alert were quick to see that here was a philosophical move designed to carry positivism beyond its restricted and polemical

cipated as early as the eighteenth century, notably by Berkeley (*A Treatise Concerning the Principles of Human Knowledge*, 1710, par. 20) and Hume (*Treatise of Human Nature*, 1728). But the analytical movement in philosophy seems traceable in the twentieth century chiefly to the work of Ludwig Wittgenstein (*Tractatus Logico-Philosophicus*, 1922; *Philosophical Investigations*, 1953) and the Oxford dons around A. J. Ayer (*Language, Truth and Logic*, Gollancz, London, 1946) and to the critical debates (during the 1930's) about logical positivism of the so-called 'Vienna Circle'. In the United States a particularly influential center of the analytical movement has developed in the Department of Philosophy at Harvard owing to the work of Willard V. O. Quine, Morton White, Henry Aiken, and Roderick Firth. Professor White and especially Aiken and Firth have been exploring the significance of the analytical philosophy for ethics. For an introductory bibliography dealing with the background, method, and problems of analytical philosophy, see Zuurdeeg, op. cit., pp. 309-11.

[1] See footnote 1 on p. 226.  [2] Zuurdeeg, op. cit., p. 13.

[3] An elaborate exposition of this procedure was put forward by C. K. Ogden and I. A. Richards in *The Meaning of Meaning*, 5th edition, Harcourt, Brace and Company, New York, 1930 (Kegan Paul, London, 1930). See also R. Carnap, *Philosophy and Logical Syntax*, Kegan Paul, Trench, Trubner Company, London, 1935.

view of signification and to provide a theoretical demonstration of the long-asserted practical irrelevance of theology. The powers of man seemed to have gained a decisive victory in the court of man's highest dignity. Reason at the service of man has been displaced by man at the service of reason.

A universe of multiple signification, however, has turned out to be less hostile to religious language than was initially claimed. God is still in exile but the boundaries are less closely guarded against him owing to a re-examination of the grounds for banishment. The revised estimate of religion is traceable in part to closely reasoned refinements of predication which have shattered the identification of what is true with what is empirically verifiable. In part, it is traceable to a fuller understanding of symbolic language.[1] But perhaps the principal route to a revised estimate of religious language has come from the investigations of ethics on the analytical model. Let us note the account of these investigations which has been given by Professor Richard B. Brandt in a book entitled *Ethical Theory*. The book is principally concerned with a *method* of ethical analysis and criticism which is identified as *meta-ethics*. Just as *meta-physics* goes beyond physics to analyze and to define the reality underlying physics, so *meta-ethics* goes beyond ethics to analyze and to define the foundations and the language of ethics.[2]

[1] One thinks, for example, of the later Wittgenstein, of John Wisdom's aphorism, for which I am indebted to Professor Hick, that the reasons for our conclusions function 'like the legs of a chair, not like the links of a chain', and, from the theological side, of A. G. N. Flew's attempted case for theism in the light of analytical philosophy. Cf. Hick, op. cit., p. 95; A. G. N. Flew, *New Essays in Philosophical Theology*, SCM Press, London, 1955.

[2] A carefully reasoned, well-documented account of this development together with a constructive suggestion as to how a 'meta-ethical' inquiry may lead to a 'normative' ethical criterion is available in Richard B. Brandt, *Ethical Theory*, Prentice-Hall, Inc., Englewood Cliffs, N. J., 1959. Indeed, Professor Brandt's book offers an admirable introduction to analytical ethics. Although Brandt argues vigorously against the view that 'theological knowledge is essential for the justification of ethical propositions' (p. 69), he does not go, as does Professor Weiss, so far as to insist that religion and ethics have nothing whatever to do with each other. On the contrary, he allows that theological propositions may imply ethical ones (p. 75) and that a 'theological rule' for the assessment of ethical judgments is possible, though to date 'no one has defended such a view at any length' (p. 252).

## 1 *Ethics on the Analytical Model*

The meta-ethical advance beyond the strictly syntactical attention to ethical language is due to the recognition of the implications for ethical theory of ordinary language. Men make ethical judgments all the time. The most obvious form of these

---

Since he is concerned in this book with ethical theory, one cannot expect more than a few hints of what on the analytical model the link between ethics and religion might be. By *normative ethics* Brandt means a philosophical 'inquiry aiming to state and defend as valid or true a complete and economic set of general ethical principles, and also some less general principles that are important for what we may call "providing the ethical foundation" of the more important human institutions' (p. 7). By meta-ethics, Brandt means *critical* ethics—but critical ethics on the analytical, *not* the Kantian, model. 'What kind of reasoning or evidence constitutes a valid "defense" or "justification" of ethical principles and how can we show that some particular kind of reasoning is a valid defense or justification?' What is 'the *meaning* of ethical terms or predicates or statements'? (p. 7). These are the questions which engage meta-ethical inquiry. They are not as dissimilar to the Kantian questions as superficially they may appear to be. The difference is traceable to the *analytical* as contrasted with the *rationalistic* context of the critical inquiry. 'Metaethics', Brandt remarks, 'thus has approximately the relation to normative ethics that the philosophy of science or epistemology or metascience has to science' (p. 7). This is very un-Kantian language but it is curiously reminiscent of the first and second *Critiques*.

The bibliographical suggestions which conclude each of Brandt's chapters are virtually a source book of the primary ethical literature of the analytical movement. Perhaps the omission of Wittgenstein from bibliography and index alike is mute attestation of the broadening of analytical interest beyond logic and grammar in the direction of ethics. Or is it a shift to a more fruitful line of investigation?

Unless otherwise indicated, the present chapter is based upon Professor Brandt's summation of the current state of analytical thinking about ethics. We are aware of the risk of misinterpretation to which such a limited consideration of the evidence exposes us. Yet we venture to think the risk defensible not only because of the obvious competence of Professor Brandt's volume but also and especially in view of the marginal relation of the analytical movement in its present phase to the focus and the purpose of this account of the methodology of Christian ethics. It may be that not least among the constructive implications of a *koinonia* ethic is the kind of 'theological rule' for the assessment of ethical judgments which meta-ethical analysis would also find admissible. But the explication of such a rule would require a full and separate treatment, a treatment which, in any event, would have to presuppose a clear methodological understanding of what is involved in Christian thinking about ethics and of what differentiates Christian from philosophical ethical interpretation.

judgments is the ethical statement. Accordingly, an analysis of the language in which such statements are commonly expressed and communicated may be expected to point to their common property, to the implicit or explicit reasoning involved, and thus to a meaningful identification of the term 'ethical' and, in consequence, to the meaning of ethical terms. Once these results have been achieved, due account may be taken of the facts that ethical statements are of diverse kinds and that the situations to which they refer are still more diverse. For the way has been prepared for a normative criterion by which statements, situations, and the appropriate behavior can be judged to be ethical.[1]

Professor Brandt, for instance, begins with what 'it is natural to say . . . is an "ethical statement" '.[2] Statements which assert that something is 'obligatory', or 'reprehensible', or 'desirable', etc., are ethical statements. In each such statement there is a 'key' word, a word which indicates that the statement is an ethical one. The key words may be called 'ethical terms'. It is noteworthy that, when ethical theory begins with a rough classification of statements in this way, it is uncommitted in advance as to the truth or falsity of ethical statements. When, then, the question of the truth or falsity of ethical statements is raised, it may be dealt with in such a way as to transcend the hitherto restrictive dogmatism in contemporary ethical theory. It is no longer necessary to assert that only statements of a scientific kind can be judged as to their truth or falsity,[3] or that the gulf between scientific and ethical statements is so great and fixed as to deny to scientific statements all ethical content and conversely to ethical statements all scientific content. In short, the radical disjunction between fact and value, whether from the side of scientific theory or from the side of ethical theory, has been overcome. Thoroughgoing positivism and thoroughgoing rationalism in ethics have thus been withered at the root.

The most important consequence of this achievement is the liberation of meta-ethical inquiry for the elaboration of a

[1] For a definition of meta-ethical and normative ethics and of the difference between them, see p. 228, note 2.

[2] Brandt, op. cit., p. 2.

[3] E.g., 'the sum total of statements rationally inferrable from observation and experiment'. Ibid., p. 37.

normative ethical criterion. Meta-ethical inquiry can arrive systematically at 'the correct method for justifying normative statements or opinions' and it can '*show* that this method *is* the correct method of justifying normative statements'.[1]

The meta-ethical course pursued by Professor Brandt carries him beyond the tests of consistency and generality as adequate to the establishment of an ethical norm. A careful assessment of what is valid and invalid about naturalistic and non-naturalistic (i.e., supernaturalistic, authoritarian) ethics leads to an examination of 'non-cognitivism' in ethics, i.e., to the various ethical proposals of linguistic analysis. Ethical naturalism holds that ethical knowledge is like the knowledge of the empirical sciences. Non-naturalism holds that ethical knowledge is like that of the basic postulates of logic. But just as ethical naturalism insufficiently considers the significance for ethics of statements other than property-referring or fact-stating,[2] so non-naturalism fails adequately 'to distinguish between merely *believing a proposition strongly* and *having rational insight into its necessity*'.[3] 'Non-cognitivism', in distinction from 'naturalism' and 'non-naturalism', is a theory of ethics which 'asserts that ethical utterances are best understood by assimilating them or likening them to commands or exclamations or sentences of some other functional speech-type different from fact statements. . . .'[4] Non-cognitivism denies that ethical terms refer to properties of objects, that ethical sentences state facts, and that there is knowledge of ethical truths in the factual sense. Some non-cognitivist positions qualify the denial to the extent of allowing some property reference or factual element in ethical statements. But whether the denial be partial or complete, the important claim is that ethical statements are non-cognitive.

What then are they? The answers to this question appear to

---

[1] Brandt, ibid., p. 8.

[2] Ibid., p. 180. For example, 'if a person is ready to call something E if and only if it is PQR', the naturalist can 'point out that the methods of science can now show him what is E, since they can show him what is PQR. But *if* the person doubts whether something that is PQR is E, the naturalist . . . cannot help him . . . .' Ibid., p. 179.

[3] Ibid., p. 201. 'Thus, we cannot say, "Anything that is PQR is desirable"; the most we can say is, "If anything is PQR and has no other ethically relevant properties, then it is desirable".' Ibid., p. 199.

[4] Ibid., p. 205.

range from the thesis that ethical sentences are verbalizations of attitudes, to the view that they are prescriptive, to the multi-functional claim that there are many things that men do with ethical words, i.e., that ethical words or sentences sometimes have one 'job', sometimes another, and that 'what a person is doing with a particular value-word at a particular time can only be discovered by examining what he says in its context. . . .'[1]

The evolving and inconclusive state of current analytical ethical theory is indicated, however, not only by the vigorous discussion of non-cognitive alternatives to previous ethical theories. A better indication is provided by the critique of non-cognitivism from within the general framework of the analytical approach to ethics. 'It is being suggested that it is not misleading to say that ethical statements are correct, valid, true or known; at least it would be more misleading to deny these things.'[2] The direction of continuing analytical inquiry is toward a correction of the non-cognitivist denial of truth-claims to ethical statements and toward achieving a methodological demonstration of 'the logical foundation of any and all ethical statements'.[3] In short, it is not sufficient to propose by analytic means a *clarification* of ethical language. Ultimately, meta-ethical inquiry is validated by its capacity to propose a normative ethical criterion.

What seems to be happening is that the gap between fact and value, between scientific and ethical statements, is being gradually closed, and by recourse to a practice familiar in moral philosophy. As we have seen, philosophical ethics tends to formulate its normative criterion in terms of a 'right rule of

[1] P. H. Nowell-Smith, *Ethics*, Penguin Books, Inc., London and Baltimore, 1954, p. 98. Quoted by Brandt, op. cit., p. 232. The attitude claim has been currently advanced chiefly perhaps by C. L. Stevenson, *Ethics and Language*, Yale University Press, New Haven, 1944 (The University Press, Oxford, 1960); the prescriptive theory may be ascribed to R. M. Hare, *The Language of Morals*, The Clarendon Press, Oxford, 1952.

[2] Brandt, op. cit., p. 241. In this connection, special attention may be drawn to S. E. Toulmin, *An Examination of the Place of Reason in Ethics*, Cambridge University Press, Cambridge, 1950; and Morton White, *Towards Re-union in Philosophy*, Harvard University Press, Cambridge, 1956 (The University Press, Oxford, 1956).

[3] Brandt, op. cit., p. 259.

reason'.[1] Analytic ethics proves to be no exception to this rule of 'the rule'. 'There is a rule or directive about the acceptance of ethical propositions. . . .'[2] And it has the singular advantage, in this instance, of providing for ethics a correlation between ethical judgments and empirical evidence. Just as scientific laws and theories do not rest upon observational evidence alone, so ethical principles rest upon more than observational evidence. Just as no general statement covers all types of scientific statement, so in ethics no general statement covers all types of ethical statement.[3] Thus, the ancient observation of Aristotle that in ethical matters utmost precision is exceedingly difficult to attain is confirmed once again by an ultra-contemporary ethical inquiry.

The analytical 'right rule of reason' parallels the 'rule of induction' under which scientific prediction on the basis of limited evidence can be made. One suggestion of such a rule has been identified as 'rule-utilitarianism'. It asserts in effect that 'a particular act is permissible if it is not prohibited, in one way or another, by the *ideal rules* of the society in which it is performed'. These rules vary in different societies. But in each case the correct set of rules for a given society 'is the one that has this characteristic: that a conscientious effort to conform to it, by everyone in the group, would *maximize the welfare* of sentient beings . . . as compared with any others of the possible sets of rules'.[4] Another suggestion is that put forward by Professor Brandt himself. For reasons which he carefully expounds but which need not concern us here, he proposes as the rule for the justification of ethical statements (the normative ethical criterion) what he calls the 'Qualified Attitude Method'. The method is a compound of a number of considerations indis-

---

[1] See above, Chapter VI, p. 169—the rule of the mean; p. 179—the categorical imperative; Chapter VII, p. 197—the pragmatic satisfaction of demand; Chapter VIII, p. 210—the primary ethical principle; pp. 220-21 —the psychoanalytical development of a productive character structure.

[2] Brandt, op. cit., p. 244.

[3] The parallelism rests upon a consideration of 'the circumstances and the kind of observational evidence which warrant a degree of confidence in a statement supported by observation'. Ibid., p. 243. Brandt uses the phrase of scientific statements. But he is discussing the point of the parallelism between scientific and ethical statements.

[4] Ibid., pp. 253-54. Italics are Brandt's.

pensable to ethical observation and analysis: (a) Particular problems are decided by appeal both to principles already more or less explicitly in mind and to preferences, feeling of obligation, etc. (b) Principles are corrected if incompatible with criticized attitudes, and criticized attitudes assist in expanding and weighing principles. (c) Judgments must be consistent, and particular ones generalizable. (d) Attitudes are discounted if they are not impartial, informed, the product of a normal state of mind, or compatible with having a consistent set of general principles not excessively complex. 'Thus ethical thinking is a complex interplay of attitudes, principles, formal requirements for principles and rules for discounting.'[1] The particular advantage attributed to the adoption of the Qualified Attitude Method in ethical thinking is that the method provides a general principle for ethical judgments 'comparable to a rule of induction. The principle is this: "Assert an ethical proposition if and only if it satisfies the conditions of the Qualified Attitude Method."'[2]

## 2  *Meta-Ethical Achievements*

The breach of the syntactical monopoly of analytic philosophy by means of the analysis of ordinary ethical language has opened up constructive possibilities not only for moral philosophy but also for the philosophy of religion. As regards ethics, it should be plain that a normative criterion, such as the one to which the Qualified Attitude Method leads, does in fact bridge the gap between fact and value, between empiricism (naturalism) and formalism (rationalism) in ethical theory. The bridge is an adroit logical construction compounded of the function, the context, and the signification of ethical terms and statements. By means of this construction men can understand and judge what ethical behavior means and what the meaning of ethical behavior is. Principles and the situation are logically and operationally linked[3]—an achievement of no small gain to

[1] Brandt, ibid., pp. 250-51. This précis of Professor Brandt's proposed rule is cited for the most part in his own words. Slight modifications, however, make the reference an exact paraphrase rather than a direct quotation.

[2] Ibid., p. 251.

[3] Professor Brandt's demonstration of this connection in interpreting such normative problems as the 'general welfare', 'human rights', 'justice and social institutions' is instructive. Ibid., chaps. 15-19.

ethical theory. The analytical moralists have transcended the post-Kantian impasse between the normative and the critical elements of ethics.[1] In so doing they have made a virtue of necessity. Aristotle's observation about the difficulty of precision in ethical matters has been transformed from a reluctantly acknowledged counsel of prudence into a resiliently adaptive counsel of procedure. The torment of moral obligation has been displaced by tentativeness, the frustration of it by flexibility, the mandatory element in it by the concern for meaning. The powers of man have so ordered the language of moral obligation as to enable man clearheadedly to keep *doing what he says he is to do*, able to accept and to await the alteration of detail, in the confidence that the direction and the goal are 'true and righteous altogether'.[2]

As regards the philosophy of religion, the recovery of the truth dimension for ethical language and the explication of an analytical rule of judgment suggest a constructive analytical approach to religious language. At least religious language with its own particular compound of fact and attitude can no longer be excluded as *prima facie* irrational or even negligible. On the contrary, the interpretation of religion on this rule conceivably opens the way to an understanding of religion, free from the debilitating and inconclusive dependence upon science and upon value as well. Thus, by a somewhat circuitous route, the interpretation of religion on the analytical model curiously confirms James' anticipation of 'a universe . . . in possession of the maximum amount of rationality practically attainable by our minds, . . . fluent and congruous with our own nature's chief demands', a universe in which men have become once more genuinely open to 'the more living divine reality with which it appears certain that empirical methods tend to connect men in imagination'.[3] If the language of religion should express 'as fluent and congruous with our own nature's chief demands', a further 'chief demand', coherent with, though not inherent in,

---

[1] And thus also between the formal and material, rational and empirical elements of ethics.

[2] Ps. 19.9. Whether the analytical achievement is an inversion or an explication of what the Psalmist reserves for the judgments of God is still an open question.

[3] See above, Chapter VII, 200.

the powers of man, it would seem to be entirely consonant with the analytical rule already noted to explore the connection between observation and imagination which such a demand conceivably also involves. Call the language expressive of this further demand 'convictional', as Zuurdeeg does; call it testimonial in distinction from statemental, as Gabriel Marcel does; call it confessional, or mythological, or theological; the point is that the phenomenon of language, once its thoroughgoing pluralism is taken seriously, may tell us more about the options of mystery and meaning actually being exercised by the 'man who speaks' than logical, metaphysical, epistemological, and syntactical reflections upon the powers of man have been able to do.[1]

As these lines are being written, a current issue of *The New Yorker* carries an account of the tercentenary observance of the founding of the Royal Society of London. Theology and politics were barred from the discussions of the early days of the Society. Instead, the Fellows were advised to use 'a close, naked, natural way of speaking; positive expression, clear senses; a native easiness, bringing all things as near to mathematical plainness as they can'. Since then mathematics has become, if not less plain, at least less ideal as a universal human discourse, and theology has begun to disclose a naked, natural-way-of-speaking quality hitherto unsuspected and at least postdating the founding of the Royal Society. As for the Society, the report observes that its Fellows 'may have been advancing the English language as well as science'.[2] As for the advance of the English language, theology has already had its turn at that, and may be in for another opportunity to contribute to the enrichment, if not to the advancement, of science. The fulfillment of these prospects depends upon the firmness of the breach of the syntactical barrier in the analysis of language, upon the further investigations of meta-language possibilities of a nonlogical kind,[3] and particularly perhaps upon the resourcefulness of

[1] Cf. Zuurdeeg, op. cit., Part I; Gabriel Marcel, *The Philosophy of Existence*, Harvill Press, London, 1948, p. 71. The phrase 'the man who speaks' I owe to Professor Zuurdeeg.

[2] 'Letter from London' by Mollie Panter-Downes, dated 27 July and published in *The New Yorker*, Vol. XXXVI, No. 25, 6 August 1960, p. 56.

[3] Zuurdeeg hints in a tantalizing way at lines along which further analytical inquiry might be pursued. Op. cit., pp. 63ff.

Christian theologians in drawing upon their own tradition and applying its insights to the frontier problem already engaging language philosophers themselves, i.e., the relation between the languages men speak and the men who speak them.

It is this relation which informs Gabriel Marcel's description of the man of 'proper pride' whose 'word is himself, for between being and the word there does exist . . . an irrefragable unity'. It is this relation which comes to expression in the curious idiom of the French language: *prendre la parole*, an idiom the implications of which have extensively engaged the reflective attention of Professor Georges Gusdorf. 'To speak up', he writes, 'is one of the major tasks of man. . . . Language does not exist before the personal initiative which sets it in motion. The given language merely offers a frame to be used by man's verbal activity. The words and the meanings formulate all kinds of possibilities. . . . The operation of language creates for us a persistent nature, beyond the present, fitting to explain the past and to engage the future.'[1] But what has been overlooked by the language philosophers (if not by the philosophers of language) and forgotten by theologians (except for a conspicuous few) is that Christian theology has from the beginning been *ex animo* a theology of language. The linguistic impulse of theology erupts powerfully in the mythology of Babel and the imagery of Pentecost. It lingers in the metaphysical patterns of the logos theology and comes alive as the theme and substance of the theology of the Reformation, only to be obscured once

[1] Gabriel Marcel, *Man Against Mass Society*, Henry Regnery Company, Chicago, 1952, p. 190; Georges Gusdorf, *La Parole*, Presses Universitaires de France, Paris, 1953, p. 35. For both these passages I am indebted to Professor Zuurdeeg, op. cit., pp. 58, 91-92. It may be objected that this relation has engaged the reflective attention not so much of the language philosophers themselves as of the philosophers who under the impact of analytical philosophy have given serious philosophical attention to the phenomenon of language. But the objection underestimates the work of the Vienna Circle at an early stage of the analytical movement as well as the growing attention to ordinary language. On the other hand, the objection may be pointing to a possible boundary between analytical philosophy and philosophical phenomenology. According to this possibility, the analytical investigation of ordinary language sooner or later suggests the question of the relation between the languages men speak and the men who speak them, the exploration of the question itself being more appropriate to phenomenological than to analytical inquiry.

more by confessional, doctrinal, and system-building theological enterprises. However proper, pressing, and perhaps unavoidable these enterprises may have been, it must be admitted that as regards the hearing each one of the other 'speaking in his own language',[1] the fundamental significance of the word for theology and of a theology of the Word has not been adequately explored.[2] Theology is neither dependent upon nor inextricably bound to any philosophical mode or model but theology can be, often has been, and must always be open to being reminded by philosophical investigation of neglected theological insights and of ways of giving contemporary significance to them. The analytical philosophy is no exception.

### 3 *'Koinonia' Ethics and Meta-Ethics*

The movement of analytical philosophical inquiry from syntactical to ordinary language, from ordinary language to the language of ethics and thence to the language of religion suggests the possibility of a parallel movement of theological inquiry. Such a movement would undertake a re-examination of the methodology of Christian ethics so as to provide a creative occasion for the linguistic impulse of theology. Such a movement would seek to show how the ethical reality of the *koinonia* and the political character of the divine activity illuminate the problem of the relation between the languages men speak and the men who speak them. To put it technically, a theological ethic as a methodological and structural analysis of the Christian life could lead to a fresh consideration of the doctrine of the church as the community of faith established and nurtured by word and sign. Obviously the parallel between analytical and Christian ethics cannot be regarded as the only option leading to a renewed reflection upon theology and language, but it may serve at least to indicate how ethics on the analytical model and ethics in the context of the *koinonia* bear upon each other.

[1] Acts 2.6.

[2] Nor is this the proper occasion to explore it. It will be enough to note such theological reflections upon language as occur in I Cor. 14; Augustine's *De Magistro*; Schleiermacher's *Essay on Language* and the discussion in the *Glaubenslehre*, pars. 18, 27, 28; Karl Barth, *Kirchliche Dogmatik*, III/2, pp. 99ff.; III/4, pp. 325ff.; and Paul Tillich's attempt to translate the language of the Church's faith into meaningful contemporary discourse.

Christian ethics and analytical ethics are not mutually exclusive. The language of Christian ethics requires the same kind of meta-ethical clarification which is currently being applied to the language of philosophical ethics. Since analytical ethics leaves open the possibility of a meta-ethical inquiry into religious and theological language (Christian and other), there would seem to be no ground in principle for excluding Christian ethical language from a meta-ethical inquiry. Even if such investigations should result in nothing beyond the refinement of translation from theological to analytical language, the gain for theological communication would be considerable. Theology, although possessed of a congenial, not to say intrinsic, language form, is not exclusively bound by that form in the communication of what theology knows.

Christian ethics and analytical ethics agree in recognizing that theological statements have ethical meaning in the qualified sense, that some but not all theological propositions imply ethical ones, and some but not all ethical propositions imply theological ones. For example, the statement 'God is one' is a theological statement which does not imply necessarily an ethical statement, i.e., the *suum cuique* that 'Justice consists in rendering to each man his due'. The statement 'God forgives' is a theological statement that does imply necessarily an ethical statement, i.e., that 'Men should deal with one another as God deals with them, *viz.*, forgive one another'. The statement 'The love of wisdom is better than the love of power' is an ethical statement that does not imply necessarily a theological statement, i.e., that 'God is omniscient and omnipotent'. The statement 'Behavior which maximizes the welfare of sentient beings is ethical behavior' is an ethical statement which does imply necessarily a theological one, i.e., either the negative theological judgment that 'Man is the measure of all things' or the positive theological judgment that 'Man is a child of God'.

Perhaps the crucial question affecting the bearing of Christian and analytical ethics upon each other is the question of the justification of ethical statements. Is there a theological rule of ethical validation? Analytical ethics tends to deny such a rule on the ground that meta-ethical inquiry leads intrinsically to the question of validation and that theology cannot supply a sufficiently inclusive normative rule for the assessment of ethical judgments. From the side of theology a similar denial has been made. On the ground that analytical ethics is concerned with the meaning and validation of moral language, whereas theological ethics has to do with the behavioral implications of the convictions of a particular confessional group, Professor Zuurdeeg bluntly affirms that 'Christian ethics is therefore a contradiction in terms, but we can speak of Christian morals, just as of Moslem, Hindu, Stoic, naturalistic morals'.[1] Analytical ethics, according to Zuurdeeg, is a philosophical inquiry in which everyone can participate. But theological inquiry is inherently subject to a convictional-confessional limitation.

We should like to suggest, however, a further possibility. We do so *not* because theological and analytical ethics must somehow correspond to, correlate with, or complement each other. The freedom to assess congenial or alien methodologies must be as fully allowed to theological as to analytical inquiry. But simply in the interest of 'bringing the evidence in', to adapt William James' phrase, the irreconcilability of theological and analytical ethics must not be prematurely assumed.[2]

It will be recalled that we have been urging the use of the term 'ethics' rather than the term 'morals' for the reflective analysis of behavior. The terminology is exactly contrary to Zuurdeeg's usage. What matters, however, is not the terminology but the point at issue, which is, not the distinction between 'behavior according to reason' and 'behavior according to custom',[3] but the question whether Christian ethics can provide a 'theological rule' for the validation of ethical judgments. This possibility has been denied by Zuurdeeg and doubted by Brandt. Yet perhaps both Zuurdeeg and Brandt have surrendered ethical complexity to tidiness of ethical analysis. It is admittedly clarifying to espouse linguistic pluralism, especially when convictional language is securely included among linguistic possibilities. It is likewise clarifying to espouse a norm of ethical validation commensurate with meta-ethical investigation of ordinary language. But what about the widen-

---

[1] Op. cit., p. 248.
[2] See above, p. 200. It may be that we shall end up with nothing more than an over-belief. But it will be a different over-belief and one more consonant with the facts.
[3] See above, Chapter I, pp. 24-25.

ing gap between logic and behavior which such analyses imply?

From the side of logic, this gap is exposed by the question of the *possibility and the limits of generalization*. Professor Brandt, for example, notes that consistency and generalization are indispensable factors of a normative criterion for the validation of ethical judgments. He notes also that consistency and generalization cannot be ultimately decisive factors in such validation. They require to be included 'in, with, and under' the Qualified Attitude Method. The latter, functioning as an ethical norm, is strikingly reminiscent of *probabilism*, long familiar to moral theologians.[1] The difference between probabilism in ethics and the Qualified Attitude Method is a difference of authorities. Probabilism transcends the limits of generalization by reference to a consensus of 'eminent divines'; the Qualified Attitude Method seeks to stay within the limits of optimum generalization by reference to a logical version of the *consensus gentium*, i.e., 'principles corrected if incompatible with criticized attitudes', 'judgments [which] must be consistent, particular ones generalizable', 'attitudes . . . impartial, informed, the product of a normal state of mind'.[2] But in either case, a haunting dissatisfaction remains with a norm that can be only proximate at best and behavior that always presents an exception. Indeed, the more normative the judgment is, the more conspicuous the exception becomes.

Perhaps the most celebrated case in point is offered by the bombing of Hiroshima and Nagasaki in 1945. By virtue of his office, the President of the United States had to assume responsibility for the decision to unleash weapons of hitherto unknown destructive power. It is not relevant to apply to the decision taken by President Truman ethical judgments informed by subsequent knowledge and experience. The question is: What were the ethical considerations involved in the judgment and the action taken *at that time*? We may assume the integrity of the President and his advisers. We know that the decision was taken and defended both militarily and ethically on the ground of hastening the end of the Second World War at a minimal loss of human life, particularly American lives. Certainly both

[1] See Chapter XII.
[2] Brandt, op. cit., pp. 250-51, and see above, p. 234, note 1.

ethical probabilism and the Qualified Attitude Method would support the normative judgment that human life is a good which must be safeguarded rather than destroyed. Yet the actual ethical situation at the time of Hiroshima and Nagasaki was that the destructive consequences of the use of nuclear weapons could not be limited by the normative judgment in terms of which the decision was taken. Here was a conspicuous exception to a conspicuous ethical norm. The measure of the disparity between the norm and the exception is not least evident from the continuing ethical uncertainty and controversy that surround that decision.

From the side of behavior, the gap between the logical norm and the concrete act is exposed by the possibility and the limits of a transvaluation of values. It could be that the authentic norm of ethics is one which expresses the disjunction of the particular from its logical subordination to the general. Such a norm, however, would also take account of the congruence of the general with the dynamics of concrete particulars. The congruence of a general ethical claim or judgment with particulars would be indicated by the recognition of a given concrete particular as a transvaluational exception. The authentic norm of ethics is one which validates behavior in terms of its transvaluational concreteness. The norm takes the form of a validating judgment, the ethical force of which is not its logical generality but its acknowledgment of the transforming power of a concrete exception.

Let us return to Hiroshima and Nagasaki. It is, of course, too much to expect the President of the United States—or any head of state—to shape public policy in terms of explicitly religious judgments. Christian faith and ethics are particularly alien to such a situation because Christianity specializes in the exception. The man healed on the Sabbath day, the woman taken in adultery, the 'good Samaritan', the 'prodigal son' are only the more vivid instances of this specialization. The bombs that fell upon Hiroshima and Nagasaki are exceptions to the logic of ethical generalization, as we have just pointed out. But can they—as concrete actions—be included in a list of ethical exceptions?

We come here upon the root of the problem of ethical valuation and transvaluation. Exceptions arise because of the relentless pressure and complexity of behavioral options. The critical question is whether an exception is ethically significant because it proves the rule or because it suspends the rule. An exception that proves the rule falls securely under the normative generalization and can be neatly disposed of with commensurate penalties. In this way its ethical significance is reduced from an exception to that of a deviation. An exception that suspends the rule challenges previously accepted ethical judgments and patterns of behavior and breaks fresh ethical ground. It breaks fresh ethical ground because it requires a transvaluation of accepted norms and values in order to take account of what has concretely occurred. Transvaluation means that the ethical inadequacy of accepted norms and values has been exposed by ethical insights and directives integrally related to the concrete situation of decision.

The decision to bomb Hiroshima and Nagasaki involved a momentous ethical risk. The risk was not the quasi-humanitarian, quasi-prudential one advanced by President Truman and his advisers. It was that the unprecedented power of nuclear energy required a bold re-examination of the ethical foundation and use of power for which existing political sovereignties and structures were incommensurate and unprepared. The displacement of the current anarchy of competing and self-justifying national sovereignties by an imaginative and self-limiting dedication to the unity and wholeness of humanity could no longer be avoided, or even deferred.

Such a risk cannot be ventured without crossing the boundary from ethics into religion. A *koinonia* ethic does not ignore the enormous difficulties which imperil every effort to relate religious faith constructively to politics. Nor does a *koinonia* ethic underestimate the political excesses and errors which abound in the history of the Christian Church. Difficulties and mistakes, however, do not justify a wall of separation between politics and piety. A *koinonia* ethic deals first of all with this ethical fact. It begins, therefore, with what is plain and revises the ethical significance of what is plain by a due consideration of the ethical exception. Clearly, without crossing the boundary from ethics into religion one can scarcely avoid adducing the wrong reasons for the right decisions, or falling into premature self-justification, or irresponsibly surrendering the claims of the future to the expediencies of the present. Having crossed the boundary, one plainly sees that a thoroughgoing revision of the problem of power is both possible and necessary.

Christian ethics recognizes that ever and again a concrete particular or set of particulars exposes just such a boundary of ethical decision. The bombing of Hiroshima and Nagasaki remains what it was *at that time*, not only ethically ambivalent but ethically confused. There was, however, *at that time*, another possibility which is still an ethical option. The particular and peculiar convergence of military, political, and human urgency upon a single moment of decision could have been ethically understood and explained as requiring an action which moved the concrete human situation to a new level of freedom, power, and order. A point of no return would thus have become instrumental to a reconstruction and reconciliation for which existing norms, values, and judgments had been exposed as inadequate. The fact is that reconciliation has become a political reality and responsibility of utmost urgency, and the exercise of this responsibility requires a context of religious faith. So long as the dynamics of such a situation and decision are understood and explained in terms of other contexts—of biological vitalism or historical materialism or the historical movement of Absolute Spirit or the freedom with justice of the 'West' or the justice before freedom of the 'East'—there would seem to be no escape from ethical expediency and the fateful fluctuation of the political order between tyranny and anarchy. Such contexts of ethical judgment and validation mean that the exception has been subordinated to a general order of valuation and so destroyed. But in so far as the dynamics of such a situation and decision are understood and explained in the context of the politics of God and as signs of what God is doing in the world for the humanization of man, a vast jungle of determined or of indeterminate possibilities and uncertainties becomes transformed into a set of possibilities and uncertainties which may be selected as bearers of reconstruction and reconciliation. This context of ethical judgment and validation means that the exception has exposed a transvaluation of values. In these terms Hiroshima and Nagasaki are signs of God's pressure toward a global implementation of the full humanity of man and to that extent are ethically significant and defensible. Here, then, the 'more living divine reality . . . of a universe . . . fluent and congruous with our own nature's chief demands' may be apprehended and heeded when biblical faith and imagination inform the correction towards 'which it appears certain that empirical methods tend'.[1]

Reformation theology has, of course, always sought to express such a transforming transvaluation by means of its conception of justification by faith.[2] Justification was explicated partly as a forensic judgment and partly as a transformation of behavioral relations between God and man. As a judgment, justification expressed itself in the 'rule' of forgiveness. In concrete behavior, forgiveness functioned as reconciliation. Here was a 'rule' which was not a rule. It could only be applied as a suspension of itself, i.e., as an exception which breaks through previously accepted ethical generalizations and revises them. Sometimes, it must be admitted, the transvaluational meaning and behavioral force of justification were espoused merely as theological formulas without due regard for the concrete conditions and context of human behavior. Yet the thrust of Reformation ethics was really toward the concrete behavior-situation and the exception within it, pressing for ethical recognition and liberation, and calling every general validation into question.

Thus as regards Reformation theology and ethics, Professor Brandt has correctly identified the theological rule for the validation of ethical judgments: The will of God as that which God approves.[3] With this rule we have already become familiar through a contextual analysis appropriate to the *koinonia* character of Christian ethics.[4] The analysis underlined the point that in the *koinonia* we do come upon a meaningful apprehension of the will of God as an ethical norm which effectively conjoins what we know with what we are to do. Such an apprehension and conjunction are possible and actual because of the political character of the divine activity. Admittedly, it was noted, the problem of a 'double standard' poses for a *koinonia* ethic a

[1] See above, Chapter VII, p. 200.

[2] Roman Catholic theology, on the other hand, has regarded justification more in sacramental than in ethical terms and kept its ethics within the framework of the *summum bonum* synthetically compounded of nature and grace.

[3] Brandt, op. cit., p. 252.     [4] See above, Chapter III, pp. 75-80.

formidable difficulty. And this same difficulty has engaged us here in the meta-ethical guise of the problem of ethical inclusiveness, or the possibility and the limits of ethical generalization. If now we consider the contextualism proposed by Christian ethics in relation to the strictures which Brandt has raised against both contextualism and a 'theological rule' for the validation of ethical judgments, the fundamental point at issue between Christian and analytical ethics emerges.

By contextualism, Brandt means the 'central claim that in the context of actual ethical problems, ethical premises are always available, and that philosophical difficulties arise only when we view problems or questions, and try to answer them outside of concrete practical contexts'.[1] This claim Christian ethics also makes, and this is the boundary which Christian ethics discerns between itself and philosophical ethics. The boundary is concrete but not on that account illogical. It marks the limits of the logical in the clarification of an ethical norm. On this boundary the logical is subordinate to what is concretely human, and what is concretely human is protected against subordination to what is logical.

It may be that contextualism as defined by Brandt assumes uncritically that 'there can be a logical re-construction of ethical belief essentially comparable to what is possible for science'.[2] We should agree that 'the rules of inductive inference permit us to pass directly from observation reports to the statements of empirical science—but not to ethical statements'.[3] But the parallelism between ethical and scientific contextualism does not involve such an inference. Ethical contextualism employs, *not* an inductive movement from scientific observation to ethical statements, but an inductive movement from ethical observation to ethical statement comparable to the movement from empirical observation to empirical statement characteristic of scientific inference. This kind of parallelism could also be claimed for the contextualism of a *koinonia* ethic.

But the real force of Professor Brandt's objection to contex-

[1] Brandt, op. cit., p. 41.

[2] Ibid., p. 49. Professor Brandt attributes this assumption to 'John Dewey and other "instrumentalists" ' (p. 45) and exempts other senses of contextualism from his objections.

[3] Ibid., p. 49.

tualism concerns its premises. In his view the contextualist assumption that the context of actual ethical problems always includes unquestioned ethical premises confuses premises that are *unquestioned* with premises that are *valid*. Thus 'the contextualist mode of reasoning cannot really justify *any* ethical principle'.[1] This objection is conclusive, if that is what contextualism involves. But when a similar objection is urged against a theological rule of validation, the tight logicality of Brandt's meta-ethical analysis begins to prove too much.

On Brandt's own admission, a theological rule would assert that 'ethical judgments are justified if they co-incide with the will of God'.[2] Such a rule, however, presupposes an identifiable source of information about the divine will. The availability of the source, in turn, may be established by one of two types of argument. There is an 'empirical' consideration, which seeks to show the correspondence between the exceptional moral insights of a religious teacher and the judgments or insights implied in ordinary ethical language. There is also a 'supernatural' argument, which does not make use of the moral perceptiveness of men but rests its case solely upon a direct connection between the ethical statements of a teacher of the will of God and the statements of God himself. In short, this is an argument from propositional revelation. The empirical argument is only as good as the correspondence between ordinary and extraordinary moral insights and is adversely affected by discrepancies. The supernatural argument is explicated by reference to 'one historically popular line of reasoning: the argument from miracles'.[3]

We could not agree more completely with Professor Brandt's strictures against a theological rule if this is the best case that can be made for it. It must also be admitted that the case is still being made and that Brandt has correctly identified 'one historically popular line of reasoning'. Yet just as a coincidental relation at best may be said to obtain between empirical science and science fiction, between moral philosophy and, shall we say, the Boy Scout Manual, so the whole apparatus of supernatural, propositional revelation and miracles bears at best only a coincidental relation to the creative and critical theological

---

[1] Brandt, ibid., p. 51.     [2] Ibid., p. 252.
[3] Ibid., p. 79. But see the whole of chap. 4 of Brandt's volume.

thought of the present century.[1] The fact is that propositional revelation and juridical expositions of the divine will are as obsolescent in Protestant theology as thoroughgoing anthropological relativism is in social ethics. Consequently, Brandt's strictures against a theological rule are wide of the mark.

There is indeed 'one major difference between the Qualified Attitude Method and any test by appeal to the will of God'.[2] But the difference is *not* the one suggested by Brandt. His method, he urges, 'is a definite account of how we do or should go about answering ethical questions. The theological method is not. It does not tell us how to ascertain the will of God. . . .'[3] If the theological method is what Brandt erroneously thinks it is, he is correct. But there is a correct theological method which does, as we have tried to show, exactly what Brandt denies. The contextual analysis of ethics required by the dynamics of the Christian *koinonia* tells us both how to ascertain the will of God and how we should go about answering ethical questions. But this information is not in the first instance propositional and tested by logical validation. It is fundamentally and initially concrete, relational, and human, indicative of what belongs to the wholeness and the fullness of man's humanity toward man. What is known in this way is translogical, not alogical— possessed of an inner logic of its own. According to this logic, the conceptual is always instrumental to the concrete, and the concrete is never self-authenticating but always being fashioned by the dynamics of the self-authenticating activity of God in, with, and under the forms of man's humanity to man of which man's language speaks.

Thus, the will of God with which Christian ethical reflection deals is what God is doing in the world to achieve the humanity

---

[1] To link Emil Brunner with E. J. Carnell is like joining Korzybski with Carnap. If 'various intelligent persons have *thought* that they', i.e., Brunner and Carnell, meant by ' "X is wrong" just "X is forbidden by God, on pain of punishment" ', the question may fairly be raised whether such persons have not overestimated their intellectual capacity to keep abreast of the range and change of human knowledge. Ibid., pp. 66-72. The fact is that the native soil of propositional revelation is Catholic theology, Greek as well as Roman, not the theology of the Reformation. Brunner is clearly in the latter tradition; Carnell, at least as patently, in the vestibule of the former.

[2] Ibid., p. 252.                    [3] Ibid.

of man, i.e., human maturity. As a theological rule for the validation of ethical judgments this would mean that statements concerning behavior which implicitly or explicitly expressed *this* relation between divine and human behavior would be valid ethical statements. But whether their validating force is their *logical* consonance with meta-ethical analysis or whether their validating force is their *indicative* congruence with the contextual self-authentication of God's political activity must remain an open question. This question awaits an extension and refinement of the dialogue between Christian and analytical moralists. Meanwhile, it may be suggested that if the validating force of ethical statements is their logical consonance with meta-ethical analysis, a *koinonia* ethic will 'not so much [have provided] an alternative method for answering ethical questions, as [have added] a supernatural dimension to the result'.[1] And then, according to Brandt, there would be no quarrel between theological and meta-ethical ethics. But if the validating force of ethical statements is their indicative congruence with God's political activity, Professor Brandt's hesitations would point to the crucial issue between Christian and analytical ethics. For let us suppose that Brandt's hesitations were directed against a constructive rather than against an obsolescent theological rule. These hesitations would then appear to be adumbrations of an ultimate incompatibility between Christian and analytical ethics. The incompatibility is really the familiar one between logic and life, this time in its meta-ethical version. A theological rule, meta-ethically arrived at, must, when applied, sooner or later expose the fact that its meta-ethical significance was formal at best. The inclusiveness and binding force of such a rule are unattainable by an ethical norm meta-ethically arrived at. On the other hand, an ethical norm meta-ethically arrived at must, when applied, sooner or later expose an inclusiveness that is proximate at best. The binding force of such a norm is the force of a logical description of ethical statements. To put the matter another way, meta-ethically speaking, logic cannot serve as the meta-language of theology, but theology might provide a more adequate meta-language than logic for meta-ethics.[2] Such a

---

[1] Brandt, ibid., p. 253.
[2] Cf. Zuurdeeg, op. cit., p. 63. 'We should admit that convictional language does not possess this "logical" structure and that therefore logic

language would conceivably be congruent with meta-ethical analysis but not validated by meta-ethics. In turn, the meta-language of theology would neither validate nor violate meta-ethical analysis. The adequacy of the language for meta-ethics would not signify a heteronomous intrusion of Christian ethics upon philosophical ethics but rather the operation of a mode of ethical discourse which could illuminate the limits and the usefulness of meta-ethics.

---

cannot serve as its metalanguage.' But the too consistent linguistic pluralism of Professor Zuurdeeg's analytical philosophy of religion prevents him from exploring the possible function of theology as a meta-language for ethics.

# X

## ON THE BOUNDARY OF ETHICS AND CHRISTIAN FAITH

WE must now return to the point from which our consideration of certain formative types of philosophical ethics began. The course of inquiry in this second part of our analysis has moved steadily toward the fundamental methodological incompatibility between Christian and philosophical thinking about ethics. 'Incompatibility' is a strong word which is readily open to the misinterpretation that Christian ethics and philosophical ethics are either in radical conflict or in radical isolation from each other. 'Incompatibility' is here used, however, to denote an inviolable boundary between Christian and philosophical ethics, a boundary which marks at the same time an inescapable impingement of the one upon the other. The relation between Christian and philosophical ethics might be characterized as one of 'dialectical tension'. But 'tension' is too tranquil a term, suggesting either a placid equilibrium or a promising resolution of outstanding differences as the ultimate state of affairs between them. The fact is that a fundamental irreconcilability divides Christian from philosophical ethics. And 'incompatibility' is the word for the dynamic and dialectical attraction and repulsion between these two disciplined accounts of what it takes to make and to keep human life human.

### I  *The Consensus of Philosophical Ethics*

The dynamic and dialectical relationship between Christian and philosophical ethics is occasioned by the human condition. Whether or not the human condition is viewed as being shaped by the divine activity and marked by man's response to it does not alter the unremitting concern and curiosity of man about the foundations of an ordered and meaningful life. This, as we have seen, is the question of ethics.[1] And the story of Christian and philosophic attention to this question is the story of a common preoccupation, despite divergent problems, and a common predicament. The formative types of philosophical ethics have pointed up three principal foci of investigation. There is the ethical object, the inquiry concerning the end or goal of human behavior. There is the ethical subject, the inquiry concerning the motive of human behavior. There is the operational shape of human behavior, the problem of the relation between the end or motive of behavior and the actual circumstances in which the pursuit of ends or motives is always entangled.

Aristotelian eudemonism, it will be recalled, is characterized principally by an analysis of ethics on the basis of the end or good toward which all things tend. Kantian legalism, on the other hand, is characterized chiefly by an analysis of ethics from the standpoint of the motive of behavior. Relativist and trans-relativist ethics have been informed mainly by the attempt to take very seriously the concrete actualities and diversities of behavior, an attempt which has involved a conspicuous reconsideration and reformulation of the normative and the behavioral aspects of ethics.

Obviously these foci of philosophical ethics are not mutually exclusive. They are differentiated by the emphasis of their respective accounts of what it really *is* that holds human society together. To Aristotle, what really holds society together, what really gives mankind its own fulfilling life, is that all things tend toward some end, that the chief end of man is happiness, and that in so far as man is governed by virtue, not by nature, he is on the way to acquiring a character that makes for happiness, and thus may be said to be a good man. To Kant, what really holds society together, what really makes it possible for men to be human beings, is that all men are under the categorical imperative of duty and that it is the good will which is integral to humanity and to the good life. In relativist and trans-relativist ethical theory, what really holds society together is a meaningful and realistic assessment and implementation of the

[1] See above, Chapter I, pp. 23-25.

directional and diverse factors in human behavior. A congeries of pluralistic, metaphysical, depth-psychological and analytical reconstructions of the tradition of moral philosophy expresses the vitality and sensitivity of relativist ethical concern. In all this, there has been at least one explicit thrust toward the ethical implications of Christian faith, namely, the ethics of Immanuel Kant. And it is difficult to see how James can be understood as he understood himself, apart from an implicit and occasionally an explicit appropriation of Christian ethical ideas.

## 2 *The Thrust of Christian Ethics Toward Philosophical Ethics*

Christian ethical theory has been more attentive to the normative than to the functional aspect of the foundations of an ordered and meaningful life. Consequently, Christian ethics has proposed its own prescriptive and programmatic ways of dealing with the range and variety of ethical problems. The problems have been superficially similar to those which have engaged philosophical ethics. And in the attempt to bring the insights and claims of Christian faith to bear upon these problems, Christian ethics has been more than a little dependent upon conceptions, procedures, and conclusions reached by philosophical ethics from quite other premises. In the discussion of ethical matters by a writer like Tertullian or Bishop Ambrose, the appropriation of philosophical ethics for purposes of Christian moral instruction is implicit. The problems are common both to Christians and to non-Christians and are considered by Christian ethical thinkers as directly as by philosophical moralists. The counsel offered does not attempt to obscure the specific ethical claim upon Christians but makes its case implicitly, that is, in the context of pagan morality and in ways that are strikingly parallel to the philosophical treatment of ethical themes. But in the case of Ritschl, the dependence of Christian upon philosophical ethics is deliberate and virtually complete. Ritschl's model was Immanuel Kant.[1]

The most influential architects of the thrust of Christian

---

[1] Cf., especially, Albrecht Ritschl, *Die christliche Lehre von der Rechtfertigung und Versoehnung*, Band III, A. Marcus, Bonn, 1874; English translation by H. R. Mackintosh, *The Christian Doctrine of Justification and Reconciliation*, Vol. III, T. & T. Clark, Edinburgh, 1900; also *Die christliche Vollkommenheit*, Vandenhoeck und Ruprecht, Goettingen, 1889.

toward philosophical ethics, however, are Augustine, Aquinas, and Schleiermacher. One may identify these approximations in various ways.[1] Let us try to understand what these three thrusts of Christian toward philosophical ethics involve by designating them respectively as *revisionist*, *synthetic*, and *dia-parallel*.

### a. The revisionist thrust: Augustine

We agree with Professor George Thomas that Augustine's treatment of philosophical ethics in the light of Christian ethics is a *revision*. But whether it is also a *transformation* is less conclusive.[2] Augustine was disposed neither to deprecate nor to disregard the problems of moral philosophy. Indeed, the eudemonistic ideal of classical ethics and the ruling conception of classical politics provided the matrix for his own ethical reflections. Thus he attempted his own formulation of the life of virtue in terms of a conspicuous revision of the Platonic scheme.[3] But Augustine had also observed that, both as regards the *highest good* and as regards *justice*, the philosophers not only often disagreed but actually tended to misread the evidence.[4] The misreading was due chiefly to the inability of reason without the illumination of faith to provide clear and reliable guidance upon ultimate issues. As a Christian thinker, Augustine was able to avoid this mistake. He recognized that, when

[1] George Thomas, for example, designates the Augustinian treatment of philosophical in the light of Christian ethics as one of 'revision' and 'transformation', and the Thomistic treatment as one of 'synthesis'; Schleiermacher is not mentioned at all. Cf. *Christian Ethics and Moral Philosophy*, Charles Scribner's Sons, New York, 1955, pp. 391-92. Karl Barth, on the other hand, does include Schleiermacher and speaks of an annexationist and isolationist attempt from the side of Christian ethics to deal with the materials of philosophical ethics. *Kirchliche Dogmatik*, Evangelischer Verlag, Zollikon-Zuerich, II/2, 1942, pp. 575-84.

[2] See note 1, above.

[3] As in the celebrated passage interpreting the Platonic virtues as forms of love. See above, Chapter I, p. 37, note 2.

[4] Cf. Augustine, *De civitate Dei*, Migne, PL, Vol. 41 [VII], Bk. XVIII, ch. xli; Bk. XIX, ch. xxiv; the English translation in *The Nicene and Post-Nicene Fathers*, First Series, The Christian Literature Company, Buffalo, Vol. II, 1887, may still be regarded as standard although some admirable fresh translations have recently appeared. Cf. the essay on the *City of God* by E. R. Hardy in Roy Battenhouse, *A Companion to the Study of Saint Augustine*, Oxford University Press, New York, 1955, chap. X.

reason is illumined by faith, the interpretation of the highest Good is altered. Thus, he considered felicity, as the fruit of faith working through love, the highest good for man, not happiness in accordance with virtue. Furthermore, the doctrine of the virtues is also revised. Justice, for example, is to be understood not as the *suum cuique* but as the agreement of reasonable beings concerning the objects of their love. In this revised sense, justice provided the sure bond of civil society.

The appealing thing about this kind of revisionism is exactly that it is *not* a transformation. It seeks to retain the philosophical matrix of ethical analysis while making room for the distinctive ethical thrust derived from Christian faith. Its genius is that Christian insights are introduced as a *corrective* of basic ethical claims derived from reason. Thus in this instance the 'rule' of love displaces the 'rule' of reason but the *structure* of the life of virtue remains. Only the ultimate instances are altered: the *suum cuique* and the *summum bonum*. A transformation would seem to call for a sharper break with the prevailing philosophical climate, for a more thoroughgoing reconstruction of the method, the problems, and the pattern of ethical interpretation. This does not occur. We have, instead, the attempt to consummate the philosophical concern with the human condition through the corrective aid of Christian faith. Indeed, this is the hallmark of Christian ethical revisionism, that it tries to say the same thing, but to say it better.

But such revisionism ill conceals the source of its own dissolution. Plato and Cicero would very probably have objected that Augustine was actually saying not something better than they were trying to say, or even should have said, but something else. The virtues as the 'forms of love' are scarcely more than formal parallels to the virtues as the forms of the good as they appear in *The Republic*.[1] Above all, justice, regarded as the political form of love, would seem to be more than formally remote from justice as the political form of equity. Revisionism always runs the unhappy risk that it arouses and nourishes the suspicion that the Christian moralist must distort the philosophical

---

[1] Compare the passage in the *De moralibus ecclesiae catholicae*, referred to above, p. 254, note 3, with Plato's *Republic*, Jowett translation, Bk. IV, 428ff.

moralist in order to make his case.[1] This is an enterprise which can scarcely be expected to elicit the confidence of the philosophical moralist in either the wisdom or the integrity of Christian ethical reflection. But even more regrettable is the effect of revisionism upon the interpretation of Christian ethics itself. It obstructs the dynamics and obscures the dialectic of the thrust of Christian ethical thinking toward the boundary on which Christian and philosophical ethics meet and divide. Revisionism involves an *implicitly* heteronomous intrusion of Christian upon philosophical ethics, an intrusion which both philosophical and Christian moralists are required by their respective ethical concerns and claims to reject.

### b. The synthetic thrust: Thomas Aquinas

Another and more formative way of dealing with the thrust of Christian ethics toward philosophical ethics is the synthesis achieved by Thomas Aquinas. As is well known, Aquinas derived his ethical model not from Plato but from Aristotle. He accepted the Nicomachean account of the nature of virtue and of the principal virtues as an accurate analysis of what reason can tell us about ethics. With the help of an Augustinian maxim, reformulated and erroneously applied, namely, that 'grace does not destroy nature but fulfills it', he then included the cardinal virtues in the Christian analysis of ethics as well.[2] This did not mean that Christian and philosophical ethics were identical. It meant that one could come by either revelation or reason along the way of ethical interpretation *up to a certain point*. For

[1] Whether Augustine's real concern was the *transformation* of philosophical by Christian ethics remains to be considered below. Certainly he has been mainly understood as the architect of Christian revisionism. And certainly, too, *revision* and *transformation* cannot *both* apply to the *same* undertaking.

[2] St. Thomas wrote *Gratia non tollit naturam sed perficit. Non quod per naturam negata sit gratia, sed potius per gratiam reparata natura*, Augustine had written in the treatise on *The Spirit and the Letter*, now part of the anti-pelagian corpus. But in the treatise on *Nature and Grace*, Augustine carefully explained that he was concerned not with the *constitution* but with the *restitution* of natural functions. *Ubi de sanandis, non de instituendis naturis agitur.* (Migne, PL, 44-45 [X], Bk. I, chap. xi [12]. I have departed from the English translation in *The Nicene and Post-Nicene Fathers*, Vol. V [1887], p. 124.) Yet medieval theologians and moralists, including Thomas, regarded natural reason and natural virtue as *constitutively* instructive, a remarkable inversion of the Augustinian point. See also Chapter XII, p. 289, note 3.

the Christian life, however, natural virtue could never be regarded as sufficient, because Christian faith brought to natural man both additional knowledge and additional power. The knowledge concerned an end higher than that of happiness in accordance with virtue, and also virtues appropriate to such a 'supernatural' end. The power concerned an infused restoration of the soul for the achievement of 'supernatural' virtues, in short, the power of grace. Thus Christian faith provided man with an ordered and meaningful life not only according to nature but according to grace. Man could now act in accordance with divine law as well as in accordance with human law. He could strive toward theological virtues of faith, hope, and charity, as well as toward cardinal virtues of wisdom, justice, temperance, and courage. He could be directed beyond happiness toward the beatific vision of God.[1]

It was clear to Aquinas that not all men could achieve the fruition of the life of grace. But what all men with the aid of grace could achieve was the optimum ethical fulfillment intrinsic to the nature of each because of the nature and power given to the human nature of all. Here was an ethic which made exacting but not exaggerated demands upon human nature. It offered man, through an ingenious combination of knowledge with power, a due assessment of the complexities, difficulties, and possibilities of responsible life. Its overarching significance, however, was, as Professor Thomas has finely put it, 'a rare spirit of inclusiveness'.[2] For range, precision, and subtlety of intellectual powers Aquinas was the peer of the incomparable master of the mind bequeathed to him by the Academy. And the pair of them, Aristotle and Aquinas, present an incomparable symbol of the most constructive combination of Christian with philosophical ethics in the long and troubled story of the relations between them. It was Aquinas who made room for *all* men within the household of faith. And he did it by an ingeniously contrived synthesis of reason and faith, nature and grace, Aristotle and the Bible, rational and theological virtue, moral philosophy and Christian ethics. On this program, the thrust of the philosophic concern with the ultimate instances of the human condition is included within the thrust of Christian

---

[1] Thomas Aquinas, *Summa Theologica*: II$^a$-II$^{ae}$, QQ. 1-27, 179-80.
[2] Op. cit., p. 392.

ethical concern with the same human condition. The 'Good' is both subordinate to and completed in 'Beatitude'. The movement here is from the human to the divine levels of ethical ends. But the movement can also be reversed and proceed from the divine to the human order. The eternal law, for example, is the norm of natural law, just as the natural law is the norm of positive law. Synthesis achieves a harmonious relation between two discrete analyses of ethics by effecting a smooth transition from the one to the other through a rationally directed movement of behavior from lower to higher claims and ends. The hallmark of Christian ethical synthesis is that it tries both to affirm and to supplement philosophical ethics, to say both the same thing and something different.

Such a synthesis, however, is deceptive. The tidy adjudication and conjunction of its components serve to prolong the suppression of a fundamental incompatibility. Eventually an unavoidable internal strain breaks apart the hierarchical symmetry of the synthesis. Although Roman Catholic moral theology still makes official and functional use of the Thomistic achievement, its efforts to do so increasingly exhibit the tenuous character of the attempt.[1] From the Christian side of the synthesis it becomes more and more necessary to break away from the schematic formalism whereby the foundations and fruits of philosophical ethics obscure the discreteness of Christian ethics. From the philosophical side, the same schematic formalism seems to deprive moral philosophy of the flexibility adequate to the concrete diversity of behavioral situations, as well as of the full fruition of its own insights into what it takes to make and to keep human life human. Why should Aristotle consent so politely to Christian baptism? And how should Christian baptism have been rightly administered where regeneration is so minimal as to be undiscernible? It could be objected in reply, 'Why not?' and 'How else?' 'Why not?' if the logic of revelation offers no abrogation of the logic of rational virtue. And 'How else?' if the infusion of grace is itself the condition of regenerative growth. But these are precisely the questions which erupt on the boundary where Christian and philosophical ethics meet and divide. These questions are rendered superfluous by the synthetic adjudication and conjunction of Christian with

[1] See Chapter XI.

philosophical ethics before the boundary is reached. The synthesis of Christian with philosophical ethics runs the risk of housing incompatibles. It imposes upon philosophical ethics ideas and goals in which it has no intrinsic interest and upon Christian ethics a dubiously congenial and less than willing partner. Synthesis involves an *explicitly* heteronomous intrusion of Christian upon philosophical ethics which both are required by their respective ethical concerns and claims to reject.

### c. The dia-parallel thrust: Schleiermacher

What, then, are the prospects of a creative thrust of Christian toward philosophical ethics? The most impressive exponent of these prospects is Friedrich Schleiermacher.

A preliminary comment is required in explanation of the term 'dia-parallel'. Why not simply say 'parallel', without the prefix? That would mean that Christian ethics and philosophical ethics are two distinct disciplines, each of which offers its own account of ethical reality. The two disciplines, moreover, do not simply coexist; they display, as regards method, history, conceptual structure, and aim, a comparable though always differentiable similarity. If, however, the prefix ('dia') is to be used, why not simply say that the relation between Christian and philosophical ethics is *dialectical*? That would mean that the two disciplines can neither ignore one another nor coincide with one another. Instead there is a tension between them which arises implicitly or explicitly from their respective formative conceptions, analytical structure, and (chiefly) the critical limits imposed by each upon the other. Further, if one wishes to take account both of *differentiation* and of *tension* in the relations between Christian and philosophical ethics, why not simply say 'correlation', or 'dialectical correlation'? To this last query the answer might well be affirmative. If all that is involved is a *description* of the relations between Christian ethics and philosophical ethics, 'correlation', or more accurately 'dialectical correlation', will do. It does cover the historical and much of the systematic evidence. This *is* what the record shows.

But such a description leaves open some very tantalizing, internal, systematic questions. Schleiermacher's refusal to leave these questions merely 'open', his painstaking clarification of inconclusive answers, and in particular his fidelity to the thrust

of Christian toward philosophical ethics give to his account of
the relation between Christian and philosophical ethics its
notable importance and significance. The term 'dia-parallel'
has been adopted for our present purpose because it points
alike to the refusal, clarification, and thrust which characterize
Schleiermacher's analysis of the methodology of a Christian
ethic.

Actually we have ventured to compound the term 'dia-
parallel' from a metaphor and an explanation of Schleiermacher
himself. During the summer of 1817 Schleiermacher lectured on
Christian ethics. He led up to his particular division of the
subject matter by an extended introduction devoted to a careful
differentiation, on the one hand, of Christian ethics from
Christian theology and, on the other, of Christian ethics from
philosophical ethics.[1] A passage in the lectures, after noting
that religion and philosophy each in its own way arrives at a
theory of ethics (*Sittenlehre*), declares:

> We must accordingly then assume that both philosophical and religious
> ethics can stand alongside each other. It is, however, very difficult to
> make clear the general nature of this juxtaposition, i.e. how it comes to
> pass. . . . The differences among religious ethical theories themselves
> cannot be denied. . . . But the differences among philosophical ethical
> theories themselves cannot be denied either. Thus between religious and
> philosophical ethics *there is nothing absolutely contradictory* (*unvertraegliches*).
> The situation is rather that the differences that mark religious ethical
> theories among themselves run parallel to the differences characteristic
> of philosophical ethical theories among themselves. Both kinds of differ-
> ences, moreover, diminish in a *parallel way*.[2]

As regards what diminishes, the parallel is evident from the
fact that religious ethical reflection and philosophical ethical
reflection each aims at a completeness which means that all
internal conflicts have been overcome. Thus, the highest result
of religious ethics is the explanation of Christianity as the fulfillment of the religious consciousness. The highest result of
philosophical ethics is the explanation of absolute and generally
acknowledged perfection. And when these results have been
achieved, 'every contradiction between Christian and philosophical ethics will have become impossible'.[3]

---

[1] Friedrich Schleiermacher, *Die christliche Sitte*, edited by L. Jonas, *Werke*,
Erste Abteilung, Bd. XII, G. Reimer, Berlin, 1843.
  [2] Ibid., pp. 26-27. Italics mine.          [3] Ibid., p. 27.

It may be that this must be regarded as Schleiermacher's considered position. There is, however, an undated letter to Jacobi, possibly from the same period, more probably a year later, which suggests how Schleiermacher viewed the continuing relation between Christian and philosophical ethics.[1] This letter seems to move a small step farther, even though only metaphorically. Unlike Jacobi, Schleiermacher thinks it possible to be both a philosopher and a Christian. Jacobi had referred to himself as being like one at sea, adrift between two currents and tossed simultaneously up and down.[2] Schleiermacher takes up this metaphor and refers to his own 'equilibrium between the two currents'. He too finds himself ceaselessly cast up and cast down, but *alternately* rather than *simultaneously*.

> My dear friend,[he wrote] why should we not be content with this? The oscillation is merely the general form of all finite existence, and there is after all an immediate consciousness of the fact that this tossing to and fro is only the two foci of my own ellipse. In this oscillation I have the whole fullness of my earthly life. My philosophy and my theology (*Dogmatik*) are firmly resolved not to contradict each other and just on that account neither wishes ever to be finished, and so long as I can think, each has always reciprocally determined and approximated the other. . . .
> One further point occurs to me in clarification of the difference between

---

[1] I am indebted to my colleague Professor Richard R. Niebuhr, whose competence in Schleiermacher's life and thought is considerable, for drawing my attention to this letter, in which Schleiermacher addresses himself summarily to the question of the relation between philosophy and theology. The position expressed here may be regarded as the basis for Schleiermacher's view of the relation between Christian and philosophical ethics. Jacobi, a prolific writer of philosophical treatises and novels and one-time President of the Munich Academy of Sciences (1807), had been in correspondence with a certain Mr Reinhold about what is involved in being a Christian and being a philosopher. Jacobi had declared that he could find no third possibility beyond continuing to philosophize or abandoning philosophy and converting to Roman Catholicism. 'Completely pagan as regards the nature and use of reason, with my whole soul a Christian', Jacobi had written (*durchaus ein Heide mit dem Verstande, mit dem ganzen Gemuete ein Christ*). And he had continued, 'I swim between two currents which refuse to combine so as to carry me. Instead they toss me about and in such a way that while the one unceasingly casts me up the other at the same time ceaselessly casts me down.' Apparently Schleiermacher had visited Jacobi and had promised to follow the visit with a letter more carefully formulating his own views. Cf. *Aus Schleiermachers Leben*, in *Briefen*, Bd. II, Zweite Auflage, G. Reimer, Berlin, 1860, pp. 348-53.

[2] See note 1, above.

us. Apropos of your image of the two irreconcilable currents, let me say that I find them irreconcilable too. But whereas you desire to unite the two and find their disjunction painful, I content myself with the separation. Reason and feeling (*Verstand und Gefuehl*) remain for me also juxtaposed. But they do make contact and constitute a *galvanic pile*. The innermost life of the spirit is real for me only in this galvanic operation: in the feeling for reason and in the understanding of feeling, wherein, however, both poles remain always turned away from one another.[1]

If we apply the metaphor of the *galvanic pile* to the parallelism between religious and philosophical ethics, we may speak of a *dia-parallel* relation between them. This means more than that they merely coexist as disciplines. It means more than that they merely correspond as regards their differences and ultimate completion. There is an internal attraction and repulsion of each toward and away from the other which give to the parallelism between them a dynamic rather than a static significance. The operation is *galvanic*, not *vegetative*. Early in the work on Christian ethics, Schleiermacher formulates what may be regarded as a kind of *law of dia-parallelism*. 'However,' he wrote, 'just as the elements of the one [philosophical ethics] cannot contradict the other [Christian ethics] *as regards content*: so *as regards form*, no element of the one is like the other. Accordingly both have this in common that in one respect they are absolutely identical, in another respect they are absolutely different.'[2] This law is really a scientific description of 'the innermost life of the spirit' in its operation. The channel of this operation is the reflective self-consciousness which at its highest levels, i.e., where the movement of spirit nears its consummation, takes philosophical and Christian ethical forms. The direction of this movement is such that the ethical is bound to be consummated by Christianity. And meanwhile it is possible and desirable, even necessary, to be content with both modes of reflective investigation.

The long methodological introduction to Schleiermacher's work on Christian ethics shows that, more than any previous Christian moralist, Schleiermacher had painstakingly faced the problem of the relation between Christian and philosophical ethics and that he tried with optimum precision to put forward a constructive proposal. The posthumously published text of the

[1] Schleiermacher, 'Letter to Jacobi', in op. cit., pp. 351, 353. Italics mine.
[2] Schleiermacher, op. cit., p. 28. Italics mine.

work allows us to follow this effort by enabling us to compare the drafts of the manuscript upon which he was at work when he died with certain formulations proposed during courses of lectures in Christian ethics given from time to time between 1817 and 1831, as well as with marginal notations both in the manuscript and in the lecture notes. One such comparison provides a further clarification of the *law of dia-parallelism* and thus seems particularly intrinsic to the present attempt to analyze the relations between Christian and philosophical ethics.

About two-thirds of the way through the introduction to *Die christliche Sitte* the argument returns to the problem of the identity of content and the diversity of form between Christian and philosophical ethics. Schleiermacher tries to specify the interrelation and differentiation between the two disciplines by means of a schematism of similar and dissimilar elements. Philosophical ethics, he notes, has been analyzed largely in terms of a doctrine of duties, a doctrine of virtues, and a doctrine of the highest good. And then he asks 'whether Christian ethics should not be structured in the same way'.[1] The answer is that it would indeed be possible to structure Christian ethics in the same way. To do so, however, would involve an important transposition of meaning which seems to be rooted in the difference between the religious and the Christian self-consciousness. A doctrine of duties is compatible with Christian ethics if due account is taken of the Christian's awareness of the conflict between flesh and spirit, and between sin and redemption. 'A dutiful act would thus be an act which expressed the triumph of spirit over flesh.' Similarly, a doctrine of virtue is compatible with a Christian ethic 'if virtue is nothing other than the power which spirit exercises over flesh, nothing other than the subordination of flesh to spirit'. As for the third doctrine of philosophical ethics, the highest good can be presented as fellowship with God through redemption wrought by the Redeemer and exhibited in the kingdom of God.

Thus far it would seem that Christian and philosophical ethics are formally distinct but interchangeable. What happens, in consequence, to the peculiar schematism of a Christian ethic? Is it not really expendable? 'Are we not required to, or rather should we not preferably adopt the forms of philosophical

[1] *Die christliche Sitte*, p. 77.

ethics?' For two very cogently argued reasons, Schleiermacher rejects such a course. The first is that in a Christian context a doctrine of virtue cannot be separated from a doctrine of the highest good. 'The description of virtues and the description of the Kingdom of God which is nothing other than the intrinsic interrelation and totality (*Gemeinschaft und Gesamtheit*) of all virtues cannot be separated at all.' The second reason is that a doctrine of duties apart from a Christian context is necessarily inconclusive because it cannot effectively relate the general form or rule or law of obligation to the individual instance. 'Thus the imperative form is always insufficient and must be assisted by the descriptive form.' On the other hand, if one starts where a Christian ethic necessarily starts, a more appropriate schematism suggests itself. The imperative (duties) and the descriptive (virtues and the *summum bonum*) analyses of action are displaced by a consideration of ethical behavior in terms of its effectiveness (*das wirksame Handeln*) and in terms of its demonstrative significance (*das darstellende Handeln*).[1]

We would seem, then, virtually to have come full circle and to have reached the point of rejecting philosophical ethics in favor of Christian ethics. But this consequence Schleiermacher refuses to draw as resolutely as he refuses to surrender Christian to philosophical ethical forms. The apparent inconsistency is superficial rather than intrinsic. Schleiermacher has not lost sight of what philosophical and Christian ethics have in common. There is a striking passage in the Lectures of the year 1824-25 which sets the record straight.[2]

Schleiermacher raises the question whether there can be really two different ethical interpretations: the one philosophical, the other Christian. 'Is there such a thing as a double ethical reality: the one understandable directly by the reason; the other derived from a Christian context?' If so, every Christian would be a *persona duplex*: 'as a rational man, he would be rationally ethical, as a Christian man, he would be ethical in a Christian sense'. As the discussion unfolds, the reader is almost transported to the lecture room and involved in the excitement with

---

[1] These paragraphs are an attempt to summarize the argument in *Die christliche Sitte*, pp. 76-83.

[2] Ibid., pp. 76-77. The passage occurs as a footnote; and to this footnote the immediately following direct citations and the interpretation refer.

which the original hearers must have followed the lecturer in the solution of this conundrum.

'It is commonplace', they would have heard him say, 'that the ethical is undivided: a Christian is expected to do nothing other than that which is expected of a rational man; and contrariwise. Yet if this were the case, the Christian community and its worship would be obligatory upon every rational man and Christian faith would be derivable from reason. But such an inference is manifestly contrary to Christian teaching which is never a matter of rational demonstration but of the exhibition of a fact. Moreover, if Christian and philosophical ethics are identical in this sense, Christian ethics is superfluous.'

'It is often said', they would have heard the lecturer say, 'that Christian ethics contains all that a rational man knows about ethics except for the addition of the obligation to do the will of God. But if this were the case, Christian ethics is really the whole of ethics under which philosophical ethics is subsumed. But such a position almost instantly encounters the stubborn fact that philosophical ethics as an independent discipline is simply "there".'

'We must', they would have heard the lecturer say, 'deal with this problem in quite another way.' And then the following proposal would have been unfolded. Suppose we begin with the point of view of philosophical ethics. Ultimately a rational analysis of ethics must lead to the possibility of adherence to a religious fellowship (*Gemeinschaft*) and in such a way as to be able to defend such adherence rationally. This recognition by philosophical ethics of the ethical reality of a religious fellowship obviously includes the way the fellowship represents the whole of life. Since philosophical ethics cannot avoid acknowledging the appropriateness of the unique Christian form of the religious community, it must recognize the Christian life as well as Christian ethics. Thus Christian ethics is acknowledged, as it were, with the approval of philosophical ethics. Supposing, however, we begin with the standpoint of Christian ethics, which is really only a description of the Christian life, we must assert that it is essential to Christian ethical reality (*Sittlichkeit*) that Christianity include all men. But plainly, only those take up Christianity who are already to a certain extent ethicized; indeed, the conscience of a Christian clearly presupposes that those who are most completely ethicized will most completely consider Christianity. Thus, Christian ethics not only can never obstruct philosophical ethics but must always desire its most complete development.

From all this, Schleiermacher concludes that philosophical and Christian ethics mutually respect each other and that it is impossible for the one to regard as ethical what the other regards as sinful. But then he makes the addition without which his conclusions would be anticlimactic indeed. Christian ethics and philosophical ethics each starts with a different principle. Therefore, the one cannot produce the content of the other. Nevertheless, both are identical to this extent (*sich so fern decken*): that each must include within its own concern what is central to the ethical reality and integrity of the other.

Undoubtedly Schleiermacher has proposed the most forth-right interpretation of the relation between Christian and philosophical ethics since the Thomistic synthesis. Here is, however, no logical and hierarchical subordination of philosophical to Christian ethics. Instead, there is an inner and organic dynamic intrinsic to the full elaboration of Christian and of philosophical ethics which presupposes and drives toward what is ethically real and central to the other. *Dia-parallelism* has replaced *revisionism* as well as *synthesis* in the effort to suggest a constructive relation between Christian and philosophical thinking about ethics.

It may be objected that Schleiermacher's view of philosophical ethics was circumscribed by too limited a conception of the role and the range of reason in ethics; and that his view of Christian ethics involved too simple a passage for the specifically Christian ethical data (the consciousness of redemption, the community of redemption, the kingdom of God) through the labyrinth of the religious consciousness to the concern and the forms of philosophical ethics. But the fact is that Schleiermacher had found what was for him a satisfactory middle term between rationality and Christian faith. The religious consciousness is the hidden ground of meeting between reason and faith. This datum of human experience explains why philosophical thought, including philosophical ethics, must organically move toward the boundary of religion; and Christian thought, including Christian ethics, must organically move toward the same boundary. 'Between these two,' Schleiermacher wrote, 'the discovery of the religious element, per se (*ueberhaupt*), and the discovery of the uniquely Christian element, there lies yet a middle term. Philosophical ethics finds the religious element identical no matter how varied its forms and maintains an identical relation to religion in whatever form. What philosophical ethics can and must establish is this, namely, that whatever man does must measure up to his religious consciousness.'[1] Christian ethics, on the other hand, finds in dogmatics the help necessary to explain and to clarify the relation between the religious consciousness and its object. Christian ethics can and must show that the ethical content of Christianity is an adequate description of the religious consciousness at the highest level of its ethical fulfillment. Thus it is this *middle term*, the religious consciousness, which enables Schleiermacher, unlike Jacobi, both to be content with the parallelism between philosophy and theology and to pursue both disciplines with enthusiasm.

Schleiermacher's enthusiasm, however, was in itself no guarantee of the success of his undertaking. The question whether the methodological parallelism between philosophy and theology can be sustained without an ultimate capitulation of one of these disciplines to the other still remains. It is this question which leads us to a consideration of the insufficiency of philosophical ethics.

[1] *Die christliche Sitte*, p. 75.

# XI

## THE INSUFFICIENCY OF
## PHILOSOPHICAL ETHICS

THE adequacy of Schleiermacher's methodological regulation of the relations between philosophical and Christian ethics must be tested by its constructive bearing upon the insufficiency of philosophical ethics. Had philosophical ethics remained within the orbit of classical and critical methodology, the prognosis would be promising. It may be that Schleiermacher is still basically correct that philosophical ethics must ultimately raise the religious question: the question about the relation between right action and the will of God. But William James is perhaps the last of the post-Kantians to provide a smooth, if tenuous, passage from philosophy to religion and thence to Christianity. Positivism, existentialism, phenomenology, and the analytical philosophy have made the going not only stormy but highly questionable. And while Kierkegaard would seem to have made it impossible to contain the religious question permanently within the limbo of irrelevance, the relation of the religious question to philosophic investigation in general, and to moral philosophy in particular, is scarcely to be understood as the organic development and consummation of rationality. Indeed, when we remember that Schleiermacher began to lecture on Christian ethics (1817) about twenty-five years after the *Critique of Practical Reason* (1788) and the treatise on *Religion* (1793) and about a quarter-century before *Either-Or* (1843) and the *Concluding Unscientific Postscript* (1846), it is difficult to know whether the law of dia-parallelism is epoch-making or episodic.[1]

[1] The contrast has been suggested by Karl Barth's treatment of Ritschl in his account of Protestant theology during the nineteenth century, where he cites a remark of Schleiermacher's concerning Frederick the Great: 'He

This uncertainty is intensified by Barth's methodological reversal and reconstruction of Schleiermacher's treatment of the relations between Christian and philosophical ethics. What Schleiermacher had tried to achieve by *dia-parallelism*, Barth proposes to correct and clarify by *dia-polemics*. Christian ethics, according to Barth, must deal with philosophical ethics not by abusive attack or in haughty isolation. Its polemics are designed neither to deprecate nor to destroy but to expose the fundamental problem which drives Christian and philosophical ethics unavoidably toward each other only to keep them apart. In the language of current international affairs, Christian ethics must deal, according to Barth, with the whole range of philosophical alternatives by 'negotiation from strength', not by 'peaceful coexistence'.[1]

## 1 *Schleiermacher and Barth*

Manuscript evidence confirms that Schleiermacher began his systematic exploration of what is involved in thinking as a Christian about ethics on 22 November 1809.[2] He commented with approval that for the previous two centuries Christian ethics had been detached from dogmatics and undertaken as a separate discipline. 'By mixing ethics with dogmatics,' he had noted, 'both lose what is distinctive of each: ethics loses scientific precision; theology loses religious precision.'[3] The published monograph firmly establishes this separation at the outset. 'Christian ethics', Schleiermacher declared, 'presupposes *as ethics* Christian theology in general . . . and so we naturally

---

did not found a school but an era.' Barth wrote of Ritschl that he 'has the significance of an episode and not . . . that of an epoch'. Cf. Karl Barth, *Die protestantische Theologie im 19ten Jahrhundert*, Evangelischer Verlag, Zuerich, 1947, pp. 379, 598. There is an English translation by Brian Cozens: *Protestant Thought from Rousseau to Ritschl*, Harper & Row, New York, 1959 (English title: *From Rousseau to Ritschl*, SCM Press, London, 1959), pp. 306, 390.

[1] Barth says '*irenisch-polemisch*', not '*schiedlich-friedlich*'. *Kirchliche Dogmatik*, Evangelischer Verlag, Zollikon-Zuerich, II/2, 1942, pp. 596, 584-85; hereinafter designated by the abbreviation *KD*.

[2] *Die christliche Sitte*, edited by L. Jonas, *Werke*, Erste Abteilung, Bd. XII, G. Reimer, Berlin, 1843, Preface, p. ix; and Appendix A.

[3] Ibid., Appendix A: '*die wissenschaftliche das strenge, die theologische das rein religioese*'.

contrast and co-ordinate Christian ethics with *dogmatics*, both part of Christian teaching in general. . . . Thus our discipline is a Christian discipline, accompanied and supplemented by dogmatics. As *Christian* ethics, our discipline is the systematic ethics of Christianity and to be contrasted with philosophical ethics as the totality of all systematic ethical inquiry. In short, our discipline seeks to be a Christian discipline but not dogmatics; an ethical discipline but not philosophical.'[1] From this initial methodological decision Schleiermacher proceeds to his dia-parallel elaboration of the peaceful coexistence between Christian ethics and moral philosophy.

We need not affirm an intrinsic connection between the dia-parallel thrust of Christian toward philosophical ethics and the methodological separation of ethics from dogmatics. As we have already seen in the case of Thomistic ethics, the inclusion of ethics within dogmatics is itself no necessary safeguard of the distinctive ethical significance of Christian faith. A synthetic co-ordination of Christian with philosophical ethics weakens the theological precision of the one and the scientific precision of the other as effectively as a dia-parallel co-ordination seems to do.[2] Schleiermacher would seem at least to have had the record on his side in support of his attempt to separate ethics and theology.

A marginal notation in the earliest manuscript on ethics indicates that methodologically at least Schleiermacher was trying to write an ethics on the Kantian model.[3] Schleiermacher appropriated not so much the Kantian scheme as the Kantian aim. With Kant, he sought to achieve scientific precision in philosophical ethics and to include Christianity 'within the limits of reason alone'. But Kant, as we have seen, was unable

[1] *Die christliche Sitte*, pp. 1-2. Italics are Schleiermacher's. Translation mine.

[2] E.g., of philosophical ethics because it is hard to see how a rational determination of the good can lead to a revealed determination of the good except as a *petitio principii*; of Christian ethics because it is hard to see how a theologically oriented ethics can avoid facing more radically than either Thomas or Schleiermacher managed to do the disjunction between the claims upon behavior arising from God's self-disclosure in Jesus Christ and claims upon behavior arising from other orientations.

[3] The notation reads: '*Dogmatische Bearbeitungen. Kantische. Das christliche als angewandte Moral, das philosophische als reine davor.*' ('Dogmatic considerations. Kantian ones. Christian ethics as applied morality, philosophical ethics contrasted as pure.') Translation mine.

to provide a rational foundation for Christian ethics, a failure by which Schleiermacher had been properly forewarned. Accordingly, he tried, by substituting the religious consciousness for the moral consciousness, to show by a scientific account of ethics how, in Kant's phrase, 'morality leads inevitably to religion', and religion to Christianity. The argument is as subtle as it is careful. For Schleiermacher never claims that the religious consciousness really arrives by an inner dynamic of its own at the specifically Christian source and substance of ethics. His point is that the dia-parallel relation between philosophical and Christian ethics can be established by reflective analysis. The result includes the prospect of the completion of philosophical by Christian ethics. As Barth sees it, this attempt can only be understood as an effort 'at least indirectly to justify Christian ethics before the forum of philosophical ethics'.[1]

Barth is convinced that the specifically Christian source and substance of ethics can be correctly and faithfully interpreted only by abandoning the separation of Christian ethics from dogmatics and including Christian ethics within a theological exposition of God's self-revelation in Jesus Christ. Thus Christian ethics is once again viewed as intrinsic to dogmatics, and Barth is launched upon an enterprise which neither Thomas nor Schleiermacher before him had been able to manage. With Thomas, Barth holds that dogmatics and ethics belong together. But unlike Thomas, Barth includes ethics under the doctrine of God, not the doctrine of man, and moves, not irenically and synthetically but irenically and polemically (and this quite deliberately), toward the boundary of philosophical ethics. With Schleiermacher, Barth holds that Christian and philosophical ethics cannot be identified. Nor can the one or the other be regarded as superfluous. But unlike Schleiermacher, the Kantian setting of the attraction and repulsion of Christian and philosophical ethics for each other is rejected. Instead, Barth attempts to explore the problem of ethics in the light of the sovereign freedom of the God who has revealed himself in Jesus Christ. 'Ethics', he declares, 'belongs to the doctrine of God because God in claiming man for himself thereby originally makes himself responsible for man. The function of ethics is fundamental explication (*Bezeugung*) of the grace of God in so

[1] Barth, *KD*, II 2, p. 577.

far as grace is man's bond of healing and of obligation. . . . The dogmatics of the Christian Church, and basically precisely the Christian doctrine of God, is *ethics* and thus is the answer to the ethical question, the eminently critical question of the Good *in* and *over* all implied goodness of human actions and ways of acting.'[1]

The immediate consequence of this reversal of the relations between ethics and dogmatics is the reconstruction of the relations between Christian and philosophical ethics. They are at once more intimate and more opposed. They are more intimate because they converge upon a common point and cannot be so neatly paralleled as separate schemata for describing separate versions of the highest good; they are more opposed because the ultimate resolution of the tension between these two ways of thinking about ethics is the rejection of Christian ethics by philosophical ethics. Peaceful coexistence has been shattered by an unabandonable dialogue of rejection. Indeed, Barth seeks to show that the relations between Christian and philosophical ethics can be rightly interpreted only in terms of the radical incompatibility between them. This is the real ground of his objection to Schleiermacher's ethics as characteristically apologetic.

The radical incompatibility between Christian and philosophical ethics is not derived from the fact that the one is oriented toward revelation, the other toward reason. Although these diverse orientations contribute to an almost unavoidable alienation between them, the basic barrier between them lies at a deeper level. Barth thinks that it is both necessary and appropriate to dogmatics to make use of terms and concepts wherever they may be found, without being committed to and bound by the usage which such terms and concepts have variously and more generally acquired. 'No concept possesses *as such* an absolutely general and intrinsically binding meaning, including the term, Ethics.'[2] He applies this judgment to the analysis of ethics by starting more explicitly with ethics in general than we have done. We have affirmed that Christian ethics is *not* chiefly concerned with the *Good* but with 'what, as a believer in Jesus Christ and as a member of his church, I am to do'. And we have found

---

[1] Barth, Ibid., pp. 564, 571. Italics and translation mine.
[2] Ibid., p. 568. Italics and translation mine.

that such a formulation led almost straight to the embarrassing problem of a double standard in ethics. Barth, on the other hand, asks, 'What is the *Good* in and above all alleged goodness of human behavior?' Or in a shorter, etymologically nearer play on words: How dependable are the stabilities?[1] He disposes almost immediately of the problem of a double standard in ethics by showing how what is after all 'only relatively common' to all ethical thinking can be taken account of by Christian ethics in spite of its rejection of philosophical ethics. 'Howsoever the relation between them may be structured,' Barth declares, 'there can be no question . . . of a positive acceptance of Christian ethics by philosophical ethics or of a connecting link between Christian and philosophical ethics, in consequence of which philosophical ethics could be said to be further developed, expanded, and enriched'.[2]

We come, then, to the radical incompatibility between Christian and philosophical ethics, to the basic barrier between them. In a word it is this: *what is a problem to the one is not a problem to the other.* To put it epigrammatically: Christian and philosophical ethics share the *same concerns* but not the *same*

---

[1] Barth, Ibid., p. 569. Italics Barth's. In the original, the etymological play is drawn from the meaning of the word τὸ ἦθος:'*die Frage nach der Richtigkeit dieser Stetigkeiten*'. With Barth's account of the etymological form of the ethical question we have agreed (see above, Chapter I, p. 24). But when a Christian analysis transposes this question into the problem of the *Good*, it seems to us that its formulation is extrinsic to the proper concern of a Christian ethic with the ethical question. Indeed, some pages later, Barth expressly declares that the problem of the Good is not strictly a problem for Christian ethics at all (see pp. 573-77). The content of Barth's analysis is not adversely affected by this somewhat alien formulation. The formulation and the implications drawn from it simply do not fit precisely. Here is an instance of a residual influence of the classical and critical tradition in ethics upon Barth's discussion. And for this reason, among others, we have ventured to transpose the etymological form of the ethical question in a different, and what seems to us strictly considered a more appropriately Christian, way.

[2] Ibid., p. 575. Barth is talking about the concept of ethics in relation to Christian ethics and uses demonstrative pronouns (*this* and *that*) and adverbs (*here* and *yonder*) to express the contrast. In broadening the contrast to that between Christian ethics and philosophical ethics as separate scientific disciplines, and in the substitution of the nominal phrases for the pronouns, I am adapting this forthright statement of the fact of incompatibility to the central thrust of Barth's argument.

*concern.*[1] Philosophical ethics is concerned with the *problem of the Good*: its actuality, its knowability, its normative relation to human behavior. But this is no problem for Christian ethics at all. For included as it is within the doctrine of God, Christian ethics may—indeed, must—presuppose what has already happened, namely, a claim upon man arising from the dynamics of God's sovereign freedom. Christian ethics always already knows the Good. The fact of this claim makes Christian ethics primarily concerned not with the normative nature and role of the Good but with the terms and the territory of obedience, with what is involved in doing the Good. The problem of obedience, on the other hand, is central to Christian ethics because the concrete situation of man has been called into question by the divine claim upon him. What has been called into question is man's actual determination (*Bindung*) by the Good, his concrete resistance to the Good and the overcoming of this resistance. But all this is no problem at all for philosophical ethics, or at least it is a marginal problem which, in the last analysis, can be left open. To begin, as Christian ethics does, with God's action as prior to and the intrinsic presupposition (*Inbegriff*) of the Good, to begin with the reality of the divine claim, with the condemnation and justification of man as sinner—that is what makes the enterprise of philosophical ethics with its questions and its answers impossible. This is the contradiction to which Christian thinking about ethics subjects the relative validity of all thinking about ethics in general.[2] To adapt another and perhaps sharper of Barth's ways of putting it: *The radical incompatibility between Christian and philosophical ethics is the irreconcilability of their respective views of human self-determination.* For philosophical ethics, 'man makes ethics', as Professor Weiss has rightly declared; and this is the secret and the guarantee of his humanity. For Christian ethics, 'God makes ethics', that is, God initiates and establishes the humanity of man. As Barth says, 'Precisely because the divine election is ultimately the determination of man, the question arises concerning the self-determination of man in the light of his determination by God'.[3]

[1] We have hinted at this incompatibility above, Chapter III, pp. 77-80.

[2] Barth, *KD*, II 2, pp. 575-76.

[3] '*Gerade in dem die Erwaehlung letztlich die Bestimmung des Menschen ist, erhebt sich die Frage nach dieser Bestimmung entsprechenden menschlichen Selbstbestimmung.*' Ibid., p. 566.

This brings us to the crucial instance of Barth's saying differently what Schleiermacher also wanted to say. Schleiermacher saw that a double standard in ethics was inadmissible. He saw that Christian and philosophical ethics converged upon a common point, and that systematic ethical analysis had to face the question of a viable differentiation between them. The thrust of Christian toward philosophical ethics must take due account of these central issues. And this Barth also sees and seeks to achieve—but by a methodological reversal and reconstruction which lead to a fundamentally altered differentiation between Christian and philosophical ethics. Schleiermacher's apologetic exposition involves merely a provisional differentiation of Christian ethics from a philosophical ethics which cannot complete itself because it cannot make its implicit theological basis explicit. This comes ingeniously close to the center of the problem and is but a hair's breadth removed from the differentiation which Barth explores. The question is: Does this *hair's breadth* make all the difference in the world or doesn't it? Barth insists that it does. The reason is that only from the other side of this thin line can the intrinsic thrust of philosophical toward Christian ethics and of Christian toward philosophical ethics be correctly acknowledged and explicated.

The difference between Christian and philosophical ethics is unbridgeable because the theological foundation of a Christian ethic is not merely expendable for philosophical ethics but must be denied. This means that in the last analysis philosophical ethics is erroneous, mistaken, and false.[1] But—and this is the point which Barth's careless readers and critics have overlooked —Christian ethics neither repudiates nor ignores philosophical ethics. Barth is neither an ethical iconoclast nor an ethical obscurantist. He has simply explicated *dia-polemically* what Calvin and Luther rightly discerned but were too simply polemical about. I think it could be said that Barth is the first Christian moralist to set the record straight. *The methodological fact is that Christian ethics need not, cannot, and does not reject philosophical ethics; it is philosophical ethics which must and does reject Christian ethics.* 'The grace of God', Barth declares, 'protests against every humanly established ethic as such. The protest, however, is positive: grace not only negates man but still more

[1] Barth, ibid., pp. 584-85.

affirms man by pursuing the solution of the ethical problem which grace provides in active refutation, resolution and suspension of all human answers to that problem.'[1]

The problem common to Christian and philosophical ethics and upon which their respective methodologies converge is the problem of the humanity of man. Schleiermacher's accent upon the religious consciousness was neither deep enough nor total enough to expose and to support the ethical predicament of man. He was, thus, methodologically nearer to the preoccupation of philosophical ethics with ethical achievement than he was to the problem of obedience which the fact of redemption makes central for Christian ethics. Barth's accent is upon the intimate connection between man's behavior and man's existence as a person. This is why the ethical problem is really nothing other than the problem of the goodness (*Guete*), integrity (*Wuerde*), rightness (*Richtigkeit*), authentic continuity (*echte Kontinuitaet*) of man's behavior, of his existence, of himself.[2] This is why, as Barth sees it, a theological ethic can and must include all ethical truth under the claim of the grace of God. 'It does not matter whether such ethical insight be rational or historical, profane or religious, ecclesiastical or socio-ethical.' The task of a theological ethic is to sharpen the discussion of the concerns, the aims, and the formulations of philosophical ethics, and in the light of its own orientation to take these concerns with utmost seriousness. Indeed, a theological ethic must take philosophical ethics seriously because such an ethic always involves the 'stuff' of its own ethical reflections. 'But just because such a relation of theological to philosophical ethics is basic and concrete, it is a critical not a collaborative (*schiedlich-friedlich*) relation. A theological ethic agrees with all other ethics in so far as the basis and origin of ethics in the command of God are explicitly or implicitly acknowledged. . . . In so far as the derivation of ethics from the command of God is obscured or denied and independent principles for ethics are proposed, a theological ethic cannot take such ethical endeavors seriously.'[3] Thus it is Christian ethics which achieves authentic ethical inclusiveness, precisely because of its explicitly exclusive point of departure. Philosophical ethics with its explicitly inclusive point

---

[1] Barth, ibid., p. 573.    [2] Ibid., p. 572.    [3] Ibid., p. 585.

of departure culminates in the exclusion of the only validating ethical possibility.

## 2  The Ethical Inadequacy of Moral Philosophy

It may be that Barth is merely saying against the background of Kierkegaard and existentialism what Schleiermacher was saying against the background of Kant and romanticism. In that case they could be expected to think and write about ethics in radically different ways. A more careful examination of the record confirms the fact that they were concerned to say the same thing though in sharp differentiation and reversal. *The methodological significance of Schleiermacher's and Barth's analysis of Christian ethics is that both started from a common orientation in the Reformation conviction that God's redemptive action in Jesus Christ is the formative fact of Christian ethical reflection, and both arrived at a recognition of the insufficiency of philosophical ethics.* Both Schleiermacher and Barth start with an awareness of the fact that the redemptive basis and orientation of a Christian ethic involves the embarrassment of a double standard. Both refuse to evade this embarrassment by breaking off relations between Christian and philosophical ethics through resort to isolationist separation or condescending assertions of the superiority of Christian over philosophical ethics. Instead, both Schleiermacher and Barth seek to overcome the embarrassment of a double standard by trying to show that philosophical ethics can neither complete itself from within itself nor escape the thrust of a Christian ethic toward philosophical ethical endeavors. In making this plain both reject revisionism and synthesis and expose the insufficiency of philosophical ethics. *The insufficiency of philosophical ethics is that the specifically and formatively ethical factor cannot be given rational generalization, and without the possibility of rational generalization, philosophical ethics cannot give interpretative structure to the ethical situation.*[1] Philosophical ethics requires 'a right rule of reason',

---

[1] This formulation is confirmed in a particularly instructive way by meta-ethical inquiry, as we have already seen (Chapter IX, pp. 241-50). Next to Kant, analytical ethics has most conspicuously and painstakingly struggled with the problem of ethical generalization. Here is perhaps the most important link between Kant and the later Wittgenstein. Analytical ethics, however, seems less aware of the radicality of evil and its bearing upon the problem of ethical generalization than was Kant. Thus, meta-ethical

however approximate, to bridge the gap between the ethical claim and the ethical act. The gap between the ethical claim and the ethical act is exactly what nullifies such a rule. Schleiermacher recognized that the insufficiency of philosophical ethics is the clue to the incompatibility between Christian and philosophical ethics.[1] Yet he continued to think in terms of an inner dynamic of ethical reflection which by a kind of organic development would ultimately provide for the consummation of philosophical by Christian ethics.[2] Barth considers the insufficiency of philosophical ethics also as the clue to the incompatibility between Christian and philosophical ethics. But he finds the incompatibility so fundamental as to displace the prospect of consummation by the ultimate rejection, *not* of philosophical by Christian ethics, but of Christian by philosophical ethics.

The foregoing account of philosophical ethics has confirmed the insufficiency which both Schleiermacher and Barth have recognized. The consensus of philosophical ethics exhibits an investigation by rational analysis of the limits and the structure of human self-determination. The ethical object, the ethical subject, the operational shape of behavior comprise the structure of human self-determination.[3] The limits of human self-

moralists, unlike Kant, regard themselves as working on the threshold of the resolution of a problem rather than on the boundary of the insufficiency of philosophical ethics. Kant seems to be unique among moral philosophers in recognizing that the practical reason was involved in a threat rather than in an unresolved problem. But what Kant did not, and perhaps could not, see was that the limit which he tried vainly to transcend was really the boundary between Christian and philosophical ethics.

[1] 'What Christian ethics requires obligates only Christians; philosophical ethics make a more *general* claim because it seeks to bind all those who can achieve the level of insight into philosophical principles from which philosophical ethics is derived.' Schleiermacher, op. cit., p. 2. Translation and italics mine.

[2] The earliest notes contain the following entries: 'Paragraph 4  *The object of both is the same.* And must be so in accordance with the material. If revelation includes more, then: either the necessity of revelation has been established by reason and reason implicitly includes everything; or else this is not the case and revelation is without foundation (*unbegruendet*). If reason includes more the principle of revelation is insufficient.' 'Paragraph 5  *The mode of Knowledge is different.*' Ibid., Appendix A, 4, 5. Italics indicate captions. Translation mine.

[3] This corresponds exactly to the schematism which Schleiermacher had

determination are defined by the nature and the possibility of ethical generalization. The Good, Aristotle had observed, belongs to the class of the limited.[1] And in this, all the philosophical moralists have followed him.[2] But intrinsic to the enterprise of moral philosophy is the impossibility of bringing the limits and the structure of human self-determination into a meaningful relationship. This impossibility is evident in a threefold way:

a. The specifically ethical factor in human self-determination is the factor of limit. There is a limit with reference to which human self-determination is validated and guided. This limit is the Good. In giving ethical direction and significance to human behavior, the Good functions as a normative criterion, a criterion which is both a binding claim and a limiting judgment. The Good can be arrived at by rational analysis only as 'a right rule of reason' which serves as a proximate link between the ethical claim and the ethical act. Thus, it is not the *specifically ethical* but the *proximately ethical*, not the validating Good but the Good as validated by reason, which makes ethical generalization possible and operable.

b. Furthermore, 'a right rule of reason' functions as a formula for differentiating ethical achievement from ethical failure. The *ethical* significance of such a rule is directly proportional to its reduction of the gap between the ethical claim and the ethical act. When applied, the rule readily supports the conclusion that one is doing better than one is. The structure of human self-determination, however, presupposes a concrete human situation which is characterized behaviorally, by a falling short of the claim by which it is directed and validated. In addition, there is a drive toward the unlimited, which in effect repudiates the claim. Biblical imagination has profoundly

---

recognized and summarily formulated as the doctrine of the highest good, of obligation, and of virtues. See above, pp. 263ff.

[1] See above, Chapter VI, p. 170.

[2] Whether as the attempt to define what is good without qualification (Kant, Chapter VI, p. 175), or as the most universal principle that the essence of good is simply to satisfy demand (James, Chapter VII, p. 197), or as the primary ethical principle (Weiss, Chapter VIII, p. 210), or as a productive character structure (Fromm, Chapter VIII, p. 220), or as a meta-ethical justification of normative statements (Brandt, Chapter IX, p. 231).

underlined the desire to transgress limits as the original temptation leading to the original sin. Ethical generalization is possible and operable only because the proximate rational good is regarded more seriously than the persistence of radical evil.

It may be, for example, that the rule of the mean—'in nothing too much'—is an effective counsel in the matter of the consumption of alcoholic beverages, so far as any given number of individuals is concerned. Yet, living by such a rule can scarcely take very sensitive account of the human waste of alcoholism both individual and social. On the other hand, a profound sensitivity to the perils of alcoholism may lead to the adoption of another 'right rule of reason', namely, 'whatever causes personal and social injury to man is to be avoided'. But, in view of the many-sidedness and the persistence of the alcoholic evil, can such a rule be seriously proposed as a general rule of conduct? The strong are, indeed, to bear the infirmities of the weak, as the New Testament suggests. But this is to be done, not under a 'right rule of reason', but in the freedom in which men were created to live. On the 'cocktail circuit' or in a fishing village ravaged by alcoholism, the 'right' course may well be total abstention. But in a situation in which drinking expresses both a proper protest against ethical legalism and an occasion through which harassed human beings may be reached, the 'right' course may well be participation. In the Christian *koinonia*, men learn how to weep with them that weep and rejoice with them that rejoice.[1]

c. The fact of ethical failure exposes the gap between the ethical claim and the ethical act, between the proximate good and the good achieved, not as a separation to be dissolved but as a cleavage to be overcome. Philosophical ethics cannot overcome such a cleavage because the rational validation of the Good, to which it is methodologically committed, functions as a principle of inclusiveness which excludes what is unlimited. Ethically speaking, evil is the unlimited, whether as resistance to limit or refusal of limit. What evil *means* ethically is that the rational Good cannot give direction and validation to human good. It cannot do so because the rational Good presupposes the possibility and applicability of ethical generalization to the structure of human self-determination. Evil cannot be excluded

[1] The allusion is to Rom. 12.15.

from the concrete ethical situation by the device of excluding it from rational generalization.

Thus the insufficiency of philosophical ethics exposes the ethical inadequacy of moral philosophy. The exposure raises the question whether there is another way of bringing the limits and the structure of human self-determination into a meaningful relationship. Is there a way of giving behavioral shape to the Good, of bringing what is specifically and formatively ethical and the concrete ethical situation meaningfully together? In particular, is there a way of doing so without recourse to a normative ethical criterion which immunizes rational generalization against the ethical threat of evil? The philosophical moralists with whom we have entered into dialogue have implicitly pointed toward such a possibility. It is, perhaps, no accident that Immanuel Kant and William James may be identified as the inaugurators of a way of thinking about ethics which, while still hampered by the insufficiency of philosophical ethics, nevertheless indicates the course along which this insufficiency may be overcome. With Kant, the rationalistic tradition in ethics ended on the boundary of religion, threatened by the fact of radical evil. The failure of ethical reflection on the classical and critical model is its inability to include the religious possibility of dealing with the ethical threat of evil within the limits of reason alone.[1] With James, the formalistic way of thinking about ethics is deliberately replaced by a contextual approach to truth and goodness only to come to a halt on the boundary of religion and before the problem of evil. Pragmatic pluralism is unable and unwilling to deny the reality of religion as experience but equally unable and unwilling to affirm religion as a 'mental mode of adaptation to reality', and evil is not so much to be overcome as 'dropped out altogether'.[2]

Meanwhile, as we have seen, the tension between ethics and religion and between the rational good and the fact of evil has intensified.[3] Kant and James were sufficiently aware of the

[1] See above, Chapter VI, pp. 183-89.

[2] See above, Chapter VII, pp. 199-202.

[3] This is perhaps the profoundest methodological significance of existentialist ethics, if not among the philosophers (Kierkegaard, Heidegger, Sartre), certainly among the novelists (Dostoevsky, Balzac, Dickens, Galsworthy), as Barth has pointed out. *KD*, p. 602. But I think one may say this also of the philosophers.

ethical bearing of Christianity to ascribe to it high priority in shaping the heart and the will if not the rational persuasiveness of the search for the Good.[1] But the resurgence of ethical humanism has changed all this. Both in its metaphysical and in its depth-psychological forms, ethical humanism finds religion, and Christianity in particular, ethically unproductive and superfluous. But neither in its metaphysical nor in its depth-psychological forms has ethical humanism been able to deal with the radicality of evil. Indeed, humanism, in contrast to eudemonism, Kantianism, and pragmatism, exhibits the intrinsic connection between the displacement of religion by the powers of man and indifference to the radicality of evil.[2]

There is, however, a way of thinking about ethics which is not bound by the insufficiency of philosophical ethics. Such an ethic provides a validating limit in terms of which human self-determination can be structured, and the radicality of evil included, within the analysis of the possibility and the power to do what is good. Such an ethic has been driven by its own concern for what it takes to make and to keep human life human toward the boundary on which the insufficiency of philosophical ethics has been exposed. Such an ethic has learned from Aristotle and especially from Kant about the limits of rationality in dealing with the concrete ethical situation, marked as it is by the cleavage between the ethical claim and the ethical act. Such an ethic has learned from William James the liberating viability open to ethical analysis when it undertakes a methodological shift from the rational to the contextual good. From ethical humanism, especially of the depth-psychological variety, such an ethic has learned to transpose the ethical question from the question of the Good to the question of human maturity, the question of the freedom of man to be what he is. And all along the line, the encounter of such an ethic with the tradition of moral philosophy has intensified the question of the terms in which the ethical claim and the ethical act can meet so as to give ethical shape to behavior. Such an ethic is the methodological option open to ethical reflection undertaken from within the *koinonia*.

The inadequacy of moral philosophy does not, of course,

---

[1] See above, Chapter VI, p. 183; Chapter VII, p. 199.
[2] See above, Chapter VIII, pp. 211f., 221ff.

establish the validity of a *koinonia* ethic. But it is just possible that the special force of humanism has made explicit what has been implicit in philosophical ethics from the first, namely, the exclusion of religion, Christianity in particular, from the humanization of man. The issue of humanization is the decisive ethical issue, and a Christian ethic that understands its proper task will not seek to have it otherwise. On the contrary, the fact that philosophical ethics must reject Christian ethics serves as a cogent reminder that only a Christian ethic that focuses upon the issue of humanization is on the right path. More often than not, a Christian analysis of ethics has blurred the focus so that its irenic openness to philosophical ethics has obscured its own polemical thrust as well as the real ground of the incompatibility between Christian and philosophical ethics. This does not mean that Kant or James or Weiss or Fromm could have—or would have—included the Christian assessment of the validating limit within which the structure of human self-determination is authenticated. It does mean, however, that Christian ethics would be rejected by philosophical ethics for intrinsic and not for spurious reasons.[1] The issue of humanization has clearly marked the incompatibility between philosophical and Christian ethics. The insights of philosophical ethics—the recognition of radical evil, of the contextual character of truth and goodness, of human maturity, of the possibility of a theological rule of meta-ethical analysis—can be appropriated by Christian ethics not as a methodological accommodation but as a confirmation of the methodological integrity of Christian ethics itself.

The 'decisive' encounter between resurgent ethical humanism and a Christian ethic that is aware of its methodological integrity has sharpened the issue of humanization in terms of the question 'What context of ethical analysis is required by an authentic account of man's freedom?'[2] The answer is: *that*

---

[1] Such as, for example, that Christianity offered 'a gnostic answer to a divine world-enigma' (James, see above, p. 201), or that 'theologies tend to confuse the fact of evil with an origin; theodicies tend to confuse the fact of evil with its locus' (Weiss, see above, p. 217), or that Christian ethics is 'authoritarian ethics' (Fromm, see above, p. 219). The point is that these strictures against a Christian analysis can be and must be admitted. But they are spurious because they miss the fundamental incompatibility between Christian and philosophical ethics.

[2] See above, Chapter VIII, p. 216.

context in which the specifically ethical (e.g., the validating limit upon human self-determination) and the concrete 'stuff' of behavior are conjoined in an environment, by a direction, and through a pattern of behavior in which the cleavage between the ethical claim and the ethical act has been overcome by an act of free obedience.[1] Such a context is the methodological contribution of a *koinonia* ethic to ethical theory. When the church is the context of ethical reflection, behavior acquires a contextual character which includes all men in the doing of what God is doing in the world to make and to keep human life human. The insufficiency of philosophical ethics does not validate the methodology of a Christian ethic. But it does clarify how and why it is that a Christian analysis of ethics resolves the problem of human behavior. Indeed, the methodological incompatibility between philosophical and Christian ethics points to the radical transposition that ethical analysis must undergo if its method and its substance are to correspond.

[1] Let those who are quickly disposed to conclude that such an answer proves nothing so much as that the mountain has labored and brought forth a mouse pause to recall the fable of 'The Lion and the Mouse'. It was the mouse that gnawed the entangled lion free.

PART THREE

# THE QUESTION OF CONSCIENCE

# XII

## A CRITIQUE OF MORAL THEOLOGY

THE differentiation of Christian ethics from moral philosophy has brought us in sight of the terms in which the cleavage between the ethical demand and the ethical act may be overcome. This cleavage is, as we have seen, the critical problem of human behavior. The problem involves unbelievers as well as believers and lends urgency to the need for an adequate method or way of thinking about ethics. What is required is a context of ethical analysis within which an authentic account of man's freedom may be given.[1] The inability of moral philosophy to meet this requirement has sharply emerged from the encounter between a Christian ethic and a resurgent ethical humanism. The way is thus open for an attempt to show how and why a Christian ethic does meet the requirement and thereby resolves the ethical problem.

The distinctive radicality of Christian ethics encounters opposition from within as well as from without. Christian ethics is in conflict not only with humanistic ethics but also with moral theology. A review of this conflict is indispensable to our present purpose for two principal reasons. The first is that moral theology is the most tested and tried attempt from within the context of the Christian Church and Christian revelation to differentiate between Christian and philosophical thinking about ethics. The second reason is that the conflict between a *koinonia* ethic and moral theology over the method and task of Christian ethics centers upon the problem of freedom and obedience in ethical behavior. It is no accident that the tradition of moral theology, both Roman Catholic and Protestant, exhibits a lively sensitivity to and struggle over the conscience. For moral theology rightly sees that the crux of the problem of

[1] See above, pp. 216, 283.

freedom and obedience is the conscience. Here is a much contested and much obscured area in the environment of humanization where the 'specifically ethical' and the concrete 'stuff' of behavior meet and give ethical shape to action. Here God and men have directly and insistently to do with one another. In this area, the aims and the direction, the motivations and the decisions, the instruments and the structures of human interrelatedness are forged into a pattern of response—*a style of life*—according to which the liberation of obedience has become the characteristic ethical fact. Men who obey under this freedom are free in this obedience. This obedient freedom is the freedom of maturity. It is the measure of development of men who do what they are.[1]

Let us turn first, then, to a critical examination of moral theology with special regard to the emergence and the significance of conscience. Moral theology proceeds on a synthetic rather than a revisionist basis; and the synthetic persuasiveness of moral theology is the notable achievement of Roman Catholic theology. Some grasp of the opportunity as well as the peril of this way of thinking about Christian ethics is a prerequisite of any attempt to take a different course.

### 1 *The Nature and Scope of Moral Theology*

The present account of the nature and scope of moral theology has been based upon the four-volume work by the Rev. Henry Davis, S.J., entitled *Moral and Pastoral Theology*.[2] The work is a

---

[1] See above, pp. 159-61.

[2] Henry Davis, S.J., *Moral and Pastoral Theology*, Sheed & Ward, London and New York, 1938, 4 vols. Volume I deals with principles; Volume II with precepts; Volumes III and IV with the seven sacraments of the church and with the way in which they are to be related to practical conduct. Perhaps the standard Continental work on moral theology is that by Joseph Mausbach, *Katholische Moraltheologie*, Elfte verbesserte Auflage, von Gustav Ermecke, Aschendorff, Muenster, Bd. I—*Die allgemeine Moral*, 1959; Bd. II—*Die spezielle Moral*, 1960; Bd. III—*Die spezielle Moral*, about to be published. The work originally appeared as *Katholische Moraltheologie*, Aschendorff Verlag, 1926-1930, and has been greatly revised and improved by the distinguished professor of moral theology at Paderborn. Its exposition is more thorough and comprehensive than the work by Father Davis. But as regards the foundation, the general structure, and the scope of moral theology, the two accounts are conspicuously similar. Indeed, the Thomistic model by which all moral theologians have been guided has meant that

clear and comprehensive exposition, and of acknowledged competence and influence.

Father Davis explains that 'moral theology is that branch of theology which states and explains the laws of human conduct in reference to man's supernatural destiny. It investigates the moral good and the moral evil in relation to man's ultimate end.'[1] Moral theology is at once distinct from and more comprehensive than ethics. It is distinct from ethics since ethics considers what is right and wrong about any given action on the basis of human reason unaided by revelation, whereas moral theology assumes a divine revelation as the basis of its analysis of conduct. What makes moral theology more comprehensive than ethics is that, in addition to divine revelation, moral theology draws upon ecclesiastical tradition and the reality of a supernatural order for its account and direction of behavior. Thus moral theology is concerned with conduct which may be rationally analyzed and guided, but conduct understood and interpreted always in the context of a divine revelation, an ecclesiastical tradition, and a supernatural order. Ethics is the handmaid of moral theology. 'If', says Davis, 'certain acts are proved to be in accordance with rational human nature, or if certain other acts are proved to be contrary to it, these conclusions are accepted and reinforced by moral theology. For rational nature is not destroyed or supplanted by its supernatural elevation but is perfected and adorned by it.'[2] Here is simply another way of stating the celebrated maxim upon which Roman Catholic anthropology and ethics rest. It is the maxim formulated by St Thomas in conspicuous dependence upon St Augustine: 'Grace does not destroy nature but perfects it.'[3] To this maxim Catholic theology and ethics have again and

---

variations of treatment concern details of arrangement rather than the fundamental scheme. Dr Ermecke's impressive scholarly achievement is perhaps best understood not only as an attempt to give full contemporaneity to the Mausbach text but also as an attempt to reaffirm the fundamental pattern of moral theology against certain vigorous revisionist efforts of contemporary Roman moralists. On Mausbach's more Augustinian (rather than Aristotelian) reading of St Thomas, see Emil Brunner, *The Divine Imperative*, The Westminster Press, Philadelphia, 1947 (Lutterworth Press, London, 1947), pp. 94-99.

[1] Davis, op. cit., Vol. I, p. 2.     [2] Ibid.

[3] '. . . *Gratia non tollit naturam sed perficit.*' Thomas Aquinas, *Summa*

again returned for support of what has come to be known as their semi-Pelagianism.[1]

In addition to being a theological science of ethics, and thus both distinct from and more comprehensive than ethics, moral theology, according to Davis, accepts the proved conclusions of dogmatics. The subject matter of moral theology is conduct. The subject matter of dogmatics is certain articles of faith. The connection between moral theology and dogmatics is supplied by canon law. Canon law is the collection of prescriptive regulations concerning man's conduct as a member of the visible society of the church. There is a *Forum Externum*, an external appeal by which the individual may guide his conduct, i.e., the appeal to the rules laid down by the church. But there is also a *Forum Internum*, which is the appeal to the obligation recognized in conscience to oppose in behavior what the church opposes.

A further point of considerable importance for the understanding of moral theology has to do with its relation to casuistry. Father Davis carefully excludes casuistry both from moral theology and from jurisprudence. 'It is', he declares, 'a separate science.' As such, casuistry is 'merely the reasoned application of law to concrete cases and it determines with all possible exactitude the limitations of law or the bearing of law upon particular cases'.[2] We have already had more than one occasion to notice the vexatious problem in all ethical theory, namely, the problem of relating the normative to the variable elements in conduct. Casuistry is perhaps the most carefully elaborated way of taking account of the diversities of behavior while retaining the integrity of the principle according to which behavior is to be judged. One could therefore say that casuistry presupposes moral theology and that moral theology functions through casuistry.

---

*Theologica*, I[a], Q. 1, Art. 8, Ad. 2. Thomas does not cite Augustine, but see the latter's treatise *On the Spirit and the Letter*, Migne, PL, 44-45 [X] chap. xxvii, 47. English translation in *The Nicene and Post-Nicene Fathers*, First Series, The Christian Literature Company, Buffalo, Vol. V, 1887, p. 103. See also Chapter X, p. 256, note 2.

[1] Brunner, op. cit., pp. 95, 98; Mausbach-Ermecke, op. cit., pp. 22, 28-29, and expressly p. 33.

[2] Davis, op. cit., Vol. I, pp. 2-3.

A final point may be mentioned which further underscores the immense versatility and persuasiveness of moral theology. This has to do with the contribution of moral theology to the problem of ethical certainty. Davis admits, as Aristotle had done long before, that in moral questions absolute certainty is very difficult to reach. By means of the science of casuistry, moral theology is able to go a long way toward reducing the moral ambiguity of behavior. Casuistry incorporates behavior within an order of tested principles by which it may be guided. 'The problem', says Davis, 'is this. In many cases, reason may prove in the abstract that a given line of conduct may be adopted. But in the concrete, taking human nature as it is, one would say that the line of conduct should be avoided.'[1] This is as clear a statement of the ethical cleavage as one could find. It poses the question of the relevance and persuasiveness of guidance in a particularly sharp way.

How does moral theology effectively connect an order of moral instruction and guidance with a frankly acknowledged moral uncertainty? If one is in doubt about the morality of any given course of conduct, there are three avenues of counsel by which one may be guided. First, there is the recourse to the common opinion of divines on the subject. Second, it is prudent to incline to those opinions which are accepted by the larger number of competent moralists. Obviously, this advice presupposes that there is no unanimity of opinion among divines about what is the right thing to do. But when the authorities are equally divided, a third counsel of conduct is available. In such a case, it is justifiable to choose either opinion. This procedure, far from being 'an abdication of reason, and a substitution of authority for argument', simply means that when a matter of conduct is doubtful in the abstract, 'my line of conduct is justified if regulated in accordance with good opinion'.[2] The justification is neither arbitrary nor irrational because good opinion is opinion in accordance with reason, and the good opinion of divines is opinion regulated in accordance with reason in the context of divine revelation, ecclesiastical tradition, and the principles of the supernatural order. It is therefore possible, after having followed these procedures, to say, as Father Davis does, 'I do not act in doubt, but with certainty'.[3]

[1] Davis, ibid., p. 4.　　　[2] Ibid., p. 5.　　　[3] Ibid.

## 2  *Moral Theology in Operation*

If now we ask how such a theological science of conduct actually applies to behavior, we must move from its way of arriving at the certainty of moral judgments to its account of the nature of a moral act. St Thomas pointed out that every moral act involves three elements,[1] and his analysis has largely shaped the teaching of moral theology on this point. Every moral act is an act of freedom. There must be a genuine alternative, a genuine choice if behavior is to be judged from the standpoint of morality. Secondly, there is the factor of 'voluntariness'. Whatever choice is made must proceed from the consent of the will. And thirdly, there must be what is called 'advertence of intellect'. By this, moral theologians mean that we must have clear knowledge of the object or end of our willing. To quote Father Davis, 'An act is perfectly voluntary when done with full advertence and full consent. It is imperfectly voluntary if advertence or consent are partial.'[2]

It is plain from the immediately foregoing remark that these three necessary constituents of a moral act are not always present in the same degree or even in full strength. One or another may be missing. How, then, is the action to be judged and the culpability determined? In such instances—and behavior for the most part consists of just these—the regulative position is assigned to the element of voluntariness. 'An object of the will', Father Davis declares, 'is directly voluntary when a positive will-act is elicited in its regard.'[3] This regulative role of consent in moral behavior takes the form in Roman Catholic ethical theory of the doctrine of intention to which we have already alluded.[4] It is *intention*—the *intention* to pursue the end, the *intention* to pursue the object of the will—which is decisive.

The negative instance of an evil action may serve to make this plain. An evil action is an intentional choice of a bad end. An intentional choice of a bad end occurs whenever three conditions are present: the results of an action could have been

[1] Thomas Aquinas, op. cit., I$^a$-II$^{ae}$, QQ. 6-15.
[2] Davis, op. cit., Vol. I, p. 12; a similar but more elaborate and refined discussion of *voluntariness* in relation to *advertence* is given in Mausbach-Ermecke, op. cit., pp. 234ff.
[3] Davis, op. cit., Vol I, p. 12.          [4] See above, pp. 128-29.

foreseen; though the results could have been foreseen, the action could have been prevented; it ought to have been prevented. Such an action is unmistakably evil and culpable. It is possible, for example, to foresee the result of an action and to know that it ought to have been prevented, but to be unable to prevent the action. In Father Davis' words, 'It is permissible to set a cause in motion in spite of its foreseen evil effect, provided the act which produces the evil effect is not itself morally wrong'.[1] Davis refers to the familiar example of the torpedoing of a neutral ship which in time of war is carrying arms to an enemy. It could be foreseen that the firing of a torpedo might have as its effect the killing of passengers aboard, or the destruction of valuable cargo. These are foreseen evil consequences. However, the *intention* is not to bring about these effects, but to torpedo the ship in order to prevent arms from reaching an enemy. In other words, the *intention* is really to bring hostilities to an end; and since this is the *intention* of the action, the action may not be regarded as morally wrong.[2] The instance of the torpedo is particularly instructive because it includes consequences which not only could have been foreseen but could have been prevented. Yet the action is not morally wrong because it ought to have been undertaken in order to bring hostilities to an end, and this was indeed the intention of firing the torpedo. If an action ought to have been pursued, even though the evil effects of the action could have been foreseen, and could have been prevented, the action is good and not evil.

A further instance of moral theology in operation may be noted with particular reference to the relation of advertence of intellect to action. Once again it is the negative case of ignorance which serves to make the point.

Ignorance, in its moral aspect, is the absence of that knowledge which we ought to have when we act. Now ignorance may be *invincible* or *vincible*. Ignorance is *invincible* when it cannot be got rid of by such reasonable diligence as is commensurate with the issue of our act and our opportunities. In some situations, reasonable diligence would mean *considerable* diligence, as when important issues are at stake, such as saving another's physical or spiritual life. Such ignorance clearly excuses from

[1] Davis, op. cit., Vol. I, pp. 13-14.
[2] It will be recalled that a similar—indeed, the identical—justification was offered for the decision of President Truman ordering the atomic bombing of Hiroshima in 1945. See above, p. 241.

moral fault, since the agent is unaware, through no fault of his own, of his obligation. *Vincible* ignorance, on the other hand, could have been got rid of by reasonable diligence. Generally speaking, *vincible* ignorance is imputable because the act is voluntary in its cause. But how imputable it is depends upon the *kind* of vincible ignorance. If vincible ignorance be fostered, it is called *affected* or *studied* ignorance. If hardly any reasonable means are taken to dispel the ignorance, it is called *crass* or *supine* ignorance. If some, but insufficient, diligence has been used trying to dispel it, it is styled simply vincible.[1]

The painstaking preoccupation of such an analysis with the nuances of behavior and with the responsibility for clear and reliable moral guidance is marked by an architectonic sobriety which to those unaccustomed to this way of thinking about ethics is likely to seem alternately tedious and amusing. Let it be noted, however, that the combination of advertence and voluntariness presupposed by such an analysis of ignorance provides a remarkably cogent and concrete way of sorting out the ethical aspects of behavior and the degree of culpability. Alternative approaches to behavior must, therefore, seriously face the question whether such alternatives have anything like the ethical clarity and pedagogical wisdom provided by moral theology.

A section on scandal exemplifies the same kind of precision of analysis. It is particularly instructive because it shows how inclusive and specific moral theology is, and how alert and adaptable it endeavors to be, as regards changes in behavioral patterns. Various kinds of scandal are carefully enumerated,[2] and then the discussion turns to a very practical application of scandal: that concerning matters of dress.

In matters of dress the custom of a civilized country excuses many, if not all, eccentricities in women. But dress that is apt to give scandal to reasonable people is certainly to be condemned as sinful. Good Catholics are rightly distressed at the change in modern times that has taken place in women's attire. Though it is possible that 'custom may stale its infinite variety', and that as young men become accustomed to the sight of hardly veiled exposures, they will think less of them and cease to be incited to lust, nevertheless, the virtue of modesty which is the peculiar adornment of women, and of charity to others, demands that women should exercise quite considerable moderation in following fashions that scandalize.

---

[1] Davis, op. cit., Vol. I, pp. 16ff. See also Mausbach-Ermecke, op. cit., pp. 218ff.

[2] Davis, op. cit., Vol. I, pp. 333-35.

Though the young woman may adopt useful fashions, she should be careful to avoid extremes, and should preferably follow the example of those who are brought up by good Catholic parents who esteem the modest bearing of their daughters a very important social virtue today. Great latitude is reasonably allowed.[1]

Davis goes on to suggest that there may come a time when a change in behavior patterns, originally in contravention of the precepts of moral theology, comes to be so generally accepted as to alter its relationship to the *intention* of action.

Plainly the approach to behavior in terms of such a structured combination of principle, precept, and the principal parts of an act is versatile, viable, and comprehensive. The Aristotelian doctrine of the mean has been transformed into 'the golden rule of intention', which, as a rational principle, enables the moral analyst and counselor to take due account of the diversity and complexity of the moral life while at the same time keeping the moral sense of direction clear. In view of the wider context in which this analysis of behavior is set, namely, the context of revelation, ecclesiastical tradition, and a supernatural order, the science of moral theology emerges as a virtually indispensable instrument of a Christian ethic in its task of attempting by reflective analysis to interpret and to shape behavior.

## 3 *The Renovation of Moral Theology: A Critique from Within by Moral Theologians*

The grounds for laying this effective instrument aside must be basic indeed. If, as we have suggested, moral theology is an ethic elaborated from within the context of the Christian revelation but to be regarded, nevertheless, as opposed to a *koinonia* ethic, it is incumbent upon us to offer a serious defense of this appraisal. We may begin by noting the growing disquiet among moral theologians themselves about the synthetic persuasiveness of a position like that of Father Davis, with its intrinsic and rigid Thomism. The clarity and strength of the Jesuit position are acknowledged, especially as regards the effective application of Thomistic theology and ethics to the pastoral practice of the church. But there is a noticeable and increasing tendency among

[1] Davis, ibid., p. 335.

Roman Catholic moralists toward a less schematic and more viable conception of moral theology.[1]

### a. Roman Catholic criticism

The current attempt at a renovation of moral theology is particularly evident in Continental Roman Catholicism. It has had no effect upon the official position of the church, which, in this as in other matters, stems from the Council of Trent. It is nevertheless significant that beneath the tranquil exterior of unanimity in matters of faith and morals, a lively ferment of intellectual inquiry and self-criticism continues. The impatience with the tradition of moral theology is rooted in the recognition that the adherence to fixed principles has tended to ignore the grave problems of concrete human behavior. These problems are continually being pressed upon the moral theologian by the poets, the novelists, the press, and by other intellectuals, particularly the sociologists and existential philosophers. The renovation does not seek a new foundation for moral theology in order to correct this grave oversight. It aims rather at a re-examination of St Thomas with the accent upon an existentialist interpretation of the relationship between charity and responsible human behavior. A brief notice of two expositions of this revisionist effort will perhaps suffice to indicate its direction and something of what it involves.

In the year 1947 a methodological essay was defended before the Faculty of Theology of the Catholic Institute in Paris. The author was Père Gérard Gilleman, S.J.[2] The essay assumes that the contemporary ethical situation is one of moral anarchy in which the massive edifice of traditional virtues is largely gone.

---

[1] For an instructive survey of the current discussion of moral theology among Roman Catholic theologians, see the article by Charles Robert, 'Théologie morale fondamentale', in *La Révue des Sciences Religieuses*, published by the Catholic Faculty of Theology in the University of Strasbourg, Vol. 29, No. 3, July 1955, pp. 267-83.

[2] Père Gérard Gilleman, S.J., 'Le Primat de la Charité en Théologie morale', *Essai Methodologique*, Paris, 1947. The essay is structured in three parts. The first sets out an account of morality according to St Thomas; the second sets out the principal argument of the essay, which is an analysis of the fundamental principle capable of leading us today toward a morality of charity; and the third offers a manual for the guidance of behavior in the light of the foregoing analysis of the principle of charity.

Thus far, that edifice has been replaced by only a vague notion of charity by which the Christian is supposed to model his behavior.

According to Gilleman, love or charity in man, left to himself, degenerates into passion and leads to tyranny in social life. Charity can, however, be convincingly shown to be the source and the end of the virtues. This is what St Thomas really wished to do. But he was prevented from doing so by the methodological climate of his time, which was excessively preoccupied with minutiae of analysis and application. We are astonished to learn from a Jesuit that Thomas was virtually an Augustinian, at least as regards the doctrine of charity. For Thomas wanted to show that all virtues are, as Augustine before him had taught, forms of love. By their schemes of virtues and vices, the manuals of moral theology have traditionally obscured the pervasiveness of charity.

This criticism of the traditional reading of St Thomas brings Père Gilleman to a most important alteration of the traditional analysis of action in moral theology. Once charity is viewed, not as the highest virtue in a hierarchical order of virtues, but as the supreme virtue of which all other virtues are forms, the regulative role of intention in evaluating behavior must be considerably modified, if not abandoned. Gilleman finds confusing and superficial the claim that, in order to make our virtues expressions of charity, it is necessary and sufficient to correct a given action by the *intention*. It is confusing and superficial because it leaves the unfortunate Christian virtually paralyzed by the preoccupation with the adjustment of his intentions. He is thus reduced to a phenomenon of the psychology of conscience. As Gilleman sees it, charity was for St Thomas *the* ontological virtue. Charity permeates the free activity of man because it is a profound spiritual tendency which affects the depths of the *being* of the Christian and so guides him toward his supernatural end. Charity at once animates the moral activity of the Christian and unites him to God as his final end. Consequently charity, which is always implicit in a virtuous action, is not always the object of an explicit intention, or even of a virtuous intention.

This displacement of intention from its regulative role in moral judgment and behavior is not meant to deprive intention of ethical significance. The aim is rather to include intention as

well as advertence and freedom within the pervasive influence
of charity. The manuals of moral theology had, according to
Gilleman, never very adequately solved the problem of how to
relate charity to the vices as well as to the virtues. When,
however, the virtues are regarded as forms of charity, it becomes
possible to make use of another Augustinian ethical doctrine,
according to which evil is to be understood as the privation of
good. This means that vice is the absence of charity. Thus the
two principles which St Thomas had placed at the beginning
of an ethic of love are adequately applied to conduct. The principles concern charity and merit. Charity, Thomas had urged,
is the form of all the virtues; and for a man in a state of grace,
every act is either meritorious or culpable. The doctrine of
privation makes it possible to recognize the culpability of action,
not so much in terms of degrees of guilt and blame, but in terms
of a loss of charity. Thus charity is truly exalted as the original
motivation and final end of behavior. In applying charity to
virtues and vices, Gilleman employs traditional classifications.
But he does so with more than the objective precision of rational
analysis, which was the strength of the tradition of moral
theology. This analysis also shows the psychological discernment which takes account both of charity as the climate of
virtue and of the light which the social sciences have shed upon
the complexity of human motivation and action. It is charity
which distinguishes the virtuous Christian from the honest
pagan.

A similar shift of accent may be noted between the renovation
of moral theology proposed by Gilleman and the renovation
proposed in the extended treatment of the subject by Bernhard
Haering.[1] The focus of attention in this work is upon the
nature of responsibility rather more than upon the nature of
virtue, upon the ethical subject rather more than upon the
ethical object.

Father Haering  regards *responsibility* as the crux of a religious
morality, and thus also of moral theology. What impresses the
reader is the conspicuously biblical way in which this interpre-

---

[1] Bernhard Haering,  *Das Gesetz Christi*, Vte Auflage, Wewel, Freiburg,
1957, 1446 pp. The volume consists of two parts; the first is called
'Fundamental Morality', 556 pp.; the second is called 'Special Morality',
769 pp.

tation of responsibility is worked out. In language remarkably reminiscent of Emil Brunner, responsibility is defined in terms of an interpersonal relationship between God and man. A dialogue is under way in which God calls and man responds. The theme of the dialogue is the prompting of men through the word of God to imitate Christ in order that they may understand how to enter into communion with the love of God. In the light of this premise, the familiar and essential themes of morality are enlivened and enriched. The subject of morality, for example, is interpreted in terms of the discipleship involved in the imitation of Christ rather than in terms of the essentials of a moral act. The obligations of discipleship are elaborated with reference to a doctrine of man which is dialectically developed according to the polarity between 'son of Adam' and 'disciple of Christ'. The movement is from the first to the second Adam, and thus the opposite of the anthropological movement presupposed by a *koinonia* ethic; but the biblical context is instructively similar. Again, the moral object is interpreted not with respect to the highest good, but with respect to the content of the call of God expressed in God's law. Virtues are still analyzed in terms of the traditional distinction between the theological and cardinal virtues, but each virtue is treated as a means of entering into communion with God and the Son of God. Thus virtues are the fruit of faith and the fruition of the imitation of Christ. Conversely, sin and temptation are regarded as an abandonment of the imitation of Christ.

The second part of Haering's treatise proposes a remedy both for a general problem which has beset moral theology and for the traditional treatment of virtues and vices. Hitherto the general problem has been that the link between the general principles of morality and the special moral situations and actions has been obscure. Casuistry has never adequately disposed of ethical ambiguity. As regards the virtues, the manuals of moral theology have variously schematized rather than synthesized them. Within the framework of the traditional scheme, Haering argues that the theological virtues are implanted in the ethical subject. This implantation is due chiefly to the virtue of charity, which can really only be presupposed because it is so intimate to the life of the believer. Haering echoes the doctrine of the virtues as forms of love, urging that the virtues introduce the divine order into various domains of life and consequently are imposed upon the conscience as means of realizing charity. Thus, through an admirable combination of doctrinal and ethical analyses, this discussion of moral theology viably relates divine revelation, ecclesiastical tradition, and a supernatural order with a morality of love.

A different kind of renovation of moral theology characterizes the ethics of Dietrich von Hildebrand, Professor of Philosophy in the Graduate School at Fordham University. von Hildebrand is an author of enormous productivity and prodigious knowledge; his work spans, as it were, two continents. His eminence as a Catholic moralist was already solidly established in Germany before he came to the United States.[1] He does not attempt a re-examination of St Thomas, but there can be no doubt about the Thomistic foundation and orientation of his thought. In further differentiation from his fellow moralists on the Continent, von Hildebrand seeks not so much to take account of the existentialist influence upon contemporary literature, sociology, and philosophy as to subject these disciplines to rigorous criticism and ultimate rejection in the light of a vigorous reaffirmation of the traditional substance of Roman Catholic theology and ethics.

It must not be supposed, however, that von Hildebrand's aggressive espousal of divine revelation, ecclesiastical tradition, and a supernatural order as the indispensable foundations of authentic morality is pursued without due regard to the corruptions of this traditionalism or without due attention to the concerns of contemporary critics of Roman Catholic moral teaching who are identified as advocates of 'circumstance ethics' and of 'sin mysticism'.

There is a 'heresy of ethos' which characterizes the attitudes and actions of 'many mediocre, conventional Christians'. It is bluntly ascribed to a 'bourgeois, conventional deformation of Christianity'.[2] Thus von Hildebrand not only agrees with the

[1] His English works on *Christian Ethics*, David McKay Company, Inc., New York, 1953, and on *True Morality and Its Counterfeits*, by the same publisher, 1955, are most directly related both to the point under discussion here and to the general thesis of this book. What his work in this country shows is a more polemical than self-critical re-examination of moral theology in the light of contemporary objections and problems.

[2] Dietrich von Hildebrand, *True Morality*, pp. 5-6.

critics in their rejection of the prescriptive formalism and juridical temper of much of the moral theology of the past. He also
directs his strictures as severely as possible against the distor-
tions of 'true morality' which have infected the practice of
moral theology in the present. Nevertheless he resolutely insists
that in their exaltation of the private conscience, the freedom of
decision, and the heroic struggle with moral complexity and
ambiguity the critics have gone too far. They have ignored, if
not repudiated, the objective basis of morality in metaphysics
and in the nature and law of God. The result is that they have
really undermined the foundations and the integrity of the
moral sensitivity which informs their work.

Professor von Hildebrand himself regards the work on *True
Morality* as an extension, and perhaps also an enrichment, of the
argument set out in *Christian Ethics*.[1] The displacement, which
he proposes in this volume, of the 'heresy of ethos' by his own
version of ethical orthodoxy may thus be regarded as a statement of his principal concern and position.

It is surprising that an analysis so conversant with the
strength and weaknesses of the traditional Roman Catholic
interpretation of morality and with contemporary ethical concerns can only offer an ethic of re-christianization. This is like
asking the critic to accept what, if he had been able in the first
instance to accept, he never would have rejected. Von Hildebrand rightly notes the protest of 'circumstance ethics . . .
against the tendency to substitute legality for morality'. But he
does not see that the 'depersonalization' which 'circumstance
ethics fears' is due not solely to the prescriptive character of the
ethical tradition.[2] It is due even less to the 'glorification of the
sinner' which von Hildebrand fears. The sober fact is that the
philosophical and ecclesiastical framework of the Christian
ethical tradition has lost both relevance and reality. Those
whom Professor von Hildebrand rebukes are more like 'sheep
without a shepherd'. They ought to be approached, therefore,
with something of the compassion born of the contrite recognition by the shepherds, as stewards of the mysteries of God, that
they have obscured what God is really doing in the world by
the heteronomous exaltation of their own traditions. von

---

[1] *True Morality*, p. 155.     [2] Ibid., p. 7.

Hildebrand's language, of course, is contemporary. But the ethical substance to which the language points is a reversion to the tradition of moral theology. 'The specific character of Christian morality' is derived from 'regard for justice itself, purity itself, veracity itself, faithfulness itself'. The commandments of Christ are said to 'refer to the basic absolute value response, that is, the response to God's infinite goodness and holiness, and the response to the ontological value of every man as an image of God'.[1] 'All human virtues', it is affirmed, 'are only a faint participation in God's infinite goodness. Every moral value is a natural revelation of God's nature. And, in an incomparably higher way, all the specifically Christian virtues, such as charity, meekness, and mercifulness, are a revelation of God's nature.'[2] And those who have lost the sense for the persuasiveness of this way of speaking about Christian morality are charged with a complete lack of the 'sensus supranaturalis' and with a defective 'obedience to holy church'.[3]

This savors of an intemperate indictment of the contemporary mind rooted in a Tridentine mentality. Its severity and exaggeration are not diminished by the subtle charm with which the qualitative difference between humanist and Christian ethics is described.[4] Above all, the indictment ignores the fact that those who in our time have become alienated from the Christian ethical tradition are the heirs of a genuine and steadily mounting disaffection from the context within which this tradition has expressed itself. The Christian ethical tradition has failed to convince the consciences of men. This was the point at issue between Roman and Reformation ethics in the sixteenth century. It is the point at issue still. The question is not whether there is a 'heresy of ethos' or an 'orthodoxy of ethos', but whether there is an authentic ethic by which men may live and die. If there is such an ethic and if the Christian gospel has anything to do with it, Christian moralists must be able to bring authentically together man's humanity and what God is doing in the world. This is the purpose and point of a *koinonia* ethic and its contextual way of understanding divine and human behavior.

---

[1] von Hildebrand, ibid., pp. 160-61.    [2] Ibid., p. 160.
[3] Ibid., p. 5.    [4] Ibid., pp. 156ff.

## b. Anglican moral theology

The dissatisfaction with the tradition of moral theology lately expressed by Roman Catholic moralists has been anticipated in Anglican moral theology both in the past and in the present. It is the peculiar character and office of Anglican thought to hold together, so far as this may be possible, both Catholic and Protestant insight and experience of the one, holy, apostolic, but divided church. Moral theology thus also comes under this 'law of Anglican existence', this winsome and instructive devotion to a *via media*.

The late Bishop of Oxford, Dr Kenneth Kirk, who, at least as regards the Catholic wing of Anglicanism, has given authoritative attention to the task and responsibility of moral theology, has clearly noted the wisdom and validity of a mediating course.[1] 'Moral theology', Bishop Kirk explains, 'must therefore steer a course between over-rigidity of definition on the one hand, and vagueness of definition on the other. It requires such a degree of exactness as will insure to the priest clear guidance in dealing with the problems that beset human conduct, without giving him the arrogance and obstinacy which are bred by a sense of absolute rightness.'[2]

Kirk rightly recognizes that Christian ethics is particularly concerned with the bearing of revelation upon behavior, or, as he puts it, 'with a society which has its roots in divine revelation'.[3] This concern has notably failed, however, in dealing with a perennial problem of all ethics: the problem of reconciling the tension between authority and individualism, between

---

[1] Bishop Kirk's attempt to formulate a sound and useful moral theology, at once free of the weaknesses of the Roman tradition and faithful to the wisdom and strength of Roman Catholic ethics, has produced three comprehensive books on the subject. We must confine ourselves here to the Bishop's central approach to the subject and to the principal limitation of his renovation. The reader will want, however, also to become familiar with the vigorous, thorough, and detailed account of a revised moral theology in operation provided by the following: Kenneth E. Kirk, *Some Principles of Moral Theology and Their Application*, Longmans, Green and Company, London, 1921; *Ignorance, Faith and Conformity, Studies in Moral Theology*, Longmans, Green and Company, London, 1925; and *Conscience, and Its Problems, An Introduction to Casuistry*, Longmans, Green and Company, London, 1927.

[2] Kirk, *Some Principles of Moral Theology*, p. 7.  [3] Ibid., p. ix.

law and liberty. Roman Catholic moral theory has failed to meet this problem owing to a too rigorous emphasis upon authority and law, whereas Protestant ethics has made the contrary mistake of overstating the case for liberty and individualism.

The Bishop of Oxford undertakes to correct these errors by addressing himself once more, and from the beginning, to what he calls 'the first business of Christian ethics'. 'The first business of Christian ethics is to enumerate the main duties of a Christian in normal circumstances.'[1] Western theologians—Ambrose, Augustine, Gregory, Aquinas, who are singled out for special mention—have inadequately attended to this business because they have chosen to base their account of the Christian ideal of life upon a pagan classification of virtue rather than upon the insights and directions of the Bible. Dr Kirk has no objection to the virtue scheme as such but thinks that it must be adapted to an ideal of life derived from the biblical view of the love of God, the nature of man, and the Christian's relation to Christ. In this context the accent would fall upon the psychological roots of the cardinal virtues, upon intelligence, appetite, and will, rather more than upon a definition of the virtues themselves and their corresponding vices. Similarly, the theological virtues would acquire significance less as the crown of the cardinal virtues than as characteristics of the Christian life.

However, as Kirk continues to spell out what is involved in the shaping of behavior by the biblical context of the Christian ideal of life, he seems to take up once again the anthropology and the penitential practice of the Roman Catholic tradition. Moral theology presupposes, according to Kirk, free will and conscience. The soul is free to choose between good and bad, right and wrong, in all its actions; and in addition, however tainted and corrupted by sin, the soul retains an innate power (conscience) both of perceiving what is good and of aspiring to it. On these presuppositions, moral theology seeks to bring together the ideal of character which God desires for each man and the means which enable the soul to progress toward that ideal. The task involves a detailed account of the laws of responsible action and their appropriateness to the natural endowments of the human soul. It involves an account of the

[1] Kirk, ibid., p. 32.

hindrances to spiritual progress, natural or acquired, and of the means by which these hindrances can be either eradicated or counteracted. It involves a discussion of the principles by which morally dubious actions are to be regulated, of the means by which the priest can co-operate with God in stimulating and fostering spiritual progress, and of the qualifications demanded of a priest in his capacity as spiritual director or guide of souls.[1] Before Bishop Kirk has gone a very great way with his renovation of moral theology, the biblical context of the Christian ideal of life has been transformed into a law of spiritual progress in obedience to which the soul's desire, intelligence, and will are transformed through purification, illumination, and union into the image of Christ.[2] The penitential theological climate of this transformation is unmistakable. The Bishop of Oxford seems almost to outdo Father Davis in the detailed schematization with which he proposes a program for the progress of the soul.[3] The analysis of moral action and the proposals for its regulation parallel the schematic and prescriptive detail provided for the soul's spiritual progress. Indeed, the more deeply and extensively Kirk moves from the renovationist intention and starting point of his analysis, the more difficult it is to see that he departs at all, except for alterations in language, from the familiar manuals of Roman Catholic moral theology.

The outcome of this elaborate attention to moral theology and its problems is the more regrettable and surprising since Kirk reckons himself as standing in the tradition not of Roman moral theology but of Caroline divinity. In the preface to the work which we have been citing, Kirk remarks that 'the only successors of St Thomas who can fairly be said to have attempted to carry out his ideal of combining the principle of authority with that of freedom are the little group of Anglican divines of the seventeenth century—Hooker, Jeremy Taylor, Sanderson, Hall, and their fellows'.[4] Frankly engaged in working out an alternative to Roman Catholic moral theology, these Caroline

---

[1] Kirk, ibid., pp. 132ff.        [2] Ibid., p. 50.

[3] The subjective requirements of penitence, for example, are set out under four headings: *internal*, that is, of the heart; *supernatural*, that is, motivated by love to God; *supreme*, that is, willing to do anything in order to escape from sin and to live a godly life; *universal*, that is, all branches of life and conditions are included.

[4] Kirk, *Some Principles of Moral Theology*, p. xi.

divines were applying to Roman teaching much the same kind
of criticism which, two hundred years later, was to come from
certain among the Roman Catholic moralists themselves. The
Caroline divines were concerned about a less formal and
schematic program of moral guidance, derived from a more
faithful adherence to Holy Scripture. They labored for an ideal
of Christian discipleship in terms of a renewed human being,
an ideal which had been obscured by the tradition of moral
theology. What contemporary Roman Catholic critics have
been exploring as a more intimate connection between the life
of virtue and life in the love of God, the Caroline moral theologians were exploring in terms of a more intimate connection
between moral theology and ascetic theology. The Carolines
were dedicated to a spirituality of 'holy living and holy
dying'.[1]

The renovation of moral theology from within must take
account of the vigorous interest of the Caroline theologians in
what they called 'practical divinity'. 'There is no formalism,
quietism, or sentimentality in the Anglican devotion of the
seventeenth century. It is thorough-going as to details, and
thinks as much in terms of moral duty as of spiritual graces.
The Divine Life in daily life might be its guiding maxim. But
if it is much concerned with the pots and pipkins of religion,
Caroline piety is not forgetful of the highest levels of the spiritual
life and labors to develop in men the faculty of seeing their daily
conduct and devotional exercises in the light of their eternal
destiny.'[2] Indeed, as the Caroline theologians saw it, the mistake
of Roman Catholic moral theology was that it failed to keep
'moral theology' and 'ascetic theology' in living connection with
each other. Roman moralists from Trent onwards, but particularly in our own time, have tended more and more to stress

---

[1] I am indebted to Professor A. T. Mollegen of the Episcopal Theological
Seminary at Alexandria, Virginia, for having drawn my attention to this
discussion of seventeenth-century Anglican theology. See H. R. McAdoo,
*The Structure of Caroline Moral Theology*, Longmans, Green and Company,
London, 1949. What follows here is based upon the textual evidence
provided by Dr McAdoo's volume. The phrase 'holy living and holy dying'
appears most influentially, perhaps, as the title of Jeremy Taylor's manual
of Caroline devotion, *Holy Living and Holy Dying*, in *The Practical Works of
Jeremy Taylor*, Henry G. Bohr, London, 1850, Vol. II.

[2] McAdoo, op. cit., p. xi.

what is necessary 'to teach the priest how to distinguish what is sinful from what is lawful' rather than to 'place high ideals of virtue before the people and train them in Christian perfection'. They have stressed 'the way of salvation, which will be attained by the observance of the commandments of God and of the church' rather than 'showing man the way of perfection'.[1] 'Practical divinity' goes far beyond such juridical impoverishment. It must, as Robert Sanderson, the Bishop of Lincoln, put it, 'when all is done, . . . bring us to Heaven; that is, it must poise our *judgments*, settle our *consciences*, direct our *lives*, mortifie our *corruptions*, increase our *graces*, strengthen our *comforts*, save our *souls*'.[2]

But Anglican moral theology of the Caroline stamp is significant not only for its critique of the Roman tradition. It also, and especially, promises to reduce the conflict between moral theology and a *koinonia* ethic. This prospect is due partly to the composite character of Caroline moral theology. More largely, it is due to the exalted, yet thoroughly human, character of its ethical sensitivity. A *koinonia* ethic which failed to nurture a similar ethical sensitivity would seriously imperil its own validity as a Christian ethic.

In a singularly instructive discussion of Caroline moral theology, Dr H. R. McAdoo notes that the Caroline divines 'read and used Aquinas and Calvin and studied the spiritual descendants of both, but refused to forget that they were Anglicans, concluding that by their Protestant reforms they had saved and restored the true and primitive Catholic Faith'.[3] Archbishop John Bramhall declared that 'we have pared away nothing which is either prescribed or practiced by the true Catholic Church', and proposed as the final test 'what hath been allowed as fit in the judgment of Antiquity, and by the long continued practice of the whole Church'.[4] John Donne observed that 'our Church, in the Reformation, proposed not

---

[1] Quoted by Dr McAdoo, ibid., pp. 10 and 11, respectively from T. Slater, S.J., *Cases of Conscience*, Benziger Brothers, New York, Vol. I, 1911, p. 36, and Father Davis, to whom we have already referred, op. cit., Vol. I, p. 4.

[2] McAdoo, op. cit., p. 10; quoted from *XXXV Sermons*, III.

[3] Ibid., p. 1.

[4] Ibid., p. 2; quoted from John Bramhall, *Works* (Library of Anglo-Catholic Theology ed.), Vol. III, p. 170.

*that* for her end, how shee might goe from Rome, but how shee might come to the Truth'.[1]

As regards the question of the bearing of Christian faith upon behavior, this Anglican concern for true catholicity promoted the search for an effective bond between what was called 'lawful authority' and 'just liberty'. Rome, as the Anglicans saw it, was offering the believer an infallible church as the solution for the problems of faith and morals, whereas Protestantism, particularly in the Puritan form in which the Carolines knew it, was offering the believer an equally rigid infallibility of Scripture. As Bishop Sanderson declared, 'The Roman infallibilism tyrannizes over conscience by striking at liberty, and the Puritan over liberty by offending against reason'.[2] Against Roman authoritarianism and legalism, Caroline moral theology sought to shape conduct by the context rather than the letter of Holy Scripture and, in a fine phrase, looked for 'not so much finality as direction'.[3] Against Puritan authoritarianism, the Caroline divines stressed holiness and rectitude of life as an exalted spiritual ideal and claim. They sought to implement this ideal and claim by a reasonable and common-sense attention to the daily details of ordinary human living and dying.

McAdoo stresses the composite character of this Anglican middle way between Romanism and Puritanism by underlining a 'traditionalist strain', a 'mixed strain', and a 'reforming strain'. The traditionalist strain relies heavily upon the doctrine of natural law and particularly upon St Thomas' account of the nature of law and of the moral act. Thomas had distinguished between eternal law and natural law, and again between divine law and human law. Eternal law is the order according to which all things are ruled by God's providence and governed by his reason. Although the whole creation participates in the eternal law by means of an inward principle of being, man, according to St Thomas, partakes of eternal law by another means also, namely, by knowledge. This knowledge of a number of the principles of eternal law is defined as natural law. Owing to the corruption of sin, however, natural law is insufficient to

---

[1] McAdoo, ibid., p. 4; quoted from John Donne, *LXXX Sermons*, XLIV. Italics mine.

[2] Ibid., p. 6; quoted from *XXXV Sermons*, V and Preface.

[3] Ibid., p. 9; quoted from Paul Elmer Moore's essay in *Anglicanism*, p. xx.

shape man's conduct, so that an additional aid to the law of reason is required. This took the form of divine law, which Thomas again subdivides into the 'old law' and the 'new law', respectively the 'decalogue' and the 'law of love'. And as divine law provides a supernatural aid to natural law, so for Thomas human law is the body of regulations which implement natural and divine law in the guidance of the practical affairs of life.[1] Hooker, says Dr McAdoo, 'whole-heartedly follows Aquinas in that he holds the natural law to be man's incomplete apprehension of the eternal law and he regards natural law as being to a certain extent mediated by human law. . . .'[2] Hooker regards eternal law and natural law as the context in which human actions are set. Since reason and will are the sources of human actions, Hooker can define a law as 'a directive rule unto goodness of operation' and declare that the law of men's nature is 'the sentence that Reason giveth concerning the goodness of those things which they are to do'.[3]

While Hooker begins with law and then comes to a discussion of human acts, Sanderson proceeds conversely and gives particular attention to actions and their relation to law. This leads Sanderson to the question of the conscience. He regards the conscience as the faculty of the practical intellect by the exercise of which a man, through reason, applies the light of judgment to particular moral actions. The immediate rule governing behavior is the rule of right reason, which takes its origin from natural law and which is 'do good and flee evil'. But the conscience as the normal and ultimate judge of the individual's conduct is always also illumined by the Holy Spirit and informed by the gospel. In this way, in Sanderson's analysis, the conscience functions as the regulator of behavior and brings the stuff of action under the control both of reason and of revelation.

If Sanderson takes a long step in the direction of a Protestant view of conscience, Jeremy Taylor takes a yet longer one in the direction of the relation of revelation to conduct. Taylor does not abandon the traditional view of natural law and its bearing upon action, but he shifts the emphasis. Revelation rather

[1] For St Thomas' account of law, see especially the *Summa Theologica*, I$^a$-II$^{ae}$, QQ. 91-93.

[2] Op. cit., p. 21.

[3] Ibid., p. 23; quoted from Richard Hooker, *Ecclesiastical Polity*, VIII, 4.

than right reason comes into the controlling position. 'Reason', Taylor declares in an astonishingly contemporary manner, 'is such a box of quicksilver that it abides nowhere; it dwells in no settled mansion; it is like a dove's neck or a changeable taffata; it looks to me otherwise than to you who do not stand in the same light that I do; and if we enquire after the Law of nature by the rules of our reason, we shall be as uncertain as the discourses of the people, or the dreams of disturbed fancies.'[1] Taylor thus goes beyond Hooker's Thomistic rationalism, according to which the law of nature is the law of reason. He regards the law of nature more widely as 'the universal Law of the World, and the Law of Mankind, concerning common necessities, . . . but . . . bound upon us only by the Commands of God'.[2] This *humanization* of the law of nature (as contrasted with its *rationality*) leads Taylor to an explicit subsumption of natural law under the law of God and the gospel. Unhappily the later Deists were to turn Taylor's advance against his own aim when they regarded Christianity as a re-publication of the religion of nature.[3] Nevertheless, Taylor's insistence that the law of nature was really a kind of re-publication of the religion of revelation, that is, of the law and the gospel, had the effect of shifting the center of gravity of moral theology in the direction of the biblical context of God's activity in the world for the salvation of mankind.[4]

Taylor's account of human action is more traditional than is his account of natural law. He accepts the Thomistic threefold structure of action, including the doctrine of intention. Yet the precision with which he explores the will in action is permeated

[1] McAdoo, ibid., p. 38; quoted from Jeremy Taylor, *Ductor Dubitantium*, Bk. II, chap. 1, rule 1.

[2] Ibid., p. 38; quoted from the same part of Taylor's work.

[3] Note, for example, Matthew Tindal's *Christianity as Old as the Creation; or the Gospel a Re-publication of The Religion of Nature*, London, first edition, 1730.

[4] The transitional character of Taylor's discussion of natural law is evident from the kind of ambivalence expressed in the following: 'All the laws of Christ concerning moral actions are the laws of nature: and all the laws of nature, which any wise nation ever reckoned, . . . are commanded by Christ.' Quoted by McAdoo, op. cit., p. 40, from the *Ductor Dubitantium*, Bk. II, chap. 1, 59. There is an echo here of the interchangeability of natural law, the Decalogue, and the law of love which occurs in the ethics of Luther and Calvin.

by another spirit than that of legalism. Taylor has a lively sense both of the ambiguity of moral choice and of what he calls 'the whole design of human nature', which is the perfection of human nature after the pattern of the perfection of Christ.[1] The laws of Jesus Christ are 'the Measures of the Spirit' and are meant to be 'perfective of the spirit'.[2]

Taylor's antilegalism enabled him also to prepare the way for a revision of the tradition of moral theology in the matter of the sinful character of actions. Traditional moral theology had made a distinction between a sinful habit and a sinful act, and regarded action but not habit as culpable. Taylor was critical of this disjunction. It presupposed a semi-metaphysical treatment of habit and by excluding habit from culpability weakened the range of responsibility and the force of guilt. He insisted upon the inseparability of habit and action.

> All sins are single in their acting; and a sinful habit differs from a sinful act, but as many differ from one, or as a year from an hour; a vicious habit is but one sin continued and repeated; for as sin grows from little to great, so it passes from act to habit: a sin is greater because it is complicated externally or internally, no other way in the world; it is made up of more kinds, or more degrees of choice; and when two or three crimes are mixed in one action, then the sin is loud and clamorous. And if these still grow more numerous and are not interrupted and disjoined by a speedy repentance, then it becomes a habit.[3]

Far from underestimating the intricacy and persistence of sinfulness, as the Carolines were sometimes accused of doing, Taylor underlined both the psychological and relational complexity of sinful behavior and its dispositional root. The dispositional root of sin is willful disobedience to God, 'a turning from Him to the creature by love and adhesion'.[4] It is the office of repentance to displace the disposition to disobedience by the disposition to 'care and labour in the ways of godliness'.[5] But the displacement of the disposition to disobedience by the disposition to repentance is a gift of grace. Taylor breaks sharply with the traditional doctrine of infused grace and

[1] McAdoo, op. cit., p. 43; quoted from *Ductor Dubitantium*, Bk. IV, chap. 1, rule I, 4.

[2] Ibid., p. 41.

[3] Ibid., pp. 49-50; quoted from *Unum Necessarium*, section II, 26.

[4] Ibid., p. 48; quoted from *Unum Necessarium*, chap. III, section V.

[5] Ibid., p. 54; quoted from *Unum Necessarium*, chap. III, section V, 55.

insists upon forgiving and enabling grace as the gift of the Holy Spirit. The doctrine of infusion erroneously shifts the analysis of sin, guilt, and renewal from an authentic human to a metaphysical level. This, as Taylor saw it, was not only unscriptural but denied the reality and role of freedom in human obedience and disobedience. God has chosen the way of free obedience as the way of human renewal and by his Spirit has bestowed 'nothing but powers and inclinations', and 'new aptnesses' for the patient perseverance in the life of grace thus begun.[1]

The renovationist character of Anglican moral theology can be correctly understood only against the background of its firm anchorage in and criticism of the Roman tradition on law, act, sin, and culpability. But Taylor's stress upon the inward character of sin and its connection with repentance, and his emphasis upon disciplined living, exhibits the mixed and reforming strains in the structure of Caroline practical divinity. According to McAdoo, the critical evidence of the mixed strain in Caroline moral theology is provided by the relation between conscience and casuistry. The mixture is compounded both of medieval and of Reformed characteristics. As regards the conscience, the Caroline divines, and indeed for the most part their contemporaries among Reformed theologians, were on the side of the Schoolmen. St Thomas had noted that the conscience had two parts. The first is the power by which we hold and understand general principles of morality, and this Aquinas called *synderesis*. The second part he called *conscientia*, meaning by this the function of the practical intellect whereby we apply the general principles of morality to specific actions in order to assess their rightness and wrongness.[2] But what the Caroline divines added to the tradition was a new emphasis on the individual conscience. 'To train the conscience', says McAdoo, 'in the use of its rightful liberty and acknowledging the authority of Scripture and Natural Law as a rule was their aim.'[3] The way was thus opened for a deepening of private moral sensitivity without courting moral anarchy. External authority was reduced to such authority (i.e., Scripture and reason) as could be readily conjoined with spontaneous decision nurtured through

---

[1] McAdoo, ibid., pp. 54-55.
[2] Ibid., p. 66. See also below, Chapter XIII, pp. 330-32.
[3] Ibid., p. 71.

a lively acquaintance with and love for the things of God. This achievement, moreover, was the fruit not of the cloister but of the parish, so that it bore the marks of wrestling with the earthiness and complexity of moral decision.

An altered view of conscience required an alteration in the theory and practice of casuistry. The question of conscience, as moral theologians look at it, is the question of doubt or certainty about the morality of an action. In pastoral practice, the principal form of this question concerns the measure of freedom permitted in an action, the moral significance of which is defined by law. Under what conditions is man free *not* to perform what the law commands and thus also free, in whole or in part, of culpability? Among Roman moralists, the position most widely adopted was that when the conscience was in doubt it was to be governed by a rule which favored freedom against strict adherence to obligation prescribed in law when opinion in support of freedom was clearly probable.[1] Caroline moral theology, however, laid greater stress upon the *spirituality* of an action than upon its *rationality*. The aim was to deal with the perplexities of conscience in terms of a more direct and internal relation between God and the soul rather than by recourse to an external consensus of reasonable opinion. This did not mean that reasoned judgment was expendable in cases of conscience. It meant that 'right reason' was ultimately determined with reference not to the operation of natural law but to the operation of the Holy Spirit in effecting a personal response to the claim and action of God, as exhibited in Holy Scripture. Jeremy Taylor could urge men to recognize that 'most of their

[1] The moral theologians identify this rule and its application as *probabilism, (certo solide probabilis)*. Probabilism is distinguished in moral theology both from a stricter and from a laxer position. The stricter position is known as *absolute tutiorism*. Its rule is that one may decide in favor of freedom and against the obligation defined in law only when the opinion of divines in favor of freedom is absolutely certain (*opinio tutior*). The laxer position is known as *probabiliorism*. Its rule is that one may decide in favor of freedom and against strict adherence to obligation imposed by law if the opinion of divines in support of freedom is at least *more probable* (*opinio probabilior*) than its opposite. Cf. Mausbach-Ermecke, op. cit., I, pars. 26-28, especially, pp. 179-88. Judged by these rules, Roman moralists were, on the whole, *probabilists*; the Caroline divines were *probabiliorists*. But Caroline moral theology, owing to the reforming strain, really presupposed a different context.

cases of conscience would cease to be problems at all if they had in them more love and simplicity'. Robert South declared that the only compass by which conscience can steer is that of the 'two grand rules of right reason and Scripture'.[1]

This simplification of authorities did not mean the substitution of individual liberty for careful rules of guidance. It meant, on the contrary, a livelier sensitivity in the governance of life to God's direct illumination of the conscience, and a casuistry 'established upon better principles, and more sober and satisfying methods'.[2]

The doctrine of sin provides, perhaps, the most radical instance of Caroline departure from the Roman tradition in moral theology. The polemics were sharp during the seventeenth century and focused upon the rejection of the traditional distinction between mortal and venial sin. The Caroline moralists found this distinction spurious because, as they saw it, all sins were laden with death, and no sin could be said to have 'an inherent right to pardon by reason of the nature of the act. . . . Though sins differ in degree, yet they differ not in their natural and essential order to death'.[3] Beneath these quasi-scholastic objections to the distinction between mortal and venial sin lay the conviction that the distinction debases the conception of holiness and the Christian life and encourages men rather to continue in their course of sinning than to seek out Christian perfection. Thus the positive side of the reforming strain of Caroline practical divinity has to do with its moving and detailed concern with repentance and holiness of life. McAdoo gathers impressive textual evidence to show that the concept of holiness is chiefly determinative of the Caroline view of repentance. As Archbishop Tillotson put it, holiness 'contains all the imitable perfections of God', and it is the 'endeavor to be habitually holy, which is our conformity to the nature of God; and actually holy, which is our conformity to the will of God'.[4] This concern for holiness might be described as 'extra-penitential' and 'extra-confessional'. Its context was not only at variance with but antithetical to the scheme under which the

---

[1] McAdoo, op. cit., p. 80; quoted from *Works* (Oxford, 1823), Vol. II, Sermon XXIII.

[2] Ibid., p. 82; quoted from the Preface to *Ductor Dubitantium*.

[3] Ibid., pp. 103, 110.     [4] Ibid., p. 121.

Roman moralists had been wont to direct the change from life under sin to life under grace. The Caroline teaching concerning holiness was personal rather than sacramental.[1] The passion for this new kind of holiness was in its own way so intense as to foster its own kind of rigidity. This should have been sufficient to dispel the charge of moral indifference and laxity. More significant, however, is the fact that, despite the strict severity of the Caroline stress upon repentance and holiness, the passion for 'holy living and holy dying', as Jeremy Taylor described it, was thoroughly rooted in Scripture and thus in the biblical account of God's way of dealing with sin and with human renewal. The result was a new and characteristic piety of its own.

Here indeed was a reforming strain in Caroline moral theology. It was an accent which seems to have carried the Caroline moralists far beyond the traditional context in which their attempt at a renovation of moral theology was conceived. The question raised by this reform is whether the 'practical divinity', i.e., the implementation of Christian faith in Christian behavior, for which the Carolines sought a more biblical and more viable context, was not bound to lead sooner or later to a rejection of moral theology altogether. It is precisely this step which the Caroline divines were unable to take. Nor could the step be expected of them. They were, however, able to document the ethical inadequacy of moral theology. The problem is not merely that traditional and reforming strains in the Anglican attempt to guide and shape behavior on the Catholic model do not effectively coalesce. A *via media* cannot mix. It can only function by postponing ultimate issues and crucial decisions, which is, in effect, to avoid them.

Eventually, the passion for 'holy living and holy dying' disrupts a *via media* because the concreteness of behavior is compounded of the ultimate and the immediate in such a way as to prevent the avoidance of decision. This means that the bond between 'lawful authority' and 'just liberty', as the Carolines put it, can be provided neither by 'Roman infallibilism' nor by 'Puritan legalism', neither by violating the conscience nor by

---

[1] McAdoo notes a reference in Matthew Scrivner's *Course in Divinity* in which Scrivner cites Ussher in rejecting 'that new Pick-lock of Sacramental Confession, obtained on men's conscience, as a matter necessary to salvation, by the Canon of the late Council of Trent'. Ibid., p. 125.

violating the reason. What is required is a context for conscience which conjoins the focus of divine activity and the focus of human responsiveness in such a way as to provide behavior with direction and decisiveness. The focus of divine activity is what God in Christ has done and is doing in the world for the humanization of man. The fulcrum of human responsiveness is the conscience—that delicate conjunction of the inner springs of human motivation and of human judgment informed by the divine activity in a single, decisive, and free act of obedience. In this context 'the two grand rules of right reason and Scripture'[1] would still be the only compass by which conscience can steer. But 'the grand rules', instead of being regulative precepts, would be indicative interpretations of the dynamics and the direction of divine activity. 'Right reason', instead of being the exercise of judgment in accordance with divine and natural law, would be the exercise of judgment sensitized by an imaginative grasp of the divine-human involvement in the doing of what it takes to make and to keep human life human. And 'Scripture', instead of being an authoritative depository of revealed truth, would be 'a well of living water', i.e., an inexhaustible reservoir of the formative images in terms of which the humanization of life may be both conceptually and behaviorally exhibited. What is required is a context for the ethical reality of conscience. Although the Caroline divines were on the nearer edge of such a context, neither Roman nor Anglican moral theology was able to supply it. We must try, by way of some appraisal of the enterprise of moral theology *per se*, to make plain the fundamental grounds for this defect and thus to underline the intrinsic incompatibility of moral theology with Christian ethics.

### 4 *A Critical Appraisal of Moral Theology*

A critical appraisal of moral theology must take seriously at least three factors which are of positive or constructive significance for Christian ethics. In the first place, moral theology is ethical reflection in the context of the church. Father Davis, it will be recalled, regards moral theology as more comprehensive than ethics and subsumes the material of ethics under the

---

[1] See above, p. 314, note 1.

directives derived from divine revelation, ecclesiastical tradition, and a supernatural order. Furthermore, in its more viable forms, moral theology draws its ideal of perfection, toward which conduct is to be directed and by which it is to be judged, from charity or holiness as the measure of 'the life of God in the soul of man'.[1] The Christian life is a pilgrimage from nature to grace and aims at the 'perfection of virtue',[2] a character development with the accent upon morality rather than upon maturity. But whether the pilgrimage be along a sacramental course or along the way of a changed interior disposition, the goal is a wholeness akin to that 'measure of development which is meant by the fullness of Christ'. Moral guidance seeks painstakingly to bring the norms and the details of behavior meaningfully together in the achievement of this goal.

In the second place, moral theology deals realistically with moral problems. The measure of this realism is broadly indicated by the way in which the moral theologians combine the certainty necessary to guide conduct with the varieties of behavioral options open to men. Indeed, it is as though the difficulty of achieving moral certainty serves the moral theologian as a kind of 'creative dare'. He is disarmingly candid about the hazard and concentrates upon surmounting it. Perhaps at no other point is the operational effectiveness of the context of this kind of ethical reflection more plain and persuasive. Moral theology proposes that the certainty that one's conduct is right or good comes, on the one hand, from the nature of the human reason and, on the other hand, from the sacramental nature of the church. The combination of what reason can determine about what is good and what is bad, about what is better and what is worse, about what is probable and what is improbable, with the sacramental power to pursue and achieve what reason can determine, is an enviable ethical

---

[1] This is the title of Henry Scougal's book. See the convenient edition by the Westminster Press, Philadelphia, 1948, with Introduction by Winthrop S. Hudson.

[2] A phrase of St Thomas. See E. Gilson, *The Christian Philosophy of St Thomas Aquinas*, Random House, New York, 1956 (Gollancz, London, 1957), pp. 342-44. As regards St Thomas himself, see *Summa Theologica*, I$^a$-II$^{ae}$, Q. 62, Art. 4, and I$^a$-II$^{ae}$, Q. 55, Art. 1, where the phrase is approximated; and II$^a$-II$^{ae}$, Q. 23, Arts. 6-8, where the phrase is justified with respect to charity.

possibility. Anyone who has ever undertaken to give ethical counsel to himself or to others might well pause a long time before rejecting it.

Thirdly, the device by which moral theology implements this combination of rational insight and sacramental power is the science of casuistry. Idealists in general, and Protestants in particular, find casuistry uncongenial. More accurately, perhaps, they find it congenial enough not to avoid it, and uncongenial enough to avoid confessing that they do *not* avoid it. This haunting suspicion of casuistry tends to be supported by the explanation that casuistry is a way of selling short a moral ideal. Casuistry, so the argument runs, is a way of finding a good reason, not for doing the good one ought to do, but for doing what one wants to do. Thus, Protestants are inclined to regard their Catholic brethren with an air of ethical superiority directly proportional to their own ethical frustration. Unlike the Caroline divines, who took up the painstaking task of a casuistry consonant with the altered view of conscience effected by the Reformation, contemporary Protestants tend to reject casuistry in theory, and implicitly or explicitly to take refuge in a kind of ethical perfectionism which always either claims or promises a moral achievement unwarranted by behavioral facts.

Casuistry, however, is not in itself a bad thing; it is a very good thing. As part of moral theology, it is not an ethical form of rationalization. On the contrary, every responsible moral theology has used casuistry as a serious attempt to deal with the cleavage between the ethical claim and the ethical act in which all ethical behavior is involved. When a man presents himself for ethical guidance, he wants to know *specifically* what he is to do. He does not welcome being told that the situation is 'awful', or that 'he ought not to have gotten himself into it'. He knows that already. What he wants to know is how he is going to get out of the situation, and how soon. It is the office of casuistical analysis to close the gap between the ethical claim and the ethical act without surrendering either the rigor of the ethical demand or the sense for the intricate difficulties of living up to the ethical demand. Moral theology, as it were, refuses to abandon a man on a sinking ship. It seeks to keep hold of him until the tempest has passed, or until he has reached a point where he can keep himself above water.

This means that *in principle* casuistry is not a science of ethical expediency. The Caroline divines did not fail to notice that casuistry is often opportunistically applied. But it is protected against sheer expediency by the authoritative role of the church in assisting man toward the achievement of his supernatural end. It is an unworthy (and still too widely fostered) suspicion among Protestants that Roman Catholic piety and moral sensitivity are a witches' brew concocted by conniving clerics for the aggrandizement of the church and the misleading or the seduction of the faithful. Such a suspicion feeds upon a painful intellectual dishonesty, particularly painful from the standpoint of a *koinonia* ethic. The dishonesty is that of judging a person or a church or an ethical position by trivialization or by setting up the best against the worst. Unless an evangelical ethic can do better with moral problems than moral theology does or than such *ad hominem* aspersions portend, the attempt at an ethic consonant with evangelical faith had better be abandoned. We in the Protestant tradition must do some sober thinking about ethical reality and about the consequence for ethics of the Reformers' rediscovery of the gospel, if what we claim to believe is going to be meaningfully and effectively related to behavior. There is a kind of covert catholicism in every human breast for the simple reason that nature is not destroyed by grace but perfected by it. All nature aspires to completion, and grace that completes both inspires and makes sense. The authentic office of casuistry is the explanation and application of the behavioral sense which grace makes.

Why, then, not be moral theologians? If the tempting device of a manual of moral instruction and guidance is not to be adopted by those whose historical roots and Christian vocation bid them to live by grace *alone*: by faith *alone* (*sola gratia: sola fide*), why not?

In the first place, moral theology, while it deals realistically with moral problems, their detail, their complexity, their call for a guidance that is confident and certain, does not deal realistically with the *ethical* problem. Serious as is its attempt to overcome the cleavage between the ethical claim and the ethical act intrinsic in the ethical predicament of man, moral theology actually prevents the discernment of the full depth and urgency of the ethical situation. The aim is to free the believer from the ethical predicament by conducting him out of the ethical situation to which the problem of the right or good action is intrinsic. Such an attempt is an ethical *tour de force* because it assumes *de facto* that the moral counselor is in a *different* situation from that of the man under instruction and guidance. The truth of the matter, however, is that the counselor and the counselee are in the *same* ethical situation. It is a *tour de force*, also, because the answer to the question 'What am I to do?' cannot be given in terms of virtues and values, rights and duties, goods and services. 'What am I to do?' seriously, not frivolously, put, implies that 'All these things have I done from my youth up'.[1] The question underlines the discovery that 'all these things' are addenda and that the real force of the ethical question is the dimension of radical disorientation and reorientation exposed by it.

This is why every ethical problem is in the last analysis a religious problem, and therefore every religious problem is in the last analysis an ethical problem. The first is the case because every authentic ethical problem raises the human question, the question who man really is, with the kind of insistence and integrity which makes the question about who God is inescapable. And the second is the case because every authentic religious problem is deeply rooted in the human problem of the wholeness or the nothingness, the greatness or the wretchedness of man. 'It's terrible what mysteries there are!' declares Mitya Karamazov. 'I can't endure the thought that a man of lofty mind and heart begins with the ideal of the Madonna and ends with the ideal of Sodom. What's still more awful is that a man with the ideal of Sodom in his soul does not renounce the ideal of the Madonna. . . . God and the devil are fighting there, and the battlefield is the heart of man.'[2] Or, Professor von Hildebrand to the contrary notwithstanding, as J. D. Salinger puts it, 'But where does by far the bulk, the whole ambulance load, of pain really come from? Where *must* it come from?'[3] It was this point which Calvin was trying to get at when he insisted upon

---

[1] Mark 10.20 and parallels.

[2] Fyodor Dostoevsky, *The Brothers Karamazov*, Universal Library edition, Grosset and Dunlap, Inc., New York, pp. 114-15.

[3] J. D. Salinger, 'Seymour', *The New Yorker*, Vol. XXXV, No. 16, 6 June 1959, p. 44.

the conjunction of the knowledge of God and the knowledge of ourselves as the substance of true wisdom. And this is why Calvinism, in one of its brighter moments of faithfulness to Calvin, insisted that 'truth is in order to goodness'.[1]

Thus, if a man seriously raises the question what he is to do, in the context of an acknowledgment that something has gone wrong with his prayer life, and if he is told to pray either more or more fervently, Christianity has been reduced to ethical trivialization, to a mystery cult. But if the man is told that the one to whom he puts the question also finds prayer empty and troublesome, that prayer is an index of impiety as well as piety, depending upon whether it conceals or opens a man as he *really* is, to God as *he* really is, then that man begins to understand the power of Christian faith to shape and transform human life. Or if a man puts the ethical question seriously in the context of an acknowledgment that he has wanted to desert his wife and in fact has done so, and if he is told to remember his marriage vows, he will be confirmed in his suspicion that Christian faith overlays the tangle and turmoil in human relationships with a veneer of sweetness and light. But if he is met with the acknowledgment 'I have done it many times; in fact, what I can't understand is why my wife hasn't run out on me', he will begin to understand that he is being ethically addressed and claimed not from an elevation of moral achievement but from the depths of the ethical predicament of man. Out of such depths, he and the one to whom he has entrusted his predicament, *together*, can say, not 'Isn't it awful?' but 'This is our situation. If what God is doing in the world has anything to do with what man is doing in the world, it is his next move!'

The crucial question is whether God has, in fact, given any hints about whether or not he is prepared to make the next move. A *koinonia* ethic turns on the point that God has given us incontrovertible evidence that the next move has already been made. The ethical predicament has been overcome—not piecemeal but by a total renewal of our humanity. Moral theology obscures this act of God. Its handling of the ethical predicament blocks the way between God's ethical activity and man's ethical impotence. Ultimately, the difference between

[1] *The Form of Government of the United Presbyterian Church in the U.S.A.*, 1958, chap. I, par. 4.

evangelical and Roman Catholic ethics is the difference in the understanding of what God is doing in the world. And this difference is as fundamental, categorical, and radical as the difference in the analysis of the ethical predicament.

The second reason for the rejection of moral theology is the theological miscalculation underlying the lack of ethical radicality. This miscalculation is twofold. The first mistake is that moral theology regards the ethical predicament as symptomatic of a disordered relation between nature and grace. Human defection is a disease rather than a corruption. Sin is a wound, not a distortion. Depravity is not ultimate but proximate.[1] Let all Protestants who are squeamish about the doctrine of total depravity consider this symptom of their own crypto-Romanism. Or let them at least consider whether or not they have been too quickly put off by the deterministic folly with which the doctrine has not infrequently been expounded. The doctrine of total depravity does not mean that a man is foredoomed to ethical frustration and helplessness. It does not undertake to estimate a man's chances of lifting himself by his own bootstraps. The doctrine of total depravity has to do instead with the pathos, sobriety, and depth of the ethical predicament of man. A man who has been unable to keep the ethical question 'What shall I do?' from breaking out, who cannot break loose from 'Sodom' and make a break for the 'Madonna', knows that if he could transcend the ethical predicament in which he finds himself he would not be in it. And it is precisely this awareness of which the doctrine of total depravity takes sober and substantive account. The doctrine simply expresses the fact that whatever it takes to overcome the ethical predicament of man does not lie within the powers of man. Human renewal is not intrinsic to human capacity; it comes to man as a gift.

The second theological mistake of moral theology is its misinterpretation of the power by which a man receives ethical renewal. Moral theology rightly calls that power 'grace'. But

[1] See Mausbach-Ermecke: 'The decisive point of controversy between Catholic and protestant ethical theory lies . . . in the doctrine of original sin.' Op. cit., p. 41. Exactly! The whole paragraph (3) is a sharp and accurate statement of the engagement and disengagement of Roman and Protestant ways of thinking about ethics.

grace, as moral theology presupposes and applies it, is a sacerdotal, quasi-physical power.[1] It is not grace as the renewing and enabling power of the divine favor, concretely operative in the confrontation of a single human being and of all men with the fact, as foretaste and prospect, of human wholeness or maturity in Jesus Christ. It is this grace by which the *koinonia* is established and sustained. It is this grace which the Caroline divines were endeavoring to acknowledge and interpret through their insistence upon a radical juxtaposition of repentance and holiness in human renewal. But it is also this grace which the Caroline divines could not dislodge from the Jesuitical context of the tradition of moral theology. Their own reading of the

[1] Some attempt is currently being made by Roman theologians to deny that Catholic theology and ethics teach that human renewal is intrinsic to human capacity or that grace is a quasi-physical power. Catholicism, so these interpreters insist, has always recognized the limits of human capacity, the personal and relational character of grace, and the fact that human renewal is a gift. Cf. for example, Hans Küng, *Rechtfertigung*, Johannes Verlag, Einsiedeln, 1957. If the denial merely means that Catholic theology and ethics also stress the divine initiative, human insufficiency, and the personal source and appropriation of grace, it must be granted. But such an acknowledgment does not touch the fundamental point at issue here. The issue is not whether grace is divinely initiated or not, personal or not; or whether human renewal involves human capacity or not. The issue is the *radicality* with which the relations between God and man are understood where grace, sin, and renewal are concerned. Radicality means that sin is a corruption, not a wound. Radicality means that the test of whether grace is really understood as a divinely initiated gift and as personal is that it comes to man not merely as a power to aid in human renewal but as a transformed relationship which *is* human renewal. It may be that the term 'habit' (*habitus*) can be applied in the relational sense. But such an application can scarcely be taken seriously so long as the Thomistic ontology remains intact. A modification here is certain to lead to a revision of the sanctions whereby dogmatic and moral theology are pursued and sustained. Of such revisions there is no clear and certainly no convincing hint to date. It is no accident that Professor Küng's attempted reinterpretation of Catholic theology occurs in response to Karl Barth's *Kirchliche Dogmatik*. If Küng is correct in suggesting that Barth's strictures against Roman theology and ethics are weakened by excessive polemics, it is also correct that Küng's insistence that Catholic theology and ethics never really taught what Barth objects to but always taught what Barth erroneously criticizes protests too much. Despite Karl Barth's laudable commendation of Küng's book, the question remains whether, had Barth not touched the issue of radicality in an unavoidable way, he would have been noticed by Roman theologians at all.

Bible had made it impossible for them to follow the tradition of moral theology in its skillful repression of the ethical predicament. But they were sufficiently dependent upon the tradition to fail of finding a way to resolve the perennial ethical tension between irrelevance and relativity, or, to use the terms of the Caroline debate, between 'ethical rigor' and 'ethical laxity'. Caroline divinity has provided us with a sober warning that at least where the ethical question is under serious consideration a *via media*, for all its perspicacity and tidiness, can neither parallel nor extend nor intersect the *via dolorosa*. 'But where does . . . the whole ambulance load of pain really come from? Where *must* it come from?'

This is still the question which underlies and exposes the ethical predicament of man. Every avenue of escape from man's inhumanity having been blocked, the insistent question is whether or not the authentic displacement of this inhumanity by the reality and resources of human renewal has occurred. The reality and resources of human renewal presuppose a context and direction of divine activity within which man's activity is set and by which his behavior can be guided. What God is doing in the world to make and to keep human life human releases behavior from the frustrating impasse between rigor and laxity, between irrelevance and relativity, and forges the authentic behavioral link between freedom and responsibility. Caroline divinity instructively documents the fact that the context and spirit of moral theology can neither forge such a connection nor give Christian shape to behavior.

Moral philosophy, as we have seen, cannot deal with the question of a behavioral link between freedom and responsibility because its methodological dependence upon rational generalization cannot take due account of the ethical predicament of man. Moral theology, as we have seen, is involved in the same methodological inadequacy but must be credited with an important methodological refinement. Owing to its basic bond with moral philosophy,[1] moral theology succumbs to the

---

[1] *Agere sequitur esse* ('action follows being'), Mausbach-Ermecke defines it (op. cit., p. 14), and proposes an appropriate ontological discipline called 'Fundamental-Moral' as the bridge between moral philosophy and moral theology. 'On the issue of the correct understanding of the relation between Being and Action (*Wirken*)', Dr Ermecke observes, 'ethical theories and

same defect. But the methodological inadequacy of moral theology is more readily concealed because of the correct identification in moral theology of the behavioral form of the ethical predicament. Moral theology rightly sees and raises the question of conscience not only as the authentic link between the freedom and the responsibility of man in ethical action but also as the link between what God is doing and what, in consequence, man is to do in the world. Thus, whereas moral philosophy gives uncertain, variable, and even marginal consideration to the question of conscience, moral theology recognizes the crucial methodological centrality of the question of conscience. But, while recognizing the pivotal role of the conscience in ethical theory and behavior, moral theology cannot provide for the ethical reality of conscience. The ethical reality of conscience requires a context within which the conscience can give behavioral shape to free obedience. A context for conscience is the methodological outcome and option of a *koinonia* ethic.

---

moral theologies divide' (ibid., p. 5). And this is one of the grounds for Karl Barth's sharp rejection of moral theology as a possibility open to a Christian interpretation of ethics (*Kirchliche Dogmatik*, Evangelischer Verlag, Zollikon-Zuerich, II/2, 1942, pp. 591-93). The point at issue could scarcely be more decisively stated. We agree both with Professor Barth and with Professor Ermecke and are concerned to underline the methodological incompatibility between Rome and the Reformation in the interpretation of ethics.

# XIII

## THE DECLINE AND FALL
## OF CONSCIENCE

THE legend of the Grand Inquisitor in Dostoevsky's novel about the Karamazovs contains a passage which focuses in words of great power upon the crucial issue at which our methodological analysis of Christian ethics has now arrived. The scene is Seville in Spain at the time of the Inquisition. The Inquisitor, an aged cardinal, has ordered the arrest of a visitor to the town who has halted a funeral cortège on its way to the Cathedral and raised from the dead a little girl. The visitor is undeniably Jesus, although Dostoevsky refers to him simply as 'the Prisoner'. At night, and in secret, the Cardinal enters the Prisoner's cell for the purpose of an interrogation, which, owing to the Prisoner's unresponding silence, turns out to be a monologue from the lips of a prince of the church.

For fifteen centuries [the Cardinal declares] we have been wrestling with thy freedom, but now it is ended and over for good. . . . Instead of taking men's freedom from them, Thou didst make it greater than ever! Didst Thou forget that man prefers peace, and even death, to freedom of choice in the knowledge of good and evil? Nothing is more seductive for man than his freedom of conscience, but nothing is a greater cause of suffering. And behold, instead of giving a firm foundation for setting the conscience of man at rest forever, Thou didst choose all that is exceptional, vague and enigmatic; Thou didst choose what was utterly beyond the strength of men, acting as though Thou didst not love them at all—Thou who didst come to give Thy life for them! Instead of taking possession of men's freedom, Thou didst increase it, and burdened the spiritual kingdom of mankind with its sufferings forever. Thou didst desire man's free love, that he should follow Thee freely, enticed and taken captive by Thee. In place of the rigid ancient law, man must hereafter with free heart decide for himself what is good and what is evil, having only Thy image before him as his guide. But didst Thou not know that he would at last reject even Thy image and Thy truth, if he is weighed down with the fearful burden of free choice.? They will cry aloud at last that the truth is not in Thee, for they could not have been left in greater confusion and suffering than Thou has caused, laying upon them so many unanswerable cares and unanswerable problems. So that, in truth, Thou didst Thyself lay the foundation for the destruction of Thy Kingdom. . . .[1]

Since the Inquisition, four further centuries of his increase of freedom have elapsed. But the Cardinal's indictment of the Prisoner still poses the decisive question of ethics: the question of what it really takes to make and to keep human life human. What it really takes is nothing other than a firm foundation for setting the conscience of man forever, not at rest, but free. Was the Cardinal right that the free conscience is defenseless against 'all that is exceptional, vague and enigmatic', leaving men 'in greater confusion and suffering', overlaid with 'so many un-answerable cares and unanswerable problems'? Or was Jesus right that 'man must hereafter with free heart decide for himself what is good and what is evil, having only [His] image before him as his guide'? Does the image support such a decision or seduce man to destruction? What *is* the context of conscience and how in this context does the conscience acquire ethical reality?

We shall be in a better position to suggest a constructive answer to these questions if we have before us, however briefly, the principal episodes in the history of the conscience in the Western ethical tradition. The semantic, philosophical and theological pilgrimage of conscience begins with the Greek tragedians of the fifth century before Christ and ends with Sigmund Freud. It is a moving, tortuous record of decline and fall which forces upon us in our time the frankest possible facing of a sharp alternative: either 'do the conscience over' or 'do the conscience in'! Ethical theory must either dispose of the conscience altogether or completely transform the interpreta-tion of its ethical nature, function, and significance.

When we describe the present ethical condition of conscience as one of decline and fall, we have two considerations chiefly in mind.[2] By the *decline* of conscience we mean the fact that the

[1] Fyodor Dostoevsky, *The Brothers Karamazov*, Universal Library edition, Grosset and Dunlap, New York, pp. 276-80.

[2] A full-length study of what has happened to conscience in the Western cultural tradition is overdue. A carefully documented and sufficiently com-

power of conscience to shape behavior both through judgment and through action has steadily lost persuasiveness and force. By the *fall* of conscience we mean the rejection of conscience as formative of, or important for, ethical behavior. What is of utmost significance for ethical theory, however, is that the conscience which has been rejected is the conscience which has declined; it is *not* the conscience which is intrinsic to ethical action which has been rejected. And this discrepancy provides the clue to a constructive interpretation of the ethical nature and function of conscience.

## 1 *The Enemy of Humanization*

The original semantic environment of the *conscience* was Greek. The Latin, *con-scientia*, was a translation of ἡ συνείδησις, which appears initially to have had two main uses, a technical-philosophical usage and an ethical usage.[1] The technical usage referred to a state of consciousness such as would be expressed as 'I am conscious of this or that within myself', or 'I am conscious within myself that this or that is the case'. Whatever it is that 'I know together with, or in common with myself' appears to include the implication of being 'desirable' or 'undesirable', but in the cognitive rather than in the ethical sense. Thus, Alcibiades declares that he is conscious that if he did not shut his ears against Socrates, 'and fly as from the voice of the siren', his 'fate would be like the others,—he would transfix me and I should grow old sitting at his feet'.[2]

---

prehensive account of what might be called 'the shape of conscience', i.e., of an interpretive framework other than that offered by moral theology in which the ethical nature and behavioral effectiveness of the conscience might once again be clearly and persuasively understood, is not at hand. Obviously, such a discussion of conscience goes beyond the limits of the present book. All that can be attempted here, and indeed is necessary to the concerns of this essay, is some indication of the principal episodes of the decline and fall of conscience and a concluding hint of a constructive ethical interpretation.

[1] The paragraphs in this chapter dealing with the Hellenistic and biblical environment and usage of the word 'conscience' are heavily dependent upon the succinct but carefully documented discussion of conscience by C. A. Pierce, *Conscience in the New Testament*, Alec R. Allenson, Inc., Naperville, 1955 (SCM Press, London, 1955).

[2] Plato, *Symposium*, 216, Jowett translation. The Greek text says: 'καὶ ἔτι γε νῦν σύνοιδ' ἐμαυτῷ. . . .'

The moral use of ἡ συνείδησις denotes the moral quality of the self's own acts or behavior, as in such variant phrases as 'to be a witness for or against oneself', 'to hug a secret to oneself', usually a guilty secret. Indeed, unless stated otherwise the connotation of ἡ συνείδησις is bad. Euripides makes Orestes say that he suffers conscience (ἡ σύνεσις, i.e., self-knowledge! knowledge privy with himself concerning himself) in that he knows with himself that he has done terrible things.

> ORESTES: I call it conscience.
>   The certain knowledge of wrong, the conviction of crime.
> MENELAUS: You speak somewhat obscurely. What do you mean?
> ORESTES: I mean remorse. I am sick with remorse.[1]

And Menander declares that he who knows anything at all with himself, no matter how brave he is, will be reduced to terror by that knowledge.[2]

Now something like a structure or configuration of meaning emerges from the foregoing uses of 'conscience', which are merely samples of innumerable others.[3] The structure suggests that ἡ συνείδησις is connected with the fixed order of things as they are. Gradually this connection tends to be traced to the gods or to God as the orderer of the universe. Conscience is also an order intrinsic to the nature of man. It refers, moreover, always to specific acts and to acts that are past. And finally, its function is that of pain. Thus Plutarch can say that conscience is 'like an ulcer in the flesh';[4] Polybius 'asserts that there is no witness so fearful, nor accuser so terrible as that which dwells in the soul of every man';[5] and Philo describes the conscience with great vividness and force: 'It is born with every soul . . . is at once both accuser and judge. . . . Never does it depart by day or by night, but it stabs as with a goad, and inflicts wounds that know no healing, until it snap the thread of that soul's

---

[1] Orestes, ll. 395ff. *The Complete Greek Tragedies*, edited by David Grene and Richard Lattimore, Vol. IV, University of Chicago Press, Chicago, 1958, p. 214.

[2] Fragment 632 (Koch collection, 1880): ' . . . ἡ σύνεσις αὐτὸν δειλότατον εἶναι ποιεῖ'. Pierce, op. cit., p. 25.

[3] How innumerable may be gleaned from the analytical index of Greek sources which Pierce has provided, op. cit., pp. 131-47.

[4] *De Tranquilitate Animi*, 476F-77A; quoted by Pierce, op. cit., p. 47.

[5] See Pierce, op. cit., pp. 40-41.

pitiful and accursed life.'[1] The meaning of conscience, then, is
that human nature is so constituted that if man oversteps the
moral limits of his nature he is certain to feel the pain of τῆς
συνειδήσεως. Just as the delight of a journey lies in the absence
of mishap, so the absence of conscience is a great joy. As a nurse
or governess will watchfully guard her charges, so the proper
office of conscience is to protect man from physical and moral
harm.[2] What is to be noted above all is that according to the
original semantic environment of conscience, the ethical significance of conscience is not that it is a teacher of morals. Its
ethical significance is that it resides in human nature as the
bearer of ethical negation and futility in the relations between
man and the order of things in which he lives.

## 2   *The Domestication of Conscience*

If now we shift the perspective and turn from the original
semantic environment of conscience toward the apex of its
cultural journey, we come upon the clearest and most influential account of its ethical nature and significance through the
mind of Thomas Aquinas. The account centers upon the distinction already alluded to between *synderesis* and *conscientia*.
'There is in the soul', Thomas wrote, 'a natural habit of first
principles of action, which are the universal principles of the
natural law. This habit pertains to synderesis. This habit exists
in no other power than reason. . . . The name *conscience* means
the application of knowledge to something. . . . Conscience . . .
is the application of any habit or of any knowledge to some
particular act.'[3] The first principles of moral action are known
to all men without deliberation. But the behavioral implementation of this knowledge requires a kind of liaison between the
principle and any given action. This bond between the principle
and the act is the conscience. What a man knows together with
himself is that this or that particular, freely chosen action is in
accordance with natural law. *Conscience is, thus, the bond between
law and responsibility.*

---

[1] *De Decalogo* 87; quoted by Pierce, op. cit., p. 46.
[2] See Pierce, op. cit., pp. 50-51.
[3] *De Veritate*, Q. 16, art. 1; Q. 17, art. 1. We quote from the English
translation entitled *Truth*, by James V. McGlynn, S.J. Chicago, Henry
Reguery Company, 1953.

Thomas is not unaware of the variety of meanings which have been attributed to *conscience*.[1] But following the advice of Aristotle that one should follow the more common signification of terms, Aquinas adheres to the tradition which derives *conscience* from *conscire*, 'to know together'.[2] As the analysis proceeds, however, a significant transformation of the ethical meaning and role of conscience takes place. The fierce and awesome internal arbiter and enemy of man is brought under the discriminating differentiation and control of the reason in the act of judging both what man knows and what man does. 'Judgment', Thomas notes, 'is two-fold: of universal [principles], which belongs to synderesis; and of particular activities, which is the judgment of choice and belongs to free choice' (i.e., the conscience).[3] Thomas explains the operation of this twofold judgment in terms of the contrast between scientific and moral knowledge, between what one 'is conscious of' and what one 'has a conscience about'.[4] In both cases there is a 'knowing together with ourselves', a 'bond betwixt two'. But in the first case, 'through scientific knowledge we look for what should be done' and 'proceed from principles to conclusions'. In the second case, 'we examine those things which already have been done and consider whether they are right' and 'reduce conclusions to principles'.[5]

This brings us to the passage in which the transformation of the ethical meaning and role of conscience is vividly formulated. 'We use the name of conscience', Thomas wrote, 'for both these modes of application [i.e., the two cases just mentioned]. For, in so far as knowledge is applied to an act, as directive of that act, conscience is said to prod or urge or bind. But, in so far as knowledge is applied to an act, by way of examining things which already have taken place, conscience is said *to accuse or*

---

[1] He alludes to Bonaventura and Alexander Hales, who use the word 'conscience' variously for the object of which one is conscious, for a power, a habit, or an act. See *De Veritate*, English translation, Q. 17, art. 1; and also p. 449.

[2] See Aristotle, *Topica*, II, 1, 109a, 27. *De Veritate*, Q. 17, art. 1, Reply.

[3] *De Veritate*, Q. 16, art. 1, Answer 15. The bracketed word appears in the English translation, p. 307.

[4] The phrases are mine, not Thomas's.

[5] *De Veritate*, Q. 17, art. 1, Reply. The first case is clearly *synderesis*; the second is *conscience*.

*cause remorse* when that which has been done is found to be out of harmony with the knowledge according to which it is examined; or to *defend or excuse* when that which has been done is found to have proceeded according to the form of the knowledge.'[1]

Something like a *domestication* of conscience has occurred. The ominous, sometimes even wildly terrifying fury of the guilty conscience has been tamed by a divine infusion of the rational soul which lightens the dark torment of negation and futility by an intrinsic power to distinguish between good and evil, and so either to defend or to accuse, to excuse or to cause remorse. The easy conscience has become the companion of the uneasy one. It must be borne in mind that the environment of conscience has also been markedly transformed from an indifferent or hostile order of inscrutable arbitrariness into an order of intellectual stability and understanding. This is the meaning of Thomas's suggestion that *synderesis* is common both to men and to angels.[2] But the change in the environment of conscience does not diminish the significance of the transformation of the conscience itself. Indeed, it is this very change which makes the domestication of conscience possible. Originally conscience had but a single function and that was negative and unbearable. Now conscience has acquired a double function, a negative and a positive one, and has become bearable. Originally conscience was that in a man which above all things else he could not endure. Now conscience can be lived with; the knowledge which a man has together with himself could be counted upon as still against him, but sometimes also—and this is the important change—as on his side.

[1] *De Veritate*, Q. 17, art. 1, Reply. Italics mine.

[2] I.e., to the next higher order of beings. Ibid., Q. 16, art. 1, Reply. See on this point especially, Étienne Gilson, *The Christian Philosophy of St. Thomas Aquinas*, Random House, New York, 1956 (Gollancz, London, 1957). Or perhaps a more existentialist interpretation of St Thomas is possible, and the environment of conscience is to be understood as an order of providence and charity. I am indebted to Professor Richard Kalter of Berkeley Divinity School, New Haven, for clarifying discussions of St Thomas' views on conscience and for this suggestion in particular growing out of his own studies looking toward the completion of a Th.D. dissertation on 'Conscience and Providence in the Thought of St Thomas Aquinas'. The re-examination of moral theology by Roman Catholic theologians considered in the foregoing chapter seems also to point to this possibility.

### 3  *Duty's Inner Citadel*

The Thomistic view of conscience is the classic statement, if not the origin, of the popular notion of the conscience as a built-in human device for spot-checking right from wrong. The pervasive hold of this position over popular morality has reached beyond the confines of the Christian ethical tradition. Within the Christian tradition its formidable influence upon ethical thinking, instructed and uninstructed alike, is due to the pivotal role of conscience in moral theology. But there is another view of conscience, strikingly similar yet strangely different, whose influence upon ethical theory and practice is perhaps second only to that of Aquinas. This influence has been initiated without the benefit of clergy. Indeed, the roles have been reversed; for the clergy have not so much bestowed as received the benefits of conscience which have been secured by Immanuel Kant.

For Kant, as for St Thomas, conscience is a faculty of judgment. It is concerned with the evaluation of action in accordance with universal moral principles and is both internal and intrinsic to human nature. With Kant, as with Thomas, the conscience both accuses and excuses. 'For conscience is practical reason which, in every case of law, holds before man his duty for acquittal or condemnation.'[1] The law, of course, is the moral law. And what makes the conscience that 'marvellous faculty in us'[2] is its function in bringing the moral law and the moral will together. *Conscience is the bond between duty and obligation.*

The argument in brief is this. The moral worth of actions is defined by the fact that the will is determined by the moral law. This means that all incentive is excluded from moral action except the constraint of the moral law itself. Thus 'morality or moral worth can be conceded only where the action occurs from duty, i.e. merely for the sake of the law'.[3] But an action done *from* duty is not in and of itself an action done *according to*

[1] Immanuel Kant, *The Metaphysical Elements of Ethics, Werke*, Vol. V, Hartenstein edition, Modes und Baumann, Leipzig, 1838, Introduction, Part XII, par. b, p. 227. Translation mine.

[2] Immanuel Kant, *Critique of Practical Reason*, Beck edition, University of Chicago Press, Chicago, 1949, p. 204.

[3] Ibid., p. 188. See also pp. 180ff.

duty. One may, for example, act *from* duty simply because the law of duty constrains, while one really desires to act in another way. The moral will is at variance with the moral law. Conversely, one may act *according to* a sense of duty without a clear command of the moral law. As Kant puts it, 'it is a very beautiful thing to do good to men because of love and a sympathetic good will or to do justice because of a love of order. But this is not the genuine moral maxim of our conduct'.[1] When this happens, a disparity has occurred between what the law of duty requires objectively (an action *from* duty) and what it requires subjectively (an action *according to* duty, i.e., as an obligation). In short, the command and the maxim of the action do not correspond. 'It is', however, 'of the utmost importance in all moral judging to pay strictest attention to the subjective principle of every maxim. . . .'[2] In the case of a good act, in the pure and proper sense of the phrase, the subjective principle of *respect for the law* (obligation) combines with the constraint of the law itself (duty). Thus, 'duty and obligation are the only names which we must ever give to our relation to the moral law'.[3] An act done both *from* duty and *in accordance with* duty is an act done both from respect for the moral law and in accordance with the moral law as the sole determining ground of the will.

Although duty and obligation define the relation of men to the moral law and thus also the moral worth of their actions, the question still remains as to how one knows that this or that action has actually met the conditions of morality. The answer is given by the moral consciousness, i.e., the consciousness of the ethical subject in the performance of a moral act. Such a man is conscious of his transcendental freedom, i.e., of his own existence as 'determinable only by laws which he gives to himself through reason'.[4] And he is also conscious of a capacity for judgment, i.e., the consciousness that at the moment of acting 'he was in possession of his freedom'.[5]

Thus, as Thomas had analyzed the moral consciousness in terms of a compound of synderesis and conscience, Kant analyzes the moral consciousness in terms of the moral reason and conscience. As Thomas had derived the content of synderesis

---

[1] Kant, ibid., p. 189.     [2] Ibid., p. 188.     [3] Ibid., p. 189.
[4] Ibid., p. 203.                                      [5] Ibid., p. 204.

from the *natural* law, Kant finds the moral reason informed by the *moral* law and respect for the moral law. What a man knows in conscience is that, in the case of any given action, duty and obligation either correspond or do not correspond. If duty and obligation are adjudged by the conscience to correspond, the conscience acquits; if duty and obligation do not correspond, the conscience condemns.

This brings us to the strangely different countenance of conscience under the careful scrutiny of Kant as compared to Aquinas. Kant's stress upon law and upon the *pure* (in contrast to the prime) principles of morality has brought a corresponding accent to the conscience in operation. The judgmental function of conscience has acquired an astringent quality. Whereas Aquinas had analyzed the conscience as a faculty of judgment, Kant makes an important addition. Conscience for Kant is *juridical as well as judgmental.* It functions not simply as the intellect or reason in the act of distinguishing good from evil but as a *tribunal*. As Kant puts it in a particularly forceful passage, 'the consciousness of an internal tribunal in man . . . is conscience. . . . This power is not something which he himself makes but it is incorporated in his being. . . . It follows him like his shadow, when he thinks to escape. . . . In his utmost depravity he may indeed pay no heed to it, but he cannot avoid hearing it. . . . Now this original intellectual and moral capacity, called *conscience*, has this peculiarity in it, that although its business is a business of man with himself yet he finds himself compelled by his reason to transact it as if at the command of another person . . . God.'[1] Thus an inner faculty of reason becomes an inner voice of judgment and the way is open for a virtual identification of the voice of conscience as the voice of God. Kant himself had cautiously written: 'the subjective principle of a responsibility of one's deeds before God'. But plainly the identification is not far removed.

The identification of the voice of conscience with the voice of God is not completely absent from the conscience as domesticated by Aquinas. In a precise sense, the juridical and the judgmental functions of conscience always belonged together as two sides of a coin. Yet just as the marked stress upon the

[1] Kant, *The Metaphysical Elements of Ethics*, Part II, par. 13, pp. 271-72. Translation mine.

awesomeness of duty inevitably overshadowed the pure rationality of the moral law, so the marked stress upon the inwardness of conscience heightened its juridical significance over its judgmental significance. The result was an operational detachment of conscience from synderesis, of the tribunal of moral judgment from the transcendent character of moral freedom. And this meant that actions could be appraised as good or bad with a heightened sense of moral certainty in proportion to the inner depth of conscience. In a more intimate and volitional sense than ever, a resurgence of the uneasy conscience had occurred. Kant had outdone the classical dramatists and moralists in juxtaposing the guilty conscience with a rational order of responsibility. And he had undone St Thomas in reaffirming the radical character of negation in relation to achievement in the evaluation of moral behavior. In the classical view, the guilty conscience, like the mark on the forehead of Cain, was the bearer of the tragedy of man's life in the world. Thomas (and moral theology with him) had displaced the tragic conscience by the easy conscience as the bearer of the dignity, and the promise of man's life as a rational being under grace. Kant had once again restored the tragic conscience to its due place in a rational analysis of the moral life. Kant has made it impossible for reason either to ignore or to suppress the conscience in the analysis of ethical sensitivity and responsibility.

However, despite the magnificence of Kant's demonstration of the impotence of conscience to shape behavior on the classical and the Thomistic model, his own achievement must also be reckoned as an extension of the conscience in decline. Perhaps it may be said that Kant was the principal architect of the decline of conscience since he most directly prepared the ground for its fall. For Kant had displaced the human significance of conscience as the link between the internal nature of man and the order in which his life is sustained. He had substituted the legal significance of conscience as an internal voice of an external authority. It is this authoritarian conscience which has so conspicuously lost its ethical persuasiveness and force today. Consequently, we must face the question whether a recovery of the ethical significance and role of conscience is either possible or desirable. If Thomas and especially Kant may be regarded as the architects of the decline of conscience, Sigmund

Freud must be regarded as the principal architect of the fall of conscience.

### 4  *The Dethronement of Conscience*

There is a passage in the *New Introductory Lectures* which vividly expresses both Freud's rejection of Kant and a hint of his own considered view of the conscience.

> The philosopher Kant once declared [Freud remarks] that nothing proved to him the greatness of God more convincingly than the starry heavens and the moral conscience within us. The stars are unquestionably superb, but where conscience is concerned God has been guilty of an uneven and careless piece of work, for a great many men have only a limited share of it or scarcely enough to be worth mentioning. . . . It is a very remarkable experience to observe morality, which was once ostensibly conferred on us by God and planted deep in our hearts, functioning as a periodical phenomenon. For after a certain number of months the whole moral fuss is at an end, the critical voice of the super-ego is silent, the ego is re-instated, and enjoys once more all the rights of man until another attack.[1]

Clearly, what Freud had discovered clinically was that the conscience did not, as Kant had claimed, express and facilitate the moralization of man. On the contrary, the net effect of the Kantian account of conscience was the dehumanization of man. Indeed, the Freudian exploration of the intimate connection between mental and moral disorder has compounded the evidence confirming the fatal role of conscience in the Western ethical tradition. With Freud the line beginning, as it were, with Euripides comes full circle round. Dramatist and scientist have met in a common documentation in depth of the ethical futility of conscience. 'The stars are unquestionably superb, but where conscience is concerned God has been guilty of an uneven and careless piece of work. . . .'

Nevertheless, Freud seems to have regarded the conscience as an inevitable rather than as an expendable datum of human nature. There is a bond between the environment of decision and the intrinsic human response to that environment which makes or breaks the emerging humanity of man. In this, Freud

[1] Sigmund Freud, *New Introductory Lectures on Psychoanalysis*, translated by W. J. H. Sprott, W. W. Norton and Company, New York, 1938 (Hogarth, London), p. 88. Kant had actually written 'the moral law within'. But as we have seen this was functionally identical with conscience.

was in agreement with Euripides, Thomas, and Kant. But unlike the theologian and the philosopher, Freud shares the pessimism about the conscience which informed its original semantic clarification. A passage in *Totem and Taboo* is virtually a prosaic duplication of the metered melancholy with which Orestes voices the suffering of conscience.

Taboo conscience is probably the oldest form in which we meet the phenomenon of conscience. For what is conscience? According to linguistic testimony it belongs to what we know most surely; in some languages its meaning is hardly to be distinguished from consciousness. Conscience is the inner perception of objections to definite wish impulses that exist in us; but the emphasis is put upon the fact that this rejection does not have to depend on anything else, that it is sure of itself. This becomes even plainer in the case of a guilty conscience, where we become aware of the inner condemnation of such acts which realized some of our definite wish impulses. . . . Whoever has a conscience must feel in himself the justification of the condemnation, and the reproach for the accomplished action. But this same character is evinced by the attitude of savages towards taboo. Taboo is a command of conscience, the violation of which causes a terrible sense of guilt which is as self-evident as its origin is unknown.[1]

[1] Sigmund Freud, *Totem and Taboo*, in *The Basic Writings of Sigmund Freud*, translated and edited by Dr A. A. Brill, The Modern Library, New York, 1938 (Kegan Paul, London), pp. 859-60. In a footnote Freud expressly alludes to the Oedipus myth, according to which the guilt of Oedipus is not canceled by the fact that it was incurred without his knowledge and will and even against them. The essay itself marks the beginning of Freud's effort to bring his clinical findings to bear upon the question of the origin of conscience, illuminating thereby also the nature of conscience. Other essays which have to do particularly with Freud's reflections upon the conscience and with the emergence of his final position on the problem are: *The Origins of Psychoanalysis*, 1910, in *General Selections*, edited by John Rickman, Hogarth Press, London, 1937; *Group Psychology and the Analysis of the Ego*, translated by James Strachey, International Psycho-analytic Press, London, 1922 (*GPE*); *The Problem of Anxiety*, translated by Henry A. Bunker, W. W. Norton and Company, New York, 1936 (*A*); *The Problem of Lay Analysis*, Introduction by Dr L. Terenczi, Brentanos, New York, 1927; *Civilization and Its Discontents*, translated by Joan Rivers, Hogarth Press, London, 1930 (*CD*); *New Introductory Lectures in Psychoanalysis* (*NIL*). The abbreviations in parentheses will be used below in identifying sources. I wish to acknowledge with special appreciation the kindness of Mr Donald Miller, a candidate for the Ph.D. degree in the history and philosophy of religion at Harvard University in making available to me his preliminary researches in connection with a dissertation upon Freud's doctrine of the conscience. Mr Miller is, of course, not accountable for the use which I have made of his findings. His assistance has helped, however, both to

The more Freud observed the results of conscience in operation, the more he endeavored to find an explanation of its origin
and formation. His earliest conjectures are characterized by an
ambivalence which the latest position tries not so much to
discard as to reconstruct. Two conceptions of conscience seem
to persist side by side as Freud tries to deal with the fact that
human nature appears unable either to avoid or to endure
conscience. 'It has long been our contention', he wrote, 'that
"dread of society" (*soziale Angst*) is the essence of what is called
conscience.'[1] Yet this contention had not been of such long
standing as to displace an earlier suggestion that 'as a substitute-
formation there arises an alteration in the ego, an increased
sensitiveness of conscience, which can hardly be called a
symptom'.[2] The point here is that conscience is a neurotic
manifestation arising from a hiatus between the instinctual
drives of the organism and reality, as presented to the organism
in its environment. The ego is the focal point of this hiatus and
responds by repressing the conflict between what Freud elsewhere calls the 'pleasure-principle' and the 'reality-principle'.[3]
In a later and perhaps more crucial discussion, a different
formulation occurs which appears to contradict 'the long-
standing contention' that conscience is a social manifestation.
It may be, however, that Freud is attempting a rather more
precise formulation of the relation between two hitherto dis-
parate conceptions of conscience. '. . . That part of the fear of
the superego which may be called social anxiety', Freud notes,
'still represents an internal substitute for an external danger,
while the other part, fear of conscience, is entirely endopsychic.'[4]
Here the term 'conscience' appears to be applied to internal
psychic responses rather than to external social pressures upon
the individual.

By whatever developmental route Freud arrived at his most

----

confirm my previous understanding of Freud's position and to facilitate the
consideration of Freud for the limited purpose of the present chapter.

[1] *GPE*, p. 10.

[2] Sigmund Freud, *Repression*, in *General Selections*, Rickman edition, 1915,
p. 109.

[3] Sigmund Freud, *Mental Functioning*, *General Selections*, Rickman edition,
1910, p. 57.

[4] *A*, p. 114.

fully elaborated view of conscience, the several elements of it are already before us. The instinctual drives, the ego responses both to these drives and to the super-ego, provide the clinical and conceptual materials which were destined to play such a formative role in the fall of conscience. As is well known, the basic elements of the psychic apparatus are the *id*, the *ego*, and the *super-ego*. The human organism arrives in the world equipped with an unorganized chaos of instinctual drives: hunger, self-preservation, sexuality, love. These drives press for and require gratification. In their elemental form they constitute the id. The id possesses the capacity to differentiate between the inexorable reality of the outer world and an inner dynamism of response, and for this part of the id Freud uses the term 'ego'. 'One can hardly go wrong,' he declares, 'in regarding the ego as the part of the id which has been modified by its proximity to the external world and the influence that the latter has had on it. . . .'[1] And just as the ego is a modified part of the id, so the super-ego is a modification of the ego. If the ego is that part of the id which protectively selects and orders its chaos anent the external world, the super-ego is that part of the ego which responds to and transmits the restrictions imposed by the external world via external authorities. 'We have posited a special function within the ego,' says Freud, 'to represent the demand for restriction and rejection, i.e., the super-ego. We can say that repression is the work of the super-ego—either that it does its work on its own account or else that the ego does it in obedience to its orders.'[2] The super-ego, at first shaped by the demands of authorities external to the ego, chiefly parental, gradually displaces these authorities and functions by its own power as a kind of internalized echo of external authorities. 'The super-ego takes the place of the parental function, and thenceforward observes, guides and threatens the ego in just the same way as the parents acted to the child before.'[3]

Thus, for Freud, the neurotic and the societal aspects of the phenomenon of conscience meet in the super-ego and its operation. In a word, conscience *is* the super-ego. Whether conscience has a positive function is not entirely clear. Freud speaks of a 'distance between an ego ideal and the real ego'[4] due apparently to the dissatisfaction of the ego with itself. But whether this ego

[1] *NIL*, p. 106.    [2] Ibid., p. 98.    [3] Ibid., p. 89.    [4] *GPE*, p. 70.

ideal is the cause or the consequence of the dissatisfaction is ambiguous. It is, perhaps, also ambiguous whether the super-ego (as the repository of parental and cultural ideals)[1] contributes positively to the socialization of the individual. Indubitably, however, the decisive operation of conscience is negative, i.e., judging and condemning, 'exercising the function of a censor'.[2] The exercise of this function is at once so intense and so aggressive as to leave the ego almost prostrate before it. As Freud describes the sequence of conscience formation its range and oppressiveness seem virtually complete. There is 'first, instinct renunciation due to dread of loss of love. . . . Then follows erection of an internal authority, and instinctual renunciation due to dread of it—that is dread of conscience. In the second case, there is the equivalence of wicked acts and wicked intentions; hence comes the sense of guilt, the need for punishment. The aggressiveness of conscience carries on the aggressiveness of authority.'[3] This aggressiveness appears to be reinforced by the super-ego of the neighbor, a phenomenon which Freud explores in terms of the relations between 'psyche' and 'alter'. 'Now it is, of course, very probable', he writes, 'that my neighbor, when he is commanded to love me as himself, will answer exactly as I have done and reject me for the same reasons. I hope he will not have the same objective grounds for doing so, but he will hope so as well. Even so, there are variations in men's behavior which ethics, disregarding the fact that they are determined, classifies as "good" and "evil". As long as these undeniable variations have not been abolished, conformity to the highest ethical standards constitutes a betrayal of the interests of culture, for it puts a direct premium on wickedness.'[4] The social pessimism which Thomas Hobbes had described in political terms three centuries earlier is here established clinically.[5]

---

[1] *CD*, chap. 1.    [2] Ibid., p. 93.    [3] Ibid., pp. 82-83.    [4] Ibid., p. 60.
[5] *Bellum omnium contra omnes*, 'the war of all against all', had been the maxim in the light of which Hobbes had proposed a theory of the political community by social contract. *Leviathan*, chap. 13. This precedent is worth recalling here not only in connection with Freud's researches but in support of Freud against those among his disciples and critics who imagine that ethical humanism offers a persuasive alternative to social pessimism. It may be that the physiological basis of Freud's social pessimism is too slender a foundation for it and certain revisions are required as regards Freud's account of the emergence of the super-ego. But this does not mean, for

What Freud seems to be saying is that 'good' and 'evil' are deterministic variants of the social and endopsychic conflict between 'psyche' and 'alter', between which the conscience operates to maintain an uneasy truce. The truce is particularly uneasy because the very obedience of 'psyche' to the demands of the super-ego provides the occasion for 'alter' to express its own aggressions unhindered by any anxiety over their being returned. This means that conscience has exchanged its ethical role and function for a psychoanalytic one. Although Freud recognized that conscience is the result both of innate constitutional and concrete environmental factors, he was unable to arrive at a depth-psychological account of the origin and significance of conscience that was otherwise than heavy with guilt and inexorability. At the end, neither individual fulfillment nor cultural development can break the stranglehold of conscience upon man's 'task of living with his fellows'. For conscience is simply 'the price of progress in civilization'.[1]

The ethical consequences of this grim doctrine are enormous. Freud seems to have done with meticulous precision what God had allegedly done with uneven carelessness. 'The moral fuss is, indeed, at an end.' But there is no 'waiting for the next attack' except for those constitutionally unable to pay the price of conscience. For the normal human course there is a way of coming to terms with the ever-present threat of dehumanization aimed at the ego by the super-ego. This is the way of the therapeutic transformation of the ethical role and function of conscience into a psychoanalytic one. Therapy seeks to illuminate the struggle between the ego and the super-ego and thereby to achieve an accommodation of the human psyche to its natural and social environment. Mature self-knowledge leads to serenity through a manageable reduction of the tensions arising from involvement in the stresses and strains of living. Consequently, an appeal to conscience in the name of morality

example, that a 'humanistic conscience' as 'the expression of man's self-interest and integrity', as 'the reaction of our total personality to its proper functioning and disfunctioning' (Erich Fromm, *Man for Himself*, p. 158) reduces or eliminates the 'direct premium on wickedness'. It means rather that the integrity of a humanistic conscience is directly proportional to its sensitivity to the dehumanizing pressures upon it.

[1] *CD*, p. 90.

or contrariwise to morality in the name of conscience is ethically sterile because humanly false, i.e., irrelevant to human nature as it actually behaves and develops. The clinical data have exposed a moral bondage upon mankind from which there is no egress. Under this bondage, the sensitivity to what it takes to make and to keep human life human is severely restricted to an attainable adjustment between self-conscious self-awareness and the relevant limits imposed by external environment. The tragic nobility of Orestes has given way before the precarious tranquillity of the measurably uninvolved life. If the uneasy conscience cannot be made easy it can at least be made evident; if it cannot be domesticated, it can at least be subdued.

> Thus conscience does make cowards of us all;
> And thus the native hue of resolution
> Is sicklied o'er with the pale cast of thought;
> And enterprises of great pith and moment,
> With this regard their currents turn awry
> And lose the name of action.[1]

Hamlet was a Freudian before Freud, a pitiful replica of Orestes, and the prototype of twentieth-century man.

Freud's greatness, like Kant's, is marked by his dedication to follow his findings regardless of consequences. On the boundary of the ethical disintegration and psychoanalytic confirmation of conscience, he has exposed the long-overdue need for a reconsideration of 'the knowledge of good and evil' as the environment of human wholeness. That he was unable himself to move toward such a reconsideration is not so much to be held against him as against the failure of the Western ethical tradition to provide an adequate context for conscience. The fall of conscience, as Freud documents it, is the rejection of the hostile conscience through the demonstration of its ethical impotence and uselessness. Such a fall could be the prelude to a rise of conscience if the loosing of conscience from its barren ethical moorings should prove to be a way of loosing it for a context within which its potential ethical role and significance could acquire ethical reality.

[1] *Hamlet*, Act III, Scene I.

# XIV

## THE ETHICAL REALITY
## OF CONSCIENCE

T HE story of the decline and fall of conscience is as much a story of conscience in search of a context as it is a record of ethical misinterpretation and default. What we are now prepared to understand is that such a context is in fact available. In the context of the *koinonia* a transformation of the nature and function of conscience occurs in terms of which conscience acquires both ethical reality and the power to shape behavior.

At the outset of the previous chapter the legend of the Grand Inquisitor put before us the pivotal question whether or not Jesus was correct that 'man must hereafter with free heart decide for himself what is good and what is evil, having only [His] image before him as his guide'. This is the question of the context of conscience and of how in such context the ethical reality of conscience is established. Having reviewed the lines along which ethical meaning and power for conscience can be neither expected nor achieved, we must take up the question once more and seek to suggest the lines of a constructive answer to it.

### 1 *A* 'Koinonia *Ethic*' *as the Context of Conscience*

The foregoing pages have attempted to show that when Christian thinking about ethics starts from and within the *koinonia* we begin to come in sight of an answer to the question 'What am I, as a believer in Jesus Christ and as a member of his church, to do?' In such a context, it makes sense to say that what I am to do is the will of God. For in this context the will of God is no general principle, no 'vague and enigmatic' rubric by which behavior may be guided. On the contrary, the will of God is the quite concrete and dynamic action of God in the world to make and to keep human life human. The will of God is expressed in the politics of God, and the clue to the understanding and interpretation of the politics of God is provided by a theology of messianism. A theology of messianism provides the conceptual apparatus whereby the political character of the divine activity may be shown to put the directional and the diverse aspects of concrete human behavior together—and this not for Christians only but for all men. For the politics of God sets up the conditions for human maturity and makes available to all men the power of human wholeness.

The full import of thinking about ethics in this way emerges from the engagement and disengagement of a *koinonia* ethic with and from moral philosophy, on the one hand, and moral theology, on the other. The methodological course which we have been following is the characteristic contribution of the Protestant Reformation to ethical theory. Indeed, it is because of this contribution that a Christian analysis of ethics requires methodological clarification and correction. Ethical thinking in the tradition of the Reformation has not yet fully and faithfully explored the insights into the bearing of Christian faith upon behavior by means of which the original Reformers, especially Luther and Calvin, broke fresh ethical ground. There have been lapses into alien methodologies, due in part to the fact that the course of history 'never does run smooth' but more to the failure to perceive the methodological revolution in ethical thinking effected by the Reformers' rediscovery of the Bible and their soteriological stress upon grace and faith alone. The *sola gratia: sola fide* ('by grace alone: by faith alone') meant for ethics an irreconcilable repudiation of the *agere sequitur esse* ('action follows being'), upon which both moral philosophy and moral theology are based. Thus what the Reformation meant for the methodology of ethical theory was liberation from the attempt to give shape to behavior in terms of *principial foundations* and *preceptual directives*. On these terms, as we have seen, neither the problem of ethical generalization nor the problem of conscience can be resolved, chiefly because there is no way of dealing constructively with the cleavage between the ethical claim and the ethical act. In the case of moral philosophy (Kant alone excepted) the cleavage is recognized but ignored; in the case of moral theology it is suppressed.

What is called for is an analysis of the environment of decision making in terms of which the shape of behavior can be concretely and conceptually described.[1] Such an environment is one in which the ethical predicament of man is overcome in the formation of conscience for obedience in freedom through the dynamics and patterns of man's involvement in God's activity. The analysis of such an environment, therefore, is one in which ethical generalization takes the form of indicative statements of the context, movement, and direction of behavior, and behavioral acts are exhibited as concretely indicative of the divine and human dimensions of maturity.

It is no accident that the authors of the first three Gospels take up this point when they report the perplexity of Jesus' disciples about the meaning of Jesus' teaching. They were evidently puzzled by the method as well as by the content of the teaching. Accustomed as they were to an ethical tradition which moved from precepts to action, from law to behavior, the disciples were thrown into confusion by Jesus' habit of juxtaposing God's action to the human situation. 'With what can we compare the kingdom of God, or what parable shall we use for it?'[2] he would say again and again. And his own reply was: 'the kingdom of heaven may be compared,' 'the kingdom of heaven is like . . . treasure hidden in a field, . . . like a net which was thrown into the sea, . . . like a grain of mustard seed . . . '.[3]

But how does one get from these similes to behavior? What have the 'grain of mustard seed' to do with telling the truth, the 'treasure hidden in a field' with supporting or condemning a steel strike, a 'net thrown into the sea' with feeding the hungry or starving the population of a town? Obviously the kind of ethical literalism which aims at a one-to-one correlation

---

[1] A contextual methodology provides this analysis and thus prepares the way for a substantive interpretation of Christian ethics (of the *content* of conscience). This volume has been chiefly concerned with a way of thinking about Christian ethics which transcends the impasse occasioned by ethical diversity between ethical irrelevance and ethical relativism. As indicated above (pp. 148, 223-24), a volume will follow in which the directional, motivational, and structural aspects of behavior will be explored.

[2] Mark 4.30.      [3] Matt. 13; Mark 4; Luke 13.

between a specific word of Jesus and a specific action misses the point of Jesus' teaching. Decision making as the Christian understands it goes on in quite another way. For the Christian, the *environment* of decision, not the *rules* of decision, gives to behavior its ethical significance. If, as we have been urging, God is at work in *this* world, doing what it takes to make and to keep human life human, no specific action can be said to express or to fulfill an ethical principle in a literal way. Telling the truth is, as already noted, not identical with optimum verbal veracity.[1] It is a matter of saying the 'right' word. The 'right' word, however, is a *sign* that human relations are going on in an environment of trust. The 'grain of mustard seed' is a *sign* that an environment of trust has been established and is being sustained by the activity of God. Thus the 'right' word is a *parable* of truth as the 'mustard seed' is a *parable* of the kingdom of heaven. In both instances, a human action has occurred which *indicates* or *points to* fundamental human relations which are both fundamental and human because of what God is doing in the world.

The genius of Reformation ethical thinking was that it discerned and made available again the New Testament understanding of decision making. Consequently, Christian ethics in the tradition of the Reformation seeks to provide an analysis of the environment of decision in which the principial foundations and preceptual directives of behavior are displaced by *contextual foundations* and *parabolic directives*. In a word, *the environment of decision is the context for the ethical reality of conscience*.

The present analysis of Christian ethics as *koinonia* ethics is an attempt to take with full seriousness the methodological revolution in ethical thinking inaugurated by the Reformation. Having noted the significance of a *koinonia* ethic for the transformation of the environment of decision into the context of conscience, we must still show how in the context of the *koinonia* the conscience can be said to acquire ethical meaning and power.

### 2  *Christian Contextualism and the Ethical Reality of Conscience*

The contextual character of Christian ethics opens up a fresh possibility for the ethical reality of conscience. It will be recalled

[1] See above, Chapter V.

that the ethical nature of conscience is already hinted at by its etymology. The word is a direct transliteration of the Latin *con-scientia*, the root of which is a *knowing*, and the prefix of which expresses a *relation* of some kind. Thus we have to do here with 'a knowing-in-relation', with a 'bond betwixt two'. But what kind of 'bond' and betwixt what 'two'; what is known in relation to what? This is the question with which Christian and philosophical moralists have wrestled painstakingly and variously, yet unsatisfactorily withal—unsatisfactorily chiefly owing to their inability to bring together the knowledge of good and evil and man's freedom to decide.

Man's freedom has been precariously caught in a squeeze between an *autonomy* which identified man's freedom to decide with the freedom of choice, and connected the knowledge of good and evil with the internally directed exercise of the will, and a *heteronomy* which identified the knowledge of good and evil with an imposed order of stability, and connected man's freedom to decide with assent and adherence to externally directed rules and regulations. Whether the order imposed itself as fate, or as providence, or as law, was ethically indifferent, since the important problem was that of the bond between moral knowledge and moral action and this bond was the crucial meaning and function of conscience. The dilemma between *autonomy* and *heteronomy* has all but rendered the conscience ethically expendable. But because the problem remains, the conscience continues to haunt the sensitivity of man with the possibility of a creative link between the knowledge of good and evil and the freedom of decision *in* that knowledge.

Could it be that there is a *theonomous* connection between the knowledge of good and evil and man's freedom? Such a possibility would mean that the knowledge of good and evil is neither the reward of a properly conducted search for the Good nor the result of a careful assessment of the powers of man. Such ways of thinking about ethics cannot give reality to man's freedom to decide for himself what is good and what is evil. Instead, the knowledge of good and evil is itself the very environment of man's humanity. In this environment, what it takes to make and to keep human life human is uninterruptedly going on and being consummated. In this environment, man's freedom of choice is not fundamentally a freedom to choose the good rather than the evil; it is fundamentally an obedient act of showing in concrete behavior where the line between God's humanizing activity and man's dehumanizing action is being drawn, and where the frontiers of human wholeness are being extended. 'It's terrible what mysteries there are!' says Mitya Karamazov. '. . . God and the devil are fighting there, and the battlefield is the heart of man.'[1] The ethical predicament of man, the cleavage between the ethical claim and the ethical act, the dilemma between ethical irrelevance and ethical relativism—all are interchangeable variants of the problem of freedom and obedience. The impasse in each instance is broken through on the boundary of man's humanity or inhumanity toward man. Here either God takes over or the devil. If man be made in the devil's image there is no egress from—in Milton's finely and precisely wrought account of Satan's plight—'the hateful siege of contraries, from deep to deeper plunged'.[2] But if God is doing in the world what in the *koinonia* he is known to be doing, then man is being hammered into humanity in the image of Christ and 'must hereafter with free heart decide for himself what is good and what is evil, having only [His] image before him as his guide'.

> History is a branding iron!
> Burn this day deeply into our memory!
> Teach us with your fire!
> Strike with your iron
> So that we may never forget!
> Brand us with the name Bataan
> and the Heroes there![3]

That was written in commemoration of an unforgettable agony of the Second World War, the battle of Bataan. But if we substitute for 'Bataan' 'Christ'; and understand 'day' to refer, not to the battle, but to the 'day of decision' and 'there' to refer, not to a place in the Philippines, but to 'the world', these lines may be appropriated as a forceful and accurate description of the conjunction of the human and the Christian experience of ethical reality.

[1] Fyodor Dostoevsky, *The Brothers Karamazov*, Universal Library edition, Grosset and Dunlap, Inc., New York, pp. 114-15.

[2] John Milton, *Paradise Lost*, IX, 122.

[3] Norman Rosten, *The Fourth Decade*, Farrar and Rinehart, New York, 1943, p. 3.

The conscience of man set, not at rest, but free is the conscience whose *theonomous* character defines what man 'knows-in-relation-to-what', what kind of bond man is involved in and 'betwixt what two'. *Conscience is the act—both of knowing and of doing—which expresses and exposes the connection between the knowledge of good and evil as the environment of humanization and the obedient response to this environment.* Thus it is the conscience which explains how and why man discerns in the knowledge of good and evil the conditions for and the behavior appropriate to what it takes to make and to keep human life human. It is the conscience—theonomously understood—which forges the link between what God is doing in the world and man's free obedience to that activity. Conscience is neither libertarian nor legalistic, neither antinomian nor nomian, but whole, i.e., unified and sensitized in the freedom wherewith Christ has set us free. In truth, Jesus Christ has laid the foundation either for the destruction of his kingdom or for its fulfillment. 'Man was created a rebel,' says the Cardinal to 'the Prisoner' at another moment in that nocturnal conversation, 'and how can rebels be happy?'[1] The answer is: in following Jesus Christ 'freely, enticed and taken captive by' him!

If some such reconstruction of the ethical nature of conscience be a possibility, the ethical significance of the reconstruction is very considerable. The question of conscience is the point of no return for the methodology of ethics. This is where our methodological analysis ends. *Fundamentally and ultimately, the validity of a Protestant as against a Roman Catholic account of ethics, and of Christian as against philosophical ethics, stands or falls upon the issue: Which account of conscience is correct?* That account of conscience is correct which sets the conscience in the kind of context in which the ethical reality of conscience is exhibited. It is incumbent upon ethics to offer a description of the nature and function of conscience in such a way as to explain the intrinsic conjunction in the ethical act, on the one hand of freedom and obedience, and on the other of free obedience with the knowledge of good and evil. If the conscience is bound to 'the rigid ancient law' in whatever form, then obedience has been sundered from 'freedom of choice in the knowledge of good and evil' and the ethical act has been surrendered to conditions alien to what it

[1] Dostoevsky, op. cit., p. 276.

takes to make and to keep human life human in the world. *Conscience has been abandoned to heteronomy.* If the conscience is viewed as a 'built-in' human device for spot-checking right from wrong, good from evil, then 'freedom of choice in the knowledge of good and evil' has been sundered from obedience and the ethical act has itself become the creator of the conditions for making and keeping human life human in the world. *Conscience has been violated by autonomy.* But if the conscience is the bond between what God is doing in the world to make and to keep human life human and man's behavior, then the ethical act is the concrete bearer of man's free obedience in the knowledge of good and evil. *Conscience is the focal instance of theonomous behavior.*

Thus the methodology of ethical analysis must pass the conscience test. By this test, the ethical inadequacy of moral theology is exposed by the fact that it delivers the conscience over to heteronomy. The ethical inadequacy of moral philosophy is exposed by the fact that the conscience is delivered over to an uneasy fluctuation between heteronomy and autonomy. And the ethical adequacy of a Protestant ethic is exposed by the fact that the *koinonia* character of such an ethic provides the context within which the conscience is theonomously free and thus acquires ethical meaning and power.

It is, however, not sufficient to rest the case for the methodology of a Protestant ethic upon a differentiation of the methodological options in accordance with the conscience test. We must try also to show how it comes about that a *koinonia* ethic provides the conscience with its proper ethical function and significance. There is a certain tautological threat to the argument we have endeavored to pursue which appears to undo what we have been trying to do by taking over at the close. Have we really only been saying that a *koinonia* ethic provides and confirms whatever ethical substance and significance the conscience has, and the conscience provides and confirms whatever ethical substance and significance a *koinonia* ethic has? A context for conscience concludes with a conscience for that context. Has the mountain merely labored to bring forth a mouse? Or is this the mouse which gnaws the lion free?[1]

The risk of tautological reasoning is a risk that every theo-

[1] See above, Chapter XI, p. 284, note 1.

logical analysis must run. If God is a major premise on the way to coherent syllogistic consequences, circularity menaces argumentation and must be disallowed. But if God is the Creator, Redeemer, and Lord of life, then circularity authenticates the exposition and cannot be avoided.

### 3  *The Roots of a Fresh Possibility*

The roots of a fresh possibility lie in the biblical way of looking at human responsibility in a world being governed and guided by the politics of God. The semantic silence of the Bible with respect to conscience is conspicuous. It would be too much to say that the word 'conscience' never occurs; but the infrequency of its use is more than coincidental. Indeed, the precise Greek construction from which the ethical meaning of conscience is derived occurs strictly but once in the Old Testament and once in the New Testament.[1] Job, steadfastly defending his righteousness before God, declares, 'My heart does not reproach me for any of my days.'[2] Paul in writing to the Corinthians declares with polemical bitterness: 'I am not aware of any thing against myself, but I am not thereby acquitted. It is the Lord who judges me.' And here we are on the edge of a Hebrew transformation of the Greek sense of conscience rather than of another distortion of the Hebrew by the Greek.

We have referred to Job's declaration not only because of the mistranslation which has befallen it but because when the Hebrew original is correctly expressed, the characteristic Old Testament alternative for conscience appears. Here, as widely throughout the Old Testament, it is not the *conscience* which connotes the fundamental 'bond betwixt two' by means of

---

[1] I.e., σύνοιδα with the dative of the reflexive pronoun, meaning a *knowing together with myself*. Following Pierce, I am accepting the equivalence of the verbal construction σύνοιδα ἐμαυτῷ with the substantival τὸ αὐτῷ συνειδέναι and ἡ συνείδησις. Even the variants, although more frequent, are not profusely evident. See C. A. Pierce, *Conscience in the New Testament*, Alec R. Allenson, Inc., Naperville, 1955 (SCM Press, London, 1955), especially pp. 29-30, 55. The passages are Job 27.6, and I Cor. 4.4, and in both the phrase σύνοιδα ἐμαυτῷ occurs.

[2] So the RSV. The LXX renders the original Hebrew as 'I do not know with myself that I have done anything amiss'. But this is characteristically so loose a rendering as to distort all but completely the Hebrew understanding of the nexus of human responsibility.

which the 'knowledge of good and evil' shapes behavior. The
Old Testament insists that it is the *heart*, not the *conscience*, which
is the nexus of human responsibility.[1] What a man knows *by
heart* is no less direct, intimate, and personal than what he knows
*in conscience*. But there is a world of difference in how a man
comes by what he knows and in the effects of such an experience
upon his humanity. The *conscience* knows by a kind of internal
sight, a cognitive seeing which condemns the knower out of the
inexorable disparity between his own nature and the order
against which he has offended. The *heart* knows by a kind of
sensitivity at once central and total which marks the person as
a whole; this relational knowledge involves man as a doer in a
behavioral response to a God whose claim upon him is the
foundation of his humanity.[2] 'As a man thinketh in his heart
so is he.'[3] 'But the word is very near to you: it is in your mouth
and in your heart, so that you can do it.'[4] Israel is bidden to
love the Lord her God with all her heart.[5] 'The fool hath said
in his heart, there is no God.'[6] And on the other hand, 'Blessed
are the pure in heart, for they shall see God.'[7] Furthermore, the
heart is good as well as evil; circumcized as well as uncircum-
cized, a heart of flesh as well as a heart of stone.[8] And whether
it is the one or the other, in no case has an internal self-judgment
occurred, still less a judgment which is uniformly negative. The
estimation of the heart is an external judgment which is possible
and which happens because man is related to God, who by his
word, or by his prophet, or by some great deed done by him
judges, and/or sustains, and/or renews the heart. Thus the heart
is the pivotal personal center of man's total response to the

---

[1] I.e., הַלֵּב, not ἡ συνείδησις.

[2] The heart is the organ of thinking and knowing in the cognitive sense
of 'mind' or 'intelligence' and also in the reflexive or intensive sense of the
involvement of the self in the act of thinking and knowing. Cognition and
the response of the self are thus conjoined in the act of knowing. Although
the Hebrew word לֵב is used primarily in the cognitive sense, it can be
and often is used in the reflexive sense. The point under discussion here,
therefore, does not rest upon an argument from language but rather upon
the semantic context conveyed by the biblical use of the word 'heart'. It is
this context rather than precise verbal evidence which supports the interpretation of what Jesus meant by 'heart'.

[3] Prov. 23.7.　　[4] Deut. 30.14.　　[5] Ibid., 6.8.　　[6] Ps. 14.1.
[7] Matt. 5.8.　　[8] Gen. 6.5; Lev. 26.41; Deut. 30.6; Ezek. 11.19.

12

dynamics, direction, and personal thrust of the divine claim upon him. In short, according to the Old Testament, the heart—not the conscience—is the focus of responsible behavior and the fulcrum of man's humanity.

Jesus follows the Old Testament both in its silence concerning conscience and in its stress upon the heart. 'Do you not see,' he asked his disciples on one occasion, 'that whatever goes into a man from outside cannot defile him, since it enters not his heart but his stomach, and so passes on? . . . What comes out of a man is what defiles a man. For from within, out of the heart of man come evil thoughts, fornication, theft, murder, adultery . . . pride, foolishness. All these evil things come from within, and they defile a man.'[1] Or again, he declares, 'The good man out of the good treasure of his heart produces good, and the evil man out of his evil treasure produces evil; for out of the abundance of his heart, his mouth speaks.'[2] We have already noted the saying concerning the pure in heart. And perhaps most significant is the formulation of the love commandment in words borrowed from Deuteronomy and Leviticus.[3]

We come then to the spirited Pauline use of 'conscience' in its familiar Greek sense.[4] '*Conscience*', it has been said, 'was introduced into Christianity under pressure from Corinth, as bound up with a controversial issue.'[5] It has usually been assumed that the Stoics provided this 'catchword of Corinth'.[6] But, as we have already seen, the word was current in the semantic environment of Hellenism so that the Stoics, far from inventing it, actually found it at hand.[7] In Corinth, the authority and integrity of Paul's apostleship were under dispute, and his critics had chosen to make their challenge a matter of conscience. In the course of Paul's defense of his apostleship, he addressed himself to a variety of problems of conduct about which his critics were saying in effect that their consciences were clear. To this the sharp rejoinder came: 'I am not aware of anything against myself, but I am not thereby acquitted' (or more freely,

---

[1] Mark 7.18-23.　　　　　　　　　[2] Luke 6.45.

[3] Mark 12.29-30; Matt. 22.37-40; Luke 10.27. See also Deut. 6.8; Lev. 19.18.

[4] See above, p. 352, note 1.　　　[5] Pierce, op. cit., p. 66.

[6] Ibid., chap. VI.

[7] This point has been cogently argued by Pierce, ibid., chap. I.

'my conscience is clear too but that does not put me in the clear'). 'This', it has been remarked, 'is the first recorded occasion in Christian history—but very far from the last—when disruptive tendencies within the Church have made a battle-cry of conscience.'[1] Since Paul not only was the first among the New Testament writers to use the term but also uses it more frequently than do other New Testament writers, his conception of conscience may be regarded as normative for New Testament thought.[2]

Already with his initial use of the characteristic Greek construction expressive of man's 'knowledge together with himself that he has done evil things', Paul hints at an eventual transformation of the ethical sense and significance of conscience. The hint is that conscience cannot be understood as an internal human faculty of judgment which functions to condemn. It is not conscience but the Lord who judges. This hint is explicated further in the Letter to the Romans as Paul's maturest view. The famous chapter on 'the powers that be' enjoins subjection to them 'not only to avoid God's wrath but also for the sake of conscience'.[3] The conspicuous parallelism between 'conscience' and the 'wrath of God' exposes the importance of a contextual ethic for the proper understanding of the true nature and function of the conscience. Superficially, Paul seems to be saying little more than the Stoics or the Greek tragedians had been saying: Man lives his life in an order of law, whether in nature or in society, and under the stern tutelage of an interior faculty of judgment, i.e., the conscience. But beneath the surface of this scheme of claim and response an explosive ingredient lurks. Paul had absorbed Hebrew as well as Greek ways of thinking about human responsibility in an ordered universe. Indeed, as one, by his own admission, 'advanced in Judaism

---

[1] Pierce, ibid., p. 65. The passage referred to is the one just quoted from I Cor. 4.4.

[2] At best, the usage is limited. Compare II Cor. 4.2; 5.11, which cannot strictly be translated by 'conscience': II Cor. 1.12 is the one clear case of a 'good conscience'; I Cor. 4.4 is the one clear case of conscience used expressly in the Hellenistic sense of 'bad conscience'; I Cor. 8.7, 10, 12; 10.25, 27, 28, 29; Rom. 2.15; 9.1; 13.5 are instances of an ironic use of 'conscience' as though it might be good but is really understood as bad. See Pierce, op. cit., p. 62.

[3] Rom. 13.5: ἀλλὰ καὶ τὴν συνείδησιν.

beyond many of [his] own age among [his] people,... extremely zealous for the traditions of [his]fathers',[1] it is not strange that he should have drawn upon the Old Testament as a resource of creativity especially when under attack, or when dealing with a difficult problem affecting the thinking and behavior of Christians. So here, in juxtaposing 'wrath' and 'conscience', the sensitivity of the Hebrew response 'from the heart' to the dynamics and purposefulness of the divine order and governance of the world transforms the context of conscience and thus also the meaning of 'conscience' itself. The relentless fate in the midst of which the humanization of man is measured by the pain of conscience is set aside. In its place, an order is acknowledged, each element of which has its instrumental function and significance within limits which concretely define the redemptive obedience of the creature to God the Creator and Redeemer. Within these limits, the integrity of the creature is secure. The violation of these limits involves the creature in the wrath of God, the divine ὀργή. The wrath of God is the disintegration of creaturehood, not as an impenetrable fate, but as an intrinsic consequence of the disregard by the creature of boundaries divinely arranged for his good out of the abundant goodness of the Creator. For man, the primary creature, such an order is an order of humanization, since the integrity of his creaturehood is the being in fact and in fulfillment what he has been created to be. Rebellion against these limits involves man both in the external and in the internal disintegration of his creaturehood. He suffers both under the wrath of God and for the sake of conscience. But—and this is the decisive point— neither the wrath of God nor the pain of conscience is a condition of humanization. Each is frankly—and contrary to the Greek context—the condition of dehumanization. Humanization, on the other hand, is a matter of obedient freedom, of free choice in the knowledge of good and evil.

The extent to which this free choice is a live and decisive option in relation to Jesus Christ is confirmed by two further uses of the word 'conscience'. Both in Rom. 9.1 and in the more influential passage concerning the conscience of the Gentiles in 2.15, the witnessing function of conscience is expressed. In the first instance, the altered context and resultant

[1] Gal. 1.14.

transformation of conscience is plain from the explicit connection of conscience with Christ and the Holy Spirit. This connection also underlies the interchangeability of 'conscience' with 'heart'. 'I am speaking the truth in Christ, I am not lying,' Paul wrote; 'my conscience (τῆς συνειδήσεώς μου) bears me witness in the Holy Spirit, that I have great sorrow and unceasing anguish in my heart.' In the second instance, 'conscience' is referred to, not in apposition to 'wrath' but rather as subordinate to it (along with the law written in the heart and conflicting thoughts). Its ethical usefulness is recognized not as intrinsic to itself but as intrinsic to the exposure by Jesus Christ of the secrets of men. 'When the Gentiles who have not the law do by nature what the law requires . . . they show that what the law requires is written on their heart, while their conscience (τῆς συνειδήσεώς) also bears witness and their conflicting thoughts accuse or perhaps excuse them on that day when, according to my gospel, God judges the secrets of men by Christ Jesus.' We need not enter here upon the question whether or not Paul was advocating a doctrine of natural revelation and natural law. What he was doing, however, was appropriating a commonly understood meaning of conscience for Christian purposes. The result was a notable shift of semantic perspective which not only drew the conscience into the orbit of the Old Testament understanding of *heart* but made the conscience instrumental to the dynamics and direction of God's humanizing activity in the world in Jesus Christ.

The behavioral consequences of this transformation of the context of conscience are tantamount to a revolution in the ethical role and significance of conscience. The most concrete and explosive case in point takes us again to Corinth and to the controversy that had arisen in the *koinonia* there over food. The question at issue was whether Christians could eat meat which had been prepared for sacrificial use in temples dedicated to idols and which could be bought at the market. In this connection, Paul makes a proposal for the ethical reality of conscience without parallel in ethical literature and containing the distinctive reconstruction of conscience effected by Christianity. There is a straight line between the God and Father of our Lord Jesus Christ, 'for whom and through whom we exist',[1] and the

---

[1] I Cor. 8.6.

liberation of conscience, for the doing 'on earth as it is in heaven'[1] of the will of God. But this contextualization of conscience, far from inaugurating ethical anarchy and irresponsibility, actually proves to be the decisive breakthrough to the ethical integrity of behavior. Obviously this is an ethical possibility for Christians only. But not so obviously—and this is what the 'moral fuss' was, at bottom, really about—'Christians only' are those who have discerned what life in the *koinonia* truly involves and who, in the vanguard of what God is doing in the world to make and to keep human life human, are open to 'the right hand of fellowship' wherever and whenever behavior in its ethical integrity is manifest.

> However, not all possess this knowledge [Paul had noted]. But some, though being hitherto accustomed to idols, eat food as really offered to an idol; and their conscience (ἡ συνείδησις αὐτῶν) being weak is defiled. Food will not commend us to God. We are no worse off if we do not eat, and no better off if we do. Only take care lest this liberty of yours somehow becomes a stumbling-block to the weak. For if anyone sees you, a man of knowledge [i.e., a Christian], at table in an idol's temple, might he not be encouraged, if his conscience is weak, to eat food offered to idols? And so by your knowledge this weak man is destroyed, the brother for whom Christ died. Thus, sinning against your brethren and wounding their conscience when it is weak, you sin against Christ. Therefore, if food is a cause of my brother's falling, I will never eat meat, lest I cause my brother to fall.[2]

Here is a repudiation of ethical legalism of every kind. But it is no less a repudiation of ethical anarchy. Indeed, the common ground between ethical scrupulousness and ethical libertarianism is the subjugation of the conscience to prescriptive regulation. In the one case, conscience is surrendered to conformity, in the other to nonconformity; in the first instance to heteronomy, in the second to autonomy. But in either case, the conscience is severed from its authenticating context and becomes the instrument of ethical irresponsibility. As far as Paul is concerned, *conscience* is not indispensable to a Christian ethic. But if it is to be appropriated for purposes of ethical analysis, it must be theonomously understood. The *theonomous* conscience is the conscience immediately sensitive to the freedom of God to do in the always changing human situation what his humanizing aims and purposes require. The *theonomous* conscience is

---

[1] Matt. 6.10.                    [2] I Cor. 8.7-13.

governed and directed by the freedom of God alone. Ultimately, it is in this freedom that the decisions of men are set, and from this freedom come the power and the transforming possibilities which give ethical shape to behavior.

The concrete instance of the theonomous conscience is the pre-eminent claim of my neighbor's conscience upon and over my own. As if to make his meaning unmistakable, Paul takes up the 'conscience-food dispute' a second time. The result is the classic and memorable statement of obedient freedom as the sum and substance of the ethical role and meaning of conscience.

> 'All things are lawful' [he declares, quoting the misguided Christian antinomians against themselves], but not all things are helpful. 'All things are lawful,' but not all things build up. Let no one seek his own, but the good of his neighbor. Eat whatever is sold in the meat market without raising any question on the ground of conscience. For 'the earth is the Lord's and everything in it.' If one of the unbelievers invites you to dinner and you are disposed to go, eat whatever is set before you without raising any question on the ground of conscience. (But if someone says to you, 'This has been offered in sacrifice' then out of consideration for the man who informed you, and for conscience' sake—*I mean his conscience, not yours*—do not eat it.) For why should my liberty be determined by another man's scruples? If I partake with thankfulness, why am I denounced because of that for which I give thanks?[1]

Why indeed? For no reason except the failure to understand that it is the *context*, not the *rule*, of conscience which provides the guidance of the conscience in the exercise of its freedom of choice in the knowledge of good and evil. Such guidance becomes available when conscience, as the internal arbiter of human action, is transposed from the self to the neighbor.[2] The neighbor's conscience can never function as a standard of conduct which applies to all people in all situations in the same way. The neighbor's conscience serves only and always as a

---

[1] I Cor., 10.23-30. Paul quotes Ps. 24.1; 50.12. Italics mine.

[2] Unless, of course, one follows those commentators who hold that Paul's use of 'conscience' in I Cor. 4.4 and Rom. 2.14-15 and 13.5 is to be understood strictly as a Greek construction without significant Hebraic alteration. In that case, it is hard to see how one can really interpret I Cor. 8.7ff.; 10.23ff., other than as a conspicuous and unresolved ambiguity in Paul's thought. We venture to assume a certain consistency in Paul's use of 'conscience' not for the sake of consistency but because such an interpretation seems to be in accord with both the texts on and the context of conscience as Paul discusses the problem.

standard of conduct which applies to different people in different situations in different ways. Not that the neighbor's conscience is itself the criterion of a good or an evil action. If such were the case, the conscience would imprison ethics within a circle as vicious as that imposed by one's own conscience. The shift from one's own conscience to the conscience of the neighbor is not a shift from a defective to a correct *criterion* of action. It is a shift from an ethically sterile subordination of conscience under law to an ethically promising perspective and relationship within which conscience can bring behavior under that criterion by which alone action may be judged as right. The neighbor's conscience is the concrete bearer of whatever ethical significance and function may be claimed for conscience. This does not mean that ethical behavior has been carried beyond the boundaries of condemnation and justification, remorse and commendation, guilt and righteousness. It means that the conscience has been deprived of its intrinsic power to accuse or to excuse—whether the conscience of my neighbor or my own. The ethical significance and function of my neighbor's conscience are concretely exhibited in the *conscience-relation* between my neighbor and myself. This *conscience-relation* is a relation of human claim and human response through which no human action is ethical in itself but all human action is instrumental to what God in Christ is doing in the world to make and to keep human life human. 'So, whether you eat or drink, or whatever you do, do all to the glory of God.'[1]

### 4 *The Nexus of Obedient Freedom*

The Pauline revolution in the understanding of the ethical role and significance of conscience has never really come into its own. It may well be that this proves nothing so much as that the revolution was misguided. It involved too sharp a break with long-standing human traditions—cultural, social, moral, and religious. In the long run, how could the Pauline view of conscience provide the conceptual, motivational, and structural clarity and power required for the shaping of behavior? The difficulties must not be underestimated. Yet for two important reasons the bond forged by the Pauline revolution between the

[1] I Cor. 10.31.

conscience and the context which gives it ethical reality cannot be ignored. The first reason is that the Pauline breakthrough on the frontier of conscience is rooted in and similar to the cultural penetration, relevance, and transformation of the Christian *koinonia*. We are dealing here with the dynamics and stuff of behavior which are more like 'leaven in the lump' than a holy crusade. Indeed, if 'conscience' is a word not wholly expendable in Christian ethics, its Pauline sense and significance must be understood and its indigenous relation to the Christian *koinonia* clearly discerned.

The second reason for taking seriously the Pauline achievement in the understanding of conscience is the story of the decline and fall of conscience in the Western ethical tradition. On this count, the issue is sharply and unmistakably focused upon the role of conscience in the humanization or dehumanization of man. To paraphrase the Freudian epigram at the conclusion of that story, *if 'conscience is the price to be paid for the progress of civilization', the* koinonia *is 'the price to be paid for the progress of conscience'*.

The contemporary mind is as little disposed to linger over the grim inevitability of conscience, which Freud could not elude, as it is to look in the direction of the *koinonia* for a context within which the conscience could acquire again the ethical stature and formative power it once held. It seems easier and more attractive to abandon the conscience altogether and to rest the case for ethical responsibility upon a humanistic faith. If the *koinonia* is the price to be paid for the progress of conscience, conscience is not worth the price.

Ultimately, this is the decisive ethical option of our time. It is unlikely, as we have tried to suggest, that a humanistic faith can nourish the ethical sensitivity necessary to a responsible life both in private and in public. It is also unlikely that the Christian *koinonia* will commend itself as an indispensable ingredient of the secular hopes and fears which increasingly inform the hearts and minds and institutions of men and nations. Such an option neither confirms nor invalidates a Christian analysis of ethics. It does expose the intrinsic significance of a Christian ethic. A day may come when the price of conscience will be unavoidable again, as the price not of frustration but of freedom. For such a day, a Christian analysis of ethics can only try to clarify its method and its content as a sign of faithfulness to its foundation and its task. At stake is the freedom of man to be human, the humanity of man in freedom.

Between Paul and the Reformation, just as between the Reformation and ourselves, the glimpses of this issue and of the price involved have been few and far between. The Reformation as shaped by the minds of Luther and Calvin may supply the complexities and ambiguities of the contemporary phase of the story of humanization and dehumanization with creative and constructive insights. But as yet these insights are little more than hints of the ethical reality of conscience and of its formative power.

Luther and Calvin were too preoccupied with the pretensions and anarchies of human sinfulness and too at home in the humanistic tradition to perceive the full revolutionary impact of the Pauline revolution upon the subjugation of the conscience in these traditions to the tight alliance between divine wrath and human guilt. Yet each in his own way had perceived something of the ferment astir in the ethical predicament of man by reason of the bond between *conscience* and *koinonia*.[1] If Luther was drawn more intently toward the motivational transformation effected by such a bond, Calvin was drawn more intently toward the structural transformation effected by a *theonomous* conscience. These differences of accent cannot be understood without taking due account of temperamental differences. 'Luther', it has been astutely remarked, 'accepted for his life work the unconquered frontier of the tragic conscience, defined as it was by his personal needs and his superlative gifts. . . .'[2] Of Calvin, it has been observed that his 'was not a deductive mind. He has passages of keen reasoning, but he often addresses himself much less to our rational judgment than to our emotion, conscience, and will. . . . He is deeply convinced and will not have us forget that every man has to do with God all his days.

[1] See Chapter II above for their insight into the *koinonia*.
[2] Erik H. Erikson, *Young Man Luther*, W. W. Norton and Company, New York, 1958 (Faber & Faber, London, 1959), p. 195. And in the area of filial relations at least, Erikson notes that 'Erasmus, Luther's cosmopolitan counterplayer, defied his father. And Calvin (in some ways Luther's Paul) reports his struggle thus. . . .' *Ibid.*, p. 97. The report concerns an influence of Calvin's father upon him analogous to that of the elder Luther upon the son.

For him this is our chief concern in all life's events and decisions. In his writings we are not in an atmosphere of fate, but in the company of the living God. . . . The life of faith is not a resigned quiescence, but is distinguished by an energizing gratitude that bears fruit in vigorous action.'[1] But these differences only reinforce the insight common to Luther and to Calvin into the formative power of conscience in the living of the Christian life.[2]

Luther began his theological career at Wittenberg with a course of lectures on the Psalms. There—in that inexhaustible treasury of Old Testament piety—he came upon the interchangeability of conscience and heart. And like Paul before him, he broke across the frontier of the tragic conscience into a fresh sensitivity to the nexus of human responsibility in the intimate confrontation between God and man. '*Locus noster,*' he said, '*in quo nos cum Deo, sponsas cum sponsa, habitare debet . . . est conscientia.*'[3] ('Conscience is our place, the place within where we must live with God as man and wife.') In another connection he could describe the conscience in words that vividly echo the melancholy of Euripides and anticipate the grim discoveries of Freud: 'Conscience is an evil beast and a wicked devil; for all authors, sacred as well as profane, have pictured this monster in horrible colors, as appears in the story of Orestes and other shameful persons. . . . Nothing is more restless and unquiet than a fearful heart, which turns pale before chance lightning, aye, even before a stirring leaf.'[4] But with like vividness he could set forth the only terms on which the conscience could make sense:

A Christian is a strange bird. Few there are who know what real christian freedom is. Most people think that freedom has to do with the body and do not know that there is a freedom of conscience and soul. This is the

---

[1] John T. McNeill, *John Calvin on the Christian Faith*, The Liberal Arts Press, New York, 1957, pp. xi, xxviii.

[2] An appropriate account of what Luther and Calvin thought about the ethical nature and function of conscience really requires a separate treatment altogether. The implications for the content of Christian ethics of the present re-examination of conscience in the light of the Pauline revolution belong to a subsequent discussion. (See above, p. 346, note 1.) Meanwhile, a brief indication of the Reformers' adoption of the Pauline transformation of conscience will suffice.

[3] Martin Luther, *Lectures on the Psalms*, WA, 3, 593, 28-29.

[4] Martin Luther, *Lectures on Genesis*, 1535-45, WA, 44, 500, 29ff.

freedom which takes it for granted that the heart and the conscience are neither pure nor righteous. If you wish to be pure and righteous, however, you must acknowledge that you become pure, righteous and happy through this king, Christ Jesus alone. . . . Christian or evangelical freedom is the freedom of conscience, through which the conscience is set free from works—not so that no works are done, but so as not to rely upon them. For conscience is not a power that shapes behavior but a power that judges behavior.[1]

As Luther saw it, however, when the conscience is set free to judge behavior, behavior acquires a nexus of obedience which displaces the concern of the individual about his ethical achievements by the claims of the neighbor upon his ethical concern. In the celebrated treatise on *Christian Liberty*, after discoursing upon the vitality of faith working through love, he takes up the claims of the neighbor upon the individual believer and strikingly inverts the Pauline statement of the neighbor's claims. The neighbor's conscience, which for Paul provided the concrete focus of free obedience, becomes, in Luther's description of the Christian's responsibility, an obligation upon the individual Christian to be a Christ to his neighbor in quite concrete ways.

Therefore, if we recognize the great and precious things which are given us, as Paul says, there will be shed abroad in our hearts by the Holy Ghost the love which makes us free, joyful, almighty workers and conquerors over all tribulations, servants of our neighbors and yet lords of all. . . . Just as our neighbor is in need and lacks that in which we abound, so we also have been in need before God and have lacked His mercy. Hence, as our heavenly Father has in Christ freely come to our help, we also ought freely to help our neighbor through our body and its works, and each should become as it were a Christ to the other, that we may be Christs to one another and Christ may be the same in all; that is, that we may be truly Christians. . . .

We conclude, therefore, that a Christian man lives not in himself, but in Christ and in his neighbor. Otherwise he is not a Christian. He lives in Christ through faith, in his neighbor through love; by faith he is caught up beyond himself into God, by love he sinks down beneath himself into his neighbor. . . .[2]

---

[1] Martin Luther, *Zweite Predigt über die Epistel Jeremia*, 23.5-8, delivered on the 26th Sunday after Trinity, 25 November 1526, WA, 20, 579, 20-26; and *De votis monasticis Martini Lutheri iudicium*, 1521, WA, 8, 606, 30-34.

[2] Martin Luther, *De Libertate Christiana*, WA, 7, English translation by W. A. Lambert, *Works of Martin Luther*, Muhlenberg Press, Philadelphia, 1943, Vol. II, pp. 338, 342.

Ethically speaking, the *neighbor-believer-conscience* relation and the *Christ-neighbor-faith-in-action* relation are identical. Luther's task, as Erikson has strikingly said, 'originated in the hypertrophy of the negative conscience inherent in our whole Judeo-Christian heritage in which, as Luther put it: "Christ becomes more formidable a tyrant and a judge than was Moses".'[1] The one conspicuous exception is, as we have seen, the Pauline revolution. And Luther, exactly as Paul had done before him, perceived the validating context of conscience and to this extent set the conscience free for its obedient ministry of humanization.

The most succinct and incisive summation of what the Pauline transformation of the conscience comes to has been provided, however, by Calvin. In the third book of the *Institutes*, Calvin takes up the behavioral question. He seeks to analyze the *means of perceiving the grace of Christ*[2]—in short, the operational consequences of the knowledge of God which had been under discussion in the first two books. Among these operational consequences, Calvin includes Christian freedom. The correct understanding of the liberty of the Christian turns upon the correct understanding of the conscience. According to Calvin, Christian liberty consists of three parts, each one a matter of conscience. The first part is that 'the consciences of believers, when seeking an assurance of their justification before God, should rise above the law, and forget all the righteousness of the law'. The second part of Christian liberty is that the consciences of believers 'do not observe the law, as being under any legal obligations but that, being liberated from the yoke of the law, they yield a voluntary obedience to the will of God'. And the third part of Christian liberty 'teaches us that we are bound by no obligation before God respecting external things, which in themselves are indifferent; but that we may indifferently some-

---

[1] Erikson, op. cit., p. 195. Dr Erikson quotes WA, 40, 562. And while he rightly regards the 'frontier of the negative conscience as the circumscribed *locus* of Luther's work', he does not, I think, allow sufficiently for the extent and the significance of Luther's crossing of the frontier: compare the stress upon a wholly new conception of *person* and *society* provided by Luther in Karl Holl, *Gesammelte Aufsaetze zur Kirchengeschichte*, Band I, *Luther*, J. C. B. Mohr, Tuebingen, J. C. B. Mohr, 1948, pp. 473-79.

[2] John Calvin, *Institutes of the Christian Religion*, Allen translation, The Westminster Press, Philadelphia, 1936, Bk. III, Title.

times use, and at other times omit them'.[1] The conclusion of the matter brings the epigrammatic formulation: 'Therefore, just as works express respect for men, so conscience is referred to God; *thus a good conscience is nothing other than inward integrity of heart.*'[2]

'All things are lawful!' We seem to hear again the Corinthian formulation unaltered except for the words 'nothing is good or bad in itself'! All things are instrumental to the doing of the will of God as God himself guides and shapes the conscience through the dynamics and the direction of what he himself is doing in the world to make human life human. In marked contrast to behavior done out of respect for men, conscience is referred to God. Loosed from its dehumanizing context, the conscience is joined instead to the knowledge of good and evil as the environment of humanization. In this context, conscience is nothing other than a good conscience, and a good conscience is nothing other than inward integrity of heart. When the stuff of human behavior is instrumental to such a context of responsibility, the motivational and the structural patterns of humanization may be regarded as taking shape under the fulfilling transformation effected by the politics of God. Bereft of every prescriptive occasion and endowed with the imaginative sensitivity of a good conscience, men may behave toward one another on the other side of the ethical predicament, in the confidence that the cleavage between the ethical claim and the ethical act has been overcome by him 'from whom and through whom are all things' and 'for whom and through whom' they exist. It is from and within the Christian *koinonia* that conscience acquires ethical reality and the power to shape behavior through obedient freedom.

See, I have set before you this day life and good, death and evil. If you obey the commandments of the Lord your God which I command you this day, by loving the Lord your God, by walking in his ways, and by keeping his commandments and his statutes and his ordinances, then you shall live and multiply, and the Lord your God will bless you in the land which you are entering to take possession of it. But if your heart turns away, and you will not hear, but are drawn away to worship other gods

---

[1] Calvin, ibid., chap. 19.2, 4, 6.

[2] '*Itaque sicut opera respectum ad homines habent, ita conscientia ad Deum refertur; ut conscientia bona nihil aliud sit, quam interior cordis integritas.*' Ibid., chap. 19.16. Translation and italics above are mine.

and serve them, I declare to you this day, that you shall perish; you shall not live long in the land which you are going over the Jordan to enter and possess.[1]

For freedom Christ has set us free; stand fast therefore, and do not submit again to a yoke of slavery. . . . For you were called to freedom, brethren; only do not use your freedom as an opportunity to the flesh, but through love be servants of one another.[2]

[1] Deut. 30.15-18.           [2] Gal. 5.1, 13.

# SELECTED BIBLIOGRAPHY

The principal sources upon which the foregoing discussion has relied have been duly annotated in the footnotes. It may be useful, however, especially to a reader concerned to know how to begin upon a study of Christian ethics, to have some indication of literature particularly suited to such a purpose. The following titles are suggested with this purpose in view and have accordingly been limited to those available either in English originally or in translation. The order is to be regarded merely as a kind of *working* classification.

A distinction has been made between basic sources, primary sources, and sources exhibiting some important encounters (whether as constructive influences or as critical alternatives) between philosophical and Christian thinking about ethics. The differentiation between *basic* and *primary* sources is admittedly a loose one. What is chiefly intended is the difference between particularly instructive and systematic contemporary discussions of Christian ethics and those treatises which have largely shaped the tradition of Christian thinking about ethics since New Testament times.

I. *Basic Sources*

Barth, Karl. *Church Dogmatics.* Volume II/2. Edited by G. W. Bromiley and T. F. Torrance. T. & T. Clark, Edinburgh, 1957.

———. *The Epistle to the Romans.* Chapters 12-15. Translated from the sixth edition by Edwyn C. Hoskyns. Oxford University Press, London, 1933.

———. *The Knowledge of God and the Service of God.* Charles Scribner's Sons, New York, 1939 (Hodder and Stoughton, London, 1928).

———. *The Word of God and the Word of Man.* Translated by Douglas Horton. Harper & Row, New York, 1957 (Hamish Hamilton, London, 1957).

Bonhoeffer, Dietrich. *The Cost of Discipleship*. Translated by R. H. Fuller. Revised edition, The Macmillan Company, New York, 1959 (SCM Press, London, 1959).

———. *Ethics*. Edited by Eberhard Bethge. The Macmillan Company, New York, 1955 (SCM Press, London, 1955).

———. *Letters and Papers from Prison*. Edited by Eberhard Bethge. Translated by R. H. Fuller. SCM Press, London, 1954 (*Prisoner for God*, Macmillan, New York, 1954).

Brunner, Emil. *The Divine Imperative*. Translated by Olive Wyon. The Westminster Press, Philadelphia, 1947 (Lutterworth Press, London, 1947).

———. *Man in Revolt*. Translated by Olive Wyon. The Westminster Press, Philadelphia, 1947 (Lutterworth Press, London, 1939).

———. *The Theology of Crisis*. Charles Scribner's Sons, New York, 1929.

Cochrane, Charles N. *Christianity and Classical Culture*. Oxford University Press, New York, 1944.

D'Arcy, M. C. *The Mind and the Heart of Love*. Henry Holt and Company, New York, 1947 (Faber & Faber, London, 1954).

Dillistone, Frederick W. *The Structure of the Divine Society*. The Westminster Press, Philadelphia, 1951 (Lutterworth Press, London, 1951).

Miller, Alexander. *The Renewal of Man*. Doubleday and Company, Garden City, N.Y., 1955 (Gollancz, London, 1956).

Niebuhr, H. Richard. *Christ and Culture*. Harper & Row, New York, 1956 (Faber & Faber, London, 1952).

———. *The Meaning of Revelation*. The Macmillan Company, New York, 1946.

Niebuhr, Reinhold. *An Interpretation of Christian Ethics*. Harper & Row, New York, 1935 (SCM Press, London, 1936).

———. *The Nature and Destiny of Man*. Charles Scribner's Sons, New York, 1955 (Nisbet, London, 1941, 1943).

Nygren, Anders. *Agape and Eros*. Translated by Philip S. Watson. SPCK, London, 1953.

Ramsey, Paul. *Basic Christian Ethics*. Charles Scribner's Sons, New York, 1950 (SCM Press, London).

———, ed. *Faith and Ethics: The Theology of H. Richard Niebuhr*. Harper & Row, New York, 1957.

Thomas, George. *Christian Ethics and Moral Philosophy*. Charles Scribner's Sons, New York, 1955.

Wright, George Ernest. *God Who Acts*. Alec R. Allenson, Inc., Naperville, Ill., 1952 (SCM Press, London, 1952).

## II. *Primary Sources*

Ambrose. *On the Duties of the Clergy*. The Nicene and Post-Nicene Fathers. Second Series. Vol. X. The Christian Literature Company, New York, 1896.

Aquinas, Thomas. *Summa Theologica: Secunda Secundae*. QQ. 1-189. American edition. Benziger Brothers, New York, 1947———.

Augustine.  *The Antimanichean Writings. The Nicene and Post-Nicene Fathers.* First Series. Vol. IV. The Christian Literature Company, Buffalo, 1887.

Benedict.  *The Rule of St. Benedict.* Edited and translated by Abbot Justin McCann. Burns, Oates and Company, London, 1952.

Calvin, John.  *The Institutes of the Christian Religion.* Especially II/6, 'Redemption in Christ'; II/8, 'Explanation of the Moral Law'; III/6-20, 'The Life of the Christian Man'; IV/20, 'Civil Government'. Two volumes. Edited by John T. McNeill. Translated by Ford Lewis Battles. The Westminster Press, Philadelphia, 1960 (SCM Press, London, 1961).

Edwards, Jonathan.  *The Nature of True Virtue.* Ann Arbor Paperbacks, University of Michigan Press, Ann Arbor, Michigan, 1960.

———.  'Religious Affections', *Works of Jonathan Edwards.* Vol. Two. Yale University Press, New Haven, 1959.

Luther, Martin.  *Lectures on Romans.* Newly translated and edited by Wilhelm Pauck. The Library of Christian Classics, Volume XV. The Westminster Press, Philadelphia, 1961.

———.  *Commentary on Galatians* (1531). Revised translation of 'Middleton' edition of English version of 1575. James Clarke and Company, London, 1953.

———.  'Treatise on Good Works' (1520). *Works of Martin Luther.* Philadelphia edition. Vol. I. Muhlenberg Press, Philadelphia, 1943.

———.  'Treatise on Christian Liberty' (1520). *Works of Martin Luther.* Philadelphia edition. Vol. II. Muhlenberg Press, Philadelphia, 1943.

Pascal, Blaise.  *Pensées.* Modern Library, New York, 1941.

Ritschl, Albrecht.  *The Christian Doctrine of Justification and Reconciliation.* T. & T. Clark, Edinburgh, 1902.

———.  *Instruction in the Christian Religion.* Translated by permission from the 4th German edition by Alice M. Swing and published in the volume *The Theology of Albrecht Ritschl* by Albert Temple Swing. Longmans, Green and Company, London and New York, 1901.

Troeltsch, Ernst.  *The Social Teaching of the Christian Churches.* Translated by Olive Wyon. Two volumes. The Macmillan Company, New York, 1949 (Allen & Unwin, London, 1931).

Wesley, John.  'A Plain Account of Christian Perfection', *The Works of the Rev. John Wesley, A.M. Sometime Fellow of Lincoln College, Oxford, with the Last Corrections of the Author.* Edited by Thomas Jackson. Vol. II. Third edition. Wesleyan Methodist Book Room, London, 1829-31.

Woolman, John.  *Journal.* Everyman's Library No. 402. J. M. Dent and Sons, London, 1922.


III. *Philosophical Ethics*

Aristotle.  *Nicomachean Ethics.* Translated by Sir David Ross. Oxford University Press, London, 1959.

Aurelius, Marcus.  'Meditations', *The Stoic and Epicurean Philosophers.* Edited by W. J. Oates. Random House, New York, 1940.

Brandt, Richard B.  *Ethical Theory: The Problems of Normative and Critical Ethics.* Prentice-Hall, Inc., Englewood Cliffs, N.J.

Epictetus. 'Discourses', *The Stoic and Epicurean Philosophers*. Edited by W. J. Oates. Random House, New York, 1940.

Fromm, Erich. *Man for Himself*. Rinehart and Company, New York, 1947 (Routledge, London, 1949).

James, William. *A Pluralistic Universe: Hibbert Lectures on the Present Situation in Philosophy*. Longmans, Green and Company, London and New York, 1909.

———. *Pragmatism: A New Name for Some Old Ways of Thinking: Popular Lectures on Philosophy*. Longmans, Green and Company, London and New York, 1907.

———. *The Will to Believe*. Longmans, Green and Company, London and New York, 1897.

Kant, Immanuel. *Critique of Practical Reason*. Translated and edited by Lewis W. Beck. University of Chicago Press, Chicago, 1949.

———. *Fundamental Principles of the Metaphysic of Morals*. Translated and edited by Lewis W. Beck. University of Chicago Press, Chicago, 1949.

———. *Religion Within the Limits of Reason Alone*. Translated with an introduction and notes by Theodore M. Greene and H. H. Hudson. Open Court Publishing Company, LaSalle, Ill., 1960.

Kierkegaard, Soren. *Either-Or, a Fragment of Life*. Vol. I translated by David F. Swenson and Lillian M. Swenson. Vol. II translated by Walter Lowrie. Princeton University Press, Princeton, N.J., 1944.

———. *Fear and Trembling*. Translated with notes and introduction by Walter Lowrie. Doubleday and Company, Garden City, N.Y., 1954 (The University Press, Oxford, 1939).

———. *Philosophical Fragments, or a Fragment of Philosophy*. Translated with introduction and notes by David F. Swenson. Princeton University Press, Princeton, N.J., 1952 (The University Press, Oxford, 1936).

———. *Purity of Heart*. Translated by D. Steere. Harper & Row, New York, 1956 (Hamish Hamilton, London, 1956).

Nietzsche, Friedrich. *Beyond Good and Evil*. Modern Library, New York, n.d.

———. *Thus Spake Zarathustra*. Modern Library, New York, n.d.

Plato. The Republic, Meno, Laches, Charmides, Protagoras, The Laws. *The Dialogues of Plato*. Translated by B. Jowett. Introduction by R. Demos. Vols. I and II. Random House, New York, 1937 (The University Press, Oxford, 1953).

Weiss, Paul. *Man's Freedom*. Yale University Press, New Haven, 1950.

Wieman, Henry Nelson. *The Source of Human Good*. University of Chicago Press, Chicago, 1946.

# INDEXES

## 1. BIBLICAL REFERENCES

**Genesis**

| | |
|---|---|
| 1 | 183 |
| 3.5 | 95 |
| 6.5 | 353 |
| 12.1-3 | 91 |
| 15 | 90n. |
| 17 | 90n. |
| 28.12 | 38 |

**Exodus**

| | |
|---|---|
| 3.13-17 | 91 |
| 13 | 90n. |
| 14 | 90n. |
| 34 | 90n. |

**Leviticus**

| | |
|---|---|
| 19.18 | 354n. |
| 26.41 | 353 |

**Deuteronomy**

| | |
|---|---|
| 5 | 90n. |
| 6.3-4 | 79 |
| 6.8 | 353, 354n. |
| 6.20-25 | 77-8 |
| 30.6 | 353 |
| 30.14 | 353 |
| 30.15-18 | 366-7 |

**Joshua**

| | |
|---|---|
| 1.11 | 90 |

**Judges**

| | |
|---|---|
| 8.22-23 | 91n. |
| 21.25 | 90-1 |

**I Samuel**

| | |
|---|---|
| 7 | 91 |
| 8-10 | 90-91 |
| 12.13-15 | 94n. |

**Job**

| | |
|---|---|
| 27.6 | 352 |

**Psalms**

| | |
|---|---|
| 14.1 | 353 |
| 19.9 | 235 |

| | |
|---|---|
| 24.1 | 359n. |
| 50.12 | 359n. |

**Proverbs**

| | |
|---|---|
| 23.7 | 353 |

**Isaiah**

| | |
|---|---|
| 6.11 | 99 |
| 11.1-10 | 98 |
| 29.13 | 79n. |
| 53 | 99 |
| 61.1-2 | 99, 114 |

**Jeremiah**

| | |
|---|---|
| 1.10 | 99 |

**Ezekiel**

| | |
|---|---|
| 3.15 | 140 |
| 11.19 | 353 |

**Matthew**

| | |
|---|---|
| 5.8 | 353 |
| 5.48 | 123 |
| 6.3 | 142 |
| 6.10 | 358 |
| 7.7-8 | 77n. |
| 7.9-10 | 204 |
| 7.21 | 52 |
| 7.29 | 94 |
| 10.16 | 142 |
| 10.29-30 | 57 |
| 11.12 | 94 |
| 13 | 346 |
| 15.1-9 | 79n. |
| 21.28-31 | 76-7 |
| 22.37-40 | 354 |
| 23.13 | 80n. |
| 24.24 | 112n. |
| 25.14-30 | 139n. |
| 26.26-9 | 100n. |

**Mark**

| | |
|---|---|
| 1.14-15 | 57 |
| 4 | 346 |

| | |
|---|---|
| 4.30 | 346 |
| 7.6-13 | 79 |
| 7.18-23 | 354 |
| 10.20 | 320 |
| 12.29-30 | 354 |
| 14.22-5 | 99-100 |

**Luke**

| | |
|---|---|
| 1.23 | 102n. |
| 1.51-2 | 99 |
| 2.11-12 | 99 |
| 2.34 | 99 |
| 4.2ff | 114 |
| 4.18-19 | 99 |
| 4.33ff | 94 |
| 6.45 | 354 |
| 10.20 | 57 |
| 10.27 | 354 |
| 10.29 | 155 |
| 11.9-10 | 77 |
| 11.52 | 80 |
| 12.37 | 52 |
| 13 | 346 |
| 14.28-30 | 80 |
| 14.33 | 80 |
| 15 | 57 |
| 16.8 | 142 |
| 17.32 | 28 |
| 19.11-27 | 139 |
| 22.17-19 | 100n. |
| 23.28 | 39 |
| 24.13-21 | 28 |

**John**

| | |
|---|---|
| 3.5 | 183 |
| 3.16-18 | 160 |
| 3.19 | 160 |
| 3.21 | 160 |
| 7.17 | 75 |
| 8.7 | 142 |
| 10 | 58n. |
| 10.16 | 156, 159 |

14.6 52
15 58n.
15.13, 14 52
19.41 214

*Acts*
1.6-8 28
2.6 238
2.22 112
16.30 99, 155

*Romans*
2.14-15 359n.
2.15 355n, 356
7 212n.
8.1-17 112n.
8.23 46
9-11 51
9.1 355n, 356
12.15 280
13.5 355, 355n, 359n.
15.27 102n.

*I Corinthians*
1.2 47n, 69n.
1.9 47
3 62
3.9-11 60
3.16 59n.
3.16-17 60
4.4 352, 355n, 359n.
5.9-13 32
6 62
6.1ff. 32
6.13 59
6.15 60
6.19 59n, 59-60
7.12ff 32
8.1ff 32
8.6 357
8.7ff 359n.
8.7, 10, 12 355n.
10 62
10.16-17 100
10.23ff. 359, 359n.
10.25, 27, 355n.
28, 29

10.31 360
11.22 69n.
12 47n, 59n, 61
13.5, 6 120
15.9 69n.
15.28 95, 97
15.29 123

*II Corinthians*
1.1 69n.
1.2 47n.
1.21-2 46
4.1ff 33
4.2 355n.
5.5 46
5.11 355n.
5.19 105
6.16 59n.
9.12 102n.
12.12 112

*Galatians*
1.2 47n.
1.13 69n.
1.14 355-6
3.28 62
4.6 62
5.1 367
5.13 367
5.16ff 112
6.6 64n.
6.15 62
6.16 51

*Ephesians*
2.19-22 61
2.21 59n.
3.1-12 48
3.14 48
3.16-19 48-9
3.18-21 90
4.1-7 49
4.11-16 49
4.13 53, 54, 85, 97, 103
4.15, 16 54
4.25-31 56
5.15-17 49

5.20 49
6.12 214

*Philippians*
1.3-5 48
1.21 161
2.17 102n.
2.30 102n.
3.14 97
4.14 64n.

*Colossians*
1.18 59n.
1.24 59n.
2.9-10 95
2.15 94
2.19 59n.
3.15 59n.

*I Thessalonians*
1.1 47n.
2.14 69n.

*II Thessalonians*
1.1 47n.

*I Timothy*
3.15 69n.
6.18 64n.

*Hebrews*
9.21 102n.
10.11 102n.
10.19 103
13.16 64n.

*I Peter*
1.10-12 47n.
2.4-10 47n.
2.9 95
2.9-10 68

*I John*
1.5f 160
1.6, 7 160
1.8-10 160-1
3.21 159

*Revelation*
1.5-6 68
11.15 95
21.1 95

## 2. PERSONAL NAMES

Adickes, Erich, 187
Aiken, Henry, 227n.
Ambrose, Bishop of Milan, 35, 36, 106, 253, 304, 369
Aristotle, 83-6, 166-71, 175, 177-8, 188, 190, 191, 192, 196, 206, 207, 211, 212, 213, 215, 220, 221, 233, 235, 252, 256, 257, 258, 279, 282, 291, 331, 370
Athanasius, 105-8
Auden, W. H., 96-7
Augustine, 37, 39, 51n, 69-70, 76, 106, 109, 110, 112, 136, 217n, 238n, 254-6, 256n, 289, 290n, 297, 304, 369
Aurelius, Marcus, 370
Ayer, A. J., 227n.

Bailey, D. S., 135n.
Balzac, Honore de, 281n.
Barth, Heinrich, 112
Barth, Karl, 13, 44, 74-5, 75n, 78n, 95, 104, 110n, 112, 118-19, 121, 137n, 138n, 205n, 238n, 254n, 268n, 269-77, 277-8, 281n, 323n, 325n, 368
Basil of Caesarea, 35
Battenhouse, Roy, 254n.
Beck, Lewis W., 172n, 333n.
Benedict, 37-9, 369
Bennett, John C., 148-54
Berkeley, George, 227n.
Berlin, Isaiah, 226n.
Berman, Harold H., 127n.
Bethge, Eberhard, 129n.
Bhave, Vinoba, 156
Bonaventura, 331n.
Bonhoeffer, Dietrich, 44, 129-30, 205n, 368
Bradley, Francis, 190n.
Bramhall, John, 307
Brandt, Richard B., 228-34, 240, 241, 245-50, 279n, 370
Brunner, Emil, 13, 27n, 43, 50n, 72n, 78n, 113n, 157, 248n, 289n, 290n, 299, 368
Buber, Martin, 91-4, 95
Bultmann, Rudolf, 90

Cadbury, Henry, 48n.

Caird, John, 196
Calixt, George, 41n.
Calvin, John, 41, 63-9, 67n, 71, 78n, 88-9, 113-15, 135, 136, 156, 157, 158, 208, 275, 307, 320-1, 345, 362-3, 365-6, 369
Carnap, Rudolf, 227n, 248n.
Carnell, Edward J., 248n.
Cicero, 255
Cochrane, Charles N., 106-7, 109n, 111, 369
Comenius, John Amos, 115
Comte, Auguste, 191
Constant de Rebecque, Henri Benjamin, 126-7
Cross, Frank M., 101n.
Cummings, E. E., 96

Danaeus, Lambert, 41n.
D'Arcy, M. C., 369
Davis, Henry, 288-95, 305, 307, 316
Dewey, John, 191, 246n.
Dickens, Charles, 281n.
Dillenberger, John, 158n.
Dillistone, F. W., 61-2, 369
Diogenes Laertius, 24
Dionysius the Areopagite, 39
Donne, John, 307-8
Dostoevsky, Fyodor, 43n, 132, 281n, 320, 326-7, 349, 350

Eddington, Sir Arthur, 83n.
Edwards, Jonathan, 369
Epictetus, 85, 370
Erasmus, Desiderius, 362n.
Erikson, Erik H., 362, 365, 365n.
Ermecke, Gustav, 134n, 288n, 290n, 292n, 294n, 313n, 322n, 324-5n.
Euripides, 329, 338, 363

Finn, James, 146n.
Firth, Robert, 227n.
Fletcher, Joseph, 132n.
Flew, A. G. N., 228n.
Francke, August Hermann, 50n.
Frederick of Saxony, 65n.
Frederick the Great, 268n.
Freud, Sigmund, 136, 327, 337-43, 361, 363
Fromm, Erich, 218-23, 279n, 283, 342n, 370

Galsworthy, John, 281n.
Gandhi, Mohandas K., 156
Gilleman, Gérard, 296-8
Gilson, Etienne, 317n, 332n.
Green, Thomas Hill, 190n.
Greene, Theodore M., 174n.
Gregory the Great, 37, 304
Grene, David, 329n.
Gusdorf, Georges, 237

Haering, Bernhard, 298-300
Hales, Alexander, 331n.
Hall, Joseph, 305
Hardy, E. R., 254n.
Hare, R. M., 232n.
Hegel, Georg Wilhelm Friedrich, 190n.
Heidegger, Martin, 281n.
Heppe, Heinrich, 31n.
Herrmann, Wilhelm, 42
Herzog, Frederick, 26n.
Heschel, Abraham, 86-7, 88, 90
Hick, John, 226n, 228n.
Hildebrand, Dietrich von, 300-2, 320
Hirsch, Emanuel, 31n.
Hobbes, Thomas, 341
Holl, Karl, 365n.
Hooker, Richard, 305, 309, 310
Hudson, Hoyt H., 174n.
Hudson, Winthrop S., 317n.
Hume, David, 227n.
Hutchison, John, 128n.

Ignatius, 53

Jacobi, Friedrich Heinrich, 261, 267
Jaeger, Werner, 170
James, William, 191, 192-204, 211, 212, 213, 215, 240, 253, 268, 279n, 281-3, 370
Jeans, Sir James, 83
Jonas, L., 260n, 269n.

Kalter, Richard, 332n.
Kant, Immanuel, 75-6, 126-9, 172-89, 190, 191, 192, 195-6, 197, 200, 201, 206, 211, 212, 213, 214, 215, 220, 221, 225n, 252, 253, 270-1, 277, 277n, 281-3, 333-7, 338, 343, 345-6, 371
Kemp-Smith, Norman, 187, 188, 189

Kierkegaard, Søren, 123, 268, 277, 281n, 371
Kinsey, Alfred C., 136
Kirk, Kenneth, 303-5
Kittel, Gerhard, 85-6, 102n, 103, 103n.
Korzybski, Alfred, 248n.
Kronecker, Leopold, 83n.
Kroner, Richard, 89
Küng, Hans, 323n.

Lagarde, Paul de, 92
Lattimore, Richard, 329n.
Lehmann, Helmut, 40n.
Luther, Martin, 40, 43n, 63-9, 78n, 134-5, 157-8, 275, 345, 362-5, 370

Marcel, Gabriel, 236, 237
Martineau, James, 190n.
Mausbach, Joseph, 134n, 288n, 290n, 292n, 294n, 313n, 322n, 324n.
McAdoo, H. R., 306n, 307-9, 311, 312, 314, 315n.
McCord, James, 81n.
McNeill, John T., 63, 67, 70, 71, 78n, 362-3
Mehl, Roger, 156-7
Menander, 329
Mendenhall, George, 93n.
Michel, Ernst, 137, 138
Mill, John Stuart, 190n.
Miller, Alexander, 369
Miller, Donald, 338-9n.
Milton, John, 349
Mollegen, A. T., 306n.
Moore, Paul Elmer, 308n.

Nehru, Jawaharlal, 156
Niebuhr, H. Richard, 369
Niebuhr, Reinhold, 13, 27n, 43, 109, 110, 207n, 369
Niebuhr, Richard R., 261n.
Nietzsche, Friedrich Wilhelm, 215, 371
Nowell-Smith, P. H., 232n.
Nygren, Anders, 35, 39, 40, 43, 369

Ogden, C. K., 227n.
Oldham, J. H., 148
Origen, 208

Panter-Downes, Mollie, 236
Pascal, Blaise, 370
Pauck, Wilhelm, 111n, 121
Pelikan, Jaroslav, 40n.
Perry, Ralph Barton, 191n, 192, 193, 195, 205
Phillips, J. B., 53n, 66n, 100n, 120
Philo, 329-30
Pierce, C. A., 328n, 329n, 330n, 352n, 354, 355, 355n.
Plato, 85, 191n, 208-9, 255, 256, 328, 371
Plutarch, 329
Polybius, 329
Protagoras, 191n.

Quine, Willard V. O., 227n.

Rad, Gerhard von, 79
Ramsey, Paul, 27n, 369
Reinhold, Ernst C. G., 261n.
Richards, I. A., 227n.
Richardson, Cyril C., 109n.
Ritschl, Albrecht, 253, 268, 370
Robert, Charles, 296n.
Rogers, Will, 74
Ross, W. D., 167n, 169n, 170n, 171, 211
Rosten, Norman, 349
Rothe, Richard, 42

Salinger, J. D., 320
Sanderson, Robert, 305, 307, 308, 309
Sartre, Jean-Paul, 281n.
Schaff, Philip, 72n, 90n, 109, 110n., 111n.
Schleiermacher, Friedrich, 13, 41, 41-2n, 238n, 254, 254n, 259-67, 268, 268n, 269-72, 270n, 275-7, 277-8
Scougal, Henry, 317n
Scrivner, Matthew, 315n.
Slater, Thomas, 307
Socrates, 225n.
Søe, N. H., 205n.
South, Robert, 314
Spencer, Herbert, 190n.
Spencer, Philipp Jacob, 50n.

Stendahl, Krister, 47n, 101n.
Stevenson, C. L., 232n.
Stitt, David L., 81n.

Taylor, Jeremy, 305, 306n, 309-14, 315
Terenczi, L., 338n.
Tertullian, 35, 253.
Thielicke, Helmut, 205n.
Thomas à Kempis, 37n, 38n, 39
Thomas Aquinas, 39-40, 254, 256-9, 270n, 271, 289, 292, 296-8, 300, 304, 305, 307, 308-9, 312, 317n, 330-37, 338, 369
Thomas, George F., 27n, 165n, 254, 257, 369
Tillich, Paul, 238n.
Tillotson, John, 314
Tindal, Matthew, 310
Tolstoy, Leo, 43n.
Toulmin, S.E., 232n.
Troeltsch, Ernst, 13, 27, 27n, 370
Truman, Harry S., 241, 243, 293n.

Ussher, James, 315n.

Venatorius, Thomas, 41n.
Visser 't Hooft, W. A., 113n, 115n, 116-17

Warren, Max, 81, 82
Weiss, Paul, 206-17, 220, 221, 223, 228n, 274, 279n, 283, 371
Welch, Claude, 108
Wellhausen, Julius, 90
Wesley, John, 370
White, Morton, 227n, 232n.
Wieman, Henry Nelson, 371
Wisdom, John, 228n.
Wittgenstein, Ludwig, 227n, 228n, 229n, 277n.
Woolman, John, 370
Wright, G. E., 79n, 92n, 93n, 369
Wyclif, John, 69

Zinzendorf, Nicolaus Friedrich von, 50n, 134
Zuurdeeg, Willem F., 225n, 226n, 227n, 236, 237n, 240, 249n.

# 3. SUBJECTS

Absolute, 198, 209-10
 Good, 214
 moral law, 184
 perfection, 260
 value, 302
Absolutism, 143, 200, 202
Adam, 119, 121, 299
 first Adam, 118
 second Adam, 51, 105, 107, 117-22, 154
Adultery, 139
Advertance, 292-3, 298
Alcoholism, 280
Analytical Philosophy, 226-8, 232-40, 246, 249, 268, 277
 See also, Meta-ethics
Anglican Moral Theology, 303-16, passim
 on authority and freedom, 304-5
 on penitence, 304-5
 see also, Caroline Divinity, Moral Theology
Anthropology, 104, 120-1, 271, 289, 299, 304
Asceticism, 36, 39
Ascetic Theology, 306
Atheism, 201
Augustan experiment, 111
Authoritarian ethics, 218-19, 223, 283, 308
 and conscience, 336
Authority, 30, 75, 312, 341
 authoritarianism, 303, 308
 of the church, 319
 and conscience, 341
 and freedom, 305, 307, 315
Autonomy, 348, 351

Bataan, 349
Beatitude, 248
Believers and Unbelievers, 50-2, 117, 152, 154-8, 160, 165
Bible, 26-7, 43, 53, 74, 78, 86, 103, 105, 109, 116, 183, 257, 304, 324, 345, 352
 see also, Scriptures
Biblical ethics, 43
 see also Christian Ethics, Ethics, New Testament Ethics

Body of Christ, 47, 49, 50, 52-5, 59-62, 66, 68
 and Humanity, 67
 and Maturity, 67
 and Temple, 59-62
Boy Scout Manual, 247
Buddhism, 165

Canon, 29, 30-1
Canon Law, 290
Capitalism, 147
Caroline Divinity, 305-16 passim
 and casuistry, 318-19
 and conscience, 312-13
 'grand rules of', 316
 and holiness, 315-15, 323
 'holy living and holy dying', 306, 315
 and koinonia ethic, 307
 and law of nature and reason, 310
 as 'practical divinity', 306-7
 and sin, 314
 and spirituality, 313
 see also, Anglican Moral Theology
Casuistry, 35, 290-1, 299, 314, 318ff.
 see also, Moral Theology
Catechisms, 78, 88
Categorical Imperative, 176-8, 188-9, 203, 211, 220, 233, 252
 maxims of, 178-9, 211
 statement of, 179
Catholic Ethics, 15, 142, 146, 250, 289-90, 300, 302-3, 322, 325
 Catholic sexual ethics, 133-4
 see also, Christian Ethics, Ethics, Moral Theology, Sexuality
Catholicism, 40, 104, 172, 261, 296, 323
 Catholic Church, 53, 65, 146, 302, 307
 Catholicity, 307
 Catholic Theology, 109, 245, 248
 Greek, 248
Charity, 38, 296-8, 297, 299, 302, 317
Chastity, 35

Christ, 33, 46, 66, 97, 100, 106-7,
109, 119, 130, 135, 157,
159-60, 310-11, 316-17, 345,
358, 360, 364, 365, 367
    as Creator, 356
    Deity of, 113
    Headship of, 52, 54-5, 68, 72
    Humanity of, 51, 113
    as Lord, 34, 52-3, 61, 77-8,
    91, 94, 355, 366
    Lordship of, 47, 49, 116, 152
    Passion of, 39
    as Redeemer, 16, 17, 356
    as Savior, 99, 133
    Three-fold office of, 105, 113-
    14, 116-17
    see also, Jesus: Son of God
Christian behaviour, 39, 75, 315
    christological foundation of,
    116
    and circumstances, 152-3
    contextual understanding of,
    302
    and decision-making, 144, 244
    defined, 15, 122
    ethical requirements of, 205
    guidance of, 129ff, 294, 316
    and maturity, 346
    and non-christian, 33
    shape of, 166, 202, 252, 288,
    328, 344, 366
    as sign, 152-3
    see also, Christian Decision-
    making
Christian community, 14, 27-29, 32,
45, 47, 50, 62, 135, 147, 158, 265
    see also, Church, *Koinonia*
Christian Economics, 147
Christian Ethics, 42-4, 205-6
    and analytical ethics, 238-9,
    246, 249-50
    as contextual, 14-15, 74-8,
    80, 124, 131, 159, 166
    defined, 25, 45, 124, 159, 272,
    344
    as 'koinonia ethics', 15-17,
    47-9, 80, 283
    and maturity, 223
    and moral philosophy, 269-70
    and New Testament ethics,
    26-9
    and philosophical ethics, 224-5,
    229, 256-9, 260-84

    as a science, 23, 25, 269-70, 273
    as a theological discipline, 15,
    25-32, 163, 165
    and a theological rule, 240
    see also, Contextualism, Ethics,
    *Koinonia*, Moral Theology
Christian liberty, 40, 78
    Calvin's doctrine of, 365f.
    Luther's treatise on, 364
    see also Freedom, Liberty
Christology,
    and ethics, 14, 17, 104-5
Church, 13, 32-6, 45-9, 55, 73,
81, 105, 116-17, 138, 140,
202-3, 238, 243, 272, 287,
303, 317, 319, 355
    Calvin's doctrine of, 71-2
    empirical, 56, 69, 70-2, 131
    ethical reality of, 54, 63
    fellowship, 50, 66-7
    institution, 50, 53, 68
    invisible and visible, 53, 68-72
    Latin, 109-10
    New Testament self-under-
    standing of, 45f, 68
    Reformation, 110
    true, 63, 68
    See also, Christian community,
    *Koinonia*
Circumstance ethics, 300
City of God, 70
Classical philosophy, 166
Communio sanctorum, 63-4, 66-8
Conscience, 15, 16, 115, 125, 140,
151, 265, 287-367 passim
    bond between duty and obliga-
    tion, 333
    bond between law and respons-
    ibility, 328-30
    Calvin's definition, 366
    context of, 316, 326-7, 343-6,
    358ff.
    decline and fall defined, 326-7
    definition of, 350
    and duty, 333-7
    ethical reality of, 316, 325,
    343-67 passim
    and freedom, 327
    Freud's doctrine of, 337-43
    fulcrum of divine activity, 354
    guilty, 336
    and heteronomy (autonomy,
    theonomy), 348, 351, 358-9

Conscience—*contd.*
    and humanization, 328-30
    judge of action, 309
    methodological importance of, 325, 350
    and moralization, 337, 343
    and neighbor, 359ff.
    in Old Testament and New Testament, 353-60
    Pauline doctrine of, 354-60
    power of soul, 304
    St Thomas' doctrine of, 312
    semantics of, 328ff.
    tragic and easy, 343, 362-3
    tribunal, 335
    voice of God, 336
    and war, 141
Consensus gentium, 168, 241
Context, 14, 44, 86, 244
    and Christian ethics, 195
    and guidance, 139ff.
    of knowledge and experience, 192
    contextual good, 281-3
    contextualism, 246-7
    see also, Christian Ethics, Conscience, Ethics, *Koinonia*
Corinth, 32
Covenant, 46, 51, 77, 91, 93, 95-6, 99
Critical ethics, 229, 235
Critical philosophy, 166, 172, 184, 190
Culpability, 293-4, 311-13
Custom, 24, 294
Cynics, 24

Decalogue, 77, 78, 310
Decision, 76
    complexity of, 313
    decision-making, 347, 349, 359
    environment of, 283-4, 346ff, 366-7
    see also, Christian Decision-making
Deist, 58
Depravity, 322
Depth-psychology, 218, 253, 282
    see also, Psycho-analysis
Desegregation, 151-3
Deuteronomy, 77-9
Dia-parallelism, 254, 259-67, 268-9, 271

law of, 262
*Didache*, 33
Discipleship, 299, 306, 346f.
Divorce, 139
Dogma, 103, 111
Dogmatics,
    and ethics, 104, 269-71, 290
Double standard, 245, 263, 273, 275
    ecclesiological, 69
    ethical, 145-59 passim
Duty, 176, 178, 180-1, 186, 188-9, 263-4, 320
    and conscience, 333-7
    see also, Conscience, Obligation

Ecclesiola in ecclesia, 50-1, 72
    see also, Church, *Koinonia*
Election, 66, 121
Empiricism, 194, 200-1, 205, 211
    Empiricists, 203, 227
Ends and Means, 167, 189, 191, 220, 258
Enlightenment, 41, 226
Eschatology, 94-5, 118, 122-3, 152
Ethical exception, 242-3, 245, 247
Ethical expediency, 131, 143
Ethical generalization, 15, 77, 130, 229, 234, 241ff, 245-6, 277-81, 324, 346
Ethical predicament, 126, 154, 165, 252, 276, 319-22, 324-5, 346, 349, 363, 366
Ethical revisionism, 254-6, 266, 288
Ethical synthesis, 254, 256-9, 266, 288
Ethics,
    branch of politics, 83ff.
    descriptive, 14
    as a discipline, 15, 168-9, 251-2, 272-3
    etymology, 23-5
    Kantian, 75
    and liturgy, 102f.
    methodology of, 15
    and religion, 15, 183-9, 197-204, 212, 216-17
    see also, Christian Ethics, Contextualism, *Koinonia*, Methodology, Moral Philosophy, Philosophical Ethics
Eucharist, 62, 65, 100-1
Eudemonism, 166, 170-2, 174, 188, 207, 252, 254, 282

Evangelical ethics, 15-16, 142, 322
  and evangelism, 82
  and faith, 319
Evil, 34, 120, 170-1, 182-3, 202, 212-
    16, 281, 283, 293, 354, 366
  radical evil, 181-4, 217, 277
  and rational good, 280, 282-3
  see also, Good
Existentialism, 268, 277, 281, 296,
    300, 332
Exodus, 93

Fasting, 35
Faith, 26, 66, 112, 139, 141-2, 144-6,
    254-5, 363-5
  and morals, 296, 308
  and obedience, 145
  rational, 186
  and reason, 257, 266
Filioque, 109-11
First Adam, 119, 154
  see also, Adam, Second Adam
Forgiveness, 139, 141, 160-1, 224,
    244, 312
Fourth Gospel, 52, 159, 183, 214
Freedom, 138, 140, 161, 172, 180-2,
    184, 209-10, 212, 244, 282,
    287-8, 356-9
  of choice, 182, 292, 301, 304,
    313, 316, 326-7, 331, 344,
    348-50, 356, 359-60, 363-7
  and authority, 305
  context of, 216, 283
  and humanity, 362
  and obedience, 312, 346
  and responsibility, 324-5
  transcendent, 334, 336
  see also, Christian Liberty,
    Liberty

Glory, 122
God, 200-1, 211, 213, 215, 228,
    239, 245, 263, 270-1, 274,
    276, 284, 288, 299, 301, 305,
    313-14, 342, 262-3, 366
  as absolute, 198
  activity, 310, 325, 349, 351-4,
    358-60, 365-6
  activity of humanization, 14,
    66, 73, 85, 112, 117, 152, 324
  being of, 184-5, 187-9, 195
  and conscience, 335-7
  creator, 97, 108, 158, 352

dynamics and direction of
    activity, 70, 77-8, 111, 141-3,
    153, 202, 248, 316, 345, 349,
    351
  economy of, 159
  faithfulness of, 160
  Father, 33, 109-11, 123, 357, 365
  Father, Son, Spirit, 108
  freedom of, 73, 144, 274, 359
  as highest Good, 174, 186
  Judge, 180, 235
  Kingship of, 91-2
  as light, 160
  people of, 46-7, 102-3, 116
  as power, 197
  purposes of, 14, 49, 70, 97,
    122-3, 144
  reality of, 321
  will of, 15, 27, 38, 43, 75-80,
    95-7, 101, 124, 131, 141,
    146, 159, 245, 248, 265, 268,
    314, 344-5, 358, 365-6
  William James' definition of,
    199
  wisdom of, 49, 51
  wrath of, 157-8
Golden mean, 169-71, 177, 233, 280
Good, 83, 122, 165-71, 173-4, 177,
    183, 185, 191, 195, 197-8,
    200, 208-9, 213, 215, 255,
    258, 270, 272-4, 278-9, 282,
    317, 348
  absolute, 210, 214
  and evil, 213-15, 326f, 341,
    343, 348-53, 356, 366
  rational, 280
  *summum bonum*, 180, 207, 245,
    254-5, 263-4, 299
  *supremum bonum*, 180, 207
  will, 175-7, 179-80, 188, 334
Gospel, 48, 57, 157, 204, 309, 319,
    357
  law and, 310
Grace, 104, 120, 256, 258, 275-6,
    311-12, 336
  of Christ, 365
  *gratia non tollit naturam sed
    perfecit*, 289, 319
  and nature, 134, 289, 319, 322
  as power, 323
  radicality of, 323
  *sola gratia, sola fide*, 319, 345
Graeco-Roman classicism, 111

Grand Inquisitor, 326ff.
Greek Orthodoxy, 42, 43
Guilt, 15, 115, 298, 311-12, 360, 362
    and conscience, 336, 338

Habit, 311, 330-1
Happiness, 167-8, 173-5, 177, 180, 186, 252
Heart, 79, 123, 183, 305, 326-7, 344, 349, 357
    and conscience, 352ff, 364, 366-7
Hebrews, history of, 46
Hedonism, 197
Hermas, 33-4
Hermeneutics, 26-7
Heteronomy, 259, 301, 348, 351
Hinduism, 25, 165, 240
Hiroshima, 241-2, 244, 293
History, 89, 110, 116, 201, 349
    historical, 46, 153, 194, 222, 276
Holy Spirit, 28, 31, 46, 52-3, 59-60, 62, 104, 106-7, 112, 156, 158-9, 309, 313, 357, 364
Homousios, 108-9
Hope, 66, 100, 132, 139, 144
Human, 16, 112, 130-1, 138, 153, 246, 258, 284, 316, 320, 324, 327, 343, 345, 347, 351, 358, 360, 366
    acts, 309
    fulfillment, 117
    life, 14, 16, 138, 251, 282, 284, 324, 327, 343, 347, 358, 366
    nature, 206, 208, 218, 222
Humanism, 205-6, 217-19, 223-4, 282-3, 287
    and conscience, 342, 361
    humanist ethics, 302
Humanity, 55-6, 66-7, 85, 116, 121, 147, 155, 158, 189, 207, 211, 243-4, 248, 252, 274, 276, 302, 321, 348-9, 353-4
    and conscience, 337f.
    and freedom, 362
    see also, Maturity, New Humanity
Humanization, 244, 283, 310, 316, 349, 357, 365-6
    and conscience, 328-30, 356
    environment of, 288
    see also, God: activity of

Idealism, 41
Idealists, 318
Idolatry, 92
Ignorance,
    invincible and vincible, 293-4
Image, (s), 88, 117, 141, 156, 316
    biblical, 90ff.
    of Christ, 305, 326-7, 344, 349
    of God, 121, 158, 302
    messianic, 98
Imagination, 86, 87-9, 95, 159, 236, 243, 279, 366
Imitation of Christ, 39, 299
Imperative, 131, 159, 178, 223, 264
Incarnation, 55, 106-8, 121, 130, 157
Indicative, 112, 131, 159, 161, 223, 248-9, 346-7
Individualism, 56ff, 60, 303-4
    Individual, 141, 199, 364
    Individuality, 219
Infusion, doctrine of, 312
Instrumentalism, 191
Intention, 128-9, 292-3, 295, 297, 310
    see also, Moral Theology
Islam, 25, 165
Israel, 46, 49, 51, 79, 91-3, 95

Jesus, 27-8, 43, 46, 57-8, 77, 79, 89, 105, 114, 122-3, 142, 155-6, 160, 326-7
    Christ, 43, 45, 47, 53, 55, 73, 133, 152, 155, 270-1, 299, 304, 323, 344, 357
    Crucifixion, 28, 160
    Resurrection, 28, 43, 55, 119
    Son of God, 54, 103, 106, 160, 299
    see also, Christ
Jewish Christian Community, 51
Judaism, 25
    Council of Rabbis of the City of New York, 146
Judgment, 120, 160, 175
    and conscience, 335-6
    ethical, 244-6
    see also, God: Judge
Justice, 36, 150-1, 180, 234, 239, 244, 254-5, 302
Justification by faith, 43, 66, 245, 274, 360, 365
    self-justification, 243

Kingdom of Christ, 95, 116, 327
Kingdom of God, 28, 57, 95, 100, 112, 186, 263-4, 346
    Kingship, 91-2, 94, 115, 117
*Koinonia* ethics, 45, 80, 111
    and casuistry, 319
    and conscience, 344ff, 351, 361-2
    and contextualism, 14, 15, 112, 145, 154, 195, 246, 302, 325
    and church, 58-9, 72
    and double standard, 159, 165
    and environment of decision, 347
    and ethical predicament, 321
    and exceptions, 243
    and humanity, 349
    and maturity, 323
    meaning of, 49-50, 112, 131, 141, 223, 245
    and meta-ethics, 229, 238ff, 248-9
    and methodological options, 282, 284, 325
    and middle axioms, 148-54
    and moral theology, 307
    and politics of God, 103, 141
    and pragmatism, 201
    and tautology, 351-2
    and truth, 133ff.
    and war, 140ff.
    and will of God, 248
    see also, Christian Ethics, Christian community, Church, Humanity, Maturity, New Humanity

Law, 78-9, 93, 134, 146-7, 312, 346, 365
    and conscience, 330, 350, 360
    eternal, 258, 308
    in heart, 357
    moral, 173-4, 177-8, 181-3, 186, 334-6, 348
    positive, 258
    St Thomas' doctrine of, 308-9
    see also, Natural Law
Legalism, 136, 166, 172, 252, 280, 308, 311, 350, 358
Legion of Decency, 146
Liberty, 304, 308, 315, 358, 365
    libertarian, 350

    see also, Christian liberty, Freedom
Liturgy, 102-3
Love, 33, 37, 39, 52, 54, 64, 66, 136, 139, 143-4, 151, 222, 224, 239, 255, 298, 300, 304-5, 314, 340, 364, 367
    of creature, 311
    commandment, 310, 354
    of God, 299, 306
    of self, 178, 219, 221

Marriage, 134-7
Materialism, 198
Maturity, 16-17, 53-6, 85, 96, 99, 101, 112, 117, 131, 146, 154, 159, 166, 211, 219-23, 249, 282-3, 317, 346
    and *koinonia*, 323
    and politics of God, 345
    see also, God activity of, Humanity, Humanization, *Koinonia* ethics, New Humanity
Mediator, 114-15, 118
Mercy, 36, 68, 302, 364
Messiah, 28, 46-7, 58, 94, 97, 99, 100-1, 111-15, 118
Messianism, 91-2, 98, 100, 102, 104, 106
    theology of, 112, 118, 130, 345
Meta-ethics, 228ff, 232, 239, 246-7, 249, 250, 277-8, 283
    see also, Analytical Philosophy
Meta-language, 236, 249, 250
Methodology, 15, 26, 41, 149, 165, 217, 224, 228-9, 238, 260, 267-8, 270, 275-6, 280-4, 296-7, 324-6, 345, 347
    and conscience, 350
Middle Ages, 37, 39, 40, 70
Middle axioms, 148ff.
Modalism, 108
Modesty, 35
Monastic, 37-8
Monism, 194
Monotheism, 92
Moral argument, 187
Moral Philosophy, 15, 37, 165, 172, 191, 206, 225, 234, 247, 253-4, 257, 268, 270, 278, 281-2, 287, 324, 345, 351

Moral Philosophy—see also, Ethics, Philosophical ethics

Moral Theology, 15-16, 129, 258, 287-325, passim, 332, 345-6, 351
  *agere sequitur esse*, 324, 345
  and casuistry, 290
  and certainty, 291, 313, 317
  and conscience, 328, 333
  critique of, 316-25
  ethical inadequacy of, 315-6, 324-5
  and moral act, 292ff.
  and scandal, 294ff.
  and theology, 289-90
  see also, Catholic ethics, Christian ethics

Morality, 23-4, 45, 173-4, 184, 270-1
  and conscience, 343
  legalistic, 40
  moralism, 36
  morals, 173
  supreme principle of, 176, 180, 188

Moravian, 50, 128

Moslem morals, 240

Motivation, 14, 35, 56, 76, 181, 190-1, 203, 252, 288, 316, 360, 366

Myth, 89, 236

Nagasaki, 241-2, 244

National Socialism, 68

Natural Law, 78, 148, 150, 154, 308-10, 312, 335, 357
  see also, Law

Natural theology, 158, 187
  natural man, 120-1
  natural revelation, 302, 357

Naturalism, 231, 240
  naturalists, 203

Neighbor, 56, 67-68, 132, 150, 219, 221-2, 341, 364-5
  and conscience, 359ff.

Neo-platonism, 40

New Humanity, 17, 51, 56, 107, 117-23, 131, 144, 152, 158, 321
  see also, Humanity, Humanization, Maturity, God: activity of, Politics of God

New Testament, 26, 32, 45-7, 57, 62, 64, 68-70, 86-7, 94, 102-3, 112, 122, 147, 155, 214, 280, 327, 352-5
  New Testament ethics, 26-9, 32-3, 35, 37, 42-3

Nicene Faith, 108

*Nichomachean Ethics*, 166-71, 174, 256

Non-cognitivism, 231-2

Normative ethics, 14, 229-32, 234-5, 241-3, 252, 274, 279

Obedience, 15, 138-9, 144-5, 274, 276, 284, 287-8, 302, 312, 316, 346, 349-51, 356, 359-60, 364-6

Obligation, 190, 208, 235, 264-5, 272, 364
  and conscience, 313, 333
  see also, Duty

Old Testament, 26, 46-7, 86-7, 92-4, 102, 352-3, 356-7, 363

Opus Posthumum, 187ff, 196

Parables, 57, 87n, 90, 122, 139, 346f.

Pentecost, 237

Perfection, 170-1, 208ff, 216, 311, 314, 317-19
  absolute, 260
  Christian, 307

Phenomenology, 237, 268

Philosophical ethics, 45, 163, 205-6, 224-5, 229, 232, 246, 250-4, 256, 258-84 passim
  see also, Ethics, Moral Philosophy

Pietism, 39, 50-1, 55, 76
  Caroline piety, 315, 319
  piety, quietism, 306
  piety and impiety, 321

Platonic, 37, 254

Pluralism, 194-4, 197, 199, 201-3, 205, 281
  pluralists, 203, 253

Politics, 81, 167-8, 243-4
  and biblical images, 90ff.
  and community, 84
  and ethics, 83ff.
  and humanization, 85
  of God, 81-101, passim, 105, 108, 112, 114, 153, 202, 244-5, 345, 352, 366
  see also, God: activity of

Positivism, 191, 230, 268
  positivists, 227

Power, 122, 168, 239, 243-4, 257
   and conscience, 331, 362
   of grace, 322-3
   logos of, 111
   sacramental, 317-18
   of spirit, 156-8
   will to, 96-7
Pragmatism, 191, 193-4, 201-2, 222, 281-2
   pragmatists, 203
Precepts, 35, 77-8, 124, 345, 347
   see also, Principles
Priesthood, 67-8, 103, 115
Principles, 77, 124, 143-4, 148-54, 171, 197, 208-10, 229, 233-4, 278, 295, 305, 312, 330f, 335, 345, 347
   supreme principle of morality, 176, 180
   see also, Legalism, Precepts,
Probabiliorism, 313
Probabilism, 241-2, 313
Protestant Council of the City of New York, 146
Protestantism, 13, 63, 116, 146-7, 308, 318
   Protestant church, 140
   Protestant ethics, 15-16, 134 (sexual), 147 (race), 287 (moral theology), 304, 350-1
   Protestant orthodoxy, 30-1
   Protestant theology, 115, 248
Psycho-analysis, 161, 223
   and conscience, 342-3
   see also, Depth-psychology
Puritanism, 308, 315
Pythagoreans, 24

Qualified Attitude Method, 233-4, 241-2, 248
   see also, Analytical Philosophy, Meta-ethics
Qumran, 47

Racial segregation, 147
   justice, 150-1, 222
Real presence, 157
Reconciliation, 244-5
Redemption, 43, 263-6
Reformation, 13, 14, 30, 40, 42, 63, 67, 71, 79, 113, 116, 135-6, 172, 237, 248, 302, 307, 318, 325, 345, 347, 362

Reformers, 31, 63, 78, 115-16, 319 345
Relativism, 15, 143, 191, 194, 197-8, 200, 202-5, 207-10, 218, 252-3, 349
Religion, 174, 181-2, 184-6, 189, 195-7, 199, 200, 211-12, 216, 218, 228, 235, 238, 243, 260, 266, 268, 271, 281-2
Repentance, 50, 57, 158, 311, 314
Responsibility, 52, 133, 211, 222, 244, 294, 311, 336, 352, 354, 364
   and conscience, 330
   and freedom, 324
   and moral theology, 298ff, 304f.
Revelation, 45, 50-1, 89, 103-5, 109-10, 149, 158, 199, 201-2, 247-8, 258, 270-1, 274, 278, 287, 291, 296, 300, 303, 309, 317
   and reason, 256
   religion of, 310
   revealed theology, 158
   self-revelation, 110
Righteousness, 33, 65, 78, 197, 224, 360, 365
   right, 188-9, 212, 235
   right action, 144, 268
   right decision, 243
   rightness, 276
Roman Catholic
   see Catholic, Church
Romanticism, 277
Royal Society of London, 236
Rule of Saint Benedict, 37-8

Sabellianism, 108
Sacrament, 64-5
Satan, 134, 349
Scandal, 294ff.
   see also, Moral Theology
Scriptures, 27, 29, 30-2, 71, 81, 90, 306, 312-16
   infallibility, 308
   Reformation maxims concerning, 30-1
   see also, Bible
Second Adam, see Adam
Second Advent, 107, 117, 122, 155
   first Advent, 100
Sects, 29, 42, 43

Secunda secundae, 39, 257, 317
Self, acceptance, 16
    determination, 274, 278-80, 282-4
    preservation, 340
    realization, 16, 221
Semi-pelagianism, 290
Septuagint, 46, 102
Sermon on the Mount, 40, 78
    see also, New Testament ethics
Sexuality, 133-4, 340
    coitus, 136
    continence, 134, 136
    and humanization, 136, 138
    lust, 135, 139
    promiscuity, 138-9
    prostitution, 138-9
Sin, 97, 263, 274, 312, 315, 322
    mortal and venial, 314
    mysticism, 300
    original, 121
Situational ethics, 32, 148-55, 234
Social gospel, 13
Spirit, 46, 49, 51, 107-9, 111-12, 114, 157-8, 262-3, 311-12
    Absolute, 244
    spiritualism, 198
Stoic, 24, 37, 58, 240, 356
Structure, 44, 50, 54-5, 222-3, 233, 243, 255-6, 278-9, 282-3, 288, 360, 366
    of action, 14
    of behavior, 44
    character, 219ff.
    of conscience, 329ff.
    of love in Moral Theology, 134
    see also, Self-determination
Supernaturalism, 201, 231, 247, 317, 302, 305
    supernatural end, 297, 319
    supernatural order, 291, 296, 300, 317
    supernaturalists, 257
Supreme Court of the United States, 150-1
*suum cuique*, 239, 255
Symbolism, ladder, 38-9
    symbolic language, 228
Synderesis, 312, 328, 330, 334
    see also, Conscience

Synoptic Gospels, 52, 58, 346

Theism, Christian, 196
    melioristic, 201, 205
    monistic, 197
    scholastic, 200
Theocracy, 92-4
Theodicy, 217, 284
Theology of language, 236, 238, 250, 299
Theonomy, 348, 350-1, 358-9, 362
Transubstantiation, 65
Transvaluation of values, 122, 242-5
Trent, Council of, 296, 302, 306
Trinity, 105-6, 108-13, 117, 155
Trust, 96
Truth, and context, 192ff.
    doing the, 159-61
    in conscience, 357
    in order to goodness, 321
    knowing the, 193ff.
    revealed, 316
    telling, 124ff., 346-7
Tutiorism, 313

*Unitas Fratrum*, 115
Utilitarianism, 190, 233

Value, 125, 207-8, 210, 220, 243-4, 320
    absolute, 260, 302
*Via media*, 303, 315, 324
Vienna Circle, 227, 237
Virginity, 35, 135-6
Virtue (s), 37, 167-9, 174, 177, 187, 216, 219-20, 252, 254-6, 258, 263-4, 296-9, 302, 304, 306-7, 320
    cardinal, 39, 254-5, 257, 299, 304
    natural, 257
    perfection of, 320
    theological, 257, 299, 304

War, 140-3, 293
    first world, 203
    second world, 241, 349
Westminster Confession of Faith, 71
Word of God, 30, 107-8
Wrath, 157-8, 356